100

D1639482

P. VERGILI MARONIS

AENEIDOS
LIBRI VII–VIII

GLASGOW UNIVERSITY PUBLICATIONS

P. VERGILI MARONIS

AENEIDOS

LIBRI VII–VIII

WITH A COMMENTARY
BY
C. J. FORDYCE

———

Introduction by

P. G. WALSH
Professor of Humanity
University of Glasgow

Edited by

JOHN D. CHRISTIE

Published for the
UNIVERSITY OF GLASGOW
by the
OXFORD UNIVERSITY PRESS
1977

Oxford University Press, Walton Street, Oxford OX2 6DP

OXFORD LONDON GLASGOW
NEW YORK TORONTO MELBOURNE WELLINGTON
IBADAN NAIROBI DAR ES SALAAM LUSAKA CAPE TOWN
KUALA LUMPUR SINGAPORE JAKARTA HONG KONG TOKYO
DELHI BOMBAY CALCUTTA MADRAS KARACHI

© *University of Glasgow 1977*

All rights reserved. No part of this publication may be reproduced, stored in a retrieval system, or transmitted, in any form or by any means, electronic, mechanical, photocopying, recording, or otherwise, without the prior permission of Oxford University Press

British Library Cataloguing in Publication Data
Virgil
    P. Vergili Maronis Aeneidos, Libri VII–VIII
    1. Latin poetry
    I. Title   II. Fordyce, C J
    III. Christie, John Duncan
    873'.01   PA6801.A5
    ISBN 0–19–713309–6

FRANCIS HOLLAND,
CHURCH OF ENGLAND SCHOOL
                    LIBRARY   •

*Printed in Great Britain
at the University Press, Oxford
by Vivian Ridler
Printer to the University*

For

KITTY FORDYCE

PREFACE

AFTER the publication in 1961 of his commentary on Catullus, Professor Christian J. Fordyce turned to the composition of a commentary on the second half of Virgil's *Aeneid*. This was to have been the third part of a three-volume 'Oxford Commentary' on Virgil's complete works, of which the second volume, on *Aeneid* I–VI, was to be composed by Professor R. G. Austin. In September of 1974 Professor Fordyce died and within a few weeks Professor Austin also died. The project was therefore abandoned.

Fordyce had virtually completed his commentaries on Books VII, VIII, and IX—though no doubt much would have been added or altered before he released his script: Books X and XI were fully drafted but awaited revision: Book XII had barely been begun. I had for some years enjoyed the privilege of discussing Fordyce's drafts. He had asked me to scrutinize them for accuracy and to offer criticisms and suggestions. During our discussions a good many modifications and additions were made, mainly to VII, VIII, and IX. Those of us who had seen some or all of these drafts were convinced that they should not be lost and persuaded the University of Glasgow to publish the present volume, comprising the commentaries on VII and VIII, which make a good pairing. I was asked to prepare the work for publication.

I should declare the extent of my editorial activity. My aim has been to keep interference with Fordyce's text to the minimum. I have tried to verify all references, quotations, and matters of fact, adjusting where necessary. Expressions of opinion I have left unaltered, even—or especially—when I may disagree. In a few places, however, I felt that it would help to cite a different view, setting it in square brackets with my initials. I have incorporated material from the draft commentaries on IX–XI, thus enhancing the scope of this volume as well as rescuing valuable comments. Whether or not the rest of the later commentaries can be published some day remains to be seen.

I have received, and am most grateful for, much expert help from all my colleagues in the Department of Humanity at Glasgow, notably from Professor Walsh, Fordyce's successor in the Chair of Humanity, who has not only contributed a scholarly Introduction but has given me the greatest possible support and encouragement. He read the original draft with typical acumen and gave me valuable counsel and help with many editorial problems. Mrs. Ruth Pepper has been a particularly assiduous helper. She was involved with the work from the outset, expertly deciphering and typing a series of amended versions, checking many references and standardizing forms. She has also offered perceptive suggestions for greater clarity and consistency of expression. I cannot express too strongly our appreciation of her patient and skilled service to this work.

I owe a special debt of gratitude to Mrs. Fordyce who has not only given the project her blessing but has been most generous in allowing me full access to her husband's papers and to the rich resources of his library. It is in the hope that she will take it as a gesture of our affection and gratitude that I have dedicated the volume to her.

Lastly my thanks are due to the Publications Officers of Glasgow University and to the skilful and vigilant readers at the Oxford Press.

JOHN D. CHRISTIE

University of Glasgow

CONTENTS

INTRODUCTION

THE two books contained in this edition have never achieved a popularity commensurate with that of the first six books of the *Aeneid*. The brilliant variety of the 'Odyssean' half of the epic—the arrival at Carthage, the narratives of the fall of Troy and of the laborious hazards of the pilgrimage westward, the tragic passion of Dido, the funeral-games in Sicily, the descent into the world of the dead upon arrival in Italy—has overshadowed the 'Iliadic' half, which has often been criticized as a more mechanical and monotonous exercise undertaken by a poet with little stomach for the martial theme which is at its centre. Yet even by this simplistic criterion the neglect of Books VII and VIII would be unjustified, for the pattern of concentrated warfare does not commence until Book IX, and the poet's versatility in variation of theme and mood is further demonstrated in these two books. In VII the focus is on the reactions of the Latins to the arrival of the Trojan immigrants, and in VIII on the visit of Aeneas to King Evander of Pallanteum, the settlement on what is to be the site of Rome. These books may escape the limbo of the 'Iliadic' *Aeneid* if the epic is visualized not only as a diptych but also as a triptych, with I–IV devoted to events at Carthage, V–VIII to the journey from Africa and initial arrival in Italy, and IX–XII to the mounting climax of the fighting. This ancillary division into three parts, undoubtedly intended by the poet, allows the reader more clearly to appreciate the distinctive themes of VII and of VIII, which are so much more than mere preliminaries to the saga of the ensuing conflict.[1]

Yet the major division in the structure of the whole is between the 'Odyssean' and the 'Iliadic' halves, and Virgil

[1] This secondary principle of division is increasingly emphasized by modern critics; see, e.g., K. Quinn, *Virgil's Aeneid* (London, 1968), 67.

indicates that his second great theme is the more important as encompassing the more considerable events: 'maior rerum mihi nascitur ordo,/ maius opus moueo'.[1] It is vital to understand the reason for this claim since it provides the key to the economy of the whole poem.[2] In his depiction in poetic legend of the events of a few weeks Virgil is attempting to encapsulate the essential character of the people ordained to govern the world—the reconciled nations which are to compose it, the emergent leaders of genius culminating in Augustus, the moral qualities, visible at the outset, on which the Roman achievement was founded. 'tantae molis erat Romanam condere gentem'; the basic theme of man's struggle over the 'demonic' element without and within[3] is set firmly in a Roman frame. The political presuppositions, echoed by Livy as well as by Virgil, that it was Rome's destiny and right to govern the world by diplomacy and war[4] may alienate us, but a full appreciation of the grand design of the *Aeneid* demands that we acknowledge them. 'The tragic parts of the *Aeneid* are most often read, and . . . we are more easily attuned to the universal aspects of the poem than the specifically Roman. Nevertheless it is the Roman theme which anchors the *Aeneid*.'[5]

I

The *Vita Vergilii* informs us that the poet (by now a celebrated literary figure some forty years old) first composed a version of the *Aeneid* in prose, dividing its content into twelve books.[6] At this preliminary stage he had to make a systematic study not only of the legends of Aeneas' journey from Troy to the West, but also of the voluminous accounts

[1] vii. 44 f.

[2] See the appropriate comments of B. Otis, *Virgil : A Study in Civilized Poetry* (Oxford, 1963), 313 ff.

[3] See V. Pöschl, *The Art of Virgil* (English edn., Ann Arbor, 1962), ch. 1.

[4] Livy i. 4. 1; *Aen.* vi. 851 ff.

[5] R. D. Williams, *Virgil* (G & R New Surveys I, Oxford, 1967), 26.

[6] Donat., *Vita Verg.* 23.

of the origins of Rome.[1] It was a laborious[2] but creative
exercise to sift the mass of legend, to select the strands
appropriate to his purpose, and from them to fashion his
new poetic history of the arrival of the Trojans and the con-
solidation of their presence in Italy. Though it is impossible
to assess fully the originality of Virgil's version, the com-
pression of the fighting into the mounting climax of a few
weeks' struggles must be his own arrangement. Further,
the pattern of duels in IX–XII (Pallas dying at Turnus'
hands, Mezentius killed by Aeneas, Turnus' death as the
climax of the poem) is the creation of the poet.

How original is the outline of events in VII–VIII? The
arrival of the Trojans by way of the Tiber is suggested by no
earlier extant writer; Virgil may have brought them by this
route to stress the importance of the river in Rome's
history.[3] The subsequent negotiations with King Latinus
are an adaptation of the vulgate version of Aeneas' landing
which had become stabilized in outline by the second cen-
tury B.C.[4] Cassius Hemina, Cato, and Dionysius of Halicar-
nassus all record the forging of an alliance between Latinus
and Aeneas, and Cato and Dionysius both mention the
marriage between Aeneas and Latinus' daughter Lavinia.[5]
Virgil's account of how the *portenta deum* impelled Latinus
to seek alliance with Aeneas—the patterning of the prodigies
of the bees and of Lavinia's fiery crown followed by the
oracular message in the grove of Faunus—bears the marks

[1] See the useful account of H. W. Prescott, *The Development of
Virgil's Art* (Chicago, 1927), 153 ff.

[2] See the poet's own comments in a letter to Augustus preserved
by Macrobius, *Sat.* i. 24. 11.

[3] See H. Boas, *Aeneas' Arrival in Latium* (Amsterdam, 1938), 53 ff.

[4] Earlier accounts, some as early as the fifth century, made Aeneas
founder of Rome, and Romulus and Remus his grandsons (see
Hellanicus cited by Dion. Hal. i. 72; Festus p. 328 L.; Dion. Hal.
i. 73), but these gave way to allow the necessary chronological interval
between the fall of Troy and the foundation of Rome.

[5] Cassius Hemina, fr. 7 P.; Cato, frr. 8 ff. P. (see W. A. Schröder,
M. Porcius Cato: *Das erste Buch der Origines* [Meisenheim, 1971]);
Dion. Hal. i. 59 f.

of his poetic originality; it has a counterpart in Dionysius, where Latinus is preparing to do battle with Aeneas when both leaders receive divine commands in dreams to seek a settlement with each other.

The role of King Latinus, *iam senior*, appears to have been wholly transformed by Virgil from vigorous warrior to dignified but impotent elder who abruptly resigns the leader's role when confronted with a concerted challenge from his subjects. In both Cato and Dionysius he is prominent in the fighting occasioned by the Trojans' arrival. In Dionysius' version, which is closer to Virgil's, the combined armies of Latinus and Aeneas crush the Rutulians under Turnus,[1] and after the campaign they co-operate in building the Trojan city which Aeneas called Lavinium after his new bride. But it was essential for Virgil's purpose that Aeneas the *fatalis dux* should be the unambiguous founder of the Roman race. Latinus becomes the passive elder who takes no part in the crushing of Italian opposition, and in the Homeric patterning of the later books he plays Priam to Turnus' Hector and Aeneas' Achilles.

The remainder of VII describes the malign influence of Juno and her agent Allecto as exercised successively upon Amata, Turnus, and the hunting-dogs of Ascanius. In his portrayal of this theological level of action Virgil has exploited earlier epic, Greek and Latin, rather than the legends of the historians. The tradition recorded by Dionysius of an unprovoked attack by the Trojans on the Latins has only the faintest echo in Virgil's account of the gratuitous assault by Ascanius on the tame stag, which rouses the country folk to seek revenge on the Trojans. The last section of the book, the 'gathering of the clans', is likewise modelled on Homer rather than on any extended prose-account.

In VIII Virgil sought to link these Laurentian activities of the Trojans with the legendary history of the site of Rome before the foundation, and this is achieved by description of a visit paid by Aeneas to Evander. The alliance between

[1] The manuscripts of Dionysius call him Tyrrhenus.

Latinus and Aeneas on the one hand and Evander on the
other was part of the received tradition, for Dionysius re-
cords that the unification of Trojans and Laurentians em-
braced also other local communities, including 'those who
had come to Italy with Evander from the town of Pallan-
teum'.[1] The encouragement to proceed to the site of Rome
is given to Aeneas in a dream by the river-god Tiberinus;
this is a significant element in the poet's patterning of
dream-messages which direct Aeneas' course of action.[2]

The history of the site of Rome which Aeneas hears from
the lips of Evander is close to the version of Dionysius. The
historian records that Evander, son of Hermes and Car-
menta, had migrated from Arcadia to the site of Rome some
sixty years before the Trojan war, when Faunus was king
in Latium. Evander's account of the arrival of Hercules and
his slaughter of Cacus is in essence the version of Dionysius
(and Livy).[3] The tour of the settlement in which Evander
points out sites of future importance is Virgil's own con-
tribution. The role of Pallas likewise reflects the poet's
creative originality. In Dionysius, Pallas is the son of Her-
cules;[4] as the young son of the aged Evander in Virgil, he
more poignantly expresses the tragic consequences of war
for Italian youth and for aged parents still alive. Pallas'
death is as vital a hinge in the *Aeneid* as is the death of
Patroclus in the *Iliad*, and Virgil concentrates his most crea-
tive efforts in shaping the role which he plays.

The final section of the book, in which Aeneas at Evander's
prompting seeks help from the city of Caere, may have been
inspired by an older tradition linking Aeneas with the
Etruscans.[5] Virgil may have developed the implications of

[1] Dion. Hal. i. 60. 3.

[2] See H. R. Steiner, *Der Traum in der Aeneis* (Berne, 1952),
66 ff.

[3] Dion Hal. i. 39; Livy i. 7. 3. See J. Bayet, *Les Origines de l'Hercule
romain* (Paris, 1926), 127 ff.

[4] By Lavinia, daughter of Evander, who, in this version, also bore
Latinus to Hercules. Polybius, vi. 11a is the oldest evidence for
Pallas as son of Hercules.

[5] See N. Horsfall, 'Corythus: the Return of Aeneas in Virgil and

this to represent the Etruscan contribution to the growth of Roman dominion. Mezentius, hated and ostracized by his fellow citizens, may represent the tyrannical element which had its historical embodiment in Tarquinius Superbus. The Olympian interludes in this book have no connection with the foundation-legends, but are further instances of the artistic imitation of Homer which we must now consider in detail.

II

Once Virgil had drawn the outline of his plot, he began the task of shaping his material to achieve his purpose. Donatus' summary describes that purpose as on the one hand a combined representation of the *Iliad* and the *Odyssey*, and on the other the depiction of the origins of Rome and of Augustus.[1] In other words, the poet sought to exploit all that was memorable in Homeric epic to shape the theme of Trojan arrival in such a way as to evoke the continuity of the living tradition of Rome, and to depict the concerns of Aeneas as being also the concerns of Augustus. To achieve this necessary connection between the heroic world and the historical Rome, the poet systematically presents the action of his epic by structural imitation of incidents in the *Iliad* and the *Odyssey*.[2]

In this evocation of Homer, Virgil has usually chosen for each of his books a single Homeric book, the action of which is pervasive. At the beginning of VII the transitional passage with its mention of Circe's demesne recalls the opening of *Odyssey* XII; this is a continuation, so to say, of the organic connection between *Aeneid* VI and *Odyssey* XI. But

his Sources', *J.R.S.* lxiii (1973), 68 ff., quoting Lycophron 1239: 'Aeneas shall come to Etruria' (and join Odysseus there). Horsfall suggests that Virgil chose Caere because of her record of co-operation with Rome in 390 B.C.

[1] Donat., *Vita Verg.* 21: '. . . argumentum uarium ac multiplex et quasi amborum Homeri carminum instar . . . et in quo, quod maxime studebat, Romanae simul urbis et Augusti origo contineretur.'

[2] See the impressive book of G. N. Knauer, *Die Aeneis und Homer* (Göttingen, 1964).

undoubtedly the chief Homeric quarry for VII is *Iliad* II. In that book Zeus sends Agamemnon a false dream to encourage him to attack the Trojans so that his forces may be routed. Agamemnon duly obeys, and the various contingents assembled to attack Troy are then described. This is the celebrated Catalogue of Ships. Virgil adopts a similar sequence of events in the later part of VII. Turnus is visited by a dream in which the Fury Allecto incites him to *furor*. So he too collects his forces, and at the end of the book comes a description of the contingents. In introducing this Catalogue, Virgil implores the goddesses on Helicon for inspiration in words almost identical with the Homeric invocation.[1] Within this controlling framework of *Iliad* II, there are numerous other reminiscences of Homeric situations.[2]

Book VIII, with its two themes of Aeneas' visit to Evander and the forging of the arms of Aeneas by Vulcan at Venus' request, has correspondingly two main sources of Homeric inspiration. Aeneas' journey to Pallanteum, his conversation with the aged Evander, and his departure all recall *Odyssey* III in which Telemachus visits the aged Nestor at Pylos. The Homeric *mise en scène* is of course quite different. The son of Odysseus goes to inquire the whereabouts of his wandering father, and nothing could be in greater contrast to Aeneas' purpose of requesting Evander's military support. Yet the patterning of journey and arrival is designedly similar. Athene provides fine weather for Telemachus' journey, just as the river-god grants Aeneas a calm passage.[3] Pallas, the son of Evander, has his counterpart in Nestor's son Peisistratus. Just as Nestor inquires ὦ ξεῖνοι, τίνες ἐστέ; πόθεν πλεῖθ' ὑγρὰ κέλευθα; and Telemachus replies, so in the Virgilian scene the boy Pallas asks the identical questions and Aeneas answers.[4] Nestor nostalgically harks back to Troy, Evander to the visit of

[1] *Aen.* vii. 641 ff., *Il.* ii. 484 ff.

[2] See vii. 15 ff. and *Od.* x. 212 ff.; vii. 170 ff. and *Od.* vii. 180 ff.; vii. 286 ff. and *Od.* v. 282 ff.; etc.

[3] viii. 86; *Od.* ii. 420 ff.   [4] viii. 112 ff.; *Od.* iii. 71 ff.

Anchises, and just as Nestor conducts Telemachus to his sleeping-quarters, so Evander personally attends Aeneas.[1]

For the Olympian scenes in this book, Virgil had recourse to *Iliad* XVIII. As Venus persuades her husband Vulcan to manufacture arms for Aeneas, and Vulcan gets the Cyclopes to work on them, so in Homer Thetis in less intimate fashion[2] persuades Hephaestus to make arms for Achilles, and there is a description of the motifs on the shield as in Virgil. (Characteristically, the shield-motifs in Virgil are more closely relevant to the theme of his poem.) And just as Thetis brings the arms to Achilles, so Venus bestows them on Aeneas, and the reactions of the two heroes are expressed in virtually identical words.[3]

Beyond this deployment of a Homeric framework for structural imitation, Virgil presses into the service of allusive imitation the insights or happy descriptions of a host of other Greek and Roman poets from Hesiod to Catullus and Lucretius. This should not be interpreted as evidence that he has insufficient thoughts and words of his own. 'Virgil profoundly and intricately makes his sources help him to give his own message and nothing else.'[4] The technique enables the deeply read poet at once to acknowledge the noble influence of a Euripides or an Ennius on his well-stocked mind, and to enlist their aid in the formulation of thoughts and images. So far as Greek influence is concerned, the epic of Apollonius Rhodius is especially frequently evoked.[5] Of

[1] viii. 154 ff. and *Od*. iii. 102 ff.; viii. 366 and *Od*. iii. 396.

[2] The sensual approach of Venus is modelled on Hera's at *Il*. xiv. 292 ff.

[3] *Il*. xix. 18: τέρπετο δ' ἐν χείρεσσιν ἔχων θεοῦ ἀγλαὰ δῶρα. *Aen*. viii. 619 f.: 'miraturque interque manus et bracchia uersat/ terribilem cristis galeam . . .'

[4] So W. F. Jackson Knight, 'Virgil's Elysium' in *Virgil* (ed. Dudley, London, 1969), 165.

[5] Note vii. 37 f. and Ap. Rhod. iii. 1 ff.; vii. 246 and Ap. Rhod. iv. 1176; vii. 514 ff. and Ap. Rhod. iv. 129 ff.; vii. 565 ff. and Ap. Rhod. ii. 737 ff.; vii. 719 ff. and Ap. Rhod. i. 120 f.; viii. 427 ff. and Ap. Rhod. i. 730 ff. See in general C. Conrady, *De Vergilio Apollonii Rhodii imitatore* (Freiburg, 1904), 54 ff.

the Latin authors Ennius becomes increasingly important
for the 'Iliadic' *Aeneid* with its numerous allusions to
Italian religious and political history. It has in fact been
suggested that in VII and VIII there are structural imita-
tions of Ennius as well as of Homer. The opening of the
temple of Janus by Juno, where there is a clear echo of a
similar gesture by Discordia in Ennius,[1] has been proposed
as a sign of extensive dependence in VII. The first passage
of VIII, where the prayer of Aeneas and the compact be-
tween Aeneas and Evander echo fragments in Ennius'
Annals, and again the description of Aeneas' shield at the
close of the book, which Servius proclaims as Ennian, are
other examples suggested.[2] In none of these instances, how-
ever, has sufficient of Ennius' poetry survived to confirm
the thesis, and given the firm deployment of Homer for
structural imitation in these books it is more probable that
imitation of Ennius is merely allusive.[3]

III

The particular function of VII is to inaugurate the second
round of tests and trials for Aeneas. In the 'Odyssean'
Aeneid he had learned to overcome the personal crises be-
setting the Homeric hero—the temptation to put personal
glory before public mission during the fall of Troy, the temp-
tation to succumb to the *labor* of the pilgrimage, the
temptation to found a Trojan-Phoenician dynasty in the
territory of Carthage. With the arrival in Italy and the de-
scent into Hades to hear from Anchises the future of the
Roman race, the pressures of the pilgrimage are lightened.
But now a second series of crises faces the archetypal

---

[1] vii. 620 ff.; Enn. *Ann.* 266 V.

[2] viii. 72 and *Ann.* 54 V.; viii. 150 and *Ann.* 32 V.; viii. 630 ff.,
and Servius ad loc. 'sane totus hic locus Ennianus est.' See E.
Norden, *Ennius und Vergilius* (Leipzig, 1915), 18 ff., 161 ff., for the
arguments for structural imitation.

[3] See now M. Wigodsky, *Vergil and Early Latin Poetry* (*Hermes
Einzelschr.* 24 [1972]), 46, 62 ff., arguing that the comment of
Servius has reference only to the Romulus–Remus scene at 630 ff.

Roman—the formidable Latin opposition which must be reluctantly crushed in order to be reconciled. After the victory over his own *furor*, after the escape from Dido's sexual *furor*, he must now face and overcome the martial *furor* of Turnus.

Virgil achieves this structural aim of emphasizing that for Aeneas 'but half of his heavy task was done' by a deliberate series of echoes from Book I.[1] In I, Juno observes the Roman fleet pressing on to Latium; she soliloquizes upon her eternal grievance. She cannot prevent Aeneas from reaching Latium ('quippe uetor fatis') but she can delay him. She summons the help of Aeolus and his winds to scatter the Roman fleet. Compare the action of VII, in which Juno sees the Trojans happily settled in Latium, and after another soliloquy ('heu stirpem inuisam et fatis contraria nostris/ fata Phrygum!') she enlists the aid of the fury Allecto to inspire opposition amongst the Latins.[2] Just as Book I begins with a brief history of Carthage, so VII has a longer account of the history of the Latins.[3] The description of the paintings in the temple at Carthage is matched by the account of the wooden carvings in the palace of Latinus.[4] Ilioneus is the preliminary spokesman for the Trojans both at Carthage and at Laurentum, and in each case Dido and Latinus express the wish for the presence of Aeneas.[5] Finally, just as Cupid, the agent of Venus, wounds Dido and rouses the *furor* of her love-passion, so Allecto, the agent of Juno, wounds Turnus and unleashes the *furor* of war.[6]

This book has three main sections, the arrival of the Trojans and their initial welcome by Latinus (1–285),[7] the

[1] See Pöschl (p. xii n. 3), ch. 1. This patterning of echoes from Book I excludes the possibility of pervasive imitation of Homer in the first part of VII. [2] i. 34 ff. and vii. 286 ff.
[3] i. 12 ff. and vii. 45 ff. [4] i. 446 ff. and vii. 170 ff.
[5] i. 521, 575 f. and vii. 212, 263 ff. [6] i. 715 ff. and vii. 445 ff.
[7] E. Fraenkel, 'Some Aspects of the Structure of *Aeneid* VII', *J.R.S.* xxxv (1945), 1 ff., explains why the book proper can begin only at lines 37 ff. It would not have been fitting to end VI with the details of the journey to the Tiber, since this would have detracted from the climax to the book.

vindictive determination of Juno to delay the alliance and
her enlistment of Allecto (286–571), and the decision to go to
war followed by the 'gathering of the clans' (572–817). The
first section has two themes to expound, the noble and
antique civilization of the Latins, and the divine ordination
that they should become allies of the Trojans. Their
genealogy is duly traced back to Saturn; the statuary and
the spoils in the *tectum augustum* confirm that Latium will
be a worthy partner in Rome's world-conquest; and Latinus
recalls that Dardanus the founder of Troy was in origin
a Latin, so that the Trojans are in fact returning home. The
conditions of their return have been already divinely pre-
scribed. Latinus, *fato diuum*, has had no male issue. His one
daughter Lavinia is courted by Turnus, the favourite of her
mother Amata—*sed portenta deum obstant*. The portent of
the bees presages external dominion; the fire which catches
Lavinia's hair and fills the house with smoke augurs the
fire of conquest which Lavinia as bride will unleash. The
prodigies have their message confirmed by the oracular
utterance of Faunus—*externi uenient generi*. Virgil depicts
these events as having occurred prior to the Trojans' arrival,
and Latinus makes the offer of marriage to Lavinia without
delay.

In the second section, Allecto is put to work by Juno to
arouse in turn the three social groupings which could put
the greatest pressure on Latinus to renounce the treaty and
to declare war on the Trojans. Allecto makes first for
Latinus' wife Amata, the natural leader of the Laurentian
matrons and a key figure at court. When she fails to per-
suade her husband to favour Turnus as son-in-law, she
becomes the embodiment of *furor*.[1] Virgil composes a strik-
ing simile of a spinning-top to describe Amata's whirling
course through the city, and every element in the simile has
a counterpart in life; Amata is the top, Allecto's serpent

---

[1] The aim of Allecto is to make her *furibunda* (348; cf. 350); after
the *furiale malum* sinks deep within her (375), Amata *furit lymphata
per urbem* (377) and *maiorem orsa furorem* (386).

is the whip, and Juno and Allecto are the playing boys.[1] She leads the matrons in a Bacchic revel which powerfully evokes the drama of Euripides. Allecto's second target is Turnus,[2] the natural military leader of the Latins at Ardea. As with Amata there is a preliminary stage before the madness takes hold, as with Amata the onset of *furor* is described by a powerful simile, in which Turnus is the bubbling water in a cauldron and Allecto the flame beneath it. Allecto leaves Turnus preparing forces for battle and prepares her third mischief, so that the alliance between *matres* and Turnus' forces may be strengthened further by the *agrestes*. Virgil achieves a brilliant variety of tone here with the affecting description of the domestic care of the tame stag, the pathos of the animal (*imploranti similis*) when wounded by Ascanius, and the excited reactions of the indignant farmers; the third balancing simile compares the countrymen to waves which under the impact of the wind (Allecto) rise high to heaven.

The general purport of this second act is clear. 'Only through the spread of a particular type of insanity can people who shortly before were leading normal and peaceful lives be brought to the state of mind in which they will resort to something so horrible as war.'[3] And perhaps the mention of *gener atque socer*[4] at the centre of this insanity would have tempted Virgil's readers to apply the lesson to the dying days of the Republic.

In the third division of the book, Virgil neatly assembles the three groups in reverse order—*pastores*, Turnus and his followers, *matres*—as a linking device with the previous section. Together they press Latinus to declare war on the Trojans. There is now a fourth simile, contrapuntal to the previous three and sustaining the imagery of the third; Latinus is like a rock unmoved by the snarling waves. But

---

[1] *Aen.* vii. 378 ff. On this facet of Virgil's art, see D. A. West, 'Multiple-correspondence similes in the *Aeneid*', *J.R.S.* lix (1969), 40 ff., and West's further contribution in *Philol.* cxiv (1970), 262 ff.
[2] On the developing characterization of Turnus, see Pöschl (p. xii n. 3), ch. 2.   [3] So Fraenkel (p. xx n. 7).   [4] vii. 317.

the storm unleashed by Juno is too much for him; *rerumque reliquit habenas.* In a favourite device to link past with present, Virgil describes how Juno opens the gates of Janus' temple, the solemn sign of a declaration of war even in Augustan times. There follows the celebrated account of the gathering of the clans. Virgil's list is less than half the length of Homer's Catalogue of Ships,[1] but this recital of the contingents of Etruscans, Latins, Sabines, Aequi, Marsi, Campanians, and Volscians is clearly intended 'to move the feeling of his Italian reader as he sees the stately procession of Italian warriors passing before him, or perchance to fill his mind with pride and pleasure at finding among them the ancient representatives of his own city or district.'[2] Beyond this purpose of arousing local patriotic pride, the Catalogue has the function also of bringing together the leading heroes who are to confront Aeneas in the final books.

In what pattern, if any, are the clans arranged? Critics from Macrobius onwards have stressed that the list follows no geographical sequence, unlike the Catalogues of Homer and Apollonius.[3] Some have suggested a patterning of heroes, and clearly the positioning of Mezentius at the beginning, and of Turnus and Camilla at the end, provides a frame into which the lesser figures are placed. But one remains sceptical of attempts to demonstrate a coherent pattern of heroes within the frame.[4] Yet it is highly unlikely that

[1] There are 28 groups in Homer and 33 in Apollonius Rhodius (i. 23 ff.) as against 13 in Virgil.

[2] W. Warde Fowler, *Virgil's 'Gathering of the Clans'*[2] (Oxford, 1918), 27.

[3] Macr. *Sat.* v. 15. 4: 'Vergilius nullum in commemorandis regionibus ordinem seruat, sed locorum seriem saltibus lacerat'. Brave attempts have been made to impose a geographical scheme; see, e.g., B. Brotherton, 'Vergil's Catalogue of the Latin Forces', *T.A.P.A.* lxii (1931), 198: 'The districts involved form a great circle in central Italy: northern Latium, southern Etruria, the lands of the Sabines, the Aequi, Marsi, Volsci, and north central Latium.' But it is admitted that three of the thirteen do not fit into the clockwise scheme suggested.

[4] Cf. R. D. Williams, *C.Q.* 1 (1961), 146 ff.; H.-D. Reeker, *Die Landschaft in der Aeneis* (Hildesheim, 1971), 102 ff.

Virgil assembled them at random; no convincing solution of their order has, however, been put forward. But all can agree about the impressive variety with which Virgil, in contrast to Homer and Apollonius, presents the various contingents. The variation lies in the selective deployment of aetiologies and genealogies, of names of towns and tribes and rivers, of the weapons carried, of their demeanour on the march, of their future fate. The stylistic techniques extend from simile and literary evocation (Camilla flying over the fields as do the horses of Erichthonius in Homer[1]) to the studied variation in position and even in the case of the individual leaders of each contingent.

IV

In VIII Virgil switches our attention from the Latins and Turnus to the Trojans and Aeneas as he makes his way to Pallanteum. He sees there the site of the future Rome, and learns more of the history to which Anchises had introduced him in Elysium. As VII harks back to I, so VIII has a connection with II, the new Rome which is to replace the old Troy. The poet planned VIII as an interlude and a change of mood between the gathering storm of VII and the outbreak of battle in IX. A key-word of the book is *mirari*, found ten times; Aeneas has leisure to marvel at Rome's future. Virgil has deployed this interlude to underline without ambiguity the links between Roman past and Roman present, to demonstrate that there is one and the same Rome, and to portray Aeneas, Hercules, Evander, and even Saturn as forerunners or 'types' of Augustus.[2] Saturn

---

[1] *Il.* xx. 226 ff.

[2] The important book of G. Binder, *Aeneas und Augustus* (Meisenheim, 1971) is virtually a commentary on Book VIII with a full bibliography. The most useful of earlier works are W. Warde Fowler, *Aeneas at the Site of Rome*[2] (Oxford, 1918); J. R. Bacon, 'Aeneas in Wonderland', *C.R.* liii (1939), 97 ff.; F. Bömer, 'Studien zum VIII. Buche der *Aeneis*', *Rh.M.* xcii (1944) 319 ff.; V. Buchheit, *Vergil über die Sendung Roms* (Heidelberg, 1963); M. C. J. Putnam, *The*

and Evander are symbols of peace in plenty and of unostentatious living, ideals for the *pax Augusta*. Hercules' conquest over Cacus, Aeneas' victory over Turnus are patterned precursors of Augustus' crushing of Antony.[1]

We have noted that the book has two interwoven themes —Aeneas' visit to and departure from Pallanteum (1–369, 454–607), and the armour of Aeneas (370–453, 608–731). But a further subtlety of structure should be noted. The events at Pallanteum and in the vale of Caere extend over three days. On the first, the events of the past are presented (102–369); on the second, the events of the present (454–607); and on the third, the events of the future, especially as depicted on the shield of Aeneas (608–731).[2] Thus Aeneas is introduced to the dynamic continuum of Roman history. Hercules is the model for Aeneas as Aeneas is to be the type of Augustus.

Aeneas' journey to Evander is proposed to him in a vision by the Tiber-god, who guarantees the authenticity of his message with the promised portent of the sow and its thirty piglets, representing the thirty years till Ascanius' foundation of Alba Longa. On rising, Aeneas offers a prayer to the Laurentian nymphs and to Tiberinus; here Virgil appropriately evokes the thought and language of Ennius.[3] He sees the sow's litter and performs the sacrifice to Juno as commanded; the sacrifice to the angry goddess ensures a calm river-journey mirrored in the diction of this tranquil passage.[4]

The arrival at Pallanteum coincides with the yearly solemnities of the cult of Hercules. Virgil's contemporaries

Poetry of the Aeneid (Harvard, 1965), ch. 3 (well written but over-speculative on poetic symbolism); and R. D. Williams's useful edition of VII–XII (London, 1973). The recent book of E. V. George, *Aeneid VIII and the Aitia of Callimachus* (London, 1974), fails to establish any fruitful connection with Callimachus.

[1] For another view see Fordyce's commentary ad locc.

[2] See Otis (p. xii n. 2) 330 ff.

[3] Not only the well-known imitation of Enn. *Ann.* 54 V. at 72, but also at 77 ('regnator aquarum' = 67 V. 'qui est omnibus princeps').

[4] viii. 68–96.

are invited here to compare past with present;[1] they would note that the date of Aeneas' arrival coincides not only with the annual festival of Hercules but also with the triumphant journey of Augustus to Rome on 12 August 29 B.C. In his honorific address, Aeneas emphasizes the common lineage of Evander and the Trojan founder Dardanus, and Evander in reply dilates upon his former meeting with Anchises. The note struck here is the interpenetration of Greeks and Trojans, and the need for alliance between the cultivated nations to bring civilization to the rude Italians. After the cult-feast Evander tells the history of Hercules and Cacus.[2] Cacus is the personification of bestiality, cruelty, and injustice; Hercules, the Stoic patron-saint, is the image of virtue and unflinching heroism in the face of anarchy throughout the world. It is notable that Hercules shows no mercy and gives his anger full rein in the destruction of the bestial cruelty for which Cacus stands; this may offer a clue to the mercilessness of Aeneas in the final episode of the poem. At the close of the story, the Trojans are invited to join in the cult-ceremony of Hercules; the description of the rite surviving in the Augustan period is yet another conscious link between past and present.

After the ceremonial all make their way to the city, and *en route* Evander, *Romanae conditor arcis*, explains the history of the site. After the primeval barbarism under the Fauns and the Nymphs, Saturn introduced the Golden Age. The patterning which makes Saturn a type of Aeneas is striking. He came as an exile, brought a golden era of peace, and was the first foreigner to become king and to rule the state of his own creation.[3] But then *belli rabies et amor suc-*

[1] viii. 98–100.

[2] See J. G. Winter, *The Myth of Hercules at Rome* (N.Y., 1910); J. Bayet, *Les Origines de l'Hercule romain* (Paris, 1926); G. K. Galinsky, *The Herakles Theme* (Oxford, 1972) and 'The Hercules-Cacus Episode in *Aeneid* viii', *A.J.P.* lxxxvii (1966), 18 ff.; H. Schnepf, 'Das Herculesabenteuer in Virgils *Aeneis*', *Gymn.* lxvi (1959), 250 ff.; Fr. Münzer, *Cacus der Rinderdieb* (Basle, 1911); V. Buchheit (p. xxiv n. 2), 116 ff.

[3] Binder (p. xxiv n. 2), 84 ff.; Buchheit (p. xxiv n. 2), 92 f.

cessit habendi; only with the advent of Evander himself, who came to the site of Rome at the call of destiny and at the instance of Carmentis and Apollo (Augustus' favourite divinity), have peace and humble living returned. He too is a type of Aeneas and of Augustus.

Evander now conducts his guest round significant landmarks of the city[1] in another passage which connects the old and the contemporary Rome. The Augustan reader could retrace the route from the Forum Boarium along the Vicus Iugarius, and the places pointed out by Evander had rich historical associations. The Porta Carmentalis commemorates the earliest Roman settlement of Evander, and the cult of Carmenta was continued in the Augustan period.[2] The Lupercal was the legendary site of the suckling of Romulus and Remus by the wolf; Augustus restored the grotto there.[3] The Asylum was the scene of the first mingling of Latin races. The Argiletum may have been mentioned for its association with the temple of Janus, again important in Augustan cult. When Evander reaches the Capitol, he pronounces the two citadels to have been the foundations of Janus and Saturn; Virgil may refer here not to the Janiculum and the Capitol but to the two eminences on the Capitol itself.[4] Finally, they make their way to the Palatine, where Evander's humble house stands, and there he bids Aeneas emulate Hercules in contempt for riches. Augustus' house too was on the Palatine, its modest dimensions consonant with this recommendation of *frugalitas*.[5] The pattern of Saturn, Hercules, Evander, Aeneas as types of Augustus is at its clearest here.

The artistic separation of the first day, which reveals the

[1] See P. Grimal, 'La Promenade d'Evandre et d'Énée à la lumière des fouilles récentes', *R.E.A.* 1 (1948), 348 ff.

[2] Ovid, *F.* i. 461 ff.

[3] Suet. *Aug.* 31.

[4] Fordyce is of a different opinion (see his note). The reference to the *Tarpeia sedes* is to the northern summit of the Capitol.

[5] Suet. *Aug.* 72: '. . . postea in Palatio, sed nihilominus aedibus modicis Hortensianis, et neque laxitate neque cultu conspicuis'. See Warde Fowler (p. xxiv n. 2), 76.

past, from the second, describing the present, is achieved
by the Olympian scene between Venus and Vulcan and the
description of Vulcan's workshop. It is right to speak here
of 'an ornate, almost baroque interlude' in which the poet
takes a holiday in brilliant and rhetorical description of
a fabulous world;[1] one should also note the humorous
element, for the god of fire is warmed by Venus' snowy arms
and feels the customary flame. At the same time, however,
this scene interlinks the divine and human levels in Virgil's
vision of the progress of the world. Just as Juno has acknow-
ledged that she can hinder but not prevent the establish-
ment of the new Troy in Latium, so Vulcan speaks here
of the temporary flexibility of fate. Jupiter and fate (here
as elsewhere identical)[2] ordain what is to be, but Venus
and Vulcan could have delayed the fall of Troy; they
personify the cosmic forces intermediate between God
and men.[3]

On the second day Evander, appropriately clad in
Italian sandals and Greek sword, holds a war-council with
Aeneas and suggests an alliance with Etruscan Caere, which
has been forewarned by its aged *haruspex* to choose a
foreign leader against Turnus and Mezentius. The pre-
figuration of the historical conquest of Latium should be
noted; not only was the Rome that dominated the Latin
League a largely Etruscan city which had shaken off Etrus-
can kingship, but Turnus is from Ardea, one of the moving
spirits of the League.[4] Aeneas' momentary dismay at the
hazards confronting him is lifted by the appearance of the
glowing arms in the sky, the fulfilment of Venus' promise.
Such a promise has not been signalled earlier in the poem,
and the presence of a half-line[5] may be an indication of in-
tended revision here. The final lines of this scene are

[1] So Williams (p. xxiv n. 2), 252.
[2] C. Bailey, *Religion in Virgil* (Oxford, 1935), 228 ff.
[3] See A. Wlosok, *Die Göttin Venus in Vergils Aeneis* (Heidelberg,
1967), 139 ff. (unfortunately not discussing this passage).
[4] Cf. Livy i. 57 (with Ogilvie's notes), iii. 71.
[5] viii. 536.

dominated by the farewell between Evander and Pallas, one of the group of Italian youth whose deaths in the ensuing books reflect Virgil's consciousness of the tragedy of necessary war.

The third day finds Aeneas in the grove near Caere, where Venus bestows the arms which are to guarantee his victory. This last scene of VIII is dominated by the description of the motifs on Aeneas' shield. There are eight representations, reflecting 'the most momentous crises in the annals of Rome, culminating in the great triumph of Augustus'.[1] The contrast with the universal themes on Achilles' shield in the *Iliad* emphasizes yet again the differing purposes of Virgil's national epic. The choice of historical exemplars notably avoids military triumphs except for Actium, but it is a mistake to see in this list merely 'escapes from terrible perils'.[2] It is a sequence representing growth through struggles *in Italy*, and it is therefore closely related to the theme of the 'Iliadic' *Aeneid*. The first scene appropriately is the suckling of the twins. The triptych on relations between emergent Rome and the Sabines—rape, war, peace— denotes the fusion through combat of the two communities. Mettius' infidelity marks the end of the challenge of Alba Longa, and the transfer of its population to Rome. The scene in which Porsenna commands the reinstatement of Tarquin and is answered by the defiant heroism of Horatius and Cloelia shows Etruscan Rome growing into liberty. The fifth scene, Manlius and the geese repelling the Gauls, recalls the new beginning of Rome after the disaster of the Allia; Camillus is to be the new Romulus. At this point, where Pyrrhus and Hannibal might have been anticipated, the nature of the scenes abruptly changes; the fact is that the theme of Rome's struggle with the foreign invader is irrelevant to the second half of the *Aeneid*.

The sixth scene emphasizes the importance of *religio*

[1] W. Y. Sellar, *Virgil*[3] (Oxford, 1897), 323. On the shield motifs see C. Becker, 'Der Schild des Aeneas', *Wien. Stud.* lxxvii (1964), 111 ff.

[2] Warde Fowler (p. xxiv n. 2), 104.

Romana, looking forward to the final depiction of Antony's retinue of Egyptian gods; the seventh, a scene in Hades, excoriates Catiline, the personification of first-century revolution, and canonizes the younger Cato, the apostle of Senatorial order and Stoic reason. It is the peace of rational order which Augustus proclaims, *pax* resting on *concordia*.[1] And so to the final scene of the battle of Actium, with Antony as the representative of discord. It is a battle not only between men but also between deities, and it is Augustus' Apollo who turns the fight.[2]

As Aeneas gazes at the shield 'he takes on his shoulder the glory and destiny of his descendants'. This final line points back to Atlas, the forebear of both Trojans and Arcadians,[3] and forward to the Augustan Age.

P. G. WALSH

[1] S. Weinstock, 'Pax and the "Ara Pacis"', *J.R.S.* l (1960), 44 ff., quoting Cic. *Leg. Agr.* i. 23, *Att.* xi. 19. 1, etc.

[2] viii. 704 f.

[3] viii. 136 ff.

SELECT BIBLIOGRAPHY

AUSTIN, R. G., *P. Vergili Maronis Aeneidos Liber Primus*, Oxford, 1971; *Liber Secundus*, Oxford, 1964; *Liber Quartus*, Oxford, 1955.

AXELSON, B., *Unpoetische Wörter*, Lund, 1945.

BAILEY, C., *Religion in Virgil*, Oxford, 1935.

BINDER, G., *Aeneas und Augustus : Interpretationen zum 8. Buch der Aeneis*, Meisenheim am Glan, 1971.

BOYANCÉ, P., *La Religion de Virgile*, Paris, 1963.

CAMPS, W. A., *An Introduction to Virgil's Aeneid*, Oxford, 1969.

CONINGTON, J., and NETTLESHIP, H., *P. Vergili Maronis Opera*, Vol. III[3], rev. Nettleship, London, 1883.

CONWAY, R. S., *P. Vergili Maronis Aeneidos Liber Primus*, Cambridge, 1935.

FOWLER, W. WARDE, *Virgil's 'Gathering of the Clans'*[2], Oxford, 1918.

—— *Aeneas at the Site of Rome*[2], Oxford, 1918.

FRAENKEL, E., 'Some Aspects of the Structure of *Aeneid* VII', J.R.S. xxxv (1945), 1–14.

HEINZE, R., *Virgils epische Technik*[3], Leipzig, 1915.

HENRY, J., *Aeneidea*, London–Dublin, 1873–92.

HEYNE, C. G., and WAGNER, G. P. E., *Virgilii Opera*[4], Leipzig–London, 1830–41.

HOFMANN, J. B., *Lateinische Umgangssprache*[2], Heidelberg, 1936.

KNAUER, G. N., *Die Aeneis und Homer*, Göttingen, 1964 (Hypomnemata, Heft 7).

LATTE, K., *Römische Religionsgeschichte*, Munich, 1960.

LEUMANN, M., *Kleine Schriften*, Zürich, 1959.

LÖFSTEDT, E., *Syntactica* i[2] (Lund, 1942), ii (Lund, 1933).

—— *Philologischer Kommentar zur Peregrinatio Aetheriae*, Uppsala, 1911.

MACKAIL, J. W., *The Aeneid of Virgil*, Oxford, 1930.

MADVIG, J. N., *Opuscula Academica*, Copenhagen, 1834–42.

MAROUZEAU, J., *Traité de stylistique latine*[4], Paris, 1962.

MEISTER, K., *Lateinisch-griechische Eigennamen*, Hft. i, Leipzig–Berlin, 1916.

NETTLESHIP, H., *Contributions to Latin Lexicography*, Oxford, 1889.

NORDEN, E., *P. Vergilius Maro, Aeneis Buch VI*[3], Leipzig, 1927.

OGILVIE, R. M., *A Commentary on Livy: Books 1–5*, Oxford, 1965.

OTIS, B., *Virgil: A Study in Civilized Poetry*, Oxford, 1963.

PAGE, T. E., *Virgil*, London, 1894–1900.

PÖSCHL, V., *Die Dichtkunst Virgils: Bild und Symbol in der Äneis*, Innsbruck–Vienna, 1950 (tr. G. Seligson, *The Art of Virgil . . .*, Michigan, 1962).

SCHULZE, W., *Zur Geschichte lateinischer Eigennamen*[2], Berlin, 1966.

SHACKLETON BAILEY, D. R., *Propertiana*, Cambridge, 1956.

TILLY, B., *Vergil's Latium*, Oxford, 1947.

VAHLEN, J., *Ennianae poesis reliquiae*[3], Leipzig, 1928.

—— *Opuscula Academica*, Leipzig, 1907–8.

WACKERNAGEL, J., *Vorlesungen über Syntax*, Basel, 1926–8.

—— *Kleine Schriften*, Göttingen, 1955.

WALDE, A., and HOFMANN, J. B., *Lateinisches etymologisches Wörterbuch*, Heildelberg, 1930–56.

WILKINSON, L. P., *Golden Latin Artistry*, Cambridge, 1963.

WISSOWA, G., *Religion und Kultus der Römer*, Munich, 1912.

Short bibliographies on particular topics will be found *passim* in the Commentary; the footnotes to the Introduction, pp. xi–xxx, contain important further references.

Abbreviations

A.L.L.   *Archiv für lateinische Lexicographie.*

K.–S.   Kühner, R., and Stegmann, C., *Ausführliche Grammatik der lateinischen Sprache*[2], Hanover, 1912–14.

P.–W.   Pauly–Wissowa (–Kroll), *Real-Encyclopädie.*

T.L.L.   *Thesaurus Linguae Latinae.*

NOTE ON THE TEXT

I am grateful to the Delegates of the Oxford University Press and to Sir Roger Mynors for their generous permission to reproduce the Oxford Classical Text (1969; revised 1972) as the basis for this Commentary.

SIGLA CODICVM

A	Schedae Vaticano-Berolinenses	saec. v
B	fragmentum Mediolanense (supra, p. vii)	saec. v/vi
F	Vaticanus lat. 3225	saec. iv
G	Sangallensis 1394	saec. v
M	Florentinus Laur. xxxix. 1	saec. v
P	Vaticanus Palatinus lat. 1631	saec. iv/v
R	Vaticanus lat. 3867	saec. v
V	fragmenta Veronensia	saec. v
p	Parisinus lat. 7906	saec. viii ex.
M²P²R²	corrector aliquis antiquus	

Codices saeculi noni:

a	Bernensis 172 cum Parisino lat. 7929 (p. x)
b	Bernensis 165
c	Bernensis 184
d	Bernensis 255+239
e	Bernensis 167
f	Oxoniensis Bodl. Auct. F. 2. 8
h	Valentianensis 407
r	Parisinus lat. 7926
s	Parisinus lat. 7928
t	Parisinus lat. 13043
u	Parisinus lat. 13044
v	Vaticanus lat. 1570
	ω consensus horum uel omnium uel quotquot non separatim nominantur
γ	Guelferbytanus Gudianus lat. 2°. 70 (p. x)
def.	deficit (uel mutilus est uel legi non potest)
recc.	codices saec. nono recentiores

P. VERGILI MARONIS

AENEIDOS

LIBER VII

Tv quoque litoribus nostris, Aeneia nutrix,
aeternam moriens famam, Caieta, dedisti;
et nunc seruat honos sedem tuus, ossaque nomen
Hesperia in magna, si qua est ea gloria, signat.
  At pius exsequiis Aeneas rite solutis,   5
aggere composito tumuli, postquam alta quierunt
aequora, tendit iter uelis portumque relinquit.
aspirant aurae in noctem nec candida cursus
luna negat, splendet tremulo sub lumine pontus.
proxima Circaeae raduntur litora terrae,   10
diues inaccessos ubi Solis filia lucos
adsiduo resonat cantu, tectisque superbis
urit odoratam nocturna in lumina cedrum
arguto tenuis percurrens pectine telas.
hinc exaudiri gemitus iraeque leonum   15
uincla recusantum et sera sub nocte rudentum,
saetigerique sues atque in praesepibus ursi
saeuire ac formae magnorum ululare luporum,
quos hominum ex facie dea saeua potentibus herbis
induerat Circe in uultus ac terga ferarum.   20
quae ne monstra pii paterentur talia Troes
delati in portus neu litora dira subirent,

   1–4 *MPR*; 5–22 *FMPR*   2 famam moriens P^1 4 signat
$R\omega$: signant *MP, utrumque Tib.*   5 Aeneas exequiis M^1R^1
6 '*Hebrus* quierant *legit*' *Seru.* (*cf. A.* iv 523)   7 portusque *P*
(*ut undecies alibi; cf. A.* iii 10)   reliquit *cd, Tib.*   8 cursus
FMPabcfr: cursum *R\omega, Tib.*   13 nocturno in lumine *Maeu*
16 sera] saeua *P*

I

Neptunus uentis impleuit uela secundis,
atque fugam dedit et praeter uada feruida uexit.

Iamque rubescebat radiis mare et aethere ab alto   25
Aurora in roseis fulgebat lutea bigis,
cum uenti posuere omnisque repente resedit
flatus, et in lento luctantur marmore tonsae.
atque hic Aeneas ingentem ex aequore lucum
prospicit. hunc inter fluuio Tiberinus amoeno   30
uerticibus rapidis et multa flauus harena
in mare prorumpit. uariae circumque supraque
adsuetae ripis uolucres et fluminis alueo
aethera mulcebant cantu lucoque uolabant.
flectere iter sociis terraeque aduertere proras   35
imperat et laetus fluuio succedit opaco.

Nunc age, qui reges, Erato, quae tempora, rerum
quis Latio antiquo fuerit status, aduena classem
cum primum Ausoniis exercitus appulit oris,
expediam, et primae reuocabo exordia pugnae.   40
tu uatem, tu, diua, mone. dicam horrida bella,
dicam acies actosque animis in funera reges,
Tyrrhenamque manum totamque sub arma coactam
Hesperiam. maior rerum mihi nascitur ordo,
maius opus moueo.

                Rex arua Latinus et urbes   45
iam senior longa placidas in pace regebat.
hunc Fauno et nympha genitum Laurente Marica
accipimus; Fauno Picus pater, isque parentem
te, Saturne, refert, tu sanguinis ultimus auctor.
filius huic fato diuum prolesque uirilis   50
nulla fuit, primaque oriens erepta iuuenta est.
sola domum et tantas seruabat filia sedes
iam matura uiro, iam plenis nubilis annis.
multi illam magno e Latio totaque petebant
Ausonia; petit ante alios pulcherrimus omnis   55

23–55 *FMPR*   26 inroseis, *id est* non roseis '*multi*' *ap. Seru.*
53 in plenis *P*

Turnus, auis atauisque potens, quem regia coniunx
adiungi generum miro properabat amore;
sed uariis portenta deum terroribus obstant.
laurus erat tecti medio in penetralibus altis
sacra comam multosque metu seruata per annos,   60
quam pater inuentam, primas cum conderet arces,
ipse ferebatur Phoebo sacrasse Latinus,
Laurentisque ab ea nomen posuisse colonis.
huius apes summum densae (mirabile dictu)
stridore ingenti liquidum trans aethera uectae   65
obsedere apicem, et pedibus per mutua nexis
examen subitum ramo frondente pependit.
continuo uates 'externum cernimus' inquit
'aduentare uirum et partis petere agmen easdem
partibus ex isdem et summa dominarier arce.'   70
praeterea, castis adolet dum altaria taedis,
et iuxta genitorem astat Lauinia uirgo,
uisa (nefas) longis comprendere crinibus ignem
atque omnem ornatum flamma crepitante cremari,
regalisque accensa comas, accensa coronam   75
insignem gemmis; tum fumida lumine fuluo
inuolui ac totis Volcanum spargere tectis.
id uero horrendum ac uisu mirabile ferri:
namque fore inlustrem fama fatisque canebant
ipsam, sed populo magnum portendere bellum.   80
    At rex sollicitus monstris oracula Fauni,
fatidici genitoris, adit lucosque sub alta
consulit Albunea, nemorum quae maxima sacro
fonte sonat saeuamque exhalat opaca mephitim.
hinc Italae gentes omnisque Oenotria tellus   85
in dubiis responsa petunt; huc dona sacerdos
cum tulit et caesarum ouium sub nocte silenti

56–8 *FMPR*; 59–87 *MPR*   60 coma *de, Non.* 349. 18
71 cum *Non.* 58. 26, 247. 39, 440. 9   72 et] ut *cd*   78 id
MPRab?rt: hoc ω   81 at] ad *M¹Pb*   84 saeuumque *Mb*
86 huic *aeuv*

3

pellibus incubuit stratis somnosque petiuit,
multa modis simulacra uidet uolitantia miris
et uarias audit uoces fruiturque deorum 90
conloquio atque imis Acheronta adfatur Auernis.
hic et tum pater ipse petens responsa Latinus
centum lanigeras mactabat rite bidentis,
atque harum effultus tergo stratisque iacebat
uelleribus: subita ex alto uox reddita luco est: 95
'ne pete conubiis natam sociare Latinis,
o mea progenies, thalamis neu crede paratis;
externi uenient generi, qui sanguine nostrum
nomen in astra ferant, quorumque a stirpe nepotes
omnia sub pedibus, qua sol utrumque recurrens 100
aspicit Oceanum, uertique regique uidebunt.'
haec responsa patris Fauni monitusque silenti
nocte datos non ipse suo premit ore Latinus,
sed circum late uolitans iam Fama per urbes
Ausonias tulerat, cum Laomedontia pubes 105
gramineo ripae religauit ab aggere classem.

   Aeneas primique duces et pulcher Iulus
corpora sub ramis deponunt arboris altae,
instituuntque dapes et adorea liba per herbam
subiciunt epulis (sic Iuppiter ipse monebat) 110
et Cereale solum pomis agrestibus augent.
consumptis hic forte aliis, ut uertere morsus
exiguam in Cererem penuria adegit edendi,
et uiolare manu malisque audacibus orbem
fatalis crusti patulis nec parcere quadris: 115
'heus, etiam mensas consumimus?' inquit Iulus,
nec plura, adludens. ea uox audita laborum
prima tulit finem, primamque loquentis ab ore
eripuit pater ac stupefactus numine pressit.

88–119 *MPR* 93 mactarat *bt* 95 subito *M*
98 uenient *MPRabcr*: ueniunt *ω*, '*melius*' *iudice Seru.* 109 in-
stituunt (*om.* -que) *cty* herbas *ω*(*praeter abfr*) 110 ipse] ille
M², *Prisc. ter*, *Seru.*, *Tib.* 119 ac] et *R*

continuo 'salue fatis mihi debita tellus   120
uosque' ait 'o fidi Troiae saluete penates:
hic domus, haec patria est. genitor mihi talia namque
(nunc repeto) Anchises fatorum arcana reliquit:
"cum te, nate, fames ignota ad litora uectum
accisis coget dapibus consumere mensas,   125
tum sperare domos defessus, ibique memento
prima locare manu molirique aggere tecta."
haec erat illa fames, haec nos suprema manebat
exitiis positura modum.
quare agite et primo laeti cum lumine solis   130
quae loca, quiue habeant homines, ubi moenia gentis,
uestigemus et a portu diuersa petamus.
nunc pateras libate Ioui precibusque uocate
Anchisen genitorem, et uina reponite mensis.'
  Sic deinde effatus frondenti tempora ramo   135
implicat et geniumque loci primamque deorum
Tellurem Nymphasque et adhuc ignota precatur
flumina, tum Noctem Noctisque orientia signa
Idaeumque Iouem Phrygiamque ex ordine matrem
inuocat, et duplicis caeloque Ereboque parentis.   140
hic pater omnipotens ter caelo clarus ab alto
intonuit, radiisque ardentem lucis et auro
ipse manu quatiens ostendit ab aethere nubem.
diditur hic subito Troiana per agmina rumor
aduenisse diem quo debita moenia condant.   145
certatim instaurant epulas atque omine magno
crateras laeti statuunt et uina coronant.
  Postera cum prima lustrabat lampade terras
orta dies, urbem et finis et litora gentis
diuersi explorant: haec fontis stagna Numici,   150
hunc Thybrim fluuium, hic fortis habitare Latinos.

120–51 *MPR*   125 accisis] ambesis (*A.* iii 257) *R*
129 exitiis *codd.* (*def. R*), *Seru. ad A.* iii 395: exiliis (*cf. A.* ii 780) *recc.*
143 manum *M¹a*   144 diditur *MPat* (*def. R*): deditur ω
145 condent *cdhv*   148 primo *Ra*

tum satus Anchisa delectos ordine ab omni
centum oratores augusta ad moenia regis
ire iubet, ramis uelatos Palladis omnis,
donaque ferre uiro pacemque exposcere Teucris.   155
haud mora, festinant iussi rapidisque feruntur
passibus. ipse humili designat moenia fossa
moliturque locum, primasque in litore sedes
castrorum in morem pinnis atque aggere cingit.
iamque iter emensi turris ac tecta Latinorum   160
ardua cernebant iuuenes muroque subibant.
ante urbem pueri et primaeuo flore iuuentus
exercentur equis domitantque in puluere currus,
aut acris tendunt arcus aut lenta lacertis
spicula contorquent, cursuque ictuque lacessunt: 165
cum praeuectus equo longaeui regis ad auris
nuntius ingentis ignota in ueste reportat
aduenisse uiros. ille intra tecta uocari
imperat et solio medius consedit auito.

    Tectum augustum, ingens, centum sublime columnis   170
urbe fuit summa, Laurentis regia Pici,
horrendum siluis et religione parentum.
hic sceptra accipere et primos attollere fascis
regibus omen erat; hoc illis curia templum,
hae sacris sedes epulis; hic ariete caeso   175
perpetuis soliti patres considere mensis.
quin etiam ueterum effigies ex ordine auorum
antiqua e cedro, Italusque paterque Sabinus
uitisator curuam seruans sub imagine falcem,
Saturnusque senex Ianique bifrontis imago   180
uestibulo astabant, aliique ab origine reges,
Martiaque ob patriam pugnando uulnera passi.
multaque praeterea sacris in postibus arma,

   152–78 *MPR*; 179–83 *FMPR*   160 ac *M²PRω*: et *M¹aberuγ*,
Seru. Latinum *abe*   161 murosque (*A*. ix 371) *R*   163 exer-
cetur *Pa*   173 hinc *ω(praeter art)*   182 Martiaque *F²PRbr*:
Martia qui *F¹Mωγ, utrumque Tib.*

captiui pendent currus curuaeque secures
et cristae capitum et portarum ingentia claustra   185
spiculaque clipeique ereptaque rostra carinis.
ipse Quirinali lituo paruaque sedebat
succinctus trabea laeuaque ancile gerebat
Picus, equum domitor, quem capta cupidine coniunx
aurea percussum uirga uersumque uenenis   190
fecit auem Circe sparsitque coloribus alas.
  Tali intus templo diuum patriaque Latinus
sede sedens Teucros ad sese in tecta uocauit,
atque haec ingressis placido prior edidit ore:
'dicite, Dardanidae (neque enim nescimus et urbem   195
et genus, auditique aduertitis aequore cursum),
quid petitis? quae causa rates aut cuius egentis
litus ad Ausonium tot per uada caerula uexit?
siue errore uiae seu tempestatibus acti,
qualia multa mari nautae patiuntur in alto,   200
fluminis intrastis ripas portuque sedetis,
ne fugite hospitium, neue ignorate Latinos
Saturni gentem haud uinclo nec legibus aequam,
sponte sua ueterisque dei se more tenentem.
atque equidem memini (fama est obscurior annis)   205
Auruncos ita ferre senes, his ortus ut agris
Dardanus Idaeas Phrygiae penetrarit ad urbes
Threiciamque Samum, quae nunc Samothracia fertur.
hinc illum Corythi Tyrrhena ab sede profectum
aurea nunc solio stellantis regia caeli   210
accipit et numerum diuorum altaribus auget.'
  Dixerat, et dicta Ilioneus sic uoce secutus:
'rex, genus egregium Fauni, nec fluctibus actos
atra subegit hiems uestris succedere terris,
nec sidus regione uiae litusue fefellit: 215
consilio hanc omnes animisque uolentibus urbem
adferimur pulsi regnis, quae maxima quondam

184–217 *FMPR*   207 penetrarit *R*: -uit *ceteri*   211 numero
P²   auget *FMPRrs, Seru.*: addit ωγ   212 dictum *M¹*

7

extremo ueniens sol aspiciebat Olympo.
ab Ioue principium generis, Ioue Dardana pubes
gaudet auo, rex ipse Iouis de gente suprema: 220
Troius Aeneas tua nos ad limina misit.
quanta per Idaeos saeuis effusa Mycenis
tempestas ierit campos, quibus actus uterque
Europae atque Asiae fatis concurrerit orbis,
audiit et si quem tellus extrema refuso   225
summouet Oceano et si quem extenta plagarum
quattuor in medio dirimit plaga solis iniqui.
diluuio ex illo tot uasta per aequora uecti
dis sedem exiguam patriis litusque rogamus
innocuum et cunctis undamque auramque patentem.   230
non erimus regno indecores, nec uestra feretur
fama leuis tantique abolescet gratia facti,
nec Troiam Ausonios gremio excepisse pigebit.
fata per Aeneae iuro dextramque potentem,
siue fide seu quis bello est expertus et armis: 235
multi nos populi, multae (ne temne, quod ultro
praeferimus manibus uittas ac uerba precantia)
et petiere sibi et uoluere adiungere gentes;
sed nos fata deum uestras exquirere terras
imperiis egere suis. hinc Dardanus ortus,   240
huc repetit iussisque ingentibus urget Apollo
Tyrrhenum ad Thybrim et fontis uada sacra Numici.
dat tibi praeterea fortunae parua prioris
munera, reliquias Troia ex ardente receptas.
hoc pater Anchises auro libabat ad aras,   245
hoc Priami gestamen erat cum iura uocatis
more daret populis, sceptrumque sacerque tiaras
Iliadumque labor uestes.'
　　Talibus Ilionei dictis defixa Latinus
obtutu tenet ora soloque immobilis haeret,   250

218–47 *FMPR*; 248–50 *FMPRV*　　221 mittit *F*　　224 con-
curreret *R*: concurritur *P*　　232 tantique *FMPb*: tantiue *Rω, Tib.*
237 ac] et *R*　　precantum *Rb*

intentos uoluens oculos. nec purpura regem
picta mouet nec sceptra mouent Priameia tantum
quantum in conubio natae thalamoque moratur,
et ueteris Fauni uoluit sub pectore sortem:
hunc illum fatis externa ab sede profectum   255
portendi generum paribusque in regna uocari
auspiciis, huic progeniem uirtute futuram
egregiam et totum quae uiribus occupet orbem.
tandem laetus ait: 'di nostra incepta secundent
auguriumque suum! dabitur, Troiane, quod optas.   260
munera nec sperno: non uobis rege Latino
diuitis uber agri Troiaeue opulentia deerit.
ipse modo Aeneas, nostri si tanta cupido est,
si iungi hospitio properat sociusque uocari,
adueniat, uultus neue exhorrescat amicos: 265
pars mihi pacis erit dextram tetigisse tyranni.
uos contra regi mea nunc mandata referte:
est mihi nata, uiro gentis quam iungere nostrae
non patrio ex adyto sortes, non plurima caelo
monstra sinunt; generos externis adfore ab oris,   270
hoc Latio restare canunt, qui sanguine nostrum
nomen in astra ferant. hunc illum poscere fata
et reor et, si quid ueri mens augurat, opto.'
haec effatus equos numero pater eligit omni
(stabant ter centum nitidi in praesepibus altis);   275
omnibus extemplo Teucris iubet ordine duci
instratos ostro alipedes pictisque tapetis
(aurea pectoribus demissa monilia pendent,
tecti auro fuluum mandunt sub dentibus aurum),
absenti Aeneae currum geminosque iugalis   280
semine ab aetherio spirantis naribus ignem,
illorum de gente patri quos daedala Circe
supposita de matre nothos furata creauit.

251–73 *FMPRV*; 274–6 *FMPR*; 277-83 *FMγR*   254 uol-
uens *F*¹   262 Troiaeque *P*²*bv*   264 sociusque *MPahs*:
sociusue *FRV*ω   281 spirantis (*G.* ii 140)] flagrantis *F*

talibus Aeneadae donis dictisque Latini
sublimes in equis redeunt pacemque reportant.   285
  Ecce autem Inachiis sese referebat ab Argis
saeua Iouis coniunx aurasque inuecta tenebat,
et laetum Aenean classemque ex aethere longe
Dardaniam Siculo prospexit ab usque Pachyno.
moliri iam tecta uidet, iam fidere terrae,   290
deseruisse rates: stetit acri fixa dolore.
tum quassans caput haec effundit pectore dicta:
'heu stirpem inuisam et fatis contraria nostris
fata Phrygum! num Sigeis occumbere campis,
num capti potuere capi? num incensa cremauit   295
Troia uiros? medias acies mediosque per ignis
inuenere uiam. at, credo, mea numina tandem
fessa iacent, odiis aut exsaturata quieui.
quin etiam patria excussos infesta per undas
ausa sequi et profugis toto me opponere ponto.   300
absumptae in Teucros uires caelique marisque.
quid Syrtes aut Scylla mihi, quid uasta Charybdis
profuit? optato conduntur Thybridis alueo
securi pelagi atque mei. Mars perdere gentem
immanem Lapithum ualuit, concessit in iras   305
ipse deum antiquam genitor Calydona Dianae,
quod scelus aut Lapithas tantum aut Calydona merentem?
ast ego, magna Iouis coniunx, nil linquere inausum
quae potui infelix, quae memet in omnia uerti,   309
uincor ab Aenea. quod si mea numina non sunt   [est:
magna satis, dubitem haud equidem implorare quod usquam
flectere si nequeo superos, Acheronta mouebo.
non dabitur regnis, esto, prohibere Latinis,

284–313 *FMγR*   288 longo *M*   290 terrae] terra
Prisc. xviii 223   292 tunc *γ*   295 num (*r⁰*)] nunc *M*
298 aut *FγRbf?r*: haud *Mω*   307 Lapithas *M²*: -this *codd.*, *Tib.*
Calydona *F²M²γbfrst* (Calydo *F¹c*), *Tib.*: Calydone *M¹Rω*   meren-
tem *FM²*(-tes *M¹*)*γcfs*, *Tib.*: merente *Rω*   *Et acc. et abl. amplectitur*
Prisc. xvii 101, *abl. Macrob.* iv 5, 6 *et Seru.*   310 uincar *M¹*
311 est *FM²Rω*: om. *M¹γc*   313 esto regnis *cdhv*

atque immota manet fatis Lauinia coniunx:
at trahere atque moras tantis licet addere rebus,　315
at licet amborum populos exscindere regum.
hac gener atque socer coeant mercede suorum:
sanguine Troiano et Rutulo dotabere, uirgo,
et Bellona manet te pronuba. nec face tantum
Cisseis praegnas ignis enixa iugalis;　320
quin idem Veneri partus suus et Paris alter,
funestaeque iterum recidiua in Pergama taedae.'
　Haec ubi dicta dedit, terras horrenda petiuit;
luctificam Allecto dirarum ab sede dearum
infernisque ciet tenebris, cui tristia bella　325
iraeque insidiaeque et crimina noxia cordi.
odit et ipse pater Pluton, odere sorores
Tartareae monstrum: tot sese uertit in ora,
tam saeuae facies, tot pullulat atra colubris.
quam Iuno his acuit uerbis ac talia fatur:　330
'hunc mihi da proprium, uirgo sata Nocte, laborem,
hanc operam, ne noster honos infractaue cedat
fama loco, neu conubiis ambire Latinum
Aeneadae possint Italosue obsidere finis.
tu potes unanimos armare in proelia fratres　335
atque odiis uersare domos, tu uerbera tectis
funereasque inferre faces, tibi nomina mille,
mille nocendi artes. fecundum concute pectus,
dissice compositam pacem, sere crimina belli;
arma uelit poscatque simul rapiatque iuuentus.'　340
　Exim Gorgoneis Allecto infecta uenenis
principio Latium et Laurentis tecta tyranni
celsa petit, tacitumque obsedit limen Amatae,
quam super aduentu Teucrum Turnique hymenaeis
femineae ardentem curaeque iraeque coquebant.　345

314–25 _FMγR_; 326–9 _FMγRV_; 330–45 _MγRV_　　317 hac] at _M_
324 dearum _FM_¹_γab?efr, Char._ 63. 30: sororum (_u._ 454) _M²Rω_
330 uerbis] dictis _γRa?_　　333 nec _Non._ 242. 11　　337 funereas
(_om._ -que) _V_¹　tibi] cui _Non._ 354. 12　　340 uelint _V_

huic dea caeruleis unum de crinibus anguem
conicit, inque sinum praecordia ad intima subdit,
quo furibunda domum monstro permisceat omnem.
ille inter uestis et leuia pectora lapsus
uoluitur attactu nullo, fallitque furentem   350
uiperam inspirans animam; fit tortile collo
aurum ingens coluber, fit longae taenia uittae
innectitque comas et membris lubricus errat.
ac dum prima lues udo sublapsa ueneno
pertemptat sensus atque ossibus implicat ignem   355
necdum animus toto percepit pectore flammam,
mollius et solito matrum de more locuta est,
multa super natae lacrimans Phrygiisque hymenaeis:
'exsulibusne datur ducenda Lauinia Teucris,
o genitor, nec te miseret nataeque tuique?   360
nec matris miseret, quam primo Aquilone relinquet
perfidus alta petens abducta uirgine praedo?
at non sic Phrygius penetrat Lacedaemona pastor,
Ledaeamque Helenam Troianas uexit ad urbes?
quid tua sancta fides? quid cura antiqua tuorum   365
et consanguineo totiens data dextera Turno?
si gener externa petitur de gente Latinis,
idque sedet, Faunique premunt te iussa parentis,
omnem equidem sceptris terram quae libera nostris
dissidet externam reor et sic dicere diuos.   370
et Turno, si prima domus repetatur origo,
Inachus Acrisiusque patres mediaeque Mycenae.'
    His ubi nequiquam dictis experta Latinum
contra stare uidet, penitusque in uiscera lapsum
serpentis furiale malum totamque pererrat,   375
tum uero infelix ingentibus excita monstris
immensam sine more furit lymphata per urbem.

346-51 *MγRV*; 352-77 *MγR*   349 pectora] corpora *R*
351 spirans *M*   356 concepit *R*   357 est *Rω*: om. *Mγ*
358 nata *Rbυ?*   363 at *γRω, Gramm., Tib.*: an *Mbr, Diom.*
464. 21, *agnoscit Seru.*   370 desidet *cdht*   dicere] poscere *M¹*
377 immensum *Heyne*

ceu quondam torto uolitans sub uerbere turbo,
quem pueri magno in gyro uacua atria circum
intenti ludo exercent—ille actus habena   380
curuatis fertur spatiis; stupet inscia supra
impubesque manus mirata uolubile buxum;
dant animos plagae: non cursu segnior illo
per medias urbes agitur populosque ferocis.
quin etiam in siluas simulato numine Bacchi   385
maius adorta nefas maioremque orsa furorem
euolat et natam frondosis montibus abdit,
quo thalamum eripiat Teucris taedasque moretur,
euhoe Bacche fremens, solum te uirgine dignum
uociferans: etenim mollis tibi sumere thyrsos,   390
te lustrare choro, sacrum tibi pascere crinem.
fama uolat, furiisque accensas pectore matres
idem omnis simul ardor agit noua quaerere tecta.
deseruere domos, uentis dant colla comasque;
ast aliae tremulis ululatibus aethera complent   395
pampineasque gerunt incinctae pellibus hastas.
ipsa inter medias flagrantem feruida pinum
sustinet ac natae Turnique canit hymenaeos
sanguineam torquens aciem, toruumque repente
clamat: 'io matres, audite, ubi quaeque, Latinae: 400
si qua piis animis manet infelicis Amatae
gratia, si iuris materni cura remordet,
soluite crinalis uittas, capite orgia mecum.'
talem inter siluas, inter deserta ferarum
reginam Allecto stimulis agit undique Bacchi.   405
    Postquam uisa satis primos acuisse furores
consiliumque omnemque domum uertisse Latini,
protinus hinc fuscis tristis dea tollitur alis
audacis Rutuli ad muros, quam dicitur urbem
Acrisioneis Danae fundasse colonis   410

378–403 $M\gamma R$; 404–10 $M\gamma RV$ 385 siluis M^1c 391 choro
M^1t: choros $M^2\gamma^2$(-rus γ^1)$R\omega$ 392 pectora ct 395 aliae]
illae M^2

praecipiti delata Noto. locus Ardea quondam
dictus auis, et nunc magnum manet Ardea nomen,
sed fortuna fuit. tectis hic Turnus in altis
iam mediam nigra carpebat nocte quietem.
Allecto toruam faciem et furialia membra   415
exuit, in uultus sese transformat anilis
et frontem obscenam rugis arat, induit albos
cum uitta crinis, tum ramum innectit oliuae;
fit Calybe Iunonis anus templique sacerdos,
et iuueni ante oculos his se cum uocibus offert: 420
'Turne, tot incassum fusos patiere labores,
et tua Dardaniis transcribi sceptra colonis?
rex tibi coniugium et quaesitas sanguine dotes
abnegat, externusque in regnum quaeritur heres.
i nunc, ingratis offer te, inrise, periclis;   425
Tyrrhenas, i, sterne acies, tege pace Latinos.
haec adeo tibi me, placida cum nocte iaceres,
ipsa palam fari omnipotens Saturnia iussit.
quare age et armari pubem portisque moueri
laetus in arua para, et Phrygios qui flumine pulchro   430
consedere duces pictasque exure carinas.
caelestum uis magna iubet. rex ipse Latinus,
ni dare coniugium et dicto parere fatetur,
sentiat et tandem Turnum experiatur in armis.'

    Hic iuuenis uatem inridens sic orsa uicissim   435
ore refert: 'classis inuectas Thybridis undam
non, ut rere, meas effugit nuntius auris;
ne tantos mihi finge metus. nec regia Iuno
immemor est nostri.
sed te uicta situ uerique effeta senectus,   440
o mater, curis nequiquam exercet, et arma
regum inter falsa uatem formidine ludit.

411–27 MγRV; 428–29 FMγRV; 430–42 FMγR   412 manet
M¹γVω: tenet M²R, Seru.   414 media nigram γ
416 uultus] cultus Arus. 513. 18   418 nectit γ   430 arua
Peerlkamp: arma codd., DSeru. ad A. i 35 (cf. A. xi 173)   para] iube
(A. x 242) M, DSeru.   436 undam] alueo (u. 303) R: unda fh

cura tibi diuum effigies et templa tueri;
bella uiri pacemque gerent quis bella gerenda.'
Talibus Allecto dictis exarsit in iras.   445
at iuueni oranti subitus tremor occupat artus,
deriguere oculi: tot Erinys sibilat hydris
tantaque se facies aperit; tum flammea torquens
lumina cunctantem et quaerentem dicere plura
reppulit, et geminos erexit crinibus anguis,   450
uerberaque insonuit rabidoque haec addidit ore:
'en ego uicta situ, quam ueri effeta senectus
arma inter regum falsa formidine ludit.
respice ad haec: adsum dirarum ab sede sororum,
bella manu letumque gero.'   455
sic effata facem iuueni coniecit et atro
lumine fumantis fixit sub pectore taedas.
olli somnum ingens rumpit pauor, ossaque et artus
perfundit toto proruptus corpore sudor.
arma amens fremit, arma toro tectisque requirit;   460
saeuit amor ferri et scelerata insania belli,
ira super: magno ueluti cum flamma sonore
uirgea suggeritur costis undantis aëni
exsultantque aestu latices, furit intus aquai
fumidus atque alte spumis exuberat amnis,   465
nec iam se capit unda, uolat uapor ater ad auras.
ergo iter ad regem polluta pace Latinum
indicit primis iuuenum et iubet arma parari,
tutari Italiam, detrudere finibus hostem;
se satis ambobus Teucrisque uenire Latinisque.   470
haec ubi dicta dedit diuosque in uota uocauit,
certatim sese Rutuli exhortantur in arma.
hunc decus egregium formae mouet atque iuuentae,

443–69 FMγR; 470–3 MγR   444 gerant M, schol. Veron.
ad A. i 1   447 diriguere ω(praeter a)   451 rapidoque Fγbcfhrv
458 ingens somnum rupit R   459 perfudit Mar   praeruptus
Fγcdtv   464 aquai Mc?ehrtuv, Seru. (cf. Quint. i 7. 18): aquae
uis FRabdfs, Macrob. v 11. 23 (aquae γ, uis add. γ²): aquae amnis
poetam reliquisse narrat (ut uidetur) Seru.   466 se iam F

hunc ataui reges, hunc claris dextera factis.

Dum Turnus Rutulos animis audacibus implet,   475
Allecto in Teucros Stygiis se concitat alis,
arte noua, speculata locum, quo litore pulcher
insidiis cursuque feras agitabat Iulus.

hic subitam canibus rabiem Cocytia uirgo
obicit et noto naris contingit odore,   480
ut ceruum ardentes agerent; quae prima laborum
causa fuit belloque animos accendit agrestis.

ceruus erat forma praestanti et cornibus ingens,
Tyrrhidae pueri quem matris ab ubere raptum
nutribant Tyrrhusque pater, cui regia parent   485
armenta et late custodia credita campi.

adsuetum imperiis soror omni Siluia cura
mollibus intexens ornabat cornua sertis,
pectebatque ferum puroque in fonte lauabat.

ille manum patiens mensaeque adsuetus erili   490
errabat siluis rursusque ad limina nota
ipse domum sera quamuis se nocte ferebat.

hunc procul errantem rabidae uenantis Iuli
commouere canes, fluuio cum forte secundo
deflueret ripaque aestus uiridante leuaret.   495

ipse etiam eximiae laudis succensus amore
Ascanius curuo derexit spicula cornu;
nec dextrae erranti deus afuit, actaque multo
perque uterum sonitu perque ilia uenit harundo.

saucius at quadripes nota intra tecta refugit   500
successitque gemens stabulis, questuque cruentus
atque imploranti similis tectum omne replebat.

Siluia prima soror palmis percussa lacertos
auxilium uocat et duros conclamat agrestis.

474–81 $M\gamma R$; 482–85 $M\gamma RV$; 486–504 $FM\gamma RV$ 475 ani-
mis Rutulos *cdhsv*   481 laborum] malorum (*A.* iv 169) *adeu,
Seru.*(?)   486 late $F^2\gamma V\omega$, *Seru.*: lati F^1MRa, *utrumque Tib.*
490 manu $FM^1\gamma$, *Tib.*   496 accensus γ 497 derexit
$F^1\gamma RV$: direxit $F^2M\omega$ 498 dextra M 502 replebat $M\gamma V^2$:
repleuit $RV^1\omega$ (*def. F*)

olli (pestis enim tacitis latet aspera siluis)   505
improuisi adsunt, hic torre armatus obusto,
stipitis hic grauidi nodis; quod cuique repertum
rimanti telum ira facit. uocat agmina Tyrrhus,
quadrifidam quercum cuneis ut forte coactis
scindebat rapta spirans immane securi.   510
  At saeua e speculis tempus dea nacta nocendi
ardua tecta petit stabuli et de culmine summo
pastorale canit signum cornuque recuruo
Tartaream intendit uocem, qua protinus omne
contremuit nemus et siluae insonuere profundae;   515
audiit et Triuiae longe lacus, audiit amnis
sulpurea Nar albus aqua fontesque Velini,
et trepidae matres pressere ad pectora natos.
tum uero ad uocem celeres, qua bucina signum
dira dedit, raptis concurrunt undique telis   520
indomiti agricolae, nec non et Troia pubes
Ascanio auxilium castris effundit apertis.
derexere acies. non iam certamine agresti
stipitibus duris agitur sudibusue praeustis,
sed ferro ancipiti decernunt atraque late   525
horrescit strictis seges ensibus, aeraque fulgent
sole lacessita et lucem sub nubila iactant:
fluctus uti primo coepit cum albescere uento,
paulatim sese tollit mare et altius undas
erigit, inde imo consurgit ad aethera fundo.   530
hic iuuenis primam ante aciem stridente sagitta,
natorum Tyrrhi fuerat qui maximus, Almo,
sternitur; haesit enim sub gutture uulnus et udae
uocis iter tenuemque inclusit sanguine uitam.
corpora multa uirum circa seniorque Galaesus,   535
dum paci medium se offert, iustissimus unus

505–7 *FMγRV*; 508–9 *FMγR*; 510–36 *MγR*   510 scinde-
bant *M*[1], *Non.* 265. 13   514 incendit *M*[1]*R*[2]   515 intonuere
cdehsuv   523 derexere *M, Tib.*: dir- *γRω*   527 nubila]
lumine *γd* (limine *v*)   528 uento *γω, Tib.*: ponto (*G.* iii 237) *MR*,
Macrob. v 13. 20   536 sese *γRacer*

qui fuit Ausoniisque olim ditissimus aruis:
quinque greges illi balantum, quina redibant
armenta, et terram centum uertebat aratris.

Atque ea per campos aequo dum Marte geruntur,   540
promissi dea facta potens, ubi sanguine bellum
imbuit et primae commisit funera pugnae,
deserit Hesperiam et caeli conuersa per auras
Iunonem uictrix adfatur uoce superba:
'en, perfecta tibi bello discordia tristi;   545
dic in amicitiam coeant et foedera iungant.
quandoquidem Ausonio respersi sanguine Teucros,
hoc etiam his addam, tua si mihi certa uoluntas:
finitimas in bella feram rumoribus urbes,
accendamque animos insani Martis amore   550
undique ut auxilio ueniant; spargam arma per agros.'
tum contra Iuno: 'terrorum et fraudis abunde est:
stant belli causae, pugnatur comminus armis,
quae fors prima dedit sanguis nouus imbuit arma.
talia coniugia et talis celebrent hymenaeos   555
egregium Veneris genus et rex ipse Latinus.
te super aetherias errare licentius auras
haud pater ille uelit, summi regnator Olympi.
cede locis. ego, si qua super fortuna laborum est,
ipsa regam.' talis dederat Saturnia uoces;   560
illa autem attollit stridentis anguibus alas
Cocytique petit sedem supera ardua linquens.
est locus Italiae medio sub montibus altis,
nobilis et fama multis memoratus in oris,
Amsancti ualles; densis hunc frondibus atrum   565
urget utrimque latus nemoris, medioque fragosus
dat sonitum saxis et torto uertice torrens.
hic specus horrendum et saeui spiracula Ditis

537–68 $M\gamma R$ 543 conuersa M^1: conuexa (A. iv 451) $M^2\gamma R\omega$,
Probus Asper Donatus ap. Seru.: conuecta *Firmiani commentarius
ibidem*   558 ille] ipse *df*   562 supera $\gamma\omega$(supra *f*): super
$MRbdr$ (*cf. A.* vi 787)   566 utrumque γd 568 horrendus
'*antiqui codices*' *teste Seru.*

monstrantur, ruptoque ingens Acheronte uorago
pestiferas aperit fauces, quis condita Erinys,   570
inuisum numen, terras caelumque leuabat.
  Nec minus interea extremam Saturnia bello
imponit regina manum. ruit omnis in urbem
pastorum ex acie numerus, caesosque reportant
Almonem puerum foedatique ora Galaesi,   575
implorantque deos obtestanturque Latinum.
Turnus adest medioque in crimine caedis et igni
terrorem ingeminat: Teucros in regna uocari,
stirpem admisceri Phrygiam, se limine pelli.
tum quorum attonitae Baccho nemora auia matres   580
insultant thiasis (neque enim leue nomen Amatae)
undique collecti coeunt Martemque fatigant.
ilicet infandum cuncti contra omina bellum,
contra fata deum peruerso numine poscunt.
certatim regis circumstant tecta Latini;   585
ille uelut pelago rupes immota resistit,
ut pelagi rupes magno ueniente fragore,
quae sese multis circum latrantibus undis
mole tenet; scopuli nequiquam et spumea circum
saxa fremunt laterique inlisa refunditur alga.   590
uerum ubi nulla datur caecum exsuperare potestas
consilium, et saeuae nutu Iunonis eunt res,
multa deos aurasque pater testatus inanis
'frangimur heu fatis' inquit 'ferimurque procella!
ipsi has sacrilego pendetis sanguine poenas,   595
o miseri. te, Turne, nefas, te triste manebit
supplicium, uotisque deos uenerabere seris.
nam mihi parta quies, omnisque in limine portus

569–85 *MγR*; 586–93 *MγRV*; 594–8 *FMγRV*   570 condita
Rfrstuv: condit *Mγabcdeh*, 'alii' *ap. Seru.*   571 leuauit *R*
573 inposuit *γ*   577 ignis *abdert*   586–615 *omiserat
olim M; add. alia manus*   586 pelago *V¹*: pelagi (*u.* 587)
ceteri rupes] moles *aeu*   589 et *om. V*   592 consilio *M²*,
agnoscit Tib.   593 testatus *Vader*: -tur *MγRω*   594 pro-
cellis *V*

funere felici spolior.' nec plura locutus
saepsit se tectis rerumque reliquit habenas.   600

   Mos erat Hesperio in Latio, quem protinus urbes
Albanae coluere sacrum, nunc maxima rerum
Roma colit, cum prima mouent in proelia Martem,
siue Getis inferre manu lacrimabile bellum
Hyrcanisue Arabisue parant, seu tendere ad Indos   605
Auroramque sequi Parthosque reposcere signa:
sunt geminae Belli portae (sic nomine dicunt)
religione sacrae et saeui formidine Martis;
centum aerei claudunt uectes aeternaque ferri
robora, nec custos absistit limine Ianus.   610
has, ubi certa sedet patribus sententia pugnae,
ipse Quirinali trabea cinctuque Gabino
insignis reserat stridentia limina consul,
ipse uocat pugnas; sequitur tum cetera pubes,
aereaque adsensu conspirant cornua rauco.   615
hoc et tum Aeneadis indicere bella Latinus
more iubebatur tristisque recludere portas.
abstinuit tactu pater auersusque refugit
foeda ministeria, et caecis se condidit umbris.
tum regina deum caelo delapsa morantis   620
impulit ipsa manu portas, et cardine uerso
Belli ferratos rumpit Saturnia postis.
ardet inexcita Ausonia atque immobilis ante;
pars pedes ire parat campis, pars arduus altis
puluerulentus equis furit; omnes arma requirunt.   625
pars leuis clipeos et spicula lucida tergent
aruina pingui subiguntque in cote securis;
signaque ferre iuuat sonitusque audire tubarum.
quinque adeo magnae positis incudibus urbes
tela nouant, Atina potens Tiburque superbum,   630
Ardea Crustumerique et turrigerae Antemnae.

   599–611 *FMγRV*; 612–31 *FMγR*   600 relinquit *b*, *Tib*.
605 Hyrcaniisque *F¹*   622 rumpit *Mabderv*: rupit *FγRcfhstu*,
Seru.   624 parant *γaeu*   628 iuuat] iubet *M*: iuuant *R*

tegmina tuta cauant capitum flectuntque salignas
umbonum cratis; alii thoracas aënos
aut leuis ocreas lento ducunt argento;
uomeris huc et falcis honos, huc omnis aratri   635
cessit amor; recoquunt patrios fornacibus ensis.
classica iamque sonant, it bello tessera signum;
hic galeam tectis trepidus rapit, ille trementis
ad iuga cogit equos, clipeumque auroque trilicem
loricam induitur fidoque accingitur ense.   640

Pandite nunc Helicona, deae, cantusque mouete,
qui bello exciti reges, quae quemque secutae
complerint campos acies, quibus Itala iam tum
floruerit terra alma uiris, quibus arserit armis;
et meministis enim, diuae, et memorare potestis;   645
ad nos uix tenuis famae perlabitur aura.

Primus init bellum Tyrrhenis asper ab oris
contemptor diuum Mezentius agminaque armat.
filius huic iuxta Lausus, quo pulchrior alter
non fuit excepto Laurentis corpore Turni;   650
Lausus, equum domitor debellatorque ferarum,
ducit Agyllina nequiquam ex urbe secutos
mille uiros, dignus patriis qui laetior esset
imperiis et cui pater haud Mezentius esset.

Post hos insignem palma per gramina currum   655
uictoresque ostentat equos satus Hercule pulchro
pulcher Auentinus, clipeoque insigne paternum
centum anguis cinctamque gerit serpentibus Hydram;
collis Auentini silua quem Rhea sacerdos
furtiuum partu sub luminis edidit oras,   660
mixta deo mulier, postquam Laurentia uictor
Geryone exstincto Tirynthius attigit arua,
Tyrrhenoque boues in flumine lauit Hiberas.

632–44 *FMγR*; 645–6 *FMPR*; 647–63 *MPR*   638 trepidus]
rapidus *M¹*   638 trementis (*cf. G.* iii 84) *FMγRaberu, Tib.*:
frementis (*A.* xii 82) *cdfhstv*   641 *'legitur et* monete' *Seru.* (*ita*
F²)   642 acciti *M*   649 hunc *M¹*

pila manu saeuosque gerunt in bella dolones,
et tereti pugnant mucrone ueruque Sabello. 665
ipse pedes, tegimen torquens immane leonis,
terribili impexum saeta cum dentibus albis
indutus capiti, sic regia tecta subibat,
horridus Herculeoque umeros innexus amictu.

Tum gemini fratres Tiburtia moenia linquunt, 670
fratris Tiburti dictam cognomine gentem,
Catillusque acerque Coras, Argiua iuuentus,
et primam ante aciem densa inter tela feruntur:
ceu duo nubigenae cum uertice montis ab alto
descendunt Centauri Homolen Othrymque niualem 675
linquentes cursu rapido; dat euntibus ingens
silua locum et magno cedunt uirgulta fragore.

Nec Praenestinae fundator defuit urbis,
Volcano genitum pecora inter agrestia regem
inuentumque focis omnis quem credidit aetas, 680
Caeculus. hunc legio late comitatur agrestis:
quique altum Praeneste uiri quique arua Gabinae
Iunonis gelidumque Anienem et roscida riuis
Hernica saxa colunt, quos diues Anagnia pascis,
quos Amasene pater. non illis omnibus arma 685
nec clipei currusue sonant; pars maxima glandes
liuentis plumbi spargit, pars spicula gestat
bina manu, fuluosque lupi de pelle galeros
tegmen habent capiti; uestigia nuda sinistri
instituere pedis, crudus tegit altera pero. 690

At Messapus, equum domitor, Neptunia proles,
quem neque fas igni cuiquam nec sternere ferro,
iam pridem resides populos desuetaque bello
agmina in arma uocat subito ferrumque retractat.

664–89 *MPRV*; 690–94 *MPR* 669 innixus *PR*
670 tunc *R* 671 fratres *MP²ar* de nomine (*A*. i 533) *P*
672 Catthillus (*om*. -que) *V¹* 677 et *om*. *P¹* 678 deficit *R*
681 late legio *M* 684 pascis *V*: pascit *ceteri* 686 currus-
que *R* 689 tegmina *P* capitis *M²V²* (*cf. uu.* 632, 742)

22

hi Fescenninas acies Aequosque Faliscos, 695
hi Soractis habent arces Flauiniaque arua
et Cimini cum monte lacum lucosque Capenos.
ibant aequati numero regemque canebant:
ceu quondam niuei liquida inter nubila cycni
cum sese e pastu referunt et longa canoros 700
dant per colla modos, sonat amnis et Asia longe
pulsa palus.
nec quisquam aeratas acies examine tanto
misceri putet, aëriam sed gurgite ab alto
urgeri uolucrum raucarum ad litora nubem. 705
    Ecce Sabinorum prisco de sanguine magnum
agmen agens Clausus magnique ipse agminis instar,
Claudia nunc a quo diffunditur et tribus et gens
per Latium, postquam in partem data Roma Sabinis.
una ingens Amiterna cohors priscique Quirites, 710
Ereti manus omnis oliuiferaeque Mutuscae;
qui Nomentum urbem, qui Rosea rura Velini,
qui Tetricae horrentis rupes montemque Seuerum
Casperiamque colunt Forulosque et flumen Himellae,
qui Tiberim Fabarimque bibunt, quos frigida misit 715
Nursia, et Ortinae classes populique Latini,
quosque secans infaustum interluit Allia nomen:
quam multi Libyco uoluuntur marmore fluctus
saeuus ubi Orion hibernis conditur undis,
uel cum sole nouo densae torrentur aristae 720
aut Hermi campo aut Lyciae flauentibus aruis.
scuta sonant pulsuque pedum conterrita tellus.
    Hinc Agamemnonius, Troiani nominis hostis,
curru iungit Halaesus equos Turnoque ferocis
mille rapit populos, uertunt felicia Baccho 725

695–725 *MPR*   695 aequosque *Seru., iustos interpretatus*
699 nubila] flumina *P*   703 examine *recc., Housman (cf. A.*
ii 727): ex agmine *codd.*   708 a] e *M*[1]   712 Rosea *P (correctum ex* Rosca *ut uid.) Rω, Seru.,* Rosa *M:* Roscia *P*[2]: roscida *a*
(roceda *r* rosda *s*)   713 montemque] amnemque (*G.* iii 37, *A.*
vi 374) *P*   722 pulsuque (*A.* xii 445)] cursuque (*u.* 807) *M*

Massica qui rastris, et quos de collibus altis
Aurunci misere patres Sidicinaque iuxta
aequora, quique Cales linquunt amnisque uadosi
accola Volturni, pariterque Saticulus asper
Oscorumque manus. teretes sunt aclydes illis   730
tela, sed haec lento mos est aptare flagello.
laeuas caetra tegit, falcati comminus enses.
    Nec tu carminibus nostris indictus abibis,
Oebale, quem generasse Telon Sebethide nympha
fertur, Teleboum Capreas cum regna teneret,   735
iam senior; patriis sed non et filius aruis
contentus late iam tum dicione premebat
Sarrastis populos et quae rigat aequora Sarnus,
quique Rufras Batulumque tenent atque arua Celemnae,
et quos maliferae despectant moenia Abellae,   740
Teutonico ritu soliti torquere cateias;
tegmina quis capitum raptus de subere cortex
aerataeque micant peltae, micat aereus ensis.
    Et te montosae misere in proelia Nersae,
Vfens, insignem fama et felicibus armis,   745
horrida praecipue cui gens adsuetaque multo
uenatu nemorum, duris Aequicula glaebis.
armati terram exercent semperque recentis
conuectare iuuat praedas et uiuere rapto.
    Quin et Marruuia uenit de gente sacerdos   750
fronde super galeam et felici comptus oliua
Archippi regis missu, fortissimus Vmbro,
uipereo generi et grauiter spirantibus hydris
spargere qui somnos cantuque manuque solebat,
mulcebatque iras et morsus arte leuabat.   755
sed non Dardaniae medicari cuspidis ictum
eualuit neque eum iuuere in uulnera cantus

726–57 *MPR*   727 patres] senes (*u.* 206) *M*²   737 pre-
mebat *R*ω: tenebat (*A.* i 622) *MPadev*   738 Sarrastris *P*²ω(*praeter
bd*)   quae *MPcd*: qua *R*ω   740 Abellae '*alii*' *ap. Seru.*: Bellae
codd., Seru.   755 iras] feras *P*²   757 in] ad *M*²   uulnera
*M*²*P*ω, *Tib.*: uulnere *M*¹*Racerv*

somniferi et Marsis quaesitae montibus herbae.
te nemus Angitiae, uitrea te Fucinus unda,
te liquidi fleuere lacus.   760
   Ibat et Hippolyti proles pulcherrima bello,
Virbius, insignem quem mater Aricia misit,
eductum Egeriae lucis umentia circum
litora, pinguis ubi et placabilis ara Dianae.
namque ferunt fama Hippolytum, postquam arte nouercae
occiderit patriasque explerit sanguine poenas   766
turbatis distractus equis, ad sidera rursus
aetheria et superas caeli uenisse sub auras,
Paeoniis reuocatum herbis et amore Dianae.
tum pater omnipotens aliquem indignatus ab umbris   770
mortalem infernis ad lumina surgere uitae,
ipse repertorem medicinae talis et artis
fulmine Phoebigenam Stygias detrusit ad undas.
at Triuia Hippolytum secretis alma recondit
sedibus et nymphae Egeriae nemorique relegat,   775
solus ubi in siluis Italis ignobilis aeuum
exigeret uersoque ubi nomine Virbius esset.
unde etiam templo Triuiae lucisque sacratis
cornipedes arcentur equi, quod litore currum
et iuuenem monstris pauidi effudere marinis.   780
filius ardentis haud setius aequore campi
exercebat equos curruque in bella ruebat.
   Ipse inter primos praestanti corpore Turnus
uertitur arma tenens et toto uertice supra est.
cui triplici crinita iuba galea alta Chimaeram   785
sustinet Aetnaeos efflantem faucibus ignis;
tam magis illa fremens et tristibus effera flammis
quam magis effuso crudescunt sanguine pugnae.
at leuem clipeum sublatis cornibus Io

758–89 *MPR*   758 montibus *M¹PRcdfh*: in montibus
M²ω   763 umentia] Hymetia *Pdfhrv, Tib.*   769 Paeonis
M¹   773 Phoebigenam *Pa?d, 'alii ut Probus' ap. Seru.*: Poeni-
genam *MRω* (Phen- *fs*), *Seru.*   ad *MPRbr*: in *ω*   undis *P¹*
778 luco . . . templisque *aeuv*

auro insignibat, iam saetis obsita, iam bos,   790
argumentum ingens, et custos uirginis Argus,
caelataque amnem fundens pater Inachus urna.
insequitur nimbus peditum clipeataque totis
agmina densentur campis, Argiuaque pubes
Auruncaeque manus, Rutuli ueteresque Sicani,   795
et Sacranae acies et picti scuta Labici;
qui saltus, Tiberine, tuos sacrumque Numici
litus arant Rutulosque exercent uomere collis
Circaeumque iugum, quis Iuppiter Anxurus aruis
praesidet et uiridi gaudens Feronia luco;   800
qua Saturae iacet atra palus gelidusque per imas
quaerit iter uallis atque in mare conditur Vfens.
  Hos super aduenit Volsca de gente Camilla
agmen agens equitum et florentis aere cateruas,
bellatrix, non illa colo calathisue Mineruae   805
femineas adsueta manus, sed proelia uirgo
dura pati cursuque pedum praeuertere uentos.
illa uel intactae segetis per summa uolaret
gramina nec teneras cursu laesisset aristas,
uel mare per medium fluctu suspensa tumenti   810
ferret iter celeris nec tingeret aequore plantas.
illam omnis tectis agrisque effusa iuuentus
turbaque miratur matrum et prospectat euntem,
attonitis inhians animis ut regius ostro
uelet honos leuis umeros, ut fibula crinem   815
auro internectat, Lyciam ut gerat ipsa pharetram
et pastoralem praefixa cuspide myrtum.

  790–817 *MPR*   801 Saturae] Asturae *'alii' ap. Seru.*
814 inhians] haesere (*A.* v 529) *P*

P. VERGILI MARONIS

AENEIDOS

LIBER VIII

Vt belli signum Laurenti Turnus ab arce
extulit et rauco strepuerunt cornua cantu,
utque acris concussit equos utque impulit arma,
extemplo turbati animi, simul omne tumultu
coniurat trepido Latium saeuitque iuuentus   5
effera. ductores primi Messapus et Vfens
contemptorque deum Mezentius undique cogunt
auxilia et latos uastant cultoribus agros.
mittitur et magni Venulus Diomedis ad urbem
qui petat auxilium, et Latio consistere Teucros,   10
aduectum Aenean classi uictosque penatis
inferre et fatis regem se dicere posci
edoceat, multasque uiro se adiungere gentis
Dardanio et late Latio increbrescere nomen:
quid struat his coeptis, quem, si fortuna sequatur, 15
euentum pugnae cupiat, manifestius ipsi
quam Turno regi aut regi apparere Latino.
   Talia per Latium. quae Laomedontius heros
cuncta uidens magno curarum fluctuat aestu,
atque animum nunc huc celerem nunc diuidit illuc   20
in partisque rapit uarias perque omnia uersat,
sicut aquae tremulum labris ubi lumen aënis
sole repercussum aut radiantis imagine lunae
omnia peruolitat late loca, iamque sub auras
erigitur summique ferit laquearia tecti.   25
nox erat et terras animalia fessa per omnis

   1–13 *MPR*; 14–26 *MPRV*   2 sonuerunt *P*[1]   10 con-
sidere (*A*. vi 67) *P*[2]   25 lacuaria '*multi*' *ap. Seru., schol. Veron.*

alituum pecudumque genus sopor altus habebat,
cum pater in ripa gelidique sub aetheris axe
Aeneas, tristi turbatus pectora bello,
procubuit seramque dedit per membra quietem.   30
huic deus ipse loci fluuio Tiberinus amoeno
populeas inter senior se attollere frondes
uisus (eum tenuis glauco uelabat amictu
carbasus, et crinis umbrosa tegebat harundo),
tum sic adfari et curas his demere dictis: 35
  'O sate gente deum, Troianam ex hostibus urbem
qui reuehis nobis aeternaque Pergama seruas,
exspectate solo Laurenti aruisque Latinis,
hic tibi certa domus, certi (ne absiste) penates.
neu belli terrere minis; tumor omnis et irae   40
concessere deum.
iamque tibi, ne uana putes haec fingere somnum,
litoreis ingens inuenta sub ilicibus sus
triginta capitum fetus enixa iacebit,
alba solo recubans, albi circum ubera nati.   45
[hic locus urbis erit, requies ea certa laborum,]
ex quo ter denis urbem redeuntibus annis
Ascanius clari condet cognominis Albam.
haud incerta cano. nunc qua ratione quod instat
expedias uictor, paucis (aduerte) docebo.   50
Arcades his oris, genus a Pallante profectum,
qui regem Euandrum comites, qui signa secuti,
delegere locum et posuere in montibus urbem
Pallantis proaui de nomine Pallanteum.
hi bellum adsidue ducunt cum gente Latina;   55
hos castris adhibe socios et foedera iunge.
ipse ego te ripis et recto flumine ducam,

27–39 *MPRV*; 40–57 *MPR*   29 pectore *M*¹   41 *addit*
profugis noua moenia Teucris (*cf. A*. x 158) '*mire quidam*' *ap. Seru.*
42–9 (cano) *seclusit Ribbeck*   43–6 = *A*. iii 390–3; 46 *om.*
hinc *MPar*, *habent R*ω   50 expedias *M*¹*P*¹*R*ω: expediam (*A*. vi
759, xi 315) *M*²*P*²*det*   56 foedere *Pbr*, *agnoscit Seru*. (*cf. A*. iv
112)

aduersum remis superes subuectus ut amnem.
surge age, nate dea, primisque cadentibus astris
Iunoni fer rite preces, iramque minasque   60
supplicibus supera uotis. mihi uictor honorem
persolues. ego sum pleno quem flumine cernis
stringentem ripas et pinguia culta secantem,
caeruleus Thybris, caelo gratissimus amnis.
hic mihi magna domus, celsis caput urbibus exit.'   65
 Dixit, deinde lacu fluuius se condidit alto
ima petens; nox Aenean somnusque reliquit.
surgit et aetherii spectans orientia solis
lumina rite cauis undam de flumine palmis
sustinet ac talis effundit ad aethera uoces: 70
'Nymphae, Laurentes Nymphae, genus amnibus unde est,
tuque, o Thybri tuo genitor cum flumine sancto,
accipite Aenean et tandem arcete periclis.
quo te cumque lacus miserantem incommoda nostra
fonte tenent, quocumque solo pulcherrimus exis,   75
semper honore meo, semper celebrabere donis
corniger Hesperidum fluuius regnator aquarum.
adsis o tantum et propius tua numina firmes.'
sic memorat, geminasque legit de classe biremis
remigioque aptat, socios simul instruit armis.   80
 Ecce autem subitum atque oculis mirabile monstrum,
candida per siluam cum fetu concolor albo
procubuit uiridique in litore conspicitur sus;
quam pius Aeneas tibi enim, tibi, maxima Iuno,
mactat sacra ferens et cum grege sistit ad aram.   85
Thybris ea fluuium, quam longa est, nocte tumentem
leniit, et tacita refluens ita substitit unda,
mitis ut in morem stagni placidaeque paludis

58–70 *MPR*; 71–88 *FMPR*   60 irasque *ω(praeter abfr)*
61 uotis] donis (*A.* iii 439) *d*   63 pinguia] singula *M*[1]
65 magna] certa (*u.* 39) *P*   67 relinquit *Raceuv*   70 sustulit
ω(praeter ar)   75 tenent *FR* (lacus *duodecies alibi plurali occurrit
numero*): tenet *MPω, Seru.*   78 tandem *d*   proprius *P*[1],
agnoscit Seru.

sterneret aequor aquis, remo ut luctamen abesset.
ergo iter inceptum celerant rumore secundo: 90
labitur uncta uadis abies; mirantur et undae,
miratur nemus insuetum fulgentia longe
scuta uirum fluuio pictasque innare carinas.
olli remigio noctemque diemque fatigant
et longos superant flexus, uariisque teguntur   95
arboribus, uiridisque secant placido aequore siluas.
sol medium caeli conscenderat igneus orbem
cum muros arcemque procul ac rara domorum
tecta uident, quae nunc Romana potentia caelo
aequauit, tum res inopes Euandrus habebat.   100
ocius aduertunt proras urbique propinquant.

  Forte die sollemnem illo rex Arcas honorem
Amphitryoniadae magno diuisque ferebat
ante urbem in luco. Pallas huic filius una,
una omnes iuuenum primi pauperque senatus   105
tura dabant, tepidusque cruor fumabat ad aras.
ut celsas uidere rates atque inter opacum
adlabi nemus et tacitos incumbere remis,
terrentur uisu subito cunctique relictis
consurgunt mensis. audax quos rumpere Pallas   110
sacra uetat raptoque uolat telo obuius ipse,
et procul e tumulo: 'iuuenes, quae causa subegit
ignotas temptare uias? quo tenditis?' inquit.
'qui genus? unde domo? pacemne huc fertis an arma?'
tum pater Aeneas puppi sic fatur ab alta   115
paciferaeque manu ramum praetendit oliuae:
'Troiugenas ac tela uides inimica Latinis,
quos illi bello profugos egere superbo.
Euandrum petimus. ferte haec et dicite lectos
Dardaniae uenisse duces socia arma rogantis.'   120

89–92 *FMPR*; 93–8 *FMPRV*; 99–118 *MPRV*; 119–20 *MPR*
90 celerant] peragunt (*A*. vi 384) *R*, *Macrob*. vi 1. 37, *Non*. 385. 7
Rumone *M*[1], *agnoscit Seru*.   92 mirantur *Fγ*   100 tunc
Rberuv, Tib.   102 sollemne *PR*, *Non*. 320. 15   108 tacitis
df, Seru.   115 tunc *R*   fatus *P*

obstipuit tanto percussus nomine Pallas:
'egredere o quicumque es' ait 'coramque parentem
adloquere ac nostris succede penatibus hospes.'
excepitque manu dextramque amplexus inhaesit;
progressi subeunt luco fluuiumque relinquunt.   125
    Tum regem Aeneas dictis adfatur amicis:
'optime Graiugenum, cui me Fortuna precari
et uitta comptos uoluit praetendere ramos,
non equidem extimui Danaum quod ductor et Arcas
quodque a stirpe fores geminis coniunctus Atridis;   130
sed mea me uirtus et sancta oracula diuum
cognatique patres, tua terris didita fama,
coniunxere tibi et fatis egere uolentem.
Dardanus, Iliacae primus pater urbis et auctor,
Electra, ut Grai perhibent, Atlantide cretus,   135
aduehitur Teucros; Electram maximus Atlas
edidit, aetherios umero qui sustinet orbis.
uobis Mercurius pater est, quem candida Maia
Cyllenae gelido conceptum uertice fudit;
at Maiam, auditis si quicquam credimus, Atlas,   140
idem Atlas generat caeli qui sidera tollit.
sic genus amborum scindit se sanguine ab uno.
his fretus non legatos neque prima per artem
temptamenta tui pepigi; me, me ipse meumque
obieci caput et supplex ad limina ueni.   145
gens eadem, quae te, crudeli Daunia bello
insequitur; nos si pellant nihil afore credunt
quin omnem Hesperiam penitus sua sub iuga mittant,
et mare quod supra teneant quodque adluit infra.
accipe daque fidem. sunt nobis fortia bello   150
pectora, sunt animi et rebus spectata iuuentus.'

121–51 *MPR*   121 percussus *MPdfhrst, Seru.*: per-
culsus *Rabceuv, Tib. (cf. G.* ii 476, *A.* i 513)   122 parente *deu*
123 ac] et *M¹, Non.* 403. 23   132 didita *MPchsu, Seru.*:
dedita *Rω*   139 fundit *P¹*   140 cuiquam *R*   creditis *P*
147 afore *P¹bfrs*: adfore (aff-) *M²P²ω* (atf- *M¹*): fore *R*: offore *fortasse
Seru.*

Dixerat Aeneas. ille os oculosque loquentis
iamdudum et totum lustrabat lumine corpus.
tum sic pauca refert: 'ut te, fortissime Teucrum,
accipio agnoscoque libens! ut uerba parentis   155
et uocem Anchisae magni uultumque recordor!
nam memini Hesionae uisentem regna sororis
Laomedontiaden Priamum Salamina petentem
protinus Arcadiae gelidos inuisere finis.
tum mihi prima genas uestibat flore iuuentas,   160
mirabarque duces Teucros, mirabar et ipsum
Laomedontiaden; sed cunctis altior ibat
Anchises. mihi mens iuuenali ardebat amore
compellare uirum et dextrae coniungere dextram;
accessi et cupidus Phenei sub moenia duxi.   165
ille mihi insignem pharetram Lyciasque sagittas
discedens chlamydemque auro dedit intertextam,
frenaque bina meus quae nunc habet aurea Pallas.
ergo et quam petitis iuncta est mihi foedere dextra,
et lux cum primum terris se crastina reddet,   170
auxilio laetos dimittam opibusque iuuabo.
interea sacra haec, quando huc uenistis amici,
annua, quae differre nefas, celebrate fauentes
nobiscum, et iam nunc sociorum adsuescite mensis.'

Haec ubi dicta, dapes iubet et sublata reponi   175
pocula gramineoque uiros locat ipse sedili,
praecipuumque toro et uillosi pelle leonis
accipit Aenean solioque inuitat acerno.
tum lecti iuuenes certatim araeque sacerdos
uiscera tosta ferunt taurorum, onerantque canistris   180
dona laboratae Cereris, Bacchumque ministrant.
uescitur Aeneas simul et Troiana iuuentus
perpetui tergo bouis et lustralibus extis.

Postquam exempta fames et amor compressus edendi,
rex Euandrus ait: 'non haec sollemnia nobis,   185

152–85 *MPR*   160 iuuentus *cdefh*   167 intertexto *P¹Rd*,
agnoscit Seru.   182 et] ac *aeuv*

has ex more dapes, hanc tanti numinis aram
uana superstitio ueterumque ignara deorum
imposuit: saeuis, hospes Troiane, periclis
seruati facimus meritosque nouamus honores.
iam primum saxis suspensam hanc aspice rupem,   190
disiectae procul ut moles desertaque montis
stat domus et scopuli ingentem traxere ruinam.
hic spelunca fuit uasto summota recessu,
semihominis Caci facies quam dira tenebat
solis inaccessam radiis; semperque recenti   195
caede tepebat humus, foribusque adfixa superbis
ora uirum tristi pendebant pallida tabo.
huic monstro Volcanus erat pater: illius atros
ore uomens ignis magna se mole ferebat.
attulit et nobis aliquando optantibus aetas   200
auxilium aduentumque dei. nam maximus ultor
tergemini nece Geryonae spoliisque superbus
Alcides aderat taurosque hac uictor agebat
ingentis, uallemque boues amnemque tenebant.
at furis Caci mens effera, ne quid inausum   205
aut intractatum scelerisue doliue fuisset,
quattuor a stabulis praestanti corpore tauros
auertit, totidem forma superante iuuencas.
atque hos, ne qua forent pedibus uestigia rectis,
cauda in speluncam tractos uersisque uiarum   210
indiciis raptor saxo occultabat opaco;
quaerenti nulla ad speluncam signa ferebant.
interea, cum iam stabulis saturata moueret
Amphitryoniades armenta abitumque pararet,
discessu mugire boues atque omne querelis   215

186–215 *MPR*   190 primum] pridem *Rbruv, agnoscit Tib.*
191 deiectae *R*   194 tenebat *M²ω*: tegebat *M¹PRabhrv, Tib.*
197 squallida *M*   202 Geryonae *Pacfh* (-ne *Mu*), *Seru. hic et ad A.*
vii 662: -ni *R*: -nis *bdt*: -nes *rv, Tib.*: -neis *e*   205 furis *M¹ω*(furi *s*),
Seru.: furiis *M²PRbrt, Tib.*   206 intemptatum *M²dhst*
211 raptor *Wakefield, collato Prop.* iv 9. 9: raptos *codd.*   212 quae-
rentes *Ru*, -tis *br*: -tem *recc.*   214 parabat *M¹*

33

impleri nemus et colles clamore relinqui.
reddidit una boum uocem uastoque sub antro
mugiit et Caci spem custodita fefellit.
hic uero Alcidae furiis exarserat atro
felle dolor: rapit arma manu nodisque grauatum   220
robur, et aërii cursu petit ardua montis.
tum primum nostri Cacum uidere timentem
turbatumque oculis; fugit ilicet ocior Euro
speluncamque petit, pedibus timor addidit alas.
ut sese inclusit ruptisque immane catenis   225
deiecit saxum, ferro quod et arte paterna
pendebat, fultosque emuniit obice postis,
ecce furens animis aderat Tirynthius omnemque
accessum lustrans huc ora ferebat et illuc,
dentibus infrendens. ter totum feruidus ira   230
lustrat Auentini montem, ter saxea temptat
limina nequiquam, ter fessus ualle resedit.
stabat acuta silex praecisis undique saxis
speluncae dorso insurgens, altissima uisu,
dirarum nidis domus opportuna uolucrum.   235
hanc, ut prona iugo laeuum incumbebat ad amnem,
dexter in aduersum nitens concussit et imis
auulsam soluit radicibus, inde repente
impulit; impulsu quo maximus intonat aether,
dissultant ripae refluitque exterritus amnis.   240
at specus et Caci detecta apparuit ingens
regia, et umbrosae penitus patuere cauernae,
non secus ac si qua penitus ui terra dehiscens
infernas reseret sedes et regna recludat
pallida, dis inuisa, superque immane barathrum   245
cernatur, trepident immisso lumine Manes.

216–46 *MPR*   221 et aerii *M²PR def?v*: aetherii *M¹γt* (et
haerii *b*): et aetherii *chu*   223 oculis *codd.*, *Seru.*, *Tib.*: oculi
'*alii*' *ap. Seru.*: oculos *γ*   238 aduolsam *M¹*   239 intonat
MP: insonat *Rω* (*cf. A.* vii 515)   244 reseret *M¹ber*, *Macrob.*
v 16. 14, *Seru.*: reserat *M²PRω*, *Non.* 41. 13   246 trepidant-
que *R*

ergo insperata deprensum luce repente
inclusumque cauo saxo atque insueta rudentem
desuper Alcides telis premit, omniaque arma
aduocat et ramis uastisque molaribus instat.   250
ille autem, neque enim fuga iam super ulla pericli,
faucibus ingentem fumum (mirabile dictu)
euomit inuoluitque domum caligine caeca
prospectum eripiens oculis, glomeratque sub antro
fumiferam noctem commixtis igne tenebris.   255
non tulit Alcides animis, seque ipse per ignem
praecipiti iecit saltu, qua plurimus undam
fumus agit nebulaque ingens specus aestuat atra.
hic Cacum in tenebris incendia uana uomentem
corripit in nodum complexus, et angit inhaerens   260
elisos oculos et siccum sanguine guttur.
panditur extemplo foribus domus atra reuulsis
abstractaeque boues abiurataeque rapinae
caelo ostenduntur, pedibusque informe cadauer
protrahitur. nequeunt expleri corda tuendo   265
terribilis oculos, uultum uillosaque saetis
pectora semiferi atque exstinctos faucibus ignis.
ex illo celebratus honos laetique minores
seruauere diem, primusque Potitius auctor
et domus Herculei custos Pinaria sacri   270
hanc aram luco statuit, quae maxima semper
dicetur nobis et erit quae maxima semper.
quare agite, o iuuenes, tantarum in munere laudum
cingite fronde comas et pocula porgite dextris,
communemque uocate deum et date uina uolentes.'   275
dixerat, Herculea bicolor cum populus umbra
uelauitque comas foliisque innexa pependit,
et sacer impleuit dextram scyphus. ocius omnes
in mensam laeti libant diuosque precantur.

247–79 *MPR*   247 luce *M*[1]*P*: in luce *M*[2]*Rω*   251 pericli est
Pcefhv (est pericli *u*), *DSeru. ad A.* iii 489 (*cf. A.* v 716)   257 iecit
MRbdrt: iniecit *Pω*   261 elidens '*multi*' *ap. Seru.*   262 exemplo *P*[1]*Rb*
atra] alta (*G.* ii 461) *P*[1]   277 innexa] inmissa *ps.Probus ad G.* ii 66

Deuexo interea propior fit Vesper Olympo. 280
iamque sacerdotes primusque Potitius ibant
pellibus in morem cincti, flammasque ferebant.
instaurant epulas et mensae grata secundae
dona ferunt cumulantque oneratis lancibus aras.
tum Salii ad cantus incensa altaria circum 285
populeis adsunt euincti tempora ramis,
hic iuuenum chorus, ille senum, qui carmine laudes
Herculeas et facta ferunt: ut prima nouercae
monstra manu geminosque premens eliserit anguis,
ut bello egregias idem disiecerit urbes, 290
Troiamque Oechaliamque, ut duros mille labores
rege sub Eurystheo fatis Iunonis iniquae
pertulerit. 'tu nubigenas, inuicte, bimembris
Hylaeumque Pholumque manu, tu Cresia mactas
prodigia et uastum Nemeae sub rupe leonem. 295
te Stygii tremuere lacus, te ianitor Orci
ossa super recubans antro semesa cruento;
nec te ullae facies, non terruit ipse Typhoeus
arduus arma tenens; non te rationis egentem
Lernaeus turba capitum circumstetit anguis. 300
salue, uera Iouis proles, decus addite diuis,
et nos et tua dexter adi pede sacra secundo.'
talia carminibus celebrant; super omnia Caci
speluncam adiciunt spirantemque ignibus ipsum.
consonat omne nemus strepitu collesque resultant. 305
    Exim se cuncti diuinis rebus ad urbem
perfectis referunt. ibat rex obsitus aeuo,
et comitem Aenean iuxta natumque tenebat
ingrediens uarioque uiam sermone leuabat.
miratur facilisque oculos fert omnia circum 310
Aeneas, capiturque locis et singula laetus

280–311 *MPR*   280 proprior *Pbcfhv*   282 flammamque
R   288 ferant *M¹*   291 Oechaliam eduros *M¹*   ut] et
Rbr, Macrob. vi 6. 14   295 Nemeae *P¹ω, Seru.*: Nemea *P²Rb,*
Nemaea *M*

exquiritque auditque uirum monimenta priorum.
tum rex Euandrus Romanae conditor arcis:
'haec nemora indigenae Fauni Nymphaeque tenebant
gensque uirum truncis et duro robore nata,   315
quis neque mos neque cultus erat, nec iungere tauros
aut componere opes norant aut parcere parto,
sed rami atque asper uictu uenatus alebat.
primus ab aetherio uenit Saturnus Olympo
arma Iouis fugiens et regnis exsul ademptis.   320
is genus indocile ac dispersum montibus altis
composuit legesque dedit, Latiumque uocari
maluit, his quoniam latuisset tutus in oris.
aurea quae perhibent illo sub rege fuere
saecula: sic placida populos in pace regebat,   325
deterior donec paulatim ac decolor aetas
et belli rabies et amor successit habendi.
tum manus Ausonia et gentes uenere Sicanae,
saepius et nomen posuit Saturnia tellus;
tum reges asperque immani corpore Thybris,   330
a quo post Itali fluuium cognomine Thybrim
diximus; amisit uerum uetus Albula nomen.
me pulsum patria pelagique extrema sequentem
Fortuna omnipotens et ineluctabile fatum
his posuere locis, matrisque egere tremenda   335
Carmentis nymphae monita et deus auctor Apollo.'
   Vix ea dicta, dehinc progressus monstrat et aram
et Carmentalem Romani nomine portam
quam memorant, nymphae priscum Carmentis honorem,
uatis fatidicae, cecinit quae prima futuros   340
Aeneadas magnos et nobile Pallanteum.
hinc lucum ingentem, quem Romulus acer asylum
rettulit, et gelida monstrat sub rupe Lupercal

312–343 *MPR*   317 parto] rapto *M*[1]   324 aurea quae
MP[2]*Rω, Aug. c.d.* xviii 15, *Lact. inst.* i 14: aureaque *P*[1]: aureaque
ut (*G.* i 247, *A.* iv 179) *ceuu*   fuerunt *Pc*   328 Ausonia *MP*:
Ausoniae *Rω*   337 aram] arma *M*[1]*R*   338 Romani *MPfhr*:
Romano *Rω*   341 nobile] nomine *P*[2]*R*

Parrhasio dictum Panos de more Lycaei.
nec non et sacri monstrat nemus Argileti   345
testaturque locum et letum docet hospitis Argi.
hinc ad Tarpeiam sedem et Capitolia ducit
aurea nunc, olim siluestribus horrida dumis.
iam tum religio pauidos terrebat agrestis
dira loci, iam tum siluam saxumque tremebant.   350
'hoc nemus, hunc' inquit 'frondoso uertice collem
(quis deus incertum est) habitat deus; Arcades ipsum
credunt se uidisse Iouem, cum saepe nigrantem
aegida concuteret dextra nimbosque cieret.
haec duo praeterea disiectis oppida muris,   355
reliquias ueterumque uides monimenta uirorum.
hanc Ianus pater, hanc Saturnus condidit arcem;
Ianiculum huic, illi fuerat Saturnia nomen.'
talibus inter se dictis ad tecta subibant
pauperis Euandri, passimque armenta uidebant   360
Romanoque foro et lautis mugire Carinis.
ut uentum ad sedes, 'haec' inquit 'limina uictor
Alcides subiit, haec illum regia cepit.
aude, hospes, contemnere opes et te quoque dignum
finge deo, rebusque ueni non asper egenis.'   365
dixit, et angusti subter fastigia tecti
ingentem Aenean duxit stratisque locauit
effultum foliis et pelle Libystidis ursae:
nox ruit et fuscis tellurem amplectitur alis.

   At Venus haud animo nequiquam exterrita mater   370
Laurentumque minis et duro mota tumultu
Volcanum adloquitur, thalamoque haec coniugis aureo
incipit et dictis diuinum aspirat amorem:
'dum bello Argolici uastabant Pergama reges
debita casurasque inimicis ignibus arces,   375
non ullum auxilium miseris, non arma rogaui

344–76 *MPR*   344 Parnasio *R*   350 siluas *R*   tenebant
*M*¹   357 arcem *M*¹*Pω*: urbem (*A*. i 5) *M*²*Rabdfr*   361 latis
*M*¹   cauernis *R*   362 uictor] nobis *br*   365 deos *P*¹

artis opisque tuae, nec te, carissime coniunx,
incassumue tuos uolui exercere labores,
quamuis et Priami deberem plurima natis,
et durum Aeneae fleuissem saepe laborem.   380
nunc Iouis imperiis Rutulorum constitit oris:
ergo eadem supplex uenio et sanctum mihi numen
arma rogo, genetrix nato. te filia Nerei,
te potuit lacrimis Tithonia flectere coniunx.
aspice qui coeant populi, quae moenia clausis   385
ferrum acuant portis in me excidiumque meorum.'
dixerat et niueis hinc atque hinc diua lacertis
cunctantem amplexu molli fouet. ille repente
accepit solitam flammam, notusque medullas
intrauit calor et labefacta per ossa cucurrit,   390
non secus atque olim tonitru cum rupta corusco
ignea rima micans percurrit lumine nimbos;
sensit laeta dolis et formae conscia coniunx.
tum pater aeterno fatur deuinctus amore:
'quid causas petis ex alto? fiducia cessit   395
quo tibi, diua, mei? similis si cura fuisset,
tum quoque fas nobis Teucros armare fuisset;
nec pater omnipotens Troiam nec fata uetabant
stare decemque alios Priamum superesse per annos.
et nunc, si bellare paras atque haec tibi mens est,   400
quidquid in arte mea possum promittere curae,
quod fieri ferro liquidoue potest electro,
quantum ignes animaeque ualent, absiste precando
uiribus indubitare tuis.' ea uerba locutus
optatos dedit amplexus placidumque petiuit   405
coniugis infusus gremio per membra soporem.
　Inde ubi prima quies medio iam noctis abactae

377–407 *MPR*   377 opisue *dt, Tib.*   378 incassumque
M¹   381 imperio *dht, Seru.*   382 nomen *P¹*   386 ferrum]
bellum *DSeru. ad A.* ii 27   391 non] haut (*u.* 414) *M*
394 deuictus *P²cdhrstu*   397 tunc *aeruv*   Teucros nobis *P¹c*
406 infusus *MP²ω, Gramm.*: infusum *P¹R, Probus et Carminius ap.
Seru.*

curriculo expulerat somnum, cum femina primum,
cui tolerare colo uitam tenuique Minerua
impositum, cinerem et sopitos suscitat ignis   410
noctem addens operi, famulasque ad lumina longo
exercet penso, castum ut seruare cubile
coniugis et possit paruos educere natos:
haud secus ignipotens nec tempore segnior illo
mollibus e stratis opera ad fabrilia surgit.   415
insula Sicanium iuxta latus Aeoliamque
erigitur Liparen fumantibus ardua saxis,
quam subter specus et Cyclopum exesa caminis
antra Aetnaea tonant, ualidique incudibus ictus
auditi referunt gemitus, striduntque cauernis   420
stricturae Chalybum et fornacibus ignis anhelat,
Volcani domus et Volcania nomine tellus.
hoc tunc ignipotens caelo descendit ab alto.
ferrum exercebant uasto Cyclopes in antro,
Brontesque Steropesque et nudus membra Pyragmon.   425
his informatum manibus iam parte polita
fulmen erat, toto genitor quae plurima caelo
deicit in terras, pars imperfecta manebat.
tris imbris torti radios, tris nubis aquosae
addiderant, rutuli tris ignis et alitis Austri.   430
fulgores nunc terrificos sonitumque metumque
miscebant operi flammisque sequacibus iras.
parte alia Marti currumque rotasque uolucris
instabant, quibus ille uiros, quibus excitat urbes;
aegidaque horriferam, turbatae Palladis arma,   435
certatim squamis serpentum auroque polibant
conexosque anguis ipsamque in pectore diuae
Gorgona desecto uertentem lumina collo.
'tollite cuncta' inquit 'coeptosque auferte labores,

408–39 *MPR*   409 calathisque Mineruae (*A*. vii 805) *dt*
412 exercens *M*   420 gemitus *P*: -tu *Md*: -tum *Rω*, *Tib.*
423 huc tum *P*; hoc *pro* huc *positum testantur Prisc.* i 34 *et* xv 6,
Seru. hic et ad A. i 4   431 horrificos *Rd*

Aetnaei Cyclopes, et huc aduertite mentem: 440
arma acri facienda uiro. nunc uiribus usus,
nunc manibus rapidis, omni nunc arte magistra.
praecipitate moras.' nec plura effatus, at illi
ocius incubuere omnes pariterque laborem
sortiti. fluit aes riuis aurique metallum   445
uulnificusque chalybs uasta fornace liquescit.
ingentem clipeum informant, unum omnia contra
tela Latinorum, septenosque orbibus orbis
impediunt. alii uentosis follibus auras
accipiunt redduntque, alii stridentia tingunt   450
aera lacu; gemit impositis incudibus antrum;
illi inter sese multa ui bracchia tollunt
in numerum, uersantque tenaci forcipe massam.
   Haec pater Aeoliis properat dum Lemnius oris,
Euandrum ex humili tecto lux suscitat alma   455
et matutini uolucrum sub culmine cantus.
consurgit senior tunicaque inducitur artus
et Tyrrhena pedum circumdat uincula plantis.
tum lateri atque umeris Tegeaeum subligat ensem
demissa ab laeua pantherae terga retorquens.   460
nec non et gemini custodes limine ab alto
praecedunt gressumque canes comitantur erilem.
hospitis Aeneae sedem et secreta petebat
sermonum memor et promissi muneris heros.
nec minus Aeneas se matutinus agebat;   465
filius huic Pallas, illi comes ibat Achates.
congressi iungunt dextras mediisque residunt
aedibus et licito tandem sermone fruuntur.
rex prior haec:
'maxime Teucrorum ductor, quo sospite numquam   470
res equidem Troiae uictas aut regna fatebor,

440–71 *MPR*   443 at] et *P¹dt*   459 Tegeaeum *Seru. ad
A.* v 299: Tegeaeum *Pω*: Tegeum *MRdf*   460 pantherea *P¹*
461 arto *Markland ad Stat. silu.* i 1. 46, *collatis uu.* 360, 455
462 procedunt *P¹*

nobis ad belli auxilium pro nomine tanto
exiguae uires; hinc Tusco claudimur amni,
hinc Rutulus premit et murum circumsonat armis.
sed tibi ego ingentis populos opulentaque regnis   475
iungere castra paro, quam fors inopina salutem
ostentat: fatis huc te poscentibus adfers.
haud procul hinc saxo incolitur fundata uetusto
urbis Agyllinae sedes, ubi Lydia quondam
gens, bello praeclara, iugis insedit Etruscis.   480
hanc multos florentem annos rex deinde superbo
imperio et saeuis tenuit Mezentius armis.
quid memorem infandas caedes, quid facta tyranni
effera? di capiti ipsius generique reseruent!
mortua quin etiam iungebat corpora uiuis   485
componens manibusque manus atque oribus ora,
tormenti genus, et sanie taboque fluentis
complexu in misero longa sic morte necabat.
at fessi tandem ciues infanda furentem
armati circumsistunt ipsumque domumque,   490
obtruncant socios, ignem ad fastigia iactant.
ille inter caedem Rutulorum elapsus in agros
confugere et Turni defendier hospitis armis.
ergo omnis furiis surrexit Etruria iustis,
regem ad supplicium praesenti Marte reposcunt.   495
his ego te, Aenea, ductorem milibus addam.
toto namque fremunt condensae litore puppes
signaque ferre iubent, retinet longaeuus haruspex
fata canens: "o Maeoniae delecta iuuentus,
flos ueterum uirtusque uirum, quos iustus in hostem   500
fert dolor et merita accendit Mezentius ira,
nulli fas Italo tantam subiungere gentem:
externos optate duces." tum Etrusca resedit
hoc acies campo monitis exterrita diuum.

472–504 MPR   472 numine P¹   477 'legimus et adfer et
adfers' Seru.   492 caedem M¹Rdft: caedes (A. viii 709, xi
648, 729) M²Pω

ipse oratores ad me regnique coronam   505
cum sceptro misit mandatque insignia Tarchon,
succedam castris Tyrrhenaque regna capessam.
sed mihi tarda gelu saeclisque effeta senectus
inuidet imperium seraeque ad fortia uires.
natum exhortarer, ni mixtus matre Sabella   510
hinc partem patriae traheret. tu, cuius et annis
et generi fatum indulget, quem numina poscunt,
ingredere, o Teucrum atque Italum fortissime ductor.
hunc tibi praeterea, spes et solacia nostri,
Pallanta adiungam; sub te tolerare magistro   515
militiam et graue Martis opus, tua cernere facta
adsuescat, primis et te miretur ab annis.
Arcadas huic equites bis centum, robora pubis
lecta dabo, totidemque suo tibi nomine Pallas.'
    Vix ea fatus erat, defixique ora tenebant   520
Aeneas Anchisiades et fidus Achates,
multaque dura suo tristi cum corde putabant,
ni signum caelo Cytherea dedisset aperto.
namque improuiso uibratus ab aethere fulgor
cum sonitu uenit et ruere omnia uisa repente,   525
Tyrrhenusque tubae mugire per aethera clangor.
suspiciunt, iterum atque iterum fragor increpat ingens.
arma inter nubem caeli in regione serena
per sudum rutilare uident et pulsa tonare.
obstipuere animis alii, sed Troius heros   530
agnouit sonitum et diuae promissa parentis.
tum memorat: 'ne uero, hospes, ne quaere profecto
quem casum portenta ferant: ego poscor Olympo.
hoc signum cecinit missuram diua creatrix,

505–34 *MPR*   512 fatum *PRω*, *DSeru.*: fata *Mc*(fato *u*)
indulget *P¹* (*correctum in* -ges) *ω*, *DSeru.* (-geet *R*): -gent *MP²cu*
514 nunc *dt*   519 tuo sibi *M¹*: suo sibi *P²*   nomine *Mω*, *Seru.*:
munere *PRb*   527 suspiciunt *Rahrv*   increpat] intonat (*A.*
ix 709) *acehuv* (insonat *f*), *Seru.*   528 nubes *Non.* 31. 17   in *om.*
M¹, *Non.*   529 tonare *M²ω* (torare *M¹*), *DSeru.*: sonare *PRc*
533 '*alii* Olympo *sequentibus iungunt*' *DSeru.*

si bellum ingrueret, Volcaniaque arma per auras 535
laturam auxilio.
heu quantae miseris caedes Laurentibus instant!
quas poenas mihi, Turne, dabis! quam multa sub undas
scuta uirum galeasque et fortia corpora uolues,
Thybri pater! poscant acies et foedera rumpant.' 540
    Haec ubi dicta dedit, solio se tollit ab alto
et primum Herculeis sopitas ignibus aras
excitat, hesternumque larem paruosque penatis
laetus adit; mactat lectas de more bidentis
Euandrus pariter, pariter Troiana iuuentus. 545
post hinc ad nauis graditur sociosque reuisit,
quorum de numero qui sese in bella sequantur
praestantis uirtute legit; pars cetera prona
fertur aqua segnisque secundo defluit amni,
nuntia uentura Ascanio rerumque patrisque. 550
dantur equi Teucris Tyrrhena petentibus arua;
ducunt exsortem Aeneae, quem fulua leonis
pellis obit totum praefulgens unguibus aureis.
    Fama uolat paruam subito uulgata per urbem
ocius ire equites Tyrrheni ad limina regis. 555
uota metu duplicant matres, propiusque periclo
it timor et maior Martis iam apparet imago.
tum pater Euandrus dextram complexus euntis
haeret inexpletus lacrimans ac talia fatur:
'o mihi praeteritos referat si Iuppiter annos, 560
qualis eram cum primam aciem Praeneste sub ipsa
straui scutorumque incendi uictor aceruos
et regem hac Erulum dextra sub Tartara misi,

535-63 *MPR*   538 unda *Rb* (*cf. A*. i 100)   543 suscitat
R (*cf. A.* v 743, viii 410)   hesternumque *Pω*: externumque *MRa*,
'*male quidam*' *ap. Seru.*   544 mactant (*A.* iv 57) *M*
555 Tyrrhena *P*   limina *Pcefsuv*: litora *MRa²bdhrt*   556 proprius-
que *PRr*   559 inexpletus *MP²bdrt* (inpletus *R; cf. G.* iv 370): -tum
P¹ω: in amplexu *ac?*   lacrimis *Md*   inexpletus, lacrimans '*multi*'
ap. Seru., -tus lacrimis '*alii*', '*honestius*' -tum lacrimans   561 pri-
mum *R*

44

nascenti cui tris animas Feronia mater
(horrendum dictu) dederat, terna arma mouenda— 565
ter leto sternendus erat; cui tunc tamen omnis
abstulit haec animas dextra et totidem exuit armis:
non ego nunc dulci amplexu diuellerer usquam,
nate, tuo, neque finitimo Mezentius umquam
huic capiti insultans tot ferro saeua dedisset 570
funera, tam multis uiduasset ciuibus urbem.
at uos, o superi, et diuum tu maxime rector
Iuppiter, Arcadii, quaeso, miserescite regis
et patrias audite preces. si numina uestra
incolumem Pallanta mihi, si fata reseruant, 575
si uisurus eum uiuo et uenturus in unum,
uitam oro, patior quemuis durare laborem.
sin aliquem infandum casum, Fortuna, minaris,
nunc, nunc o liceat crudelem abrumpere uitam,
dum curae ambiguae, dum spes incerta futuri, 580
dum te, care puer, mea sola et sera uoluptas,
complexu teneo, grauior neu nuntius auris
uulneret.' haec genitor digressu dicta supremo
fundebat; famuli conlapsum in tecta ferebant.

Iamque adeo exierat portis equitatus apertis 585
Aeneas inter primos et fidus Achates,
inde alii Troiae proceres; ipse agmine Pallas
it medio chlamyde et pictis conspectus in armis,
qualis ubi Oceani perfusus Lucifer unda,
quem Venus ante alios astrorum diligit ignis, 590
extulit os sacrum caelo tenebrasque resoluit.
stant pauidae in muris matres oculisque sequuntur
puluaeram nubem et fulgentis aere cateruas.

564–93 *MPR* 566 tum *br* 569 finitimos *P*[1] umquam
Mabdhs?t: usquam *PRcefruv* 572 at *M*[2]ω: ad *M*[1]*PR*
577 patiar *P*[2]*cefhv* 579 nunc o nunc *R* (*cf. A.* ii 644)
581 sola et sera *MR*ω, *Auson. cento* 88, *Seru.*: sera et sola *Pbr*, *Seru.*
ad A. ix 480 582 complexus *M*[2]*Rr* ne *P*[2]ω (*om. c*, nec *v*),
Non. 315. 13, *Don. ad Ter. Hec.* 637 583 dicta] maesta (*A.* iii
482) *M*[1] 588 it *Markland ad Stat. silu.* v 1. 245: in *codd.*

olli per dumos, qua proxima meta uiarum,
armati tendunt; it clamor, et agmine facto   595
quadripedante putrem sonitu quatit ungula campum.
est ingens gelidum lucus prope Caeritis amnem,
religione patrum late sacer; undique colles
inclusere caui et nigra nemus abiete cingunt.
Siluano fama est ueteres sacrasse Pelasgos,   600
aruorum pecorisque deo, lucumque diemque,
qui primi finis aliquando habuere Latinos.
haud procul hinc Tarcho et Tyrrheni tuta tenebant
castra locis, celsoque omnis de colle uideri
iam poterat legio et latis tendebat in aruis.   605
huc pater Aeneas et bello lecta iuuentus
succedunt, fessique et equos et corpora curant.
    At Venus aetherios inter dea candida nimbos
dona ferens aderat; natumque in valle reducta
ut procul egelido secretum flumine uidit,   610
talibus adfata est dictis seque obtulit ultro:
'en perfecta mei promissa coniugis arte
munera. ne mox aut Laurentis, nate, superbos
aut acrem dubites in proelia poscere Turnum.'
dixit, et amplexus nati Cytherea petiuit,   615
arma sub aduersa posuit radiantia quercu.
ille deae donis et tanto laetus honore
expleri nequit atque oculos per singula uoluit,
miraturque interque manus et bracchia uersat
terribilem cristis galeam flammasque uomentem,   620
fatiferumque ensem, loricam ex aere rigentem,
sanguineam, ingentem, qualis cum caerula nubes
solis inardescit radiis longeque refulget;
tum leuis ocreas electro auroque recocto,
hastamque et clipei non enarrabile textum.   625
illic res Italas Romanorumque triumphos

594–626 *MPR*   610 egelido *M¹acfuv, Seru.*: et gelido
M²PRbdhrt (gelido *e*)   620 minantem *P*   621 loricamque
aer?uv

haud uatum ignarus uenturique inscius aeui
fecerat ignipotens, illic genus omne futurae
stirpis ab Ascanio pugnataque in ordine bella.
fecerat et uiridi fetam Mauortis in antro　　　　　　　630
procubuisse lupam, geminos huic ubera circum
ludere pendentis pueros et lambere matrem
impauidos, illam tereti ceruice reflexa
mulcere alternos et corpora fingere lingua.
nec procul hinc Romam et raptas sine more Sabinas　　635
consessu caueae, magnis Circensibus actis,
addiderat, subitoque nouum consurgere bellum
Romulidis Tatioque seni Curibusque seueris.
post idem inter se posito certamine reges
armati Iouis ante aram paterasque tenentes　　　　　640
stabant et caesa iungebant foedera porca.
haud procul inde citae Mettum in diuersa quadrigae
distulerant (at tu dictis, Albane, maneres!),
raptabatque uiri mendacis uiscera Tullus
per siluam, et sparsi rorabant sanguine uepres.　　　645
nec non Tarquinium eiectum Porsenna iubebat
accipere ingentique urbem obsidione premebat;
Aeneadae in ferrum pro libertate ruebant.
illum indignanti similem similemque minanti
aspiceres, pontem auderet quia uellere Cocles　　　650
et fluuium uinclis innaret Cloelia ruptis.
in summo custos Tarpeiae Manlius arcis
stabat pro templo et Capitolia celsa tenebat,
Romuleoque recens horrebat regia culmo.
atque hic auratis uolitans argenteus anser　　　　　655
porticibus Gallos in limine adesse canebat;
Galli per dumos aderant arcemque tenebant
defensi tenebris et dono noctis opacae.

627–58 *MPR*　　　　628 omnipotens *M*　　　　633 reflexa
M²PRabrt: reflexam *M¹ω*　　　　640 aras *Rbdt*　　pateramque *M*
642 medium *M¹*　　　652 Manlius *M²Pcfrst*: Manulus *M¹*: Malius
R: Mallius *ω*　　　657 Galli] olli *R*

47

aurea caesaries ollis atque aurea uestis,
uirgatis lucent sagulis, tum lactea colla   660
auro innectuntur, duo quisque Alpina coruscant
gaesa manu, scutis protecti corpora longis.
hic exsultantis Salios nudosque Lupercos
lanigerosque apices et lapsa ancilia caelo
extuderat, castae ducebant sacra per urbem   665
pilentis matres in mollibus. hinc procul addit
Tartareas etiam sedes, alta ostia Ditis,
et scelerum poenas, et te, Catilina, minaci
pendentem scopulo Furiarumque ora trementem,
secretosque pios, his dantem iura Catonem.   670
haec inter tumidi late maris ibat imago
aurea, sed fluctu spumabant caerula cano,
et circum argento clari delphines in orbem
aequora uerrebant caudis aestumque secabant.
in medio classis aeratas, Actia bella,   675
cernere erat, totumque instructo Marte uideres
feruere Leucaten auroque effulgere fluctus.
hinc Augustus agens Italos in proelia Caesar
cum patribus populoque, penatibus et magnis dis,
stans celsa in puppi, geminas cui tempora flammas   680
laeta uomunt patriumque aperitur uertice sidus.
parte alia uentis et dis Agrippa secundis
arduus agmen agens, cui, belli insigne superbum,
tempora nauali fulgent rostrata corona.
hinc ope barbarica uariisque Antonius armis,   685
uictor ab Aurorae populis et litore rubro,
Aegyptum uirisque Orientis et ultima secum
Bactra uehit, sequiturque (nefas) Aegyptia coniunx.
una omnes ruere ac totum spumare reductis
conuulsum remis rostrisque tridentibus aequor.   690

659–90 *MPR*   660 tunc *P*: cum *dt*   661 coruscant
MRadfht: -cat *Pbceruv*   672 spumabant ω: -bat *MPRbrt*,
utrumque (*ut uid.*) *Seru.*   680 stat *Rbr*   cui] huic *P²*
690 stridentibus (*cf. A.* v 143) *Rω* (*praeter b*); -que *om. ch*

alta petunt; pelago credas innare reuulsas
Cycladas aut montis concurrere montibus altos,
tanta mole uiri turritis puppibus instant.
stuppea flamma manu telisque uolatile ferrum
spargitur, arua noua Neptunia caede rubescunt.   695
regina in mediis patrio uocat agmina sistro,
necdum etiam geminos a tergo respicit anguis.
omnigenumque deum monstra et latrator Anubis
contra Neptunum et Venerem contraque Mineruam
tela tenent. saeuit medio in certamine Mauors   700
caelatus ferro, tristesque ex aethere Dirae,
et scissa gaudens uadit Discordia palla,
quam cum sanguineo sequitur Bellona flagello.
Actius haec cernens arcum intendebat Apollo
desuper; omnis eo terrore Aegyptus et Indi,   705
omnis Arabs, omnes uertebant terga Sabaei.
ipsa uidebatur uentis regina uocatis
uela dare et laxos iam iamque immittere funis.
illam inter caedes pallentem morte futura
fecerat ignipotens undis et Iapyge ferri,   710
contra autem magno maerentem corpore Nilum
pandentemque sinus et tota ueste uocantem
caeruleum in gremium latebrosaque flumina uictos.
at Caesar, triplici inuectus Romana triumpho
moenia, dis Italis uotum immortale sacrabat,   715
maxima ter centum totam delubra per urbem.
laetitia ludisque uiae plausuque fremebant;
omnibus in templis matrum chorus, omnibus arae;
ante aras terram caesi strauere iuuenci.
ipse sedens niueo candentis limine Phoebi   720
dona recognoscit populorum aptatque superbis
postibus; incedunt uictae longo ordine gentes,
quam uariae linguis, habitu tam uestis et armis.

691–723 *MPR*   692 altis *ah, 'alii' ap. Seru.*   701 dirae
M¹Pabcerv: diuae (*cf. A.* iv 473) *M²Rdfhstu*   704 tendebat.*P*
722 gentes] matres (*A.* ii 766) *R*

hic Nomadum genus et discinctos Mulciber Afros,
hic Lelegas Carasque sagittiferosque Gelonos   725
finxerat; Euphrates ibat iam mollior undis,
extremique hominum Morini, Rhenusque bicornis,
indomitique Dahae, et pontem indignatus Araxes.
    Talia per clipeum Volcani, dona parentis,
miratur rerumque ignarus imagine gaudet   730
attollens umero famamque et fata nepotum.

724–31 *MPR*   724 hinc *Pbs*   Mulcifer *ω*   725 hinc
Pbcfsuv   731 fata] facta *cesuv, utrumque agnoscit DSeru.*

COMMENTARY ON BOOK VII

*Works cited in abbreviated form appear in full
in the Select Bibliography on pp. xxxi f.*

1–36. *After burying his nurse Caieta in the place that still bears
her name, Aeneas sails through the night along the coast, passing
the land of Circe, and at dawn reaches the mouth of the Tiber.*

1. **tu quoque:** i.e. like Misenus (vi. 234 f.) and Palinurus (vi.
381 ff.), Trojan refugees who are said to have given their
names to their last resting-places in Italy. On the device of
apostrophe see on 49.

   litoribus nostris: Virgil rarely speaks in the first person in
the *Aeneid*, but cf. viii. 332 'diximus', ix. 446 'si quid mea
carmina possunt'. Caieta, on the borders of Latium and
Campania, was a busy harbour in Cicero's time (*Leg. Man.*
33 'portum Caietae celeberrimum et plenissimum nauium').

   Aeneia nutrix: cf. x. 156 'Aeneia puppis', 494 f. 'Aeneia
hospitia'; so, e.g., 252 'sceptra Priameia', ii. 542 f. 'corpus
Hectoreum', viii. 287 f. 'laudes Herculeas', 384 'Tithonia
coniunx', x. 394 'Euandrius ensis'. This use of the possessive
adjective in preference to the genitive was a native Latin
idiom, as is shown by such standard formulas as *flamen
Dialis, ostium Tiberinum, campus Martius*, and such early ex-
pressions as *sacerdos Veneria* (Plaut. *Rud.* 329), *uim Vol-
caniam* (Lucil. 606 M.). Early Greek shows the same use of
proper adjectives (e.g. Homer's Νεστορέη νηῦς, Γοργείη κεφαλή,
βίη Ἡρακληείη; cf. the regular Ἄρειος πάγος), which the language
of tragedy adopted and the Alexandrian poets made into a
mannerism; in Latin verse the influence of Greek practice
and metrical convenience combined to commend it. Ordinary
language shows the same idiom with such 'common' adjec-
tives as *erilis* and *patrius*: for Virgil's use of these, cf. 490
'mensae erili', viii. 462 'gressum erilem', vii. 636 'patrios
ensis', 653 'patriis imperiis'. See J. Wackernagel, *Vorlesun-
gen* ii. 70 ff., *Kl. Schr.* ii. 1358 ff.; E. Löfstedt, *Synt.* i². 107 ff.,
Per. Aeth. 76 ff.; J. Marouzeau, *Traité de stylistique latine*,
205 ff.

3. **seruat honos sedem tuus,** 'the honour paid you still haunts
your resting-place and your name marks your bones'. For
seruat cf. vi. 507 (of the tomb of Deiphobus) 'nomen et arma

locum seruant'; for *sedes* in this context cf. vi. 152 'sedibus hunc refer ante suis et conde sepulcro', 328 'sedibus ossa quierunt'.

honos: the original nominative form, invariable (as *arbos* is) in Virgil (it occurs fourteen times in the *Aeneid*) and usual in Cicero. The second vowel is long; in the later form *honor*, formed by analogy from the oblique cases, in which -*r*- was the regular development of intervocalic -*s*-, it is shortened on the analogy of other types of substantive in -*or* (e.g. nouns of agent), but Virgil preserves the original quantity in *pauor* (ii. 369), *amor* (xi. 323, xii. 668), *dolor* (xii. 422) and *labor* (*Geo.* iii. 118: at vi. 277 he uses *labos*).

nomen: for the derivation of the Italian place-name from a figure of Graeco-Italian legend cf. vi. 234 f. 'monte sub aerio qui nunc Misenus ab illo / dicitur aeternumque tenet per saecula nomen', 381 ff. 'aeternumque locus Palinuri nomen habebit / . . . gaudet cognomine terra', x. 143 ff. 'adfuit . . . / et Capys: hinc nomen Campanae ducitur urbi' (i.e. *Capuae*). The turn belongs to the learned tradition of Hellenistic poetry: so when Propertius embarks on aetiological poetry in the manner of Callimachus, he describes his theme as *cognomina prisca locorum*: the significant name is an αἴτιον of the place. So also 671 'Tiburti dictam cognomine gentem', i. 276 f. 'Romulus . . . Romanos . . . suo de nomine dicet', 533 'Italiam dixisse ducis de nomine gentem', v. 117 ff. (the gentes Memmia, Sergia, and Cluentia from Mnestheus, Sergestus, and Cloanthus), xi. 246 f. (Argyripa or Arpi from Argos Hippion), viii. 51 ff. (the Palatine from Pallas), 330 ff. 'Thybris / a quo post Itali fluuium cognomine Thybrim / diximus; amisit uerum uetus Albula nomen'. (See Norden on *Aen.* vi. 234 f.) For another type of etymological aside see viii. 322 ff. 'Latiumque uocari / maluit, his quoniam latuisset tutus in oris'. For etymology brought out by an adjective see on 684.

4. **Hesperia in magna,** 'in the great Land of the West': Dido gives the same proud name to Italy in i. 569. The name of the 'Westland' for Italy is, of course, Greek; the name is not found as a substantive (ἑσπερία χθών is Italy in Ap. Rhod. iii. 311 and in the elegiac poet Agathyllus quoted by Dion. Hal. i. 49), but it may go back to Stesichorus (see D. Page, *Poetae Melici Graeci*, p. 111). Ennius had already used it, *Ann.* 23 V. 'est locus Hesperiam quam mortales perhibebant': Horace has it twice for Italy, *Od.* iii. 6. 8, iv. 5. 38, but in *Od.* i. 36. 4 'Hesperia ultima' is Spain.

si qua est ea gloria, 'if that renown is anything (is any renown at all)'. The parenthesis is a pathetic reflection: 'if

glory by which the living set store means anything to the
dead'. There is a close parallel in x. 827 f. 'teque parentum /
manibus et cineri, si qua est ea cura, remitto' ('if concern
for that means anything to you').

signat: i.e. is a *signum* of: cf. Tac. *Germ.* 28 'manet adhuc
Boihemi nomen signatque loci ueterem memoriam' ('attests
the old tradition of the country').

5. **at pius Aeneas:** *at* as usual marks a transition: Aeneas turns
to his further duty. *pius* in Virgil's use is not a mere stock
epithet but can be seen to have relevance to the contexts in
which it is placed, contexts as various as the implications
of the word. The *pietas* of Aeneas may be revealed in the
observance of ritual duties, in patient submission to the will
of heaven, in human feeling for loved ones, in concern for
those who look to him as their leader. See Austin on iv. 393;
N. Moseley, *Characters and Epithets* (London, 1926), 81 ff.;
U. Knoche in *Festschrift Bruno Snell* (Munich, 1956), 89 ff.

6. **aggere . . . tumuli:** cf. v. 44 'tumuli ex aggere': the *tumulus*
consists in the *agger*: similarly 106 'ripae ab aggere'.

6f. **alta . . . aequora:** 'deep waters' or 'high seas'? While in
some particular contexts *altus* applied to the sea clearly
refers to depth (e.g. *Geo.* iv. 528 'se iactu dedit aequor in
altum'), it seems likely that in set phrases such as this (or
362 'perfidus alta petens . . . praedo', iii. 192 'altum tenuere
rates', ix. 81 'pelagi petere alta parabat') it represents (like
our 'high seas' and such expressions as *decurrere, deferri, de-
mittere* applied to ships, sometimes with the addition of *ex
alto*: cf. also i. 381 'conscendi nauibus aequor') the point of
view of an observer on land seeing the sea rise towards the
horizon.

7. **tendit iter uelis:** cf. vi. 240 'tendere iter pennis', i. 656 'iter
ad nauis tendebat': similarly i. 410 'gressum tendit'.

tendit iter uelis portumque relinquit: for Virgil's charac-
teristic practice of representing an action under two aspects
by the use of two clauses connected by *et* or *-que* see E.
Norden, *Aeneis VI*, pp. 379 f.; T. E. Page in *C.R.* viii
(1894), 203 f.; A. S. McDevitt in *C.Q.* lxi (1967), 316 ff.; so
viii. 125 'progressi subeunt luco fluuiumque relinquunt',
iv. 154 f. 'agmina . . . fuga glomerant montisque relinquunt',
x. 819 f. 'uita . . . / concessit maesta ad Manis corpusque re-
liquit'; similarly, e.g., iii. 662 'altos tetigit fluctus et ad
aequora uenit', v. 292 'inuitat pretiis animos et praemia
ponit', vi. 115 'ut te supplex peterem et tua limina adirem'.
In these cases the time of the two clauses is the same (for
relinquit means not 'departs from' but 'leaves behind him').
But the second clause often conveys an aspect which is prior

in time to that of the first; Virgil prefers the vivid directness of co-ordination where prose writers or earlier poets would use a subordinate clause or a participle (as Virgil himself occasionally does: iii. 300 'progredior portu classis et litora linquens', vi. 157 'ingreditur linquens antrum'): so ii. 353 'moriamur et in media arma ruamus', 749 'ipse urbem repeto et cingor fulgentibus armis', vi. 365 f. 'tu mihi terram / inice, namque potes, portusque require Velinos', viii. 85 '(suem) mactat sacra ferens et cum grege sistit ad aram', 611 'talibus adfata est dictis seque obtulit ultro'.

8. **in noctem,** 'as night came on', as in *Geo.* iv. 189 f. 'siletur in noctem'. That this is the meaning of the phrase, and not 'right into the night', is shown by Celsus vii. 27. 1 'si febris . . . in noctem augetur'; Sen. *Agam.* 576 'cecidit in lucem furor'. Similarly Lucretius has vi. 712 'Nilus in aestatem crescit' ('with the summer'), vi. 875 'umor et in lucem tremulo rarescit ab aestu' ('as the light comes on'). The breeze does not fall at sunset as usual (cf. iii. 568 'fessos uentus cum sole reliquit') and they do not have to spend the night ashore as the ancient sailor was accustomed to do.

9. **tremulo sub lumine,** 'in the quivering light': cf. viii. 22 f. 'aquae tremulum labris ubi lumen aenis / sole repercussum aut radiantis imagine lunae'. The phrase is Ennian (*Sc.* 292 V.): 'lumine sic tremulo terra et caua caerula candent'. On the repetition *lumine . . . lumina* (13) see on 491.

10. **proxima . . . raduntur,** 'closely they skirt the shore'; *proxima* explains the following lines: they are close enough to hear the sounds on shore. For *radere* of 'brushing along' a coast cf. iii. 700, v. 170.

Circaeae . . . terrae: Homer had made Circe's home an island (*Od.* x. 135) and Virgil follows him in iii. 386 ('Aeaeae insula Circae'); post-Homeric legend, which identified Odysseus' ports of call with places in Italian waters, making Lipara the island of Aeolus and placing the Laestrygones at Formiae, found Circe's island of Aeaea on the coast of Latium. In fact Circei (originally *Cercei*: see Hülsen, P.–W. s.v.) was a promontory, now Monte Circello, an isolated spur of the Volscian hills (799 'Circaeum iugum'), rising steeply out of the sea and running back into the low ground of the Pomptine marshes, but early sailors may well have been misled by the lie of the land into taking it for an island. One account attempted to reconcile fact and fiction by making it an island which had become attached to the mainland (Varro *ap.* Serv. iii. 386; Pliny, *N.H.* ii. 201). In historical times the people of the town of Circei, planted on the neck of the promontory as a Roman colony against the Volsci and later a popular summer resort, still recognized their legendary connection with Circe (Cic. *N.D.* iii. 48 'Circen quoque coloni nostri Circeienses religiose colunt') and Strabo (v. 3. 6) speaks of a 'temple of Circe' there which had Odysseus' cup as a relic.

11-18. Almost every word contributes to the vivid romantic imagery of these lines. Virgil's picture of Circe's island home, with its atmosphere of mystery and horror, is very different from Homer's matter-of-fact account (*Od.* x. 148 ff.). There too it is set in a clearing in the woods, smoke rises from it (though not from perfumed cedar) and Circe is singing at her loom: but the lions and wolves, victims of her magic, that prowl around are tame and effusively welcoming. (Ovid shatters romance and makes Circe the busy director of a well-organized witch's laboratory: *Met.* xiv. 268 ff. 'ipsa quis usus / quoque sit in folio, quae sit concordia mixtis, / nouit et aduertens pensas examinat herbas'.)

11. inaccessos, 'unapproachable': for this use of negatived participial adjectives cf. i. 257 f. 'manent immota tuorum / fata tibi', iii. 420 'implacata Charybdis', v. 591 'indeprensus et inremeabilis error', viii. 559 'inexpletus lacrimans', x. 174 'inexhaustis . . . metallis', 242 f. 'clipeum cape quem dedit ipse / inuictum ignipotens', 391 f. 'simillima proles / indiscreta suis'. For *lucos* see on 29.

Solis filia: Circe is the daughter of Helios and Perse (Hom. *Od.* x. 138 f.) and the sister of Aeetes, Medea's father; there is magic in the family.

12. resonat: the transitive use, 'makes to resound', is found elsewhere only in Silius' imitation of this passage, xiv. 30.

13. urit . . . cedrum : Virgil transfers this romantic touch from Homer's picture of Calypso's cave, *Od.* v. 59 ff. πῦρ μὲν ἐπ' ἐσχαρόφιν μέγα καίετο, τηλόθι δ' ὀδμὴ / κέδρου τ' εὐκεάτοιο θύου τ' ἀνὰ νῆσον ὀδώδει / δαιομένων· ἡ δ' ἔνδον ἀοιδιάουσ' ὀπὶ καλῇ / ἱστὸν ἐποιχομένη χρυσείῃ κερκίδ' ὕφαινεν.

nocturna in lumina, 'to give light through the night': for *in* expressing purpose cf. 664 'gerunt in bella dolones'; Lucan i. 306 'in classem cadit omne nemus'.

14. arguto . . . telas, 'as she sweeps across the delicate web with the whistling shuttle': the line is repeated from *Geo.* i. 294 'arguto coniunx (the farmer's wife) percurrit pectine telas'. *pecten* is the technical term for the comb whose teeth are inserted in the web to close up the cross-threads of the weft (Ovid, *Met.* vi. 57 f. '(subtemen) inter stamina ductum / percusso pauiunt insecti pectine dentes', *F.* iii. 820 'rarum pectine denset opus'), but neither *percurrens* nor *arguto* suits that operation. Here *pecten* must be the shuttle, usually

radius, which is shot across the upright threads on the loom
carrying the cross-thread behind it (Ovid has the same verb,
F. iii. 819 'stantis radio percurrere telas') and whistles or
sings as it goes (so Ar. *Ran.* 1316 κερκὶς ἀοιδός; *A.P.* vi. 174
κερκίδα δ' εὐποίητον, ἀηδόνα τὰν ἐν ἐρίθοις, vi. 288 κερκίδα τὰν ἱστῶν
μολπάτιδα). Henry's suggestion that *pecten* is applied to the
shuttle because it strikes the hanging threads just as the plec-
trum (which is *pecten* in *Aen.* vi. 647) strikes the strings of
the lyre (conversely the lyre-strings are *stamina* in Ovid, *Met.*
xi. 169) is unnecessary: the shape of the shuttle with project-
ing teeth at either end to hold the thread justifies the use of
the word.

arguto: the adjective is used of that which makes a clear,
sharp impression on the senses—usually, as here, that of
hearing (cf. *Ecl.* 7. 24 'arguta fistula', 8. 22 'argutum nemus',
9. 36 'argutos olores', *Geo.* i. 143 'argutae serrae', 377
'arguta hirundo') but sometimes that of sight (*Geo.* iii. 80
'argutum caput' ('clear-cut head'); Cic. *Leg.* i. 27 'oculi
arguti', *de Or.* iii. 220 'manus arguta') and even that of smell
(Pliny, *N.H.* xv. 18 'odor argutior') or of taste (Pall. iii.
25. 4 'argutos sapores'). Hence it comes to be used meta-
phorically of lively, racy speech (e.g. Cic. *Att.* vi. 5. 1 'litteras
quam argutissimas') and of quickness of mind (Hor. *A.P.* 364
'argutum acumen').

15. **exaudiri:** the infinitive of narration (often, not very hap-
pily, called the historic infinitive) taking the place of a finite
verb in narrative has its origin in a primitive stage of lan-
guage which conveys ideas in mere names and in which the
infinitive, in its essential character of verbal noun, simply
names an action without particularization of time or person.
In comedy, in Cicero's letters (and his early speeches) and
in Petronius the idiom (usually with two or more infinitives)
is seen in everyday use for brisk emphatic description. (Its
effect may perhaps be roughly judged from the exaggerated
use of a similar way of speech in the narratives of Dickens's
Mr. Jingle, who dispenses with finite verbs.) In literary lan-
guage it was developed (in particular by the extension to
passive infinitives) and exploited (especially by the his-
torians[1]) as a dramatic way of presenting a situation, with an
emphasis on sheer fact, in a series of sharp strokes. Virgil has
thirty-two examples of it, of which eight have single in-
finitives and ten have passives: for a list, see J. J. Schlicher
in *C.P.* ix (1914), 380 f. Sometimes it conveys the feeling of

---

[1] Notably Sallust and Tacitus: its absence from the unemotional
narrative of Caesar is significant.

general excited movement (so, e.g., at i. 423 ff., ii. 685 f., vi. 491 f., xi. 142) : here it heightens the sense of supernatural mystery, as it does (with the same verb) in vi. 557 f. 'hinc exaudiri gemitus et saeua sonare / uerbera'; similarly in 78 below, 'id uero horrendum ac uisu mirabile ferri'. For another use in which the infinitive expresses a habitual action see iv. 421 f. 'solam nam perfidus ille / te colere', xi. 822 'quicum partiri curas'. See P. Perrochat, *L'Infinitif de narration en latin* (Paris, 1932).

gemitus iraeque, 'growls of anger' : what the grammarians label 'hendiadys' (as Servius labels this) is the poet's device of making a more vivid impact on his reader's mind by splitting a complex idea into its components and presenting these side by side in co-ordinated substantives—a device which may also have its metrical convenience (see on 142). For *gemere* of wild beasts cf. Lucr. iii. 296 ff. 'leonum / pectora qui fremitu rumpunt plerumque gementes / nec capere irarum fluctus in pectore possunt' (a passage which Virgil probably had in mind here); Hor. *Epod.* 16. 51 'circumgemit ursus ouile'.

irae : as at 755 the word has a plural reference : but see on 445.

16. **rudentum** : the verb is most often used of asses, but in *Geo.* iii. 374 it is used of deer, in *Aen.* viii. 248 of the monster Cacus.

18. **magnorum ululare luporum** : the repetition of *o* and *u* (and of *u* in 16) is clearly deliberate; Virgil has the assonance of genitive plural elsewhere at 324 'dirarum ab sede dearum', xi. 361 'caput horum et causa malorum', xii. 649 'magnorum haud umquam indignus auorum'.

formae . . . luporum cf.: iii. 591 'ignoti noua forma uiri', vi. 289 (of Geryon) 'forma tricorporis umbrae'. The periphrasis (not strictly applicable here, since presumably they did not see the animals) enhances the effect of mysterious terror. Similarly in 650 'corpore Turni' emphasizes the handsomeness of Turnus, in viii. 194 'Caci facies' the repulsiveness of Cacus.

19. **potentibus herbis** : again in xii. 402 : *potens* often has the implication of magical or supernatural virtue : cf. vi. 247 'Hecaten caeloque Ereboque potentem'; Ovid, *Her.* 5. 147 'herba potens ad opem', 12. 168 'Hecates sacra potentis'.

20. **induerat . . . in uultus** : Virgil has the same unusual construction of *induere* in *Geo.* i. 187 f. 'cum se nux plurima siluis / induet in florem'. (At *Geo.* iv. 142 f. he uses the normal ablative construction in a similar context, 'quot . . . pomis se fertilis arbos / induerat'.) It is not confined to poetry but

in prose it is always metaphorical and refers to involvement in something disagreeable or unwelcome: cf. Cic. *Diu*. ii. 41 'cur igitur uos induitis in eas captiones quas numquam explicetis?', 44 'cum autem (uenti) se in nubem induerint', *Verr*. ii. 2. 101 'uidete in quot se laqueos induerit'.

terga ferarum: for *tergum* (or *tergus*), 'hide', cf. v. 351 'tergum Gaetuli immane leonis', 403 'duro intendere bracchia tergo' (of a boxing-glove), vi. 243 'nigrantis terga iuuencos', i. 634 f. 'horrentia centum / terga suum (i.e. sues horrenti tergo)'. The meaning is most neatly illustrated in Pliny, *N.H.* viii. 30 'durissimum dorso tergus'.

21. quae . . . talia, 'these uncanny things, so dreadful': cf. x. 298 f. 'quae talia postquam / effatus Tarchon': so in prose Cic. *Phil*. ii. 71 'quibus rebus tantis talibus gestis', *Att*. i. 18. 8 'ex eis quae scripsimus tanta'.

monstra paterentur: cf. iii. 583 f. 'immania monstra / perferimus' (of the noises of Etna). *monstrum* (earlier *monestrum, from *moneo*) is originally a religious term used of a supernatural phenomenon which conveys a portent or an omen: so below 81 'sollicitus monstris', 376 'ingentibus excita monstris', ii. 171 'nec dubiis ea signa dedit Tritonia monstris'. The flame on Iulus' head (ii. 680), the branch that drips blood (iii. 26), the transformation of the ships into nymphs (ix. 120) are all *mirabile monstrum*. Hence it comes to be applied to any uncanny creature or thing, usually with the sinister implication of a threat of evil (but not always: in Cat. 64. 15 the ship Argo is a *monstrum*): Virgil uses it of the Trojan horse (ii. 245), of the Harpies (iii. 214), of Polyphemus (iii. 658), of Fama (iv. 181), of the sea (v. 849), of the Fury Allecto (vii. 328), of Cacus (viii. 198), of Io's gadfly (*Geo*. iii. 152), and, with playful mock-solemnity, of the pests of the stockyard (*Geo*. i. 185); Horace of Cleopatra (*Od*. i. 37. 21), Cicero of Catiline (*Cat*. ii. 1). So in the exaggeration of colloquial language, *monstrum mulieris* (Plaut. *Poen*. 273), *monstrum hominis* (Ter. *Eun*. 696). (The popular diminutive *mostellum*, a ghost, is preserved in the title of Plautus' *Mostellaria*.)

pii: the point is the same as in iii. 265 f. 'di, talem auertite casum / et placidi seruate pios': cf. i. 603 ff., ii. 689 ff. The Trojans' *pietas* deserves divine protection in return.

22. litora dira: *dirus* is another word of religious language, 'illboding', 'sinister': cf. i. 293 f. 'dirae . . . Belli portae', viii. 349 f. 'religio . . . dira loci'. See on 324.

24. uada feruida: the 'boiling shallows' of a rocky coast: cf. i. 536 'uada caeca', v. 221 'breuibus uadis', x. 678 'saeuis uadis . . . syrtis'. *uadum* properly refers to shallows (it is a cognate of *uado* and first applied to fordable water: cf. the proverbial *in uado esse*) but elsewhere Virgil follows the poetic freedom which had made it a synonym of *undae* and *aequora* (cf. Cat. 64. 58 'pellit uada remis'): so, e.g., v. 158 'longa sulcant uada salsa carina', 615 f. 'tot uada fessis / . . . superesse', viii. 91 'labitur uncta uadis abies'.

25 f. To describe the dawn Virgil follows a Homeric cliché only at iv. 584 f., repeated with expansion at ix. 459 ff. Elsewhere his descriptions are varied and vivid: cf. ii. 801 f., iii. 521, iv. 6 f., v. 42 f., 104 f., xii. 113 ff.

25. iamque . . . cum: this vivid formula of transition, common in Virgil, belongs to the epic style; it is not found in earlier epic, but the two instances in Horace (*Sat.* i. 5. 20, ii. 6. 100 f.) are parody of the epic manner. At i. 223 Virgil has the variation *et iam . . . cum. iamque* without a following *cum*-clause is also a common transition (e.g. 160 below).

rubescebat: Virgil uses the verb four times but it is not found earlier: other 'inceptive' verbs which appear first in Virgil are *crebresco, madesco, nigresco, inardesco.*

26. roseis . . . lutea: Ovid has the same combination (to which Bentley incautiously objected here), *F.* iv. 714 'Memnonis in roseis lutea mater equis'. *luteus* is a reddish, orange yellow, the colour of the bride's *flammeum* (Pliny, *N.H.* xxi. 46; Lucan ii. 361): Gellius (ii. 26. 8) places it among the reds and Nemesianus (*Cyn.* 319) writes 'rubescere luto'. For *in bigis*, 'behind a pair', cf. xii. 164 'bigis . . . in albis'.

27. posuere, 'fell': so x. 103 'tum Zephyri posuere'; Ovid, *Her.* 7. 49 'iam uenti ponent'. This intransitive use (and that of *turbare* in vi. 800 'turbant trepida ostia Nili'; Varro, *R.R.* iii 17.7 'cum mare turbaret') is perhaps technical. But such a use is not uncommon with other verbs—e.g. *uertere, mouere, mutare, uariare, minuere, praecipitare, rugare*: Virgil has intransitive uses of *flectere* (ix. 372) and *iungere* (x. 240). For nautical terms in Virgil cf. (*terram*) *abscondere* (iii. 291: so Servius), *stare*, 'ride' (iii. 403, vi. 901), *superare*, 'make' (i. 244, viii. 95: see note there).

omnisque repente resedit: the rhythm, with trochaic caesura in both fourth and fifth foot, giving the line a 'false ending' in the middle of the fifth foot, is unusual. Virgil has about a hundred examples (many of them with *-que* and some with *-que . . . -que*): see E. Norden, *Aeneis VI*, pp. 176, 428; Austin on ii. 380. In a few lines the rhythm may be felt to be expressive (here it has been suggested that its 'undulating movement' is meant to contrast with the expression of effort in the highly spondaic line following), but in most cases (e.g. in 43 below) no particular sound-effect is discernible. (Twice the words consist of proper names: xi. 612, xii. 661.) The pattern of this line is repeated twice elsewhere, at ii. 380 'trepidusque repente refugit' and 465 'ea lapsa repente ruinam', and had precedent in Enn. *Ann.* 47 V. 'germana, repente recessit'.

28. lento marmore, 'the listless sea'. The basic meaning of *lentus* seems to be that of yielding under pressure: thence it develops along two opposite lines according as emphasis is laid (*a*) on the unwillingness to yield ('stiff', 'tough', 'sticky', 'slow', 'lazy') or (*b*) on the yielding ('pliant', 'flexible', 'supple'). For (*a*) cf. *Geo.* iv. 170 (*massis*), *Aen.* v. 683 (*uapor*), vii. 634 (*argento*), xi. 650 (*hastilia*), xii. 781 (*stirpe*), of persons xii. 237 (*lenti consedimus*); for (*b*) *Geo.* iv. 558 (*ramis*), *Aen.* vi. 137 (*uimine*), vii. 731 (*flagello*), xi. 829 (*colla*).

The use of *marmor* as a poetic word for the sea (cf. *Geo.* i. 254 'infidum remis impellere marmor'), which goes back to Ennius (*Ann.* 384 V. 'marmore flauo') was based on Homer's ἅλς μαρμαρέη, 'the sparkling sea': the noun μάρμαρος from which *marmor* was derived (with an analogical change of termination) is not itself found so used.

tonsa is also a word of the Ennian vocabulary (*Ann.* 230 V. 'pectora pellite tonsis', 231 'referunt ad pectora tonsas'): it has been connected with the root of *tendo*, but ancient etymology (Fest. 488 L. 'tonsa quod quasi tondeatur ferro') may have stumbled on the truth and it may well be the participle of *tondeo*, 'lopped' (*tondere* in this sense is a technical term of arboriculture), *arbor* or *abies* being understood. (See Walde–Hofmann s.v.; E. Schwyzer in *Zeit. f. vergl. Sprachforschung* lxiii [1936], 53 f.) Virgil uses *tonsa* for *remus* only here and at x. 299 'consurgere tonsis': Norden (on vi. 88) suggests that in both places he was concerned to avoid repeating the preceding syllable -*re*, but (despite Servius' stricture on ii. 27 'Dorica castra') he allows himself such repetition (even without a difference in quantity) many times and actually has 'incumbere remis' at viii. 108.

29. atque: for *atque* introducing a dramatic turn in the action or presenting a sudden new picture, cf. i. 227, iv. 261, 663, vi. 162, viii. 655, x. 219.

ingentem . . . lucum: again at viii. 342, 597 (cf. vii. 676 f. 'ingens / silua'). *ingens* is a word of the solemn epic style, already used by Ennius, and a favourite epithet of Virgil's; he uses it 168 times in the *Aeneid*, 31 times in the *Georgics* (never in the *Eclogues*). Whatever its origin (and that has been much disputed: Schwyzer connected it with *gens*, 'with-

out origin', Brugmann with γίγας, Lindsay with the root of
gn-osco, 'unknown'), it is much more than an intensification
of *magnus*: it is a word of feeling (see Conway on i. 114, 453),
usually conveying an overtone of mystery or awe like English
'vast'. In prose it is rare except in the coloured style of the
historians Sallust, Livy, and Tacitus; in the speech of
comedy it is a term of colloquial exaggeration (like our
'tremendous' or 'enormous'). Sometimes its emotional sug-
gestions are enhanced by its position (170 'tectum augustum,
ingens', vi. 552 'porta aduersa ingens', iv. 181 'monstrum
horrendum, ingens', xii. 897 'saxum antiquum ingens') or by
emphatic repetition (xii. 896 f.: cf. xii. 640). On the other
hand, as Henry pointed out in his light-hearted (and not
very perceptive) note on *ingens* 'the maid of all work' (v.
118), it sometimes looks like a *tibicen* or stopgap; a word can
hardly retain its expressivity when it is used five times—
three times of Cerberus, once of Aeneas himself, and once of
the *uagitus* of the shades—in 27 lines (vi. 400–26).

lucum: Servius' attempt (on i. 310) to distinguish between
the three words for 'wood'—'lucus est arborum multitudo
cum religione, nemus uero composita multitudo arborum,
silua diffusa et inculta'—is too precise. *lucus* (originally a
clearing in a wood: compare the technical terms *collucare*,
sublucare, *interlucare*) and *nemus* both have religious associa-
tions, but the poets (and especially Virgil who has *lucus*
fifty times) use them freely as 'affective' terms of romantic
colouring: Festus (159 L.) comes near that when he says
'nemora significant siluas amoenas'.

The coast at the mouth of the Tiber was probably still
wooded in Virgil's day, but the picture of trees, river, and
singing birds is not realistic description but romantic scene-
painting in the Hellenistic tradition. (See on 82 f.)

30. hunc inter: the use of *inter* with a singular, 'in the midst of',
is rare in reference to space but not uncommon in reference
to time: cf. *inter cenam, inter noctem, inter uiam.*

Tiberinus : Virgil's name for the Tiber is *Thybris*, the
Hellenized form of an Etruscan name. His preference is
clear: he uses *Thybris* eighteen times in the *Aeneid*, *Tiberis*
only once (vii. 715: see note there), and when he reproduces
Ennius' line (*Ann.* 54 V.) 'teque, pater Tiberine, tuo cum
flumine sancto' (an adaptation of the prayer-formula quoted
by Servius, 'Adesto, Tiberine, cum tuis undis'), it becomes
(viii. 72) 'tuque, o Thybri tuo genitor cum flumine sancto'.
Here and in three other places in the *Aeneid* (vi. 873, vii.
797, viii. 31) the adjective *Tiberinus* used substantively of
the river-god, the *pater Tiberinus* of Ennius, provides an

alternative. But the eponymous hero who had his corpus of
varying legends and is Tiberinus in Livy (i. 3. 8) is also
Thybris in Virgil (viii. 330). It may well be that *Thybris* was
a Virgilian innovation in poetry: as the name of the river it is
not found before the *Aeneid* (unless the uncertain *Catalepton*
13 is to be dated then)— and in the solemn closing passage of
Georgic i Virgil had himself used the ordinary name: '(Vesta)
quae Tuscum Tiberim et Romana Palatia seruas'—but that
fact is the less conclusive since in what remains of earlier
poets *Tiberis* appears only twice and *Tiberinus* only once.
Ovid follows Virgil's example in the *Metamorphoses* (and
the later epic poets do the same) but uses both *Thybris* and
Tiberis in the *Fasti*: Horace and Propertius have only
Tiberis and *Tiberinus*. On the form and origins of the name
see K. Meister, *Lat.-griech. Eigennamen*, i. 53 ff.; P. Kretsch-
mer, *Glotta* i (1909), 295; F. Bömer, *Gymn.* lxiv (1957), 134 ff.;
on Virgil's usage A. Momigliano, *Terzo contributo alla storia
degli studi classici* (Rome, 1966), ii. 609 ff.

   fluuio ... amoeno (repeated at viii. 31) is a descriptive
ablative; in the next line both *uerticibus rapidis* and *multa
arena* are probably attached to *flauus*, though *uerticibus
rapidis* and *multa flauus arena* may be taken as parallel de-
scriptive phrases modifying *prorumpit*.

   amoeno: in poetry *amoenus* is always a word of physical
description, used of what gives pleasure to the eye: so
v. 734 f. 'amoena piorum / concilia Elysiumque', vi. 638
'amoena uirecta' (from Ennius) 'amoena salicta', *Ann.* 39
V.): Cicero is fond of using *amoenitas* of natural scenery.

31 f. flauus ... prorumpit: Ovid borrows the phrase, *Met.*
xiv. 448 'in mare cum flaua prorumpit Thybris harena'.
flauus is a regular description of the Tiber (Hor. *Od.* i. 2. 13,
i. 8. 8, ii. 3. 18; Ovid, *Tr.* v. 1. 31): when Father Tiber calls
himself *caeruleus* at viii. 64, he is using the standard epithet
of a river-god. The lower Tiber is still a yellow river, carrying
down large quantities of eroded rock which in the centuries
have so silted up its estuary that Ostia, in Virgil's time close
to the sea, is now some three miles upstream.

32 f. uariae ... uolucres: cf. *Geo.* i. 383 'uariae pelagi uolucres'.
Virgil (like other Latin poets) is fond of using *uarius* of bright,
gay, contrasting colours (so with *colores*, *Ecl.* 4. 42, *Geo.* i.
452, *Aen.* iv. 701, v. 89; *flores*, *Ecl.* 9. 40 f.; *serta*, *Aen.* iv.
202; *arma*, *Aen.* viii. 685, xii. 123), but that picturesque
effect is probably not intended here: for the phrase is
Lucretian (i. 589, ii. 344) and in Lucretius it means only 'in
their several kinds' (similarly he has *uariae pecudes*, *uariae
gentes*).

circumque supraque : for the double *-que* see on 186. Virgil has the quantity *sŭpra* only here, *sūpra* in 381, 784, and in fifteen other places.

33. **alueo** : a dissyllable (as in 303) by synizesis, the coalescence of two adjacent vowels, a device (first found in Catullus) which enables the use of some forms whose prosody would otherwise prevent it: so (*eo*) viii. 292 *Eurystheo*, ix. 716 *Typhoeo*, xii. 847 *uno eodemque*; (*ea*) vii. 190, i. 698 *aurea*; (*ei*) vii. 609, xii. 541 *aerei*, vi. 280 *ferrei*, x. 496 *baltei*, i. 726, v. 352, viii. 553 *aureis*, vii. 249 *Ilionei*, viii. 383, x. 764 *Nerei*. See also on 142, and, for a similar device, on 175.

34. **mulcebant** : properly of a caressing touch, 'stroke'. Lucretius uses the phrase of birds, but not with reference to sound (iv. 136 'aera mulcentis motu': cf. Cic. *Arat.* 88 '(aquila) igniferum mulcens tremebundis aethera pinnis'): Ovid imitates Virgil's phrase, *F.* i. 155 'tepidum uolucres concentibus aera mulcent'.

35 f. **flectere . . . imperat:** the infinitive with *impero*, which occurs only here in Virgil (in three other places *impero* is followed by an accusative and passive infinitive clause, as it regularly is in prose), is favoured by the poets. In general the advantages of the infinitive in directness and manipulability over a subordinate clause or a gerundial construction lead to a great extension of its prolative use with verbs both in comedy and in later poetry: for Virgilian examples see v. 485 f. 'certare inuitat', vii. 112 f. 'uertere adegit', 214 'subegit succedere', ix. 114 'trepidate defendere', x. 118 f. 'instant sternere', 354 'expellere tendunt'. See also on 591.

36. **laetus** : no doubt because he had come to the promised land of which Creusa had told him (ii. 781 f.) and which he had had before him through all his wanderings (iii. 500), though he did not know exactly where it was (v. 83 'Ausonium, quicumque est, quaerere Thybrim'). But in that case there is some inconsistency: he does not know until line 151 that the river he has reached is the Tiber.

37-45. The quiet close of Book VI marked a turning-point in the fortunes of Aeneas, with the confirmation of his destiny: appropriately a new book opened with the last stage of his journey and the romantic description of the voyage from Cumae to the landing in Latium. With that landing comes another turning-point, this time for the poet: he has come to his main theme, the story of the founding of the new Troy in Italy, to which the story of the wanderings has been a prelude, and he announces that new beginning and assumes his greater commitment, *maius opus*, in another invocation and a second prologue.

At the beginning of the poem Virgil, like Homer, had addressed his Muse without a name: for the 'Catalogue' in this book he calls on all the Muses (641 ff.), for the battle-scenes at ix. 525 on Calliope, *maxima Musarum* (Ovid, *Met.* v. 662), with her sisters. The choice of Erato to be his inspiration here is surprising: for the Muses are *diuersae nouem sortitae iura puellae* (Prop. iii. 3. 33) and Erato, *nomen amoris* (Ovid, *F.* iv. 195 f.), is always associated with the poetry of love. Apollonius had appropriately invoked Erato in the opening lines of his third book, the love-story of Jason and Medea, and Virgil might well have followed his example in Book IV when he told the story of Aeneas and Dido; there, as in Apollonius, by divine contriving the wandering hero and his hostess fall in love and Dido dominates the one story as Medea the other. Here, as in Apollonius, the hero has reached his journey's end and enters on a new stage, the second half of his adventure: but the resemblance goes no further. Virgil's present theme is no Hellenistic love-story; he makes more of the motive of Turnus and Lavinia than earlier tradition, as his rehandling of the legend enables him to do (see on 56), but the love-interest remains in the background. The beautiful Lavinia is *causa mali tanti*, as the Sibyl predicted (vi. 93: the words are picked up at xi. 480), and her importance has been foreshadowed (anonymously) in Creusa's prophecy (ii. 783) and (by name) in that of Anchises (vi. 764); but she is a silent, shadowy figure, like a well-bred Roman daughter of later days. Aeneas never sees her and her father's offer of a marriage of convenience is made to him through a messenger. The only indication of her own feelings comes in the last book (xii. 64 ff.), when Amata's words to Turnus bring a blush to her cheek and in his short reply the enamoured Turnus refers to her for the first time. Compared with Medea's story, this is meagre material for the patronage of Erato which Apollonius has put into Virgil's mind.[1]

37 ff. nunc age . . . expediam: the same formula appears at vi. 756 ff. (the opening of Anchises' prophecy), *Geo.* iv. 149 f. (the opening of a new chapter in the story of the bees).

The punctuation of the Oxford Text attaches *rerum* to *status*: *status rerum* is a common phrase in prose (e.g. Livy viii. 13. 2 'iam Latio is status erat rerum'; Tac. *Hist.* i. 11 'hic fuit rerum Romanarum status', iv. 11, *Ann.* i. 2), but the

---

[1] It was left to the medieval French poet of the *Eneas*, with indirect assistance from Ovid, to make Lavinia not merely an articulate lover but an analyst of love (see H. C. L. Laurie in *M.L.R.* lxiv [1969], 283 ff.).

echo of Lucr. v. 1276 'sic uoluenda aetas commutat tempora rerum' (cf. Ovid, *Tr.* i. 1. 37 f. 'iudicis officium est ut res ita tempora rerum / quaerere') and the structure and rhythm of the sentence both point to taking *rerum* with *tempora*.

38. **quis . . . status**: no distinction can be drawn between *quis* and *qui* as respectively the substantival and the adjectival form of the interrogative pronoun. Though the matter is one in which manuscripts are obviously liable to error, the weight of evidence is enough to show that in both uses *quis* is much the commoner form and to suggest that *qui* was a development from *quis* due to the nature of the following sound. *quis deus* is almost invariable (and so, in another common cliché, is *quis furor*) : on the other hand (*scire*) *qui sim* (*sis, sit*) is universally preferred to *quis sim*. In Virgil the proportion of *quis* to *qui* in the substantival and in the adjectival use is much the same: in each the examples of *quis* greatly outnumber those of *qui* and of the undisputed examples of *qui* most are followed by *s*-. The variation which P presents at v. 648 f., 'qui spiritus illi, / quis uultus', is the less surprising and at ix. 723 P's *quis* would not be exceptional. With the indefinite pronoun the preference is even more marked: Virgil (like Ovid and Juvenal) uses only *quis*. See E. Löfstedt, *Synt.* ii. 79 ff.

39. **Ausoniis . . . oris**: Αὔσονες was the Greek form of the name given to themselves by an Oscan-speaking people of central Italy: in Latin it appears, with normal rhotacism and a Latin suffix, as Aurunci. In historical times their home was the country between the Liris and the Volturnus in northern Campania, with Suessa as its capital: from there they come to join the forces of Turnus in this book (206, 727). They were neighbours there of the Greek settlements of Magna Graecia and as such they were vaguely known to Hecataeus and Hellanicus in the fifth century. In Hellenistic poetry Αὐσονία was taken up as a 'learned' or romantic name for Italy—so Apollonius (iv. 660) has Αὐσονίης ἀκτὰς Τυρσηνίδας—and from there Virgil and his successors adopted it.

40. **primae exordia pugnae**: the regular Latin idiom by which a word is reinforced by another part of speech which does not add to its meaning but emphasizes it (cf. Cat. 63. 19 'mora tarda', 64. 236 'laeta gaudia'; Ovid, *Met.* vii. 184 'muta silentia'; Hor. *Ep.* ii. 1. 12 'supremo fine') is particularly common in phrases conveying the notion of beginning: so *Aen.* iv. 284 'quae prima exordia sumat?', vii. 371 'si prima domus repetatur origo'; Enn. *Sc.* 248 f. V. 'neue inde nauis inchoandi exordium / coepisset'; Lucr. i. 383 'initium primum capiat . . . mouendi'; Tac. *Ann.* xiii. 10 'ut principium

anni inciperet mense Decembri'. Sometimes in prose the
expression is not only doubled but trebled: cf. Livy iii. 54. 9
'prima initia incohastis libertatis uestrae', xxxvii. 19. 5
'instauremus nouum de integro bellum'. For other examples
see E. Löfstedt, *Synt.* ii. 179 f.; Gudeman on Tac. *Dial.* 11. 8.

41. uatem: the *uates* is one whose utterance is inspired and the
word was the name for the poet, the inspired spokesman of
the Muses, until the new Hellenism displaced it by the
adoption of *poeta*, 'maker', from Greek. Thereafter it was con-
fined to the sense of 'prophet' (sometimes with a derogatory
implication: Enn. *Sc.* 319 V.; Lucr. i. 102, 109; Cic. *N.D.*
i. 55), and in that sense Virgil uses it many times. But Virgil
and Horace restore it to its old use as the poet's solemn title of
honour: so it is used twice in the *Eclogues* (9. 33 f. 'sunt et mihi
carmina, me quoque dicunt / uatem pastores', 7. 28) and
again here: for Horace's use of it cf. *Epod.* 17. 44, *Od.* i. 1. 35,
iv. 3. 15, iv. 6. 44, *A.P.* 400. On the origin of the word and its
history see M. Runes in *Festschrift Kretschmer* (Vienna, 1926),
202 ff.; H. Dahlmann in *Philol.* xcvii (1948), 337 ff.: on its
use by the Augustans, see J. K. Newman, *Augustus and the
New Poetry* (Brussels, 1967), ch. 4, who, however, makes too
much of its implications concerning the poet's function in
his society.

tu . . . tu: the repetition belongs to the prayer-style: cf. 49.

mone, 'remind'. The Muse remembers (hence she is a
daughter of Mnemosyne) and reminds her poet: cf. 645
'meministis enim, diuae, et memorare potestis'. The con-
nection is etymologically sound: μοῦσα (from earlier *μόνσα)
is cognate with *moneo* (and with *mens* and *mind*).

horrida bella: the words are repeated in the Sibyl's pro-
phecy in vi. 86 f. 'bella, horrida bella, / . . . cerno'; the
phrase is perhaps Ennian.

42. actos . . . reges, 'princes driven by courage to meet death':
for the plural *animi* in a variety of contexts cf. i. 722, ii. 386,
iv. 414, viii. 228, ix. 144, 249, x. 250, xi. 366, 438.

43. Tyrrhenam manum: the Etruscans whose assistance
Evander secures for Aeneas: see esp. viii. 478 ff.

44. maior . . . ordo, 'a grander succession of events opens be-
fore me'. The phrase is reminiscent of *Ecl.* 4. 5 'magnus ab
integro saeclorum nascitur ordo'.

45–106. *The situation in Latium. King Latinus' daughter has
been sought in marriage by the Rutulian chief Turnus, but
warning portents are confirmed by an oracle which declares that
she is destined to have a foreign husband and to have descendants
who will rule the world.*

45. arua Latinus et urbes: the rare rhythm occurs only twice elsewhere in the *Aeneid* (vi. 167 'insignis obibat et hasta', viii. 229 'huc ora ferebat et illuc') and once in the *Georgics* (iii. 86 'iactata recumbit in armo').

46. longa in pace: cf. viii. 325 '(Saturnus) placida populos in pace regebat'. The words seem to be inconsistent with what is said later: for lines 423–6 imply that Turnus had already assisted Latinus in a war with the Etruscans and in viii. 55 Evander's Arcadians 'bellum adsidue ducunt cum gente Latina'.

47 ff. Virgil builds a romantic past out of Italian legend. Latinus, an eponymous abstraction—like Italus and Sabinus, who are vaguely reckoned among his ancestors in line 178—from the name of his country and its people, belongs to the traditional story. His royal lineage here is created (by Virgil himself, it seems: in Hesiod's *Theogony* (1011 ff.) he is the son of Odysseus by Circe) out of three figures from primitive Italian belief whose history is hard to disentangle. Saturnus, whatever his provenance and his earliest character (the connection of his name with *sero* is discredited in favour of an Etruscan origin: see G. Wissowa, *Rel. u. Kult.* 204 ff.; K. Latte, *Röm. Relig.* 137, 254 f.) has assumed, when he is first known to us, the character of an agricultural deity (so he is represented as carrying a *falx*, *Geo.* ii. 406). Very early he had come to be identified with the Greek Cronos: a link was provided by the story that when he was expelled from Olympus by his son Zeus, Cronos settled in Italy and there presided over Italy's Golden Age (cf. viii. 319 ff.). (Hence on the one hand Jupiter, Juno, and Neptune, as the accepted counterparts of Zeus, Hera, and Poseidon, and on the other Italy itself in poetry share the epithet *Saturnius*.) Picus, originally an animal-deity, the woodpecker of folklore (see Frazer on Ovid, *F.* iii. 54), sometimes reduced to the status of satellite or sacred bird of Mars (Ovid, *F.* iii. 54; Plut. *Q.R.* 21; Pliny, *N.H.* x. 40), is also a rustic *numen* (Ovid, *F.* iii. 291 f.): in 187–91 he is represented in the costume and with the appurtenances of an augur-king and has attached to him the hysteron-proteron legend of a transformation into bird shape by Circe's magic.

Faunus is a perplexing figure whose identity has suffered by conflation with Pan: he too is a rural *numen* of the woods and the flocks (Hor. *Od.* iii. 18) who as the source of supernatural voices has also a prophetic function out of which, formalized and Hellenized, Virgil has made the incubation-oracle of lines 81 ff. (see note there). The multiplicity of Fauni (*Ecl.* 6. 27, *Geo.* i. 10, *Aen.* viii. 314) which appears as

early as Ennius may be merely an assimilation to the Πᾶνες
of Greek poetry: but it may go back to an original conception
of undifferentiated spirits of the woods and the countryside
from which the figure of a single Faunus came to emerge.
(See K. Latte, *Röm. Relig.* 83 f.)

47. Laurente Marica: the nymph Marica is elsewhere associated
with the region of the river Liris in the extreme south of
Latium (Hor. *Od.* iii. 17. 7 f. 'innantem Maricae / litoribus . . .
Lirim'; Mart. x. 30. 9) and she had a cult and a *lucus* at
Minturnae at its mouth (Livy xxvii. 37. 2; Plut. *Marius* 39. 4).
Laurens seems to be loosely used here to mean 'Latin' with-
out special reference to the *ager Laurens*: with less im-
propriety the adjective is applied to Turnus from Ardea in
650, to the Tiber in v. 797, and to the nymphs of the Tiber
valley in viii. 71. See also on 63.

48. accipimus, like *fertur* (735, v. 588), *ferunt fama* (765), *fama
est* (205, iii. 578, vi. 14), *dicitur* (409), *ut perhibent* (iv. 179,
viii. 135), *si uera est fama* (iii. 551), is a cliché inherited from
the Alexandrians (witness the repeated use of it in Catullus
64 and 68), a formula of the scholarly poet who is concerned
to claim the authority of tradition.

49. te, Saturne: the device of apostrophe, already used by
Homer (but rarely: e.g. *Il.* iv. 127 f.), became a mannerism
of Hellenistic poetry, designed to give at once dramatic
variety and a touch of subjective intimacy to a narrative:
Catullus had already exploited it in Latin. In Virgil it is used
sparingly and its poetic value is often unmistakable: it evokes
the reader's sympathy in a pathetic situation (as in ii.
429 ff., vi. 30 f., vii. 759 f.), gives emotional colour to enliven
a battle-scene (so it is common in Book X: e.g. 324 ff.,
390 ff., 402 f., 411, 514), diversifies a catalogue (as here or
in vii. 684 f.). In his successors, and especially in Ovid, who
is lavish with it, and Lucan, it often degenerates into a piece
of mechanical technique commended by metrical convenience.
See E. Norden, *Aeneis VI*, pp. 122, 126; J. Endt in *Wien.
Stud.* xxvii (1905), 106 ff.

  refert: 'claims' Saturn as his father: cf. Ovid, *Met.* xiii.
141 f. 'rettulit Aiax / esse Iouis pronepos'. Elsewhere in
similar contexts in Virgil the meaning is 'reproduce', 'recall':
iv. 328 f. 'paruulus . . . Aeneas qui te tamen ore referret',
xii. 348 'nomine auum referens, animo manibusque paren-
tem'.

  auctor: founder, originator, of the line: cf. iv. 365 'generis
. . . auctor'. For a study of the word see H. Nettleship, *Con-
trib. to Lat. Lex.* 360 ff.

50. filius . . . prolesque uirilis: the expansion emphasizes the situation which makes Lavinia a political bride. For the characteristic Virgilian idiom cf. i. 258 f. 'urbem et promissa Lauini / moenia', vi. 282 'ramos annosaque bracchia', xi. 22 'socios inhumataque corpora'.

51. nulla . . . erepta, 'was no more but had been taken from him': Latin regularly uses a co-ordinating conjunction to connect clauses which are negative and positive expressions of the same fact, whereas English idiom prefers to stress the difference of emphasis with an adversative: cf., e.g., Cic. *de Or.* ii. 147 'nihil te effugiet atque omne quod erit in re occurret'. For *nullus esse*, 'not to exist', cf., e.g., Cic. *Tusc.* i. 87 'de mortuis loquor qui nulli sunt', *Acad.* ii. 47 'conantur ostendere multa posse uideri esse quae omnino nulla sint', and the common use of *nullus sum* in comedy.

    oriens: the nearest parallels to this use seem to be Hor. *Ep.* ii. 1. 130 f. 'orientia tempora . . . / instruit exemplis'; Vell. ii. 99. 2 'orientium iuuenum . . . initiis'.

52. seruabat: here not merely 'kept to' the house, as in vi. 402 'casta licet patrui seruet Proserpina limen' or the traditional encomium of the Roman matron, *domum seruauit (Carm. Epigr.* 52 B.), but with the implication of maintaining the position of the establishment (*tantas sedes*) as heiress.

53. matura uiro: so Hor. *Od.* i. 23. 12 'tempestiva uiro'.

54. multi illam: the opening is reminiscent of Cat. 62. 42 'multi illum pueri, multae optauere puellae'.

55. ante alios pulcherrimus omnis: again in iv. 141 of Aeneas himself; a comparative is similarly strengthened i. 347 'ante alios immanior omnis'. Livy adopts the poetic pleonasm: e.g. i. 15. 8 'ante alios acceptissimus'.

56. Turnus: the name is emphatically placed at his first appearance. Turnus had become associated with the Aeneas legend in its Roman form at an early state in the tradition, but the part assigned to him varies in the versions of which we have evidence. The Lavinia motive first appears in the later version represented (with some discrepancies) by Livy (i. 2) and Dionysius (i. 59–60, 64), where the slighted Turnus is the common enemy of Latins and Trojans after the two peoples have been united and their union sealed by a political marriage. Virgil goes back to the earlier version represented by Cato (Servius on i. 267, iv. 620), in which Turnus joins the Latins against the incomers, combining it with the Lavinia story and giving Turnus the leadership of Italian resistance, and so is enabled both to develop the character of Turnus and to present a picture of a united Italy. See J. Perret, *Les Origines de la légende troyenne de Rome* (Paris, 1942), 524 ff.

    auis . . . potens: i.e. with prestige and prosperity secured

by his lineage: *potens* often has reference to material wealth:
cf. Cat. 61. 149 f. 'domus . . . potens / et beata uiri'.

56 f. quem . . . adiungi . . . properabat: for the rare use of a
noun-clause after *propero* cf. Sall. *Cat.* 7. 6 'se quisque hostem
ferire . . . properabat'. The use of a simple infinitive (as in
264 'iungi hospitio properat') is common.

57. amore: 'desire' (not 'love'), as in the common phrase 'si
tantus amor' (ii. 10, xi. 323; cf. vi. 133).

59 ff. laurus erat . . . huius: for this formula of description see
on 563 ff.

59. tecti medio: for the substantival use of the neuter adjective
cf. 563 'Italiae medio', iii. 354 'aulai medio', xi. 547 'fugae
medio': similarly 64 'huius summum', iii. 232 'ex diuerso
caeli'. So without a partitive genitive 566 'medio', viii. 675
'in medio', xii. 273 'ad medium'.

   Virgil, who is no archaeologist, no doubt has in mind the
open court or *peristylium* behind the living quarters which
was a usual feature of the large Roman town-house of his
own day: there is a similar picture of Priam's palace in ii.
512 f. 'aedibus in mediis nudoque sub aetheris axe / ingens
ara fuit iuxtaque ueterrima laurus' and the same plan is
implied for Dido's palace in iv. 494, where she builds her
pyre 'tecto interiore sub auras' (cf. 504 'penetrali in sede sub
auras').

60. sacra comam: i.e. its foliage is protected from the pruner's
knife. The limiting accusative attached to an adjective (or,
less commonly, to a verb) to define the respect in which it is
applied (the 'accusative of respect' of grammarians) is a
Greek construction which makes its first appearance in Latin
in Virgil's immediate predecessors: thereafter it becomes
common. Virgil uses it both with adjectives, as here (so
i. 320 'nuda genu', v. 285 'Cressa genus', *Geo.* iii. 58 'faciem
tauro propior': with a pronoun viii. 114 'qui genus?'), and
with verbs (*Geo.* iii. 84 'tremit artus', already in Lucretius):
on the use with passive participles and its relation to the
'middle' construction, see on 503.

   metu seruata: cf. ii. 714 f. 'antiqua cupressus / religione
patrum multos seruata per annos'.

61 ff. quam . . . ab ea: the continuation of a relative by a
demonstrative in another case is a normal Latin idiom: cf.,
e.g., Cic. *Or.* 9 'quam intuens in eaque defixus', *Brut.* 258
'qui nec extra urbem hanc uixerant neque eos aliqua bar-
baries domestica infuscauerat'. Alternatively, after a re-
lative in an oblique case the pronoun in a continuation
which demands a different case is regularly suppressed (cf.,
e.g., Cic. *Verr.* ii. 4. 9 'mancipium . . . quo et omnes utimur

et non praebetur a populo'): so ix. 593 f. 'cui Remulo cog-
nomen erat, Turnique minorem / germanam nuper thalamo
sociatus habebat', xii. 225 f. 'cui genus a proauis ingens . . .
et ipse acerrimus armis', 943 f. 'Pallantis pueri, uictum quem
uulnere Turnus / strauerat atque umeris inimicum insigne
gerebat'; and so, even after a relative in the nominative,
ix. 387 f. 'locos qui post . . . dicti / Albani (tum rex stabula
alta Latinus habebat)'. See Madvig on Cic. *Fin.* i. 42 and
v. 26; Munro on Lucr. i. 718–20; K.–S. ii. 2. 324 f.

63. ea: the oblique cases of *is* are little used in elevated poetry
after Lucretius: only the neuter accusative *ea* occurs with
any frequency and most forms are very rare. Virgil has *eā*
once in the *Aeneid*, *eo* twice, *eum* six times, and *eos* once.
See B. Axelson, *Unpoetische Wörter*, 70 ff.; M. Hélin in
R.É.L. v (1927), 60 ff.

Laurentisque . . . colonis, 'gave his settlers the name
Laurentes': *Laurentis* stands in apposition to *nomen* without
the normal 'attraction' to the dative (which Virgil has at
i. 267 f. 'cui nunc cognomen Iulo / additur', ix. 593 'cui
Remulo cognomen erat'): in prose the construction appears
first in Livy (i. 1. 11 'cui Ascanium parentes dixere nomen',
xxxv. 47. 5 'filiis duobus Philippum atque Alexandrum et
filiae Apamam nomina imposuerat'). At *Aen.* iii. 18 'Aenea-
dasque meo nomen de nomine fingo', where there is no dative,
the apposition is unremarkable: at *Geo.* i. 137 f. 'stellis
numeros et nomina fecit / Pleiadas, Hyadas' it is necessitated
by the presence of *numeros*.

This aetiological legend is contradicted by Virgil himself at
171, where Picus, Latinus' grandfather, already is called
Laurens.

The Laurentes had an existence in history as one of the
Latin peoples (Cato fr. 58 P.: they appear in inscriptions
from the site of Lavinium) and *ager Laurens* remained the
description of the coastal region of north Latium between
the Tiber and Antium. But there is no evidence for the
continued existence of Latinus' town (which Virgil does not
name)—if it ever existed at all: the town of the region was
Lavinium.

64. huius . . . summum: see on 59.

65. liquidum trans aethera, 'through the clear sky': cf. vi. 202
'liquidumque per aera lapsae', v. 525 'liquidis in nubibus',
vii. 699 'liquida inter nubila', x. 272 'liquida nocte'.

66. per mutua, 'reciprocally', is found only here, but compare
the common *per uices*, 'alternately', and such other modal
uses as *per ludum, per speciem, per scelus*; so ix. 31 'per
tacitum'. See also on 86.

68. continuo: the dramatic value of *continuo* makes it a favourite word of Virgil's (sixteen times in *Aen.*, twelve in *Geo.*): after him it is rare.

In Homer and in Apollonius speeches invariably begin and end with the beginning and ending of a line: Catullus follows the same practice. In Virgil, on the other hand, speeches beginning or ending within a line are frequent.

69 f. easdem . . . isdem: they come from the same quarter as the bees, i.e. from the sea, and to the same quarter, i.e. the *arx*.

70. dominarier: the context here is solemn, but the archaic form of the passive infinitive is commended by its metrical convenience and elsewhere Virgil uses it without any such colour: *Geo.* i. 454 *immiscerier*, *Aen.* iv. 493 *accingier*, viii. 493 *defendier*, ix. 231 *admittier*, xi. 242 *farier* (following *fari* in 240).

71. adolet: a ritual term of complex history in which two distinct notions appear to have coalesced. The verb *adolere* certainly meant 'set alight', 'burn' a sacrificial offering. That meaning is clear in such early texts as the *Acta Fratrum Arualium* (*C.I.L.* vi. 2107), 'arborum . . . adolendarum . . . causa', or Valerius Antias, fr. 61 P., 'eo . . . uituli uiginti et septem coniecti et ita omnia adulta sunt'; it persists in such instances as *Ecl.* 8. 65 'uerbenasque adole pinguis et mascula tura', *Aen.* iii. 547 'Iunoni . . . iussos adolemus honores'; Ovid, *Her.* 16. 335 'adolebunt cinnama flammae', in all of which the object of the verb is the burned offering: the word is even extended to non-sacrificial contexts, Ovid, *Met.* i. 492 'leues stipulae demptis adolentur aristis'; Gell. xvii. 10. 7 (Virgil's instruction to his executors) 'petiuit ̄ . . . ut *Aeneida* . . . adolerent'. The compound *adolefacere* is also used in the *Acta Fratrum Arualium* and the noun *adoletum*, a place for burning victims, is cited in the glossaries (*C.G.L.* ii. 564. 19). But this verb has been 'crossed' with the intransitive *adolesco* (a cognate of *alo* and of *indoles*, *suboles*, and *proles*) and has come to be treated as the corresponding transitive, with the sense of *augere* (for the ritual meaning of which see on 111), and analogy has produced *abolere* as its opposite. From this fusion is derived the use in which the object of the verb is the altar on which, or the deity to which, sacrifice is made: so here 'adolet altaria taedis' is the transitive equivalent of *Geo.* iv. 379 'adolescunt ignibus arae'; cf. Lucr. iv. 1236 f. 'sanguine . . . / conspergunt aras adolentque altaria donis'; *Aen.* i. 704 'flammis adolere penatis' (on which Servius notes 'proprie est augere': cf. Non. 58 M. 'significat uotis uel supplicationibus numen auctius facere'). This use is later taken up by Tacitus, *Ann.* xiv. 30 'cruore captiuo adolere aras', *Hist.* ii. 3 'precibus et igne puro altaria adolentur'. See A. Ernout, *Philologica* i (Paris, 1946), 53 ff.

castis . . . taedis: the epithet which properly applies to the performer of the ritual is transferred as in iv. 637 'pia uitta', v. 745 'farre pio'.

73–80. Alliteration is marked throughout these lines.

73. uisa: *uideri* regularly introduces a supernatural phenomenon: cf. *Geo.* i. 477 f. 'simulacra modis pallentia miris / uisa sub obscurum noctis', *Aen.* iii. 90 'tremere omnia uisa', iv. 460 f. 'hinc exaudiri uoces et uerba uocantis / uisa uiri, nox cum terras obscura teneret', vi. 257 'uisaeque canes ululare per umbram', viii. 525 'ruere omnia uisa repente', ix. 110 f. 'ingens / uisus ab Aurora caelum transcurrere nimbus'.

nefas: the exclamation of horror again in viii. 688, x. 673.

comprendere, 'catch the flame in her hair': cf. Caes. *B.G.* v. 43. 2 'hae (casae stramentis tectae) celeriter ignem comprehenderunt', *B.C.* iii. 101. 4 'flamma ab utroque cornu comprensa': at *Geo.* ii. 303 ff. Virgil makes *ignis* the subject of the verb, 'ignis / qui furtim . . . / robora comprendit'.

74. ornatum: her dressed hair: *crines* (or *capillos*) *ornare* is regularly used of elaborate coiffure. For the accusatives *ornatum, comas, coronam,* see on 60 and 503.

crepitante cremari: the alliterative phrase is Lucretian, vi. 155 'flamma crepitante crematur'.

75. regalisque . . . coronam: -*que* must connect the two *accensa*-phrases without a balancing -*que* in the second, as in x. 313 f. 'perque aerea suta, / per tunicam', xi. 171 'Tyrrhenique duces, Tyrrhenum exercitus', 641 'ingentemque animis, ingentem corpore et armis'. For a similar usage with *et* see on 327. (The -*que* cannot be taken as connecting *cremari* and *inuolui*, since *tum* (76) in accordance with Virgilian practice must introduce a new clause: cf., e.g., *Geo.* ii. 296, *Aen.* xi. 724.)

76. lumine fuluo: like other colour-words, *fuluus* has a range of use which makes it difficult to define, but it seems to mean a bright reddish yellow. In the poets it is a cliché for gold (e.g. 279, x. 134, xi. 776) and for sand (e.g. xii. 276): Virgil uses it of the jasper (iv. 261), of fair hair (x. 562, xi. 642) and of a cloud (presumably radiant) surrounding a divinity (xii. 792); Tibullus of the stars (ii. 1. 88); Ovid of the pollen of a lily (*Met.* x. 191); Manilius of the dawn (ii. 942). It is also a standard epithet for the lion (first in Lucr. v. 901: four times in Virgil) and the eagle (first in Cic. *Leg.* i. 2 (verse): twice in Virgil): Virgil has it of the wolf (688, i. 275), and in

Pliny's prose it is applied to bulls (xxii. 9), to beeswax (xxi. 83) and to wine (xiv. 80). A. Burger in *R.É.L.* viii (1930), 227 ff. connects the word with *fulgeo*: but see M. Leumann in *Glotta* xxi (1933), 195.

77. Volcanum: for the metonymy see on 113.

78. id uero: '*that*, following on the earlier portent': for *uero* thus marking a climax cf. *hic uero* (*Geo.* iv. 554, *Aen.* ii. 438, 699, viii. 219), *tum uero* (ii. 228, iv. 450, v. 659, 720), *at uero* (*Geo.* iii. 322, *Aen.* iv. 279, x. 762, 821, xii. 216).

　　ferri : 'historic' infinitive, 'was noised abroad', 'put about': see on 15.

79. canebant: of oracular utterance as in 271 (again with subject unexpressed), ii. 176, iii. 373, 559, vi. 99, viii. 49, 340, 499, x. 417, xii. 28.

80. ipsam: emphatically placed in enjambment with a following pause to point the contrast: a subject for *portendere* is to be understood out of *id ferri*.

81 ff. A dream which decided Latinus' attitude to the Trojans was part of the original story: in Dionysius' version (i. 57. 4) on the night before he was to attack Aeneas' party an ἐπιχώριος δαίμων appeared in him and bade him welcome the strangers: ἥκειν γὰρ αὐτοὺς μέγα ὠφέλημα Λατίνῳ καὶ κοινὸν Ἀβοριγίνων ἀγαθόν. (At the same time Aeneas was visited by his πατρῷοι θεοί, who told him to make friendly overtures to Latinus.) Out of this Virgil has built up his own composite picture. The supernatural voice from the wood is Italian (for such warning voices attributed to Faunus or the Fauni cf. Cic. *Diu.* i. 101, *N.D.* ii. 6) and so is the scene, a place of volcanic exhalation: but with these Virgil has combined the formal associations of a Greek oracle and the characteristically Greek notion of incubation (see on 87 ff. below). And by changing the sequence of events he gives the oracle a new importance in the story: its occasion is not now the appearance of an invading army but portents which have occurred before the Trojans reach Italy, and it bids Latinus not only admit these strangers but make a marriage-alliance with them.

82 f. sub alta . . . Albunea: Servius notes 'alta quia est in Tiburtinis altissimis montibus', and Albunea is known as the name of a Tiburtine water-spirit (Hor. *Od.* i. 7. 12 'domus Albuneae resonantis'; Varro *ap.* Lact, *Inst.* i. 6. 12 'decimam (Sibyllam) Tiburtem, nomine Albuneam, quae Tiburi colatur ut dea iuxta ripas amnis Anienis'), which may have had its origin either in a sulphurous spring or in the white falls of the river. But the distance between Laurentum and Tibur and the unconvincing vagueness of Servius' note have suggested that Virgil's Albunea should be looked for elsewhere. The

name could belong to any of the sulphurous springs of the
region with their white deposits (cf. 517 'sulpurea Nar albus
aqua': for the name Albula given to sulphurous springs in
the region cf. Vitr. viii. 3. 2; Mart. i. 12. 2; Stat. S. i. 3. 74 f.):
a suitable place has been found in the neighbourhood of
Ardea, in lands now significantly called Zolforata from their
extinct sulphur-mines, and a particular site in a cave there
close to the line of the Roman road to Ardea.

Attempts at identification are based on a misunderstand-
ing of the ways of ancient poets in general and of Virgil in
particular. The realism of many of his descriptions of local
scenery is a realism of romantic imagination, not of observa-
tion. It is as unlikely that he toured Latium in search of
local colour as that he visited Amsanctus (see on 565). Here,
as elsewhere, he is exploiting the associations of a name (and
the Tiburtine Albunea was a familiar name) and clothing
it with an imaginary scene which serves his poetic purpose,
not a detailed eyewitness description of a real one. For him
Albunea is a great dark wood (*altus* is a favourite epithet
with him for *lucus, nemus,* and *silua*) which rises above a
mysterious spring and holds an oracle which is itself a piece
of poetic fantasy.

On the Ardea site see B. Tilly, *Vergil's Latium,* 103 ff.;
M. Guarducci, in *Studi in onore di Gino Funaioli* (Rome,
1955), 120 ff., would place Virgil's Albunea in the region of
Laurentum; B. Rehm, *Philol.* Supp. xxiv. 2 (1932), 75 ff.,
concludes that the description is imaginary.

84. **mephitim:** *mefitis* is an Italic word belonging to the region
where the phenomena of sulphurous exhalation and volcanic
eruption were common: the spelling with -*ph*- is a Graeciza-
tion. As a common noun it occurs only here and in an extra-
vagant phrase of Persius 3. 99, 'gutture sulpureas . . .
exhalante mefites': elsewhere it is personified, as the name
of a deity who had shrines in various parts of South Italy—
there was one at Amsanctus (Pliny, *N.H.* ii. 208; see on 565)
—and as far north as Cremona, and a temple on the Es-
quiline at Rome (Varro, *L.L.* v. 49; Fest. 476 L.).

85. **Italae:** the invariable lengthening of the first vowel of
Italia/'Iταλία was an artificial device adopted by Hellenistic
poets to accommodate the name to dactylic verse. In the
adjective the long vowel appears first in Catullus (1. 5):
Virgil has three instances of it (643, iii. 185, ix. 698) against
more than forty of the short. (See M. Leumann, *Glotta* xix
[1931], 249.) For other variations of quantity in proper names
see on 359 *Lauinia,* viii. 416 *Sicanium.*

Italia, the Latin name of the country, is, curiously enough,

a Greek word. The name which appears in Oscan as *Viteliú*
belonged to the south-western extremity of the peninsula:
the derivation from *uitulus* (which Dion. Hal. i. 35 gives with
a legend to explain it) is a piece of folk-etymology. The in-
habitants of the Greek-speaking colonies which were planted
on the seaboard of the region Graecized it as 'Ιταλία and it was
in that form that the speakers of Latin adopted it. The Italic
name was extended to cover first the whole of the South and
then the Central regions of the peninsula (víTELIÚ was the
legend on the coinage struck by the Italians at Corfinium in
the Social War), and the Latin *Italia* kept pace with it.

Oenotria: cf. i. 530 ff. 'est locus, Hesperiam Grai cogno-
mine dicunt, / terra antiqua, potens armis atque ubere
glaebae; / Oenotri coluere uiri; nunc fama minores / Italiam
dixisse ducis de nomine gentem'. Oenotria was an old name
(Herod. i. 167) for the region in the toe of Italy whose in-
habitants were later known as Bruttii: legend gave it an
eponymous King Oenotrus and made him a brother of the
eponymous Italus.

86. in dubiis: the substantival use of the neuter plural adjec-
tive is common in Virgil (especially in adverbial phrases):
cf. 66 'per mutua', xii. 424 'in pristina'.

87 ff. The practice of 'incubation' (ἐγκοίμησις) at an oracular
shrine, where the inquirer slept, often wrapped in the skin
of an animal sacrificed to the god or hero, and had his answer
revealed to him in a vision, was well-known in Greece (Paus.
i. 34. 5 [Amphiaraus]; Lyc. 1050 ff. [Podalirius]) and prob-
ably also in Magna Graecia (Strabo vi. 3. 9 records it at a
shrine of Calchas in Apulia). But there is no evidence that
it was indigenous in Italy: apart from this passage it appears
only in Ovid, *F.* iv. 649 ff., which is based on Virgil's narra-
tive, and in Plautus, *Curc.* 216 ff., which clearly comes from
a Greek source.

88. somnosque petiuit: on Virgil's use of the singular and
plural of *somnus* see Austin on ii. 9. He seems to prefer to
use the plural of the deep sleep in which the sleeper is relaxed
or (as here) transported: cf. 754 'somnos' (of charmed
snakes), *Geo.* ii. 470 'mollesque sub arbore somni', *Aen.* ii. 9
'suadentque cadentia sidera somnos'. So 'in a dream' is
regularly (seven times in Virgil) *in somnis* (see E. Löfstedt,
Synt. i². 55 ff.).

89. modis . . . miris: the phrase is Lucretian; cf. Lucr. i. 123
'quaedam simulacra modis pallentia miris', which Virgil bor-
rows at *Geo.* i. 477. He uses it again, always with an emo-
tional suggestion, at *Geo.* iv. 309, *Aen.* i. 354, x. 822. As
Austin shows on i. 354, the evidence of comedy suggests

that Lucretius and Virgil gave an overtone of mystery to an old-fashioned expression of common speech.

90. fruitur: cf. viii. 468 'licito tandem sermone fruuntur'.

91. imis ... Auernis: a local ablative with *adfatur*; he is transported in sleep to the underworld: Acheron stands for the powers of the lower world as in 312 'Acheronta mouebo'. Virgil uses the singular *Auernus* and the plural *Auerna* three times each: other Virgilian examples of neuter 'poetic' plurals for masculine place-names (a relic of the original collective meaning of the neuter plural: in practice a convenient device for producing dactyls, which Ennius had introduced and Lucretius continued) are *Tartara* (thirteen times; *-us* once), *Maenala* (twice; *-us* twice), *Ismara* (once; *-us* once), *Massica* (once, 726; *-us* once), *Taygeta* (once), *Dindyma* (twice), *Gargara* (twice).

92. et tum: i.e. on this as on previous occasions; the regular custom is followed in a particular case and *petens responsa* looks back to *responsa petunt* (86): cf. 616.

93. mactabat: *mactare* is formed from *mactus, itself a verbal adjective from the verb *mago, 'make great' (cf. *magnus*, *magis*, *ma(g)ior*). *mactus survives only in the form *macte* used, with *esto* expressed or understood, (*a*) in ritual address to a god ('honoured with ...'), as in the prayer-formula quoted by Cato (134. 3) 'Iupiter, macte isto fercto esto, macte uino inferio esto'; (*b*) in formal address to persons ('bless you for ...', 'be honoured with/for'), as in the stereotyped phrase *macte uirtute (esto)*, 'bravo'[1] (Hor. *Sat.* i. 2. 31 f.; Cic. *Att.* xii. 6. 3:[2] so Pacuv. 146 R. 'macte esto uirtute operaque omen adproba'; *Aen.* ix. 641 'macte noua uirtute, puer, sic itur ad astra'; Livy x. 40. 11 'macte uirtute diligentiaque esto'; Stat. *Theb.* vii. 280 'macte animo'; Pliny, *Pan.* 89. 3 'macte uterque ingenti in rem publicam merito')[3]. The indeclinable use (cf. Livy ii. 12. 14 'iuberem macte uirtute esse', vii. 36. 5 'macte uirtute, milites Romani, este') suggested to Nettleship (*Contrib. to Lat. Lex.* 520) that *macte* might originally have been the adverb (though the *-e* is short in verse) and the idiom parallel to that of *bene sum*: more probably it is a fossilized vocative originally addressed by itself to a god and later supplemented by *esto* when its force had been forgotten.

---

[1] Cf. Sen. *Ep.* 66. 50 '"macte uirtute esto" sanguinulentis et ex acie redeuntibus dicitur'.

[2] Cicero also has *macte!* alone, *Att.* xv. 29. 3.

[3] Martial substitutes a genitive for the ablative, xii. 6. 7 'macte animi'.

The denominative verb *mactare* means 'make *mactus*': it is a technical term for honouring a god with sacrifice (Cic. *Vat.* 14 'puerorum extis deos manis mactare') but is also used more generally: so Enn. *Ann.* 301 V. 'Liuius inde redit magno mactatus triumpho'; Cic. *Rep.* i. 67 'eos . . . ferunt laudibus et mactant honoribus'. It also acquired, especially in popular language, the ironical inverted sense of loading someone with what is unwelcome: so the common phrase of comedy *mactare aliquem infortunio*, e.g. Plaut. *Amph.* 1034, *Trin.* 993; Ter. *Ph.* 1028 'faxo tali eum mactatum atque hic est infortunio'; similarly Cic. *Vat.* 36 'maiore es malo mactandus', *Cat.* i. 27 'summo supplicio mactari'.[1]

In its technical religious use the verb underwent a change of construction, the offering becoming the direct object (cf. the double construction of *dono*), as early as Cato, 134. 2 'fertum Ioui . . . mactato'; so Pacuv. 289 R. 'coniugem macto inferis'.[2] Usually the reference is to animal sacrifice, as it is here and elsewhere in Virgil (e.g. ii. 202, viii. 85, xi. 197), and from this use the verb is extended to mean simply 'kill' without any reference to sacrifice: e.g. Acc. 52 R. 'quod utinam me suis arquitenes telis mactasset dea'; Cic. fr. 22 M. 26 'auis taetro mactatas dente (draconis)': so *Aen.* ii. 667 'alterum in alterius mactatos sanguine', viii. 294 f. 'tu Cresia mactas / prodigia et uastum Nemeae sub rupe leonem', x. 413. See R. Wünsch, *Rh. Mus.* lxix (1914), 127 ff.; O. Skutsch and H. J. Rose, *C.Q.* xxxii (1938), 220 ff.

bidentis: *bidens* is the ritual term for a two-year-old sheep, not because it has only two teeth (see Gellius' smug anecdote of the ignorant lecturer, xvi. 6) but because ruminants at that age acquire their first two permanent teeth, which stand out prominently among the surviving milk-teeth. See M.-A. Kugener in *Mélanges Paul Thomas* (Bruges, 1930), 493 ff.

94 f. tergo stratisque . . . uelleribus: the *strata uellera* are the *tergum* (see on 20).

96. ne pete: the use of *ne* with the imperative, which is regular in comedy, had gone out of standard use by the first century and in prose it is extremely rare: see J. Wackernagel, *Vorlesungen* i. 214: the only instances appear to be Livy iii. 2. 9; Sen. *Contr.* i. 2. 5 (quoted from Arellius Fuscus), *Dial.* ii.

[1] A comedian can even combine the two uses: Novius 39 R. (from a *fabula Atellana*: addressed to a god?) 'macto te his uerbenis, macta tu illanc infortunio'.

[2] Note the formulas of *deuotio* in Livy: ix. 40. 9 'eos (sc. hostes) se Orco mactare . . . dictitans', x. 28. 13 'iam ego mecum hostium legiones mactandas Telluri ac dis manibus dabo'.

19. 4: the poets find the archaism convenient and in Virgil
it is common.

conubiis: Virgil has *conūbia* at iii. 319, iv. 213, 535, ix. 600,
xii. 42. If the *-u-* was invariably long (as it is in *nubo*), then
conubiis here (and at 333, iii. 136, iv. 168, xii. 821) and
conubio at 253 (and i. 73, iv. 126) must be trisyllabic, *-i-* being
given consonantal value by a prosodic licence not uncommon
in Virgil (see on 175); the same applies to Lucretius iii. 776;
Catullus 62. 57; Ovid, *Met.* vi. 428, and no fewer than sixteen
places in Statius. In view of the general practice of these
poets, it is more likely that the quantity was variable and
the writer's choice a matter of convenience, the original
quantity being *conŭbium* (cf. *pronŭba*) and *conūbium* an alter-
native 'literary' prosody adopted for a word which in the
general sense of 'marriage' (as opposed to the strict technical
sense) is practically confined to hexameter verse. See P.
Maas, *A.L.L.* xiii. 433 ff.; J. Wackernagel, *Kl. Schr.* ii.
1280 ff.

97. o: see on 360.

neu crede: *natam* is not to be understood as object: cf.
Ecl. 2. 17 'nimium ne crede colori', *Geo.* iv. 48 'altae neu
crede paludi', 192 'aut credunt caelo aduentantibus Euris',
Aen. ix. 42 'neu struere auderent aciem neu credere campo',
xi. 807 f. 'nec iam amplius hastae / credere . . . audet'.

paratis, 'ready made', 'to hand', ἑτοίμοις: so iv. 75 'osten-
tat opes urbemque paratam'; Cat. 62. 11 'non facilis nobis
. . . palma parata est'; Petr. 15. 9 'nec uictoria mi placet
parata'; Pliny, *Pan.* 88. 4 'paratum id quidem et in medio
positum'.

98. generi: the reference is to Aeneas only, but the generalizing
plural is appropriate to the oracular style: cf. viii. 503 'ex-
ternos optate duces'.

sanguine: i.e. by contributing their blood to our race: the
first intimation of the blending of the two nations with which
the poem is to end (xii. 833 ff.).

98 ff. qui . . . ferant, quorumque . . . nepotes . . . uidebunt: the
final clause (cf. i. 19 f. 'progeniem . . . Troiano a sanguine
duci / audierat Tyrias olim quae uerteret arces', 286 f. 'nas-
cetur . . . Caesar, / imperium Oceano, famam qui terminet
astris') is combined with direct prophecy.

100 f. utrumque . . . Oceanum: i.e. the Ocean bounding the in-
habited world on east and west: so *Geo.* iii. 33 'utroque ab
litore gentis'; Prop. iii. 9. 53 'currus utroque ab litore
ouantis'; Ovid, *Met.* xv. 829 f. 'gentes ab utroque iacentes /
Oceano'.

101. uertique regique, 'see the whole world moving in obedience

at their feet': *uerti* perhaps combines the notion of the
natural movement of things with the figurative one of de-
pendence (cf. Cic. *Verr.* i. 20 'omnia in unius potestate ac
moderatione uertentur'; Livy xxxvii. 7. 9 'totum id uertitur
in uoluntate Philippi'). For *-que . . . -que* see on 186.

103. **ipse** strengthens *suo*: in such phrases Latin attaches *ipse*
to the subject and prefers *suo ipse* to *suo ipsius*.

   non . . . premit ore, 'does not hold it close in his mouth'
i.e. refrain from repeating it: cf. iv. 332 'curam sub corde
premebat'.

105. **Ausonias:** see on 39.

   Laomedontia : i.e. Trojan, as in viii. 18 'Laomedontius
heros', without the implicit reference to Laomedon's
treachery (cf. *Geo.* i. 501 f., *Aen.* iv. 541 f.) which *Laomedon-
tiadae* has in iii. 248.

   pubes : so 219 'Dardana pubes', 794 'Argiua pubes', 429 f.
'armari pubem . . . para'. *pubes* is a collective term for an
adult male population (cf. the parody of an edict in Plaut.
Pseud. 125 f. 'dico omnibus, / pube praesenti in contione,
omni poplo'). In prose it is rarely found and always with a
formal-heroic or archaic suggestion: Cic. *Mil.* 61 'omnem
Italiae pubem'; Livy i. 16. 2 (at a *contio*) 'Romana pubes . . .
aliquandiu silentium obtinuit' (similarly i. 9. 6, i. 28. 8). See
E. Benveniste, *R. de Ph.* xxix (1955), 7 ff.

106. **ab aggere:** for the construction cf. iii. 76 'errantem
(Delum) Mycono e celsa Gyaroque reuinxit'; Ovid, *F.* iv. 331
'querno religant a stipite funem'.

   ripae . . . aggere : i.e. the bank consisting of an *agger*: cf.
6 'aggere . . . tumuli'. Virgil uses *agger* of a river-bank again
in ii. 596 f. 'aggeribus ruptis cum spumeus amnis / exiit',
of a road in v. 273 'uiae deprensus in aggere serpens'.

107–47. *The Trojans take a meal on landing : when in their
hunger they eat the wheaten cakes they had used as plates, they
fulfil a prophecy and Aeneas knows that he has reached his jour-
ney's end.*

107. **Iulus:** this alternative name for Ascanius appears first in
literature in Virgil, who uses the two names an almost equal
number of times. The origin of *Iulus* is obscure: Virgil him-
self derives it (i. 268) from an earlier *Ilus* and ancient ety-
mologists gave even more fanciful explanations. However it
found its way into the story (Servius on i. 267 has been taken
to imply that it came into Cato's account), it had no doubt
been exploited by Caesarian propaganda concerned to con-
nect the *gens Iulia* with the Trojan settlement of Italy. In
reference to Ascanius the name is always trisyllabic: it is a

disyllable when Horace, *Od.* iv. 2. 2, gives it to Antony's son, who bore it as a *praenomen*.

108. An interesting piece of reminiscence: Virgil has interlocked two half-lines of Lucretius (i. 258 'corpora deponunt', ii. 30 'sub ramis arboris altae').

109. adorea liba: both are ritual terms: *ador* is a kind of spelt (*far*) used in sacrifice, *libum* a sacrificial cake made with wheaten flour, cheese, and egg (for the recipe see Cato 75).

110 ff. The expression of these lines, to our taste turgid and pretentious, represents the poet's concern to invest commonplace notions with a distinction consonant with their place in a heroic narrative. For ancient doctrines of 'enhancement' in poetry and oratory, and in particular the relation of vocabulary to the *genus dicendi* and the avoidance of 'humilia' which are 'infra dignitatem rerum aut ordinis' (Quint. viii. 2. 2), see Aristotle, *Rhet.* iii. 6–7; *ad Her.* iv. 18; Hor. *Ep.* ii. 2. 111 ff. Virgil rarely indulges in this 'euphuistic' style, but cf. i. 174 ff.

110. subiciunt: i.e. they use the flat cakes to put their food on.

  Iuppiter ipse MPR: *ille* M², which Priscian, Servius, and Donatus confirm. *ille* here cannot be directly supported by those passages in Virgil where similar formulas are put into the mouth of a speaker—558 'haud pater ille uelit, summi regnator Olympi', ii. 779 'ille sinit superi regnator Olympi', x. 875 'sic pater ille deum faciat, sic altus Apollo': these (and the imitations in Stat. *Theb.* v. 688 'uidet haec, uidet ille deum regnator' and *Siluae* iii. 181 'monet hoc pater ille deorum') represent the archaic idiom which occurs in comedy (Plaut. *Most.* 398, *Pseud.* 923 'ita ille faxit Iuppiter', *Amph.* 461 'quod ille faxit Iuppiter', *Curc.* 27 'nec me ille sirit Iuppiter') and in Apuleius (*Met.* iii. 29 'sed tandem mihi inopinatam salutem Iuppiter ille tribuit'), in which the original force of *ille* is deictic, 'Jupiter above there' (cf. Cic. *Cat.* iii. 22 'ille, ille Iuppiter restitit', where Cicero is pointing to the Capitol as he speaks). If Virgil wrote *ille* here in narrative, the phrase must be taken to be a false archaism: he probably wrote *ipse*.

  monebat, 'inspired'; see on 41. On Virgil's use of the Hellenistic device of parenthesis see G. Williams, *Tradition and Originality in Roman Poetry* (Oxford, 1968), 730 f.

111. solum, 'the base', i.e. the cake: Virgil has another unparalleled use of *solum* in v. 199, of the sea surface on which a ship rests.

  augent, 'heap with country fruits': *augere* is a ritual term of sacrifice as in Plaut. *Merc.* 675 f. 'aliquid cedo / qui (i.e. quo) uicini hanc nostri augeam aram (Apollinis)'; cf. ix. 407 f.

'si qua tuis umquam pro me pater Hyrtacus aris / dona tulit,
si qua ipse meis uenatibus auxi'.

112. **hic,** 'thereupon'.

forte, 'as luck would have it': the emphasis, as usual, is not
on accident but on coincidence: see on 509 'ut forte'.

112 f. **uertere . . . adegit:** see on 35 f.

113. **penuria edendi,** 'scarcity of eating', an unparalleled ex-
pression: the sense is that of *penuria cibi* in Lucr. v. 1097 or
penuria uictus in Hor. *Sat.* i. 1. 98, but the substitution of the
abstract *edendum* (which cannot mean 'something eatable')
for the concrete is an unexpected turn. Four centuries after
Virgil the phrase took Ammianus' fancy (xxvi. 6. 4).

exiguam in Cererem : the form of metonymy (the Latin
technical term is *denominatio, ad Her.* iv. 43; Quintilian in-
cludes it under *hypallage,* viii. 6. 23) by which the names of
gods are used for the objects with which they are concerned
or associated is already in Homer, *Il.* ii. 426 σπλάγχνα δ' ἄρ'
ἀμπείραντες ὑπείρεχον Ἡφαίστοιο ('fire'): so in the oracle quoted
by Herod. vii. 141 ὦ θείη Σαλαμὶς, ἀπολεῖς δὲ σὺ τέκνα γυναικῶν / ἤ που
σκιδναμένης Δημήτερος ('corn') ἢ συνιούσης. But in Greek it does
not become common before the Hellenistic period. Latin
poetry took it over as early as Ennius (*Ann.* 487 V. 'cum
magno strepitu Volcanum uentus uegebat') and used it very
freely. So much was the metonymic use of *Ceres, Liber/Bac-
chus, Vulcanus, Mars, Neptunus, Minerua/Pallas,* and *Vesta*
felt to be a mere piece of conventional embellishment ('grauis
modus in ornatu orationis et saepe sumendus', Cicero calls it,
de Or. iii. 167) that the most earnest of atheists could condone
it (Lucr. ii. 655 ff. 'si quis mare Neptunum Cereremque uocare
/ constituit fruges et Bacchi nomine abuti / mauolt quam
laticis proprium proferre uocamen, / concedamus ut hic terra-
rum dictitet orbem / esse deum matrem, dum uera re tamen
ipse / religione animum turpi contingere parcat'[1]) and the
most sensitive of poets could combine it with epithets glaringly
inconsistent with the personal implication of the names. For
exigua Ceres cf. *Geo.* i. 297 'rubicunda Ceres medio succiditur
aestu', *Aen.* i. 177 'Cererem corruptam undis . . . expediunt';
an extreme case is viii. 180 f. 'onerantque canistris / dona
laboratae Cereris', where *dona* and *laboratae* represent different
notions of Ceres: similarly viii. 409 'tolerare colo uitam
tenuique Minerua', *Geo.* i. 344 'tu lacte fauos et miti dilue
Baccho'; Ovid, *Her.* 19. 44 'Pallade . . . pingui tinguere

[1] Cf. Cic. *N.D.* iii. 41 'cum fruges Cererem, uinum Liberum dicimus,
genere nos quidem sermonis utimur usitato, sed ecquem tam amen-
tem esse putas qui illud quo uescatur deum credat esse?'; ii. 60, 71.

membra'. *deus* alone can stand for *Bacchus* and so for *uinum* (ix. 336 f. 'multo . . . / membra deo uictus'): Ovid and Statius can take artifice a stage further by substituting a personal description for the name, *Met.* xi. 125 'miscuerat puris auctorem muneris (i.e. Bacchum) undis', *Silu.* iii. 1. 41 '(Herculem) confectum thiasis et multo fratre (i.e. Baccho) madentem'. See O. Gross, 'De metonymiis sermonis latini a deorum nominibus petitis', *Diss. Phil. Halenses* xix (1911).

115. patulis . . . quadris, 'the flat quarters': the circular *placenta* was marked into four *quadrae* by two cross-cuts at right angles: so the farmer doing his own baking in *Moretum*, 46 ff. 'subactum ('kneaded') opus . . . dilatat in orbem / et notat impressis aequo discrimine quadris': cf. Mart. ix. 90. 17 f. 'libetur tibi candidas ad aras / secta plurima quadra de placenta'. (So in Greek τρύφος and βλωμός: Hesiod, *W.D.* 442 ἄρτον δειπνήσας τετράτρυφον ὀκτάβλωμον: Athen. iii. 114 E. βλωμιαίους ἄρτους τοὺς ἔχοντας ἐντομάς, οὓς Ῥωμαῖοι κοδράτους λέγουσι.) Hence the use of *quadra* of a meagre ration ('slice'): Sen. *Ben.* iv. 29. 2 'quis beneficium dixit quadram panis?'; Juv. 5. 2 'aliena uiuere quadra'.

116. heus is an interjection of colloquial language (common in comedy and found a dozen times in Cicero's letters but almost unknown outside familiar idiom) with which a speaker peremptorily calls another's attention to an order or admonition, a question (as here), or (rarely) an apposite proverbial saying. (See J. B. Hofmann, *Lat. Umgangsspr.* 15 f.; W. S. Watt in *Glotta* xli [1963], 138 ff.). Here the ejaculation suits the excitement of young Iulus' innocent surprise— 'Look here, are we eating our tables as well?': Virgil uses it once elsewhere (i. 321), with an imperative, in the mouth of Venus disguised as a young huntress.

mensas . . . consumimus: Servius alleges (on i. 736: cf. iii. 257) that *mensa* was the term for a wheaten cake used as a plate to hold offerings to the gods (Donatus on iii. 257 connects the practice with the worship of the Penates): there is no other evidence for this usage. On the other hand, there is evidence that *mensa* was a technical term of sacrifice: Festus (112 L.) quotes the formula *mensa frugibusque iurato* (explaining it as 'per mensam et fruges'), and the corresponding Umbrian form *mefa* occurs several times in the Iguvine Tables in reference to sacrificial offering, usually accompanied by the term *spefa* (presumably representing a Latin **spensa*, which can be connected with a verb **spendo*, corresponding to the Greek σπένδω). Whatever the origin of the word may have been (a reasonable conjecture is that it is the verbal adjective of *metior* and originally meant 'measured portion' or the like), the extension of meaning from a sacred cake used as a plate for sacrificial offerings first to the altar-table on which such offerings are placed (for this sense cf. ii. 764 'mensae deorum'; Naev. 3 R. 'sacra in mensa penatium ordine ponuntur') and then to a table of ordinary use is not implausible. If this is the history of the word, the story of the 'eating of the tables' looks like an aetiological legend invented to account for the special sacrificial meaning of *mensa*. Such a legend must, of course, be of Italian origin: the story appears in Greek versions (Lyc. 1250 τράπεζαν εἰδάτων πλήρη κιχών: Dion. Hal. i. 55 σέλινα μὲν πολλοῖς ὑπέστρωτο καὶ ἦν ταῦτα ὥσπερ τράπεζα τῶν ἐδεσμάτων, ὡς δέ φασί τινες ἴτρια καρποῦ πεποιημένα πυρίνου καθαρότητος ταῖς τροφαῖς ἕνεκα) but their use of τράπεζα entirely obscures its linguistic significance. See P. J. Enk, *Mnem*. xli (1913), 386 ff.; P. Kretschmer, *Glotta* viii (1917), 79 ff.

117. adludens, 'jesting': cf. Cic. *de Or.* i. 240 'Galba autem adludens ('playfully') uarie et copiose multas similitudines ('analogies') adferre'; Suet. *Iul.* 22 'responderit quasi adludens'.

118. primam serves to reinforce *prima* and to emphasize the instantaneity of the action.

119. eripuit, 'caught it up as he spoke': cf. Val. Max. i. 5. 3 'arripuit omen'. So *omen accipere* is used of picking up a chance word which has for the hearer an unintended meaning; cf. Cic. *Diu.* i. 103 (and other examples quoted in Pease's note); Livy v. 55. 2.

  numine: i.e. by the manifestation of divine purpose: cf. ii. 123, iii. 363, viii. 78.

  pressit: 'checked', so that he would not add more and spoil the omen, is the obvious interpretation in view of ix. 324 'sic memorat uocemque premit', where a speaker is checking his own utterance: the slight zeugma by which *uocem* with *eripuit* refers to his actual words, with *pressit* to his utterance, is natural enough. It is no objection to say that he had stopped already: *nec plura* gets its meaning from the following *eripuit . . . pressit*—he said no more because he was not given the chance. Henry translates 'held fast', i.e. held the accidental word fast so that the omen it conveyed should not escape: but the only examples he can cite refer to physical action (Ovid, *Met.* viii. 37 with 'frena'; Sil. v. 670 with 'ferrum') and the figurative use is very dubious. Even less likely is the semi-technical use of *premere*, 'drive home', 'clinch' (Cic. *Tusc.* i. 88 with 'argumentum').

120. continuo, 'without more ado': see on 68.

fatis is ablative here: in vi. 66 f. 'non indebita posco / regna meis fatis' it may be either ablative or dative.

121. fidi ... penates: because they have not abandoned him and the promise they made to him in a vision in Crete (iii. 148 ff.), that he would find his home in Italy, has come true.

122. hic domus, haec patria: perhaps Virgil wishes to avoid the repetition of either *haec* or *hic* (cf. viii. 39 'hic tibi certa domus'); in iv. 347 'hic amor, haec patria' *hic* is probably masculine and the idiom the same as in vi. 129 'hoc opus, hic labor est', x. 858 f. 'hoc decus illi, / hoc solamen erat', xi. 739 'hic amor, hoc studium', xii. 572 'hoc caput, o cives, haec belli summa nefandi'.

namque: the postponing of connective particles begins with Catullus and may well have been suggested by the practice of Hellenistic poets with καί and ἀλλά. Virgil postpones *nam* and *namque* to the second place in the sentence not infrequently (*nam* seven times, *namque* six times): he has *nam* in the third place twice (ix. 803, xii. 206) and *namque* in the fourth, as here, at least once elsewhere (v. 733; perhaps x. 614). Extreme cases are *namque* in the sixth place at *Ecl.* I. 14 and *sed enim* in the fifth at *Aen.* ii. 164. On Virgil's practice see E. Norden, *Aeneis VI*, pp. 402 ff.: on that of the elegists M. Platnauer, *Latin Elegiac Verse* (Cambridge, 1951), 93 ff.

123. Anchises: there is an inconsistency here. The prophecy has been uttered not by Anchises but by the Harpy Celaeno (iii. 255 ff.), to whom Virgil transferred it—in the traditional story it is either the oracle of Dodona or a 'Sibyl' of Erythrae (Dion. Hal. i. 55. 4) that tells the Trojans to go West till they come to a land where they eat their tables and continues with the prophecy of the white sow: see on viii. 42 ff.— and on Celaeno's lips it is not a promise but a parting threat of revenge which, when the fortunes of the Trojans seem to be set fair and the Penates in Crete have sent them on their way to Italy, leaves them disconsolate till Helenus in Epirus reassures them (iii. 394 f. 'nec tu mensarum morsus horresce futuros: / fata uiam inuenient aderitque uocatus Apollo').

fatorum arcana: so Jupiter declares, i. 262 'uoluens fatorum arcana mouebo', and the Sibyl's prophecies, vi. 72, are 'arcana fata'.

125. accisis, 'clipped': for the metaphorical sense cf. Hor. *Sat.* ii. 2. 113 f. 'integris opibus noui non latius usum / quam nunc accisis'.

126. sperare ... memento, 'bear in mind to expect'.

127. moliri aggere tecta: the phrase seems to combine the ideas

of *moliri tecta* and *cingere aggere tecta*. For *moliri* cf. 158
'molitur locum', 290 'moliri tecta': it is one of Virgil's
favourite verbs, which he uses in a wide variety of contexts,
always implying effort: its object may be either the instru-
ment which is handled (so *Geo.* i. 329 'fulmina', *Aen.* x. 131
'ignem' (of fire-darts), xii. 327 'habenas') or the result which
is produced (concrete as here and in i. 424 'aram', iii. 5
'classem', or abstract as in i. 414 'moram', ii. 108 'fugam',
xii. 851 'letum . . . morbosque'). The addition of *manu* re-
gularly emphasizes personal exertion: e.g. 621 'impulit ipsa
manu portas', *Geo.* ii. 156 'tot congesta manu praeruptis
oppida saxis', *Aen.* iv. 344 'recidiua manu posuissem Per-
gama uictis', vi. 835 'proice tela manu'.

128. haec erat illa fames: for *hic . . . ille* thus identifying some-
thing realized in the present with something predicted or
imperfectly understood in the past cf. 255 f. 'hunc illum
fatis . . . / portendi generum', 272 'hunc illum poscere fata',
iv. 675 'hoc illud, germana, fuit?': so Ter. *And.* 125 f. 'hoc
illud est, / hinc illae lacrumae'; Tac. *Ann.* xiv. 22. 4 'hunc
illum numine deum destinari credebant'. (οὗτος/ὅδε and ἐκεῖνος
are similarly used: e.g. Soph. *El.* 1178 τόδ' ἔστ' ἐκεῖνο: Ar. *Ach.*
41 τοῦτ' ἐκεῖν' οὑγὼ 'λεγον).

The same point is emphasized by the imperfect: for this
idiomatic use of it to indicate realization of a state of affairs
already existing ('was all along, if we had known') cf. Hor.
Od. 1. 27. 19 f. 'quanta laborabas Charybdi, / digne puer
meliore flamma', *Ep.* i. 4. 6 'non tu corpus eras sine pectore'.
The use is much more common in Greek, often pointed by
ἄρα: Aesch. *Cho.* 243 πιστὸς δ' ἀδελφὸς ἦσθ' ἐμοὶ σέβας φέρων: Hom.
Od. xiii. 209 f. οὐκ ἄρα πάντα νοήμονες, οὐδὲ δίκαιοι / ἦσαν Φαιήκων
ἡγήτορες: Soph. *O.C.* 1697 πόθος καὶ κακῶν ἄρ' ἦν τις. See E. Fraen-
kel, *Horace* (Oxford, 1957), 324 n. 3.

129. One of six incomplete lines in this book: the others are
248, 439, 455, 702, 760. In the whole poem there are nearly
sixty, varying in length from one foot to four and very un-
evenly distributed—Book II has ten while VI and XI have
only two each and XII one: only in one line (iii. 340) is the
sense left incomplete.

That there were incomplete lines in the 'authentic' text
published after Virgil's death we know from Donatus' *Life*
(41, 'edidit . . . Varius sed summatim emendata ut qui uersus
etiam imperfectos si qui erant reliquerit'): but we have no
assurance that it had not either more or fewer of them than
now appear. For the evidence of the indirect tradition shows
that the interpolation of supplements for incomplete lines
began early in the history of the text and editions incorporat-

ing them were in circulation. Seneca (*Ep.* 94. 28) quotes x.
284 in a complete form and Servius knew of complete versions
of ii. 787 and viii. 41. Two lines which are complete in our
tradition are suspect: the ending of v. 595, though it is
unexceptionable, has weak manuscript authority and that
of xii. 218, though it is given by all the manuscripts, does not
fit the context and can hardly be genuine. Interpolations
may have established themselves where we have no ground
for suspecting them. On the other hand the knowledge that
interpolations existed may have led to attempts to purify the
text which condemned as spurious and removed from the
tradition some line-endings which, though perhaps weak and
not indispensable to the sense, were genuine.

That Virgil regarded these incomplete lines as having their
final form or had an artistic purpose in leaving them as they
stand it is impossible to believe. The importance in Latin
poetry (and not least in Virgil) of precedent and convention
in matters of form makes it significant that there is no pre-
cedent either in Latin or in Greek for the broken lines; that
they were not a piece of deliberate technique is at least sug-
gested by the fact that there are no such lines in the *Georgics*,
and that they were not so understood by the fact that Virgil's
admirers and sedulous imitators, the later epic poets, no-
where reproduce this distinctive feature of the *Aeneid*.

The most natural assumption is that which is suggested by
Donatus' account of Virgil's method of composition: (23)
'Aeneida . . . particulatim componere instituit, prout liberet
quidque, et nihil in ordinem arripiens. ac, ne quid impetum
moraretur, quaedam imperfecta transmisit, alia leuissimis
uersibus ueluti fulsit, quae per iocum pro tibicinibus inter-
poni aiebat'. Virgil, that is, left a line incomplete when a way
of completing it which satisfied him had not presented itself
or when he had still to work into a context a passage con-
ceived and composed as a unit of thought. That some of these
lines are rhetorically satisfying in bringing a movement to
a dramatic, perhaps an epigrammatic, close (as, e.g., 455 and
760 may be said to do) is precisely what one might expect
on this assumption, and the fact that a number of them con-
sist of formulas introducing a speech (e.g. iii. 527, ix. 295,
x. 17, 490, 580—an extreme case, the two words 'cui Liger')
or resuming the narrative after one (v. 653 'haec effata') or
of the concluding words of a speech (e.g. 455, v. 815, x. 284,
876) points in the same direction. (As for the weak lines
which Virgil consciously used as temporary stop-gaps—*tibi-
cines*, struts or scaffolding, as he called them, to hold the
structure up till they could be replaced by permanent building

—we may sometimes think that we can recognize one; but that is only guessing.)

For discussion see F. W. Shipley, 'Virgil's Verse Technique' in *Washington University Studies*, Humanistic Series xii (1924), 115 ff.; J. Sparrow, *Half-lines and Repetitions in Virgil* (Oxford, 1931); J. Perret, *Virgile* (Paris, 1952), 142 ff.; O. Walter, *Die Entstehung der Halbverse in der Äneis* (Giessen diss. 1933); W. Warde Fowler, *Virgil's 'Gathering of the Clans'*, 93 ff.; J. W. Mackail, *The Aeneid*, Introduction x–xi.

exitiis: so the manuscripts, confirmed by Servius (who quotes the line on iii. 395), probably rightly. *exsiliis* (for the plural cf. ii. 780) has been supported by R. D. Williams (*C.R.* lxxv [1961], 195 f.) on the ground that even as a rhetorical exaggeration *exitiis* is here impossible since the Trojans had survived their sufferings and there was no *exitium* for the new Troy, but the passages from Cicero which he quotes—*Mil.* 3 'rapinis et incendiis et omnibus exitiis publicis', *Leg.* i. 34 'id (sc. utilitatem a iure seiungere) enim querebatur (Socrates) caput esse exitiorum omnium'—in fact represent a rhetorical use not very different. The same question arises at x. 850, where Servius supports *exsilium* against *exitium* of MPR.

130. **laeti:** of the cheerful response to a command as at 430, iv. 294 f., x. 14.

   primo . . . cum lumine: for the temporal use cf. *Geo.* iii. 324 'Luciferi primo cum sidere'; Cic. *Att.* iv. 3. 4 'cum prima luce', *Diu.* ii. 33 'cum luna'.

131. **quiue habeant homines:** Latin idiom often prefers *et* or *-que* where English would use 'or', and *-ue* where English would prefer 'and', in cases where either a copulative conjunction or a disjunctive is logically justified, though they represent different points of view. The variation can be most easily seen in some numerical phrases (*bis terque*, 'twice and in fact three times': *bis terue*, 'twice or for that matter three times') and in corrective phrases (Cic. *Verr.* ii. 3. 11 'magna atque adeo maxima', *Q.F.* ii. 13. 1 'magna uel potius maxima'), and the interchangeability of the two uses is shown by such pairs as Tac. *Ann.* i. 9 'uita eius uarie extollebatur arguebaturue' and i. 25 'diuersis animorum motibus pauebant terrebantque'; Pliny, *N.H.* ii. 229 'fons eodem quo Nilus modo ac pariter cum eo decrescit augeturue' and (a few lines below) 'pariter cum aestu maris crescunt minuunturque'. The fact that the two ways of expression can be used indifferently in many cases where ideas can be associated equally well in either way leads to (*a*) the extension of *et* (or

-*que*) to cases in which it cannot be logically justified, (*b*) the use of -*ue* (or *aut*), especially in rapid interrogative clauses (direct or indirect), as here, where a copulative conjunction is called for, and (*c*) the combination of the two forms of expression. So (*a*) *Geo.* iii. 121 '(equus) patriam Epirum referat fortisque Mycenas', *Aen.* x. 708 f. 'aper multos Vesulus (in the Alps) quem pinifer annos / defendit multosque palus Laurentia (on the coast of Latium)'; Lucr. v. 984 f. 'fugiebant saxea tecta / spumigeri suis aduentu ualidique leonis'; (*b*) *Aen.* ii. 74 f. 'hortamur fari quo sanguine cretus / quidue ferat', 150 f. 'quis auctor? / quidue petunt?', ix. 376 'quae causa uiae? quiue estis in armis?', x. 149 f. 'memorat nomenque genusque / quidue petat quidue ipse ferat'; Livy vii. 14. 1 'quaenam haec res sit aut quo acta more percontatur'; (*c*) Lucr. iii. 551 f. 'manus atque oculus naresue seorsum / secreta a nobis nequeunt sentire'; *Aen.* vi. 608–14 'quibus . . . aut qui . . . quique . . . quique'. On these usages see E. Löfstedt, *Synt.* i². 348 f., *Per. Aeth.* 200 f.; W. H. Kirk in *A.J.P.* xlii (1921), 1 ff.

133. pateras libate: cf. iii. 354 'libabant pocula'.

134. reponite: 'duly place' (not 'replace': there is no suggestion that the *uina* had been removed), as in *Geo.* iii. 527 'epulae repostae', iv. 378 f. 'epulis onerant mensas et plena reponunt / pocula'. But the sense is 'replace' in viii. 175 f. 'dapes iubet et sublata reponi / pocula'.

135. sic deinde effatus: cf. v. 14 'sic deinde locutus'. Virgil regularly gives *deinde* an unemphatic position: e.g. i. 195 ff. 'uina bonus quae deinde cadis onerarat Acestes . . . diuidit', iii. 609 'hortamur quae deinde agitet fortuna fateri', viii. 481 f. 'hanc multos florentem annos rex deinde superbo / imperio . . . tenuit'. Rare exceptions are *Geo.* i. 106, iv. 161, *Aen.* viii. 66.

ramo: Aeneas puts on a wreath to perform a ritual act: so in v. 71 he and his men put on wreaths of myrtle to approach Anchises' tomb.

136. genium loci: the place, like the person, has its *genius* or immanent spirit: so Aeneas sees the serpent at Anchises' tomb (v. 95 f.), 'incertus geniumne loci famulumne parentis / esse putet'.

136 f. primam deorum Tellurem: for the acknowledged priority of Earth cf. Aesch. *Eum.* 1 f. πρῶτον μὲν εὐχῇ τῇδε πρεσβεύω θεῶν / τὴν πρωτόμαντιν Γαῖαν: Soph. *Ant.* 337 f. θεῶν τε τὰν ὑπερτάταν Γᾶν.

138. orientia: the stars are coming out as he speaks. *noctis signa* is Lucretian (v. 1190 'luna dies et nox et noctis signa seuera': cf. Enn. *Ann.* 433 V. 'nox . . . signis praecincta').

139. Idaeumque Iouem Phrygiamque . . . matrem: in iii. 104 f.
King Anius speaks of the origins of the Trojan race in Crete,
Jupiter's island, and the Cretan Mount Ida, the refuge of
Jupiter's infancy. But here Aeneas is addressing the gods
of his own homeland and here, as in Homer (*Il.* iii. 276
Ζεῦ πάτερ, "Ἰδηθεν μεδέων, xvi. 604 f. Διὸς . . . 'Ιδαίου) the reference
is to Mount Ida in the Troad. The *Phrygia mater* is Cybele,
the Anatolian mother-goddess whose worship was associated
with 'Phrygia', i.e. north and central Asia Minor, and in parti-
cular with the mountains of Ida and Dindymus (cf. x. 252
'alma parens Idaea deum, cui Dindyma cordi').

ex ordine: probably 'in succession' (as in *Geo.* iii. 341
'totum ex ordine mensem'; cf. 177 below) rather than 'duly',
of ritual regularity, as Servius takes it here and (again
dubiously) in v. 773 '. . . iubet soluique ex ordine funem':
'duly' is *ordine* in *Geo.* iv. 376, *Aen.* iii. 548, v. 102.

140. duplicis: a mere convenience for *ambo* or *duo* as in i. 93
'duplicis palmas'; Lucr. vi. 1146 'duplices oculos'.

caeloque Ereboque parentis: Venus and Anchises: for the
local ablative attached to a noun cf. 269 f. 'plurima caelo /
monstra', iv. 26 'pallentis umbras Erebo', viii. 419 'ualidique
incudibus ictus'. For *-que . . . -que* see on 186.

141. ter: the magical or ritual number: cf. *Ecl.* 8. 73 f. 'terna
. . . triplici . . . ter', *Geo.* i. 345, iv. 384 f., *Aen.* vi. 229, xi. 188 f.

141 f. clarus . . . intonuit: 'loud', 'distinctly': *clare* (and
clara uoce) is regularly so used but there is no parallel to the
adverbial use of the adjective. Thunder in a clear sky was an
omen of special significance (cf. ix. 630 f.; Hor. *Od.* i. 34. 5 ff.;
Ovid, *F.* iii. 369), but *clarus* cannot mean *claro caelo*.

142 f. 'displays from heaven a cloud blazing with rays of golden
light as he brandishes it in his hand'. As Conington observes,
this cannot be merely a cloud gilded by the sun like that in
viii. 622 f., 'cum caerula nubes / solis inardescit radiis
longeque refulget': for that would be no omen—and anyhow
it is night-time (138). Virgil's picture must have been sug-
gested by the phenomenon of a cloud discharging electricity.

142. radiis et auro: hendiadys has a poetic purpose (see on 15),
but Virgil's repeated use of it with *auro* is no doubt en-
couraged by the metrical awkwardness of *aureus*: so *Geo.*
ii. 192 'pateris . . . et auro', *Aen.* i. 648 'signis auroque',
iii. 467 'hamis auroque', viii. 436 'squamis auroque', ix. 26
'pictai uestis et auri', 707 'squama et auro'.

144. diditur . . . rumor: cf. viii. 132 'tua terris didita fama'.
didere is a favourite word of Lucretius': elsewhere it is rare.

145. debita: cf. 120 'fatis . . . debita tellus'.

quo condant, 'on which to found': cf. 98 f.

146. instaurant, 'begin anew' (as in viii. 283): the phrase is curiously inconsistent with line 113 and the whole motive of the preceding passage. *instaurare* is technically used of performing a ceremony over again to remove or prevent a flaw (cf. Livy ii. 36. 1). Virgil uses it in religious contexts with similar implication at iii. 62 'instauramus Polydoro funus' (i.e. give him a proper funeral this time), v. 94 'inceptos . . . instaurat honores' (an offering is resumed after an interruption), and (more boldly) iv. 63 'instauratque diem donis' (the distraught Dido keeps on making fresh starts with her offerings): more generally, of making a fresh start with new vigour, at ii. 451 'instaurati animi', 669 f. 'instaurata . . . proelia', vi. 529 f. 'di, talia Grais / instaurate', x. 543 'instaurant acies'. On his use of the word see Henry's note on iii. 62.

omine magno: with *laeti*; cf. v. 522 f. 'magno augurio', ix. 21 'omina tanta'.

147-8. Both lines occur elsewhere with change of one word, at i. 724 and iv. 6.

147. uina coronant: so i. 724: cf. *Geo.* ii. 528 'socii cratera coronant'. The phrase is clearly suggested by Homer's κρητῆρας ἐπεστέψαντο ποτοῖο (*Il.* i. 470; cf. viii. 232 πίνοντες κρητῆρας ἐπιστεφέας οἴνοιο) which must mean 'crowned the bowls (i.e. filled them to the brim) with wine': but the explicit iii. 525 f. 'magnum cratera corona / induit impleuitque mero' shows that Virgil had the putting of a garland round the bowl in mind (cf. Tib. ii. 5. 98 'coronatus stabit et ipse calix').

148-285. *Next morning Aeneas sets about building a settlement and sends ambassadors to King Latinus. The king receives them hospitably, recalling the old connection between their people and his, assures them of his goodwill and offers his daughter in marriage to Aeneas as the foreign husband of whom the oracles had spoken.*

148. The resort to the device of alliteration on *p* and *l* may stress the excitement of a new situation: that is not to say that the sounds are themselves expressive. See Appendix.

lampade: so iii. 637 'Phoebeae lampadis instar', iv. 6 f. 'Phoebea lustrabat lampade terras / . . . Aurora': Lucretius had used the word in the same reference (v. 610 'rosea sol alte lampade lucens', vi. 1198 'nona reddebant lampade uitam', 'on the ninth day').

lustrabat: for *lustrare* thus used of a heavenly body traversing the earth cf. iv. 6 f. (quoted above), 607 'Sol, qui terrarum flammis opera omnia lustras'. For the development of the word see on 391: Warde Fowler suggests that something of the notion of purification survives in these uses,

but i. 607 f. 'montibus umbrae / lustrabant conuexa' makes
that unlikely.
150. **diuersi:** i.e. turning in different directions: cf. ix. 416
'diuersi circumspiciunt'.

Numici: the Numicius (or Numicus: Virgil has only the
genitive and both forms of the nominative are found),
which appears again along with the Tiber in 242 and 797, is
one of the small streams which wind across the Campagna;
it has generally been identified with the Rio Torto flowing
between Lavinium and Ardea. (See B. Tilly, *Vergil's Latium*,
66 ff.; F. Castagnoli in *Arch. Class.* xix [1967], 235–47.)
Virgil makes no explicit reference to its connection with the
Aeneas legend, but that connection was still alive in his day.
It was on the Numicius that Aeneas, in the course of fighting
with the Rutulians, was said to have been killed or to have
disappeared from human sight and became identified with
a *deus indiges* of the place. Following the annalists (cf.
Cassius Hemina, fr. 7 P. 'apud Numicium parere desiit . . .:
patris indigetis ei nomen datum') Livy cautiously says
(i. 2. 6) 'situs est, quemcumque eum dici ius fasque est (i.e.
whether god or hero) super Numicum flumen: Iouem in-
digetem appellant'. Virgil himself, ending his story with the
death of Turnus, leaves the fate of Aeneas unrecorded, but
in Jupiter's words at xii. 794 f. the legend is implicit: 'in-
digetem Aenean scis ipsa et scire fateris / deberi caelo fatisque
ad sidera tolli'. (Ovid repeats it, making his mother Venus
rescue him and give him immortality, *Met.* xiv. 607 f. 'con-
tigit os fecitque deum, quem turba Quirini / nuncupat in-
digetem temploque arisque recepit': cf. Tib. ii. 5. 43 f. 'illic
sanctus eris, cum te ueneranda Numici / unda deum caelo
miserit indigetem'; Juv. 11. 63 'alter (Aeneas) aquis, alter
(Hercules) flammis ad sidera missus'.) Dionysius of Hali-
carnassus (i. 64. 5), travelling in Virgil's time, saw on the
Numicius a ἡρῷον dedicated to Aeneas under the title of πατὴρ
θεὸς χθόνιος (i.e. *pater indiges*): the Verona scholia on *Aen.* i.
259 offer the information that the consuls and the pontifices
went out to the shrine of 'Aeneas Indiges' on the Numicius
once a year to offer sacrifice. On the significance of these
titles and of that of 'Lar Aineias' on an inscription found
near Lavinium see A. Alföldi, *Early Rome and the Latins*
(Michigan, 1963), 252 ff.
151. **Thybrim:** see on 30.
152. **satus Anchisa:** the same epic periphrasis in v. 244, 424,
vi. 331.

　　ordine ab omni: Servius bravely attempts to explain 'ex
omni qualitate dignitatum, quod apud Romanos in legatione

mittenda hodieque seruatur', but the phrase looks like a
tibicen (see on 129).

153. centum oratores: *orator* has its old sense of 'spokesman'
as in viii. 505, xi. 100, 331: so in Ennius, *Ann.* 207 V. 'orator
sine pace redit regique refert rem' and in formal phrases in
Plautus (*Stich.* 290 f. 'aequiust eram . . . oratores mittere ad
me donaque', 490 f. 'oratores sunt populi, summi uiri: Am-
bracia ueniunt huc legati publice') and in Livy (e.g. ii. 32. 8
'placuit oratorem ad plebem mitti Menenium Agrippam',
xxxvi. 27. 2 'pacis petendae oratores ad consulem miserunt').
The extravagant number (repeated for Latinus' proposed
embassy to Aeneas, xi. 331) is a piece of heroic colour or
'*Märchenatmosphäre*', like the hundred pillars of Latinus'
palace (170), Galaesus' hundred plough-oxen (539), Latinus'
three hundred horses (275), or the three hundred temples
dedicated by Augustus on the shield (viii. 716).

   augusta ad moenia: cf. 170 'tectum augustum' (the only
other appearance of the adjective in the *Aeneid*). Servius'
explanation of *augusta* as *augurio consecrata* is essentially
right (cf. Ovid, *F.* i. 609 f. 'sancta uocant augusta patres:
augusta uocantur / templa sacerdotum rite dicata manu';
Suet. *Aug.* 7 'loca . . . in quibus augurato quid consecratur
dicantur'), though it is too narrow. *augustus*, belonging to
the family of *augere* (as Ovid rightly says, *F.* i. 611 f. 'huius
et augurium dependet origine uerbi / et quodcumque sua
Iuppiter auget ope'), is used of what has received divine
blessing: *augustus* is formed from a noun-stem **augus* (as
angustus from **angus*) which survives also in the masculine
augur for the person who conveys blessing. The religious use
of the adjective is common in Cicero (e.g. *Har. Resp.* 12
'quod tres pontifices statuissent, id semper . . . satis sanctum,
satis augustum, satis religiosum esse uisum est', *Verr.* ii. 5. 186
'augustissimo et religiosissimo in templo', *Dom.* 137 'in loco
augusto consecratam aram', *N.D.* ii. 62 'auguste sancteque
Liberum . . . consecrauerunt') and in Livy.

154. ramis uelatos Palladis: i.e. carrying olive branches in their
hands, the sign of peace or of supplication (cf. xi. 101
'uelati ramis oleae ueniamque rogantes', viii. 116 'paci-
feraeque manu ramum praetendit oliuae'): they were often
wreathed with wool (viii. 128 'uitta comptos uoluit prae-
tendere ramos'). For the use of *uelatus* cf. Plaut. *Amph.* 257
'uelatis manibus orant ignoscamus peccatum suom';
uelamenta was the technical term for these suppliant's
tokens: cf. Livy xxix. 16. 6 'uelamenta supplicum, ramos
oleae, ut Graecis mos est, porgentes'; Ovid, *Met.* xi. 279
'uelamenta manu praetendens supplice'.

155. pacem exposcere: a ritual phrase, 'ask for peace' (*posco*, from earlier **porc-sco*, is a cognate of *prec-or*): cf. iii. 261 'uotis precibusque iubent exposcere pacem'; Livy i. 16. 3 'pacem precibus exposcunt', vii. 40. 5 'quod deos immortales inter nuncupanda uota expoposci'.

156. haud mora: the paratactic phrase is common in Virgil: e.g. *Geo.* iv. 548, *Aen.* iii. 207, 548, v. 140, 368, vi. 177.

157. humili . . . fossa, 'with a shallow trench': cf. v. 755 'urbem designat aratro'. Servius says that the plough was drawn by a bull and a cow and that care was taken that the earth should be thrown to the inside.

158. molitur locum: cf. *Geo.* i. 494 'agricola incuruo terram molitus aratro', and see on 127.

159. pinnis atque aggere: the settlement is fortified like a Roman camp. *pinna,* 'feather' (the word is often confused in manuscripts with *penna,* 'wing', with which it is probably unconnected), is used in a variety of technical senses: here of the twined boughs or stakes fixed on the top of a *uallum* as an 'entanglement' or *chevaux de frise*: so in Caesar, e.g. *B.G.* vii. 72. 4 '(uallo) loricam ("parapet") pinnasque adiecit'.

160. Latinorum: the hypermetric hexameter, in which the final syllable is elided into the following line, is found before Virgil only in isolated instances in Lucilius (547 M.), Lucretius (v. 849) and Catullus (64. 298: there may be a second in the elegiac 115. 5); that it appeared in Ennius may be implied by Seneca's observation quoted by Gellius xii. 2. 10: 'Vergilius . . . non ex alia causa duros quosdam uersus et enormes et aliquid supra mensuram trahentes interposuit quam ut Ennianus populus agnosceret in nouo carmine aliquid antiquitatis'. Virgil has twenty other instances, one with *-em* (*Geo.* i. 295), two with *-a* (*Geo.* ii. 69, iii. 449), the rest with *-que* (usually the second of a pair of *-ques*) or *-ue*. It has been suggested that the practice was adopted from Hellenistic poets who, with their taste for the unusual, derived it from some Homeric lines in which $Z\hat{\eta}\nu$ ending a line was taken to be an elided $Z\hat{\eta}\nu a$, but it is not found in extant Alexandrian hexameter verse and the only Greek example is in an elegiac epigram of Callimachus (41 Pf. οὐκ οἶδ' / εἰ). Virgil's use of it seldom seems to convey any rhetorical or dramatic effect: for possible exceptions see iv. 629 (where Dido's last speech ends with a hypermetric *-que*), x. 781. Later epic poets rarely use it. The list of hypermetric lines given by Lachmann, Lucr. p. 81, is supplemented by L. Quicherat in *R. de Ph.* xiv (1890), 51 ff.

161. muroque subibant: so the manuscripts here (except R, which has *murosque*), supported by Servius: at ix. 371 in the same phrase they are divided between *muroque* and *murosque* and Priscian there supports the dative. Virgil's practice seems to have been variable: cf. vi. 13 'subeunt Triuiae lucos', viii. 125 'subeunt luco'.

163. domitant . . . currus: i.e. their teams: cf. *Geo.* i. 514 'neque audit currus habenas', iv. 389 'iuncto bipedum curru . . . equorum', *Aen.* xii. 287 'infrenant alii currus', 350.

164. aūt ācrīs tēndūnt ārcūs: the heavily spondaic opening, contrasting with the liveliness of 163, conveys the sense of effort: the effect is repeated in ix. 665 'intendunt acris arcus': similarly vii. 380 (of children fascinated by a top) 'intenti ludo exercent', vi. 643 (of wrestlers) 'contendunt ludo et fulua luctantur harena'. For other examples of the dramatic effect of a succession of spondees see i. 118 'apparent rari nantes in gurgite uasto', v. 256 'longaeui palmas nequiquam ad sidera tendunt', ix. 30 f. 'ceu septem surgens sedatis amnibus altus / per tacitum Ganges', iv. 404–6 (three lines with fourteen spondees). For the assonance in *acris . . . arcus* see on 491.

   acris . . . arcus: *acer* is elsewhere applied to human beings (and occasionally to animals), to emotional concepts like *animus, sensus, cura, dolor*, or to objects which make a sharp impact on the senses (e.g. *tibia* Hor. *Od.* i. 12. 1 f., *hiems Od.* i. 4. 1, *sonitus* Virgil, *Geo.* iv. 409, *umores* Cic. *N.D.* ii. 59, *rubor* Sen. *N.Q.* i. 14. 2, metaphorically *egestas* Lucr. iii. 65, *bellum* Cic. *Balb.* 14, *supplicium* Cic. *Cat.* i. 3). The use of the adjective here (repeated in ix. 665) is unparalleled: it must be taken to refer to the 'sharp, quick spring of the bow' (Page). A contrast with *lenta* (a regular epithet for the tough shaft of a missile: cf. xi. 650 'lenta hastilia': see on 28) seems to be intended, but the antithesis is not exact.

165. lacessunt: i.e. *alius alium*.

   ictu : in boxing: cf. v. 377 'uerberat ictibus auras', 428 abduxere . . . capita ardua ab ictu', 457 'dextra ingeminans ictus'.

166. cum takes up *iamque* of 160 after the parenthetical description of 162–5.

167. ingentis: 'bene nouitatis ostendit opinionem: ingentes enim esse quos primum uidemus opinamur' (Servius).

   in ueste: for *in* used of costume cf. iv. 518 'in ueste recincta', v. 179 'madidaque fluens in ueste', xii. 169 'puraque in ueste sacerdos'; Prop. iv. 2. 37 f. 'ibo / mundus demissis institor in tunicis': so in prose, Cic. *Phil.* viii. 32 'cum est in sagis ciuitas', *Cat.* ii. 4 'quem amare in praetexta coeperat': similarly of other accompaniments, iii. 595 'patriis

ad Troiam missus in armis', v. 37 'horridus in iaculis et pelle
Libystidis ursae'; Enn. *Ann.* 506 V. 'leuesque secuntur in
hastis'; Man. ii. 241 'fulget Centaurus in arcu'; Stat. *Theb.*
i. 712 'horruit in pharetris'; Pliny *N.H.* xxxiii. 30 'maior
pars iudicum in ferreo anulo fuit'; Tac. *Hist.* iv. 3. 2 'pati-
bulo adfixus in isdem anulis quos acceptos a Vitellio gesta-
bat'; Apul. *Met.* iii. 5 'cum me uiderent in ferro'.

   reportat, 'carries the news that ...': cf. ix. 193 'uiros qui
certa reportent': the use with a noun-clause occurs only here
in classical Latin.

169. medius: i.e. surrounded by his court: cf. *Geo.* iv. 436 'con-
sedit scopulo medius' ('with his herd round about him'),
Aen. xii. 564 'celso medius stans aggere fatur'.

170 ff. In this anachronistic picture of the massive, colonnaded
temple-palace crowning the citadel of Latinus' town Virgil
clearly has in mind the Capitoline temple of his own day (see
W. A. Camps, *C.Q.* liii [1959], 54): all the details of his de-
scription have their counterparts there—the use of the temple
as a council-chamber, the statues of kings (Appian, *B.C.* i. 16)
and *uiri illustres* (Suet. *Cal.* 34) in the forecourt, the *epulum
Iouis* on 13 September when after sacrifice the senate
feasted in the temple as the guests of the Capitoline triad
(Livy xxxviii. 57. 5; Val. Max. ii. 1. 2; Gell. xii. 8. 2), and
the ceremonial inauguration there of the consuls, successors
of the king, at the beginning of their year of office (Ovid, *F.*
i. 79).

170. The heavy line of spondees suggests the solemnity of the
scene. For *ingens* giving weight to the line cf. 791, iv. 181,
vi. 552, 616, xii. 897: for Virgil's use of the word see on 29.
   augustum: see on 153.

170–3. tectum ... hic: for the formula of description see on
563 ff.

171. urbe ... summa: i.e. on the citadel or *arx*.
   Laurentis ... Pici: Virgil has forgotten that in 61 he makes
Latinus himself found the town and bestow the name
Laurentes.

172. horrendum siluis et religione: cf. viii. 597 f. 'lucus ... /
religione patrum late sacer'. *religio* is man's natural feeling
of awe in the presence of what he finds inexplicable by his
own experience and ascribes to the supernatural: thence it
comes to include the worship or ritual in which that feeling
is expressed: on the history of the notion see W. Warde
Fowler, *Roman Essays and Interpretations* (Oxford, 1920),
7 ff.; H. Nettleship, *Contrib. to Lat. Lex.* 570 ff.

174. omen erat: i.e. the performance of the ceremony here
was necessary to give an auspicious start to the reign. The

reference to the *fasces* is an anachronism: archaeological evidence (see H. H. Scullard, *The Etruscan Cities and Rome* [London, 1967], 223) supports the statement of Silius (viii. 483 ff.) that the use of the *fasces* as a symbol of authority originated in Etruria: presumably it came to Rome with the Etruscan kings.

erāt: the 'irrational' lengthening of a short final syllable under the ictus before a vowel is a common feature of Virgilian prosody. There are five other instances with *-at* (*Ecl.* i. 38, *Geo.* iv. 137, *Aen.* v. 853, x. 383, xii. 772) and fifty-one with other terminations: *-et, -it, -ut* (once), *-or, -er, -ur, -as* (once), *-is, -us,* and *-ul* (once); of the possible total of 57, 29 occur at a caesura in the 3rd foot (with *Aen.* iii. 504 and xii. 232 included), fourteen in the 4th (if x. 67 has 'fatis petiit'), seven in the 2nd, and seven in the 5th (see also on 398). A number of these types are already found in Ennius: the others also may have had Ennian precedent. In some cases (notably *-at* and *-or*) the lengthening might represent an original prosody which is observed by Plautus: but in the majority it cannot be so explained as an archaic survival: the nominative termination *-us,* lengthened both by Ennius and by Virgil, was never long, and *-it* is lengthened by both not only in the perfect, where *ī* was the original quantity, but in the 3rd conjugation present.

Such 'irrational' lengthenings are already common in Homer; some can be explained there as relics of an original quantity or as the effect of a lost consonant, *y* or *ϝ*, at the beginning of the following word, but most appear to be due to the influence of the ictus and to a following pause: so, e.g., *Il.* i. 153 δεῦρο μαχησόμενός, ἐπεὶ . . . , 491 οὔτε ποτ' ἐς πόλεμὸν, ἀλλὰ . . ., v. 287 ἤμβροτες οὐδ' ἔτυχες, ἀτὰρ . . ., *Od.* viii. 283 εἴσατ' ἴμεν ἐς Λῆμνον. The practice was continued by the Hellenistic poets.

It is impossible to find any dramatic purpose in Virgil's practice (there is none discernible in Homer's) and unnecessary to look for technical explanations (F. Vollmer in *Sitz. Bay. Akad.,* Phil.-Hist. Kl. 1917, 19 ff.; R. G. Kent in *Mélanges Marouzeau* [Paris, 1948], 302 ff.; F. W. Shipley in *T.A.P.A.* lv [1924], 142 ff.). Virgil's purpose is literary, not dramatic, suggestion: he is recalling Ennian effects and, like Ennius, echoing Homeric rhythms. For a special case of such reminiscence, the lengthening of a short final syllable in the fifth foot before a Greek word, see on 398; for the irregular lengthening of *-que* see on 186.

175. **ariete:** for the trisyllabic scansion, *-i-* being given consonantal value, cf. xi. 890 *arịetat,* ix. 674 *abịetibus,* xi. 667

abiete, ii. 442, v. 589 *parietibus*, vii. 769 *Paeoniis*, xii. 401
Paeonium, *Geo.* ii. 482 *fluuiorum*, iv. 243 *stelio*, *Aen.* vi. 33
omnia, vii. 237 *precantia*. This device, already found in
Ennius (*Ann.* 94 V. *auium*, 436 *insidiantes*), and often serving
(as here) to admit a word whose quantities make it other-
wise unusable in verse, is to be distinguished from synizesis,
the coalescence of two vowels: see on 33 'alueo'. *u* is simi-
larly given consonantal value in v. 432, xii. 905 *genua*, *Geo.*
i. 397, ii. 121 *tenuia*.

176. **perpetuis mensis:** they sat on benches at long undivided
tables in the manner of the heroic age instead of reclining
on couches: cf. Ovid, *F.* vi. 305 f. 'ante focos olim scamnis
considere longis / mos erat et mensae credere adesse deos.'
The old practice survived in the country (cf. Columella's rule
for the *uilicus*, xi. 1. 19 'nec nisi sacris diebus accubans
cenet'): even after the introduction of couches for men the
custom was for women (Val. Max. ii. 1. 2) and children eating
with their elders (Suet. *Claud.* 32; Tac. *Ann.* xiii. 16) to sit.

177. **ueterum:** see on 204.

ex ordine, 'one after another', 'in a row': cf. 139 above.

177 f. **effigies . . . e cedro:** for the prepositional phrase at-
tached to a noun cf. v. 266 'geminos ex aere lebetas', xi. 10
'clipeum ex aere': similarly iv. 457 'fuit . . . de marmore
templum', xi. 15 f. 'de rege superbo / primitiae'.

178. **antiquo e cedro:** for the wooden statues of primitive times
cf. Tib. 1. 10. 19 f. 'tunc melius tenuere fidem cum paupere
cultu / stabat in exigua ligneus aede deus', ii. 5. 28 'facta
agresti lignea falce Pales'; Prop. iv. 2. 59 f. 'stipes acernus
eram, properanti falce dolatus, / ante Numam grata pauper
in urbe deus'.

Virgil's *cedrus* (cf. 13) is probably not the tall oriental
conifer (the cedar of Lebanon) which we call cedar but a
juniper (*juniperus oxycedrus*) which is native to central Italy.

Italusque paterque Sabinus: there is clear evidence of lack
of revision in the fact that Latinus is here given a quite dif-
ferent pedigree from that assigned to him in lines 47–9. There
he is descended from Saturn through Picus and Faunus:
Picus is here, in a prominent place, and so is Saturn, but
Faunus has disappeared; Italus and Sabinus, eponyms of
Italian peoples, are also among his forebears and another
Italian deity, Janus, keeps Saturn company (cf. viii. 357 f.).
For *-que . . . -que* see on 186.

e cedro, Italusque: hiatus after a long vowel under the
ictus at a caesura occurs in Virgil:

    (*a*) in the third foot (as here and at 226) seventeen times
    (six times in *Ecl.*, four in *Geo.*, seven in *Aen.*);

(b) in the fourth foot nine times (once in *Ecl.*, twice in
Geo., six times in *Aen.*);
(c) in the second foot five times (three times in *Geo.*, twice
in *Aen.*);
(d) in the fifth foot (see on 631) thirteen times (three times
in *Ecl.*, twice in *Geo.*, eight times in *Aen.*).

All these types have precedent in Homer and are continued
by the Alexandrians: (d) is common in Theocritus. In some
instances, particularly those of (a) in *Ecl.*,[1] those of (c) in
Geo. and those of (d), reminiscence of Greek rhythm is other-
wise suggested by the presence of Greek words and/or by
a spondaic fifth foot. While in some cases the hiatus occurs
at a marked pause, more often there is no marked break in
sense: often the line consists of an enumeration and the
hiatus is followed by *et* or *aut*, and while dramatic point
has been read into such instances as *Aen.* iii. 606 'si pereo,
hominum manibus periisse iuuabit', or iv. 235 'quid struit?
aut qua spe inimica in gente moratur', elsewhere (as in the
Homeric instances) there seems to be none, e.g. xii. 535 f.
'ille ruenti Hyllo animisque immane frementi / occurrit'.

There is one example of hiatus after an unstressed long
syllable at the end of the first foot (which also has Homeric
precedent, e.g. *Il.* ii. 209, *Od.* xi. 188)—*Geo.* i. 437, a transla-
tion of a line of Parthenius from which it takes over not this
but two other metrical Graecisms.

Twice a short final vowel stands in hiatus, once at the
caesura in the third foot (*Ecl.* 2. 53 'addam cerea pruna:
honos erit huic quoque pomo'), once at a marked pause at
the end of the fourth (*Aen.* i. 405 'et uera incessu patuit dea.
ille ubi matrem'). Both patterns are Homeric.

179. uitisator: Accius uses the compound of Dionysus, fr.
240 R. (*Bacchae*) 'o Dionyse, optime pater, uitisator, Semela
genitus'. The *falx*, the vine-dresser's knife, is the symbol of
Saturn (Fest. 432 L.; Plut. *Q.R.* 42: cf. Ovid, *F.* i. 234 'fal-
cifer ... deus', v. 627 'falcifero ... seni'; Juv. 13. 39 f.), but
this line must refer to Sabinus.

seruans sub imagine falcem, 'keeping his knife in repre-
sentation': Ovid is fond of the phrase *sub imagine*, but always
qualifies it with an adjective or a genitive, *Met.* i. 213 'deus
humana lustro sub imagine terras', iii. 250 '(canes) dilacerant
falsi dominum sub imagine cerui', xiii. 714 f. 'uersique uident
sub imagine saxum / iudicis', *F.* vi. 613 'signum erat in solio

---

[1] *Ecl.* 7. 53 has both (a) and (d): *Geo.* i. 281 has both (a) and at the
end of the fifth foot the shortening of a long vowel in hiatus, regular
in Greek but rare in Latin.

residens sub imagine Tulli': cf. Man. v. 408 'institor aequoreae uaria sub imagine mercis'.

180. Iani bifrontis: Janus is the god of the city-gate and appears in that role in 610 below as guardian of the Gates of War: for the legend which made him a king in Latium (and co-ruler with Saturn), see on viii. 357 f.

182. ob, 'in the cause of': not a common use but regular in this reference (so, e.g., Cic. *Sest.* 83 'ob rem publicam interfecto'). The line is repeated from vi. 660 'hic manus ob patriam pugnando uulnera passi'.

183. sacris in postibus arma: cf. iii. 286 f. 'aere cauo clipeum, magni gestamen Abantis, / postibus aduersis figo', v. 359 f. 'clipeum efferri iussit . . . / Neptuni sacro Danais de poste refixum'.

184. captiui . . . currus: cf. ii. 765 'captiua uestis': the use is common in prose, e.g. Caes. *B.C.* ii. 5 'captiuae naues'; Livy x. 46. 6 'captiua pecunia'. The chariot of heroic times was light: Conington cites *Il.* x. 505, where Diomede speaks of carrying off Rhesus' chariot over his shoulder.

 curuae . . . secures: i.e. battle-axes with a curved edge: the *securis* is carried by Italian warriors in 510 and 627, by the Amazons in xi. 656, by Camilla in xi. 696.

185. cristae capitum: cf. Lucr. ii. 632 'terrificas capitum quatientes numine cristas': similarly *Aen.* x. 638 f. 'iubas . . . capitis'.

 portarum . . . claustra: bars from the gates of captured cities.

186. spiculaque clipeique: the repeated *-que* connecting a pair of words, usually parallel in sense or in form, usually nouns but sometimes verbs or other forms (e.g. iv. 83 'auditque uidetque', 581 'rapiuntque ruuntque', 589 'terque quaterque', vii. 32 'circumque supraque', ix. 787 'miseretque pudetque'), is an epic mannerism, an artificial device going back to Ennius, who adopted it to secure the metrical convenience of Homer's τε . . . τε. For the use of it in Plautus, always significantly in passages with some elevation of style, and in Horace see E. Fraenkel, *Plautinisches im Plautus* (Berlin, 1922), 209 ff.; E. Löfstedt, *Synt.* ii. 306. Virgil uses it more than 150 times in the *Aeneid*: occasionally the *-que*s connect units of more than one word, e.g. i. 87 'clamorque uirum stridorque rudentum', ii. 313 'clamorque uirum clangorque tubarum': rarely the phrases connected are not parallel, e.g. v. 521 'ostentans artemque pater arcumque sonantem', viii. 277 'uelauitque comas foliisque innexa pependit'.

 For the lengthening of the first *-que* under the ictus cf.

xii. 89 'ensemque clipeumque'. Virgil has sixteen other in-
stances, all but one, like these, in the second foot, and all
but two before two consonants (e.g. *Ecl.* 4. 51, *Geo.* iv. 222
'terrasque tractusque', *Geo.* i. 371 'Eurique Zephyrique',
Geo. iv. 336 'Drymoque Xanthoque', *Geo.* i. 352 'aestusque
pluuiasque', *Aen.* xii. 181 'fontisque fluuiosque', ix. 767
'Noemonaque Prytanimque', xii. 443 'Antheusque Mnestheus-
que', viii. 425 'Brontesque Steropesque'): two occur before
single consonants (*Aen.* iii. 91 'liminaque laurusque', xii.
363 'Chloreaque Sybarimque'). The practice is an imita-
tion of Homer's lengthening of τε both regularly, according
to Greek usage, before two consonants and irregularly before
a single consonant (e.g. εἶδός τε μέγεθός τε: ἀπήμονά τε λιαρόν
τε: *Aen.* ix. 767 comes directly from Homer): it is not found
in the extant fragments of Ennius, but Accius ends a
hexameter with *metellique caculaeque* (fr. 2 M.). Ovid con-
tinues the practice (with twelve instances) and lengthens
-que before a single consonant oftener than Virgil.

Apart from this treatment of *-que*, lengthening of a final
short vowel appears only at two places, *Aen.* iii. 464 and
xii. 648: both lines have been plausibly emended (see A. E.
Housman in *C.Q.* xxi [1927], 10).

187 f. sedebat ... gerebat: far from avoiding the 'jingle' pro-
duced by 'grammatical rhyme' at the end of successive lines,
Virgil has sixteen instances of it, nearly all with imperfect or
participial forms. (For an extreme instance see viii. 646–8,
653, 656–7.) Some of these have been taken to emphasize a
continuity of action, some to mark a conclusion; but any such
significance is hard to find in vi. 843 f. 'potentem ... seren-
tem' or x. 804 f. 'arator ... uiator' and harder still to find
in vii. 796 f. 'Labici ... Numici'. Nor can these cases pro-
perly be separated from (*a*) similar rhymes occurring at other
points in successive lines (e.g. in the fifth foot at xi. 843 f.
'coluisse Dianam / ... gessisse pharetras'), (*b*) similar
rhymes within one line (often 'framing' a line, e.g. iv. 505
'erecta ingenti taedis atque ilice secta', vi. 518 'ducebat
Phrygias; flammam media ipsa tenebat', xi. 886 'defenden-
tum armis aditus inque arma ruentum'), (*c*) the large number
of final assonances which just fall short of rhyme (e.g. vi.
485 f. 'tenentem ... frequentes', viii. 359 f. 'subibant ...
uidebant', ix. 250 f. 'tenebat ... rigabat'), and (*d*) those
cases in which an unemphatic word is repeated at the same
point in successive lines (e.g. v. 71 f. 'tempora ramis. / ...
tempora myrto', vi. 900 f. 'litore (*codd.*; limite *recc.*, which
Mynors accepts) portum / ... litore puppes'). So far as these
assonances are deliberate, one is driven to the conclusion

that, like many instances of alliteration (see Appendix), they have no significance in themselves but constitute a formal element of symmetry the principles of whose particular application elude us. (See H. T. Johnstone in *C.R.* x [1896], 9 ff.; R. G. Austin in *C.Q.* xxiii [1929], 46 ff.; E. Norden, *Aeneis VI*, pp. 392 f.) For successive lines ending with the same word see on viii. 271 f.

Picus (see on 47 ff.) occupies the place of honour (*ipse*) seated and ceremonially arrayed. The *lituus* was a staff curved at the end (Livy i. 18. 7 'baculum sine nodo aduncum tenens')—a form of the priestly or magic wand which appears in many primitive religions—associated in historical times with the augurs (Cic. *Diu*. i. 30 'lituus iste uester quod clarissimum est insigne auguratus'). The *trabea* was a short ceremonial garment (*parua* contrasts it with the long *toga*) worn by the king (Livy i. 41. 6, of Servius Tullius: cf. *Aen*. xi. 334 'sellam regni trabeamque insignia nostri'), by the consuls, as his successors, on solemn occasions (so at the opening of the gates of Janus in 612 below), by the *flamines Dialis* and *Martialis* (Servius on 190), by the Salii (Dion. Hal. ii. 70. 2 χιτῶνας ποικίλους χαλκαῖς μίτραις κατεζωσμένοι καὶ τηβέννας ἐμπεπορπημένοι περιπορφύρους φοινικοπαρύφους ἃς καλοῦσι τραβέας), and by augurs: Servius on 612, quoting Suetonius, *de genere uestium*, distinguishes three forms of *trabea*; 'unum dis sacratum quod est tantum de purpura, aliud regum quod est purpureum, habet tamen album aliquid, tertium augurale de purpura et cocco'. A similar garment seems to have been part of regal costume in Etruria—a wall-painting from Caere shows a king wearing a short embroidered garment of purple: see H. H. Scullard, *The Etruscan Cities and Rome* (London, 1967), pl. 100—and the *trabea*, like the *fasces* (see on 174), may well have been introduced at Rome by the Etruscan kings. Both *trabea* and *lituus* are associated in Roman tradition with Romulus-Quirinus (Ovid, *F*. i. 37 'trabeati cura Quirini', ii. 503 f. 'trabeaque decorus / Romulus', vi. 375 'lituo pulcher trabeaque Quirinus'; Juv. 8. 259 'trabeam et diadema Quirini': cf. Plut. *Rom*. 22. 1, *Cam*. 32. 5): hence the anachronistic description *Quirinali* here and in 612 below. The *ancile* was a shield with a curved indentation on each side (Varro, *L.L.* vii. 43 'ab utraque parte ut Thracum incisa'): the Salii carried *ancilia*, attributed by legend to the time of Numa, in their rites in honour of Mars—a vestige, presumably, of the accoutrements of the primitive warrior. But to find here a connection in Mars-worship between the king and his costume, betwen Picus the bird-satellite of Mars (see on 47 ff. above), Quirinus the Sabine god who was associated

with Mars and with whom Romulus mysteriously came to be
identified, and the *ancile* and *trabea* which in historical times
belonged to the priests of Mars, is to credit Virgil with the
knowledge of a modern anthropologist: all he is doing here is
to give to these ritual objects (as he gives to the civic symbol
of the *fasces* in 173 above) an antiquity even more remote
than familiar legend gave them.

lituo appears to be attached by zeugma to *succinctus*,
which properly applies only to *trabea*. (Or is *Quirinali lituo*
a descriptive ablative parallel to *succinctus trabea*?)

189 ff. Picus ... alas: the story in Ovid, who relates it at length
(*Met.* xiv. 312 ff.), is that Circe, the Sun's daughter, fell in
love with Picus at first sight and when he repelled her ad-
vances, remaining faithful to his *coniunx* Canens, took her
revenge by turning him into a bird by her magic. That fits
capta cupidine here but not *coniunx*. Servius gets out of the
difficulty by explaining that *coniunx* means 'non quae erat
sed quae esse cupiebat': but while there are places where
coniunx means 'intended bride' (cf. iii. 330 f., ix. 138), there
is none where it means 'intending bride'. On the other hand
two later passages seem to imply that Latinus was descended
from Circe: at vii. 282 she has given Latinus horses from the
stock of her father the Sun and at xii. 164, though she is not
mentioned, Latinus has the Sun as his *auus*.

Here Virgil seems to be conflating the picturesque love-
story with an account in which the father of Latinus is Picus
(not Faunus as in line 47) and his mother not Marica (as
there) but Circe. In [Hesiod], *Theogony* 1011 ff. there is yet
another combination: there Circe is Latinus' mother and
Odysseus his father.

189. equum domitor represents ἱππόδαμος, a common heroic
epithet in Homer: Virgil has it again in 651 (of Lausus) and
in 691 (of Messapus).

equum: the original *-um* form for the second declension
genitive plural survived in regular use in a number of formal
and official expressions, e.g. *numerum, iugerum, modium,
medimnum, socium, fabrum, liberum, triumuirum* (on the ques-
tion of usage see Cic. *Orat.* 155–6); the *-orum* form which sup-
planted it was introduced by analogy from the *-arum* of the
first declension. The archaism belongs to the epic style:
Virgil uses it in *diuum, deum, uirum, superum, equum,
iuuencum, socium, famulum,* in the adjectives *omnigenum* and
magnanimum and in the proper names *Danaum, Teucrum,
Pelasgum, Graium, Italum, Aetolum, Achiuum, Tyrrhenum*:
by a reversal of analogy it is extended to the first declension in
caelicolum, Graiugenum, Aeneadum, Dardanidum, Lapithum.

capta cupidine coniunx: the triple alliteration in the second hemistich is a continuation of an Ennian stylistic pattern which goes back to Saturnian verse: see Appendix. Virgil has about a dozen examples of threefold alliteration in this position (so 486 'custodia credita campi', iv. 29 'secum seruetque sepulcro', viii. 603 'Tyrrheni tuta tenebant', ix. 635 'Rutulis responsa remittunt', 693 'portas praebere patentis'): threefold alliteration in the first hemistich (e.g. xi. 209 'certatim crebris conlucent') is less common. See E. Wölfflin in *A.L.L.* xiv. 515 ff.

190. aurea: for the disyllabic value see on 33.

uersum uenenis, 'transformed by her potions': 'love-charm' is the original meaning of *uenenum* (**uenes-nom* from the stem of *uenus*, a neuter common noun later personified as a feminine): cf. Afranius 380 f. R. 'aetas et corpus tenerum et morigeratio, / haec sunt uenena formosarum mulierum'. So Horace uses it of Medea's potions, *Epod.* 5. 61 f. 'dira barbarae . . . uenena Medeae', *Od.* ii. 13. 8 'uenena Colcha'. Marcian in *Dig.* 48. 8. 3 defines *uenenum* as a 'nomen medium', covering drugs given with beneficial and with harmful intention and including 'id quod amatorium appellatur'.

192. tali intus templo: *templo* is a local ablative and *intus* adverbial (cf. Plaut. *Rud.* 689 f. 'in fano hic intus / Veneris'; Livy xxiv. 10. 6 'in aede intus Sospitae Iunonis'): Munro on Lucr. iv. 1091 argued for the use of *intus* as a preposition with the ablative, but in all his examples (e.g. Lucr. vi. 1169 'flagrabat stomacho flamma ut fornacibus intus') it can be taken as adverbial, as it must be in Lucr. ii. 965 'trepidant in sedibus intus'.

192 f. patria . . . sede sedens: for the combination of noun and verb cf. vi. 506 'magna manis ter uoce uocaui', xii. 482 f. 'magna / uoce uocat'. For the co-ordination of the local ablative and the adjectival phrase cf. v. 327 f. 'iamque fere spatio extremo fessique sub ipsam / finem aduentabant', 498 'extremus galeaque ima subsedit Acestes'.

194 ff. The passage corresponds closely to the description of the first meeting of the Trojans with Dido in i. 520 ff. There also Ilioneus is the spokesman; Dido, who, like Latinus, has been prepared for the strangers and divinely instructed to welcome them, knows, like him, the history of Troy and has her own link with it (*atque equidem memini* at 205 as at i. 619); the Trojans make their request and promise their gratitude in similar terms (for verbal resemblances see vii. 228, 233, 235 and i. 524, 548 f., 545); Dido and Latinus are both presented with treasures from Troy. But while in Book I Ilioneus speaks first and reveals the identity of his party, here Latinus apparently can guess without being told who *ingentes uiri ignota in ueste* must be.

194. placido ... ore (again at xi. 251), 'kindly utterance': *placidus* regularly conveys the notion of good will (as its opposite *implacidus* means 'unkind', not 'unquiet'): see T. E. V. Pearce in *C.R.* lxxxii (1968), 13 f.

195. Dardanidae: the king's opening words show at once that he knows the ties of kinship which bring the Trojans to Italy.

195 f. neque enim ... -que: see on 581.

196. auditi, 'heard of', a not uncommon use: e.g. Plaut. *Curc.* 593 f. 'mulierem peiorem ... non uidi neque audiui'; Prop. iv. 9. 37 'audistisne aliquem, tergo qui sustulit orbem?'; Hor. *Od.* ii. 1. 21 'audire magnos iam uideor duces'; Cic. *Verr.* ii. 2. 79 'quod unquam huiuscemodi monstrum ... audiuimus aut uidimus?'; for the passive use cf., e.g., Ovid, *Met.* vi. 170 f. 'quis furor auditos ... praeponere uisis / caelestes?'; Cic. *N.D.* ii. 6 'auditam esse eam pugnam', *Pis.* 2 'honorem ... uirtuti perspectae non auditae nobilitati deferebat'.

197 f. quae causa rates aut cuius egentis (uos) ... uexit: the expression is illogical; two forms of question, 'quae causa rates aut cuius egestas ... uexit' and 'qua causa aut cuius egentes ... uecti estis', are conflated.

198. uada: see on 24.

199. errore uiae, 'mistaking of the way': cf. iii. 181 'errore locorum'; Livy xxiv. 17. 4 'errore uiarum'. The use of the genitive is not uncommon in prose: so Cic. *Sest.* 82 *nominis, Caec.* 50 *uerborum.*

200. qualia multa reproduces the Homeric formula οἷά τε πολλά: e.g. *Od.* viii. 160 ἄθλων οἷά τε πολλὰ μετ' ἀνθρώποισι πέλονται.

201. portu: i.e. the river-mouth.

202. ignorate: probably 'do not fail to understand (i.e. be assured) that the Latins are the stock of Saturn' (for the omission of *esse* cf. iii. 602 'scio me Danais e classibus unum'): but perhaps 'do not mistake the Latins, Saturn's stock' (for this use of the verb cf. Ter. *Heaut.* 105 'erras si id credis et me ignoras'; Cic. *Rab. Post.* 33 'si me inuitum putas ... defendisse causam, et illum et me uehementer ignoras', *Acad.* ii. 4).

203. Saturni: see on 47 ff.

203 f. haud uinclo ... tenentem: *uinclo* is opposed to *sponte sua, legibus* to *more*: compare Ovid's description of the Golden Age, *Met.* i. 89 f. 'aurea prima sata est aetas quae uindice nullo / sponte sua sine lege fidem rectumque colebat'.

Latinus means that the way of life of the *Saturnia regna*, the
Golden Age of primitive innocence, still has force in his
kingdom: but the picture of a society in which law is un-
necessary hardly fits with the conception of the *fasces*, the
symbol of the enforcement of law, in line 173, and Virgil
adopts a quite different conception in viii. 314 ff., where
man's primitive state is savage and Saturn is the law-giver
who makes the Golden Age by imposing a civilized way of
life.

For the rare combination *haud . . . nec* cf. i. 327 f., iii. 214.

204. ueteris dei: i.e. Saturn: for *uetus* of a legendary figure cf.
177 'ueterum . . . auorum', 254 'ueteris Fauni', 795 'ueteres
Sicani', viii. 356 'ueterum . . . monimenta uirorum', 600
'ueteres . . . Pelasgos'; Cat. 7. 6. 'Batti ueteris . . . sepul-
crum'; Hor. *Od.* ii. 12. 9 'Saturni ueteris'; Stat. *S.* iii. 4. 47 f.
'ueterisque penates / Euandri'; Val. Fl. ii. 473 'nos Ili
ueteris quondam genus'.

se tenentem: equivalent to *se continentem*, living a dis-
ciplined life.

205. atque equidem memini: cf. i. 619 'atque equidem Teu-
crum memini Sidona uenire', *Geo.* iv. 116 ff. 'atque equidem
. . . forsitan . . . canerem'. The use of *atque* to introduce a
fresh point by way of confirmation belongs to the idiom of
ordinary speech: so often in comedy and oratory (e.g. Plaut.
Capt. 354 f. 'soluite istum nunciam, atque utrumque',
584 f. 'uide sis ne quid tu huic temere insistas credere. / atque
ut perspicio, profecto iam aliquid pugnae edidit').

obscurior annis: cf. Ovid, *F.* vi. 103 f. 'obscurior aeuo /
fama'.

206. Auruncos: see on 39.

ferre : after *memini* Virgil prefers the present infinitive,
by which a speaker vividly pictures in his mind's eye an
event which he has witnessed and makes it live again (so
Ecl. 7. 69, 9. 52, *Aen.* i. 619, viii. 157 ff.); he has the perfect,
by which the speaker merely recalls an event as something
in the past, only once, at *Geo.* iv. 125 ff. 'memini . . . uidisse
senem'. *ita* anticipates the following *ut*-clause ('how').

his . . . agris is not to be taken literally: Dardanus'
legendary origins were in Italy but, as the following lines
explain, in another region of it.

207. Dardanus: the Italian version of the legend of Dardanus
which Virgil uses (whatever his source may have been:
Varro [Servius on iii. 167] had followed the Greek tradition
which placed Dardanus' birth in Arcadia) gives him an
origin in Etruria, from which he made his way to Samothrace
and thence to Phrygia: there he became the founder of the

royal house of Troy, which derives its descent from Jupiter
(i. 380, viii. 36) through him. The stemma is:

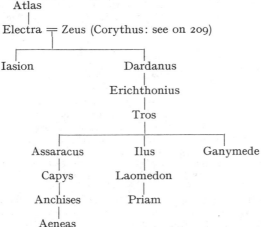

Atlas
|
Electra = Zeus (Corythus: see on 209)
|
┌─────────┴─────────┐
Iasion   Dardanus
                     |
                Erichthonius
                     |
                   Tros
                     |
┌──────────────┬─────┴──────┬──────────────┐
Assaracus   Ilus   Ganymede
| |
Capys   Laomedon
| |
Anchises   Priam
|
Aeneas

penetrarit: so only R, but the indicative *penetrauit* of the
other manuscripts is impossible.

208. Threiciamque ... fertur: Virgil's most prosaic line. The
island off the Thracian coast is Σάμος Θρηικίη in Homer (*Il.*
xiii. 12 f.; Σάμος alone in *Il.* xxiv. 78); the compound Σαμο-
θρηικίη appears in Herodotus.

209. Corythi: Corythus was the legendary name of a town in
Etruria which has generally been identified (as it is by Silius
iv. 720 f.) with Cortona in the foothills of the Apennines near
Lake Trasimene. For its eponymous founder Corythus (whose
name in Greek legend is connected with Arcadia, Diod. iv.
33. 11) we have only the evidence of Servius, who makes him
the mortal husband of the Atlantid Electra who (viii. 135 f.)
is the mother of Dardanus by Jupiter. In iii. 167 ff. the
Trojan Penates, appearing to Aeneas in a vision in Crete, had
told them of their origins in Italy (from which they had pre-
sumably been brought by Dardanus) and had given the
message 'Corythum terrasque requirat / Ausonias'. (For an
attempt to identify Corythus with Tarquinii see N. Horsfall,
J.R.S. lxiii [1973], 68 ff. [discussed by E. L. Harrison and N.
Horsfall in *C. Q.* xxvi (1976), 293-7, J.D.C.])

Corythi Tyrrena ab sede: for the defining genitive of a
place-name cf. iii. 687 'angusta ab sede Pelori' (so Cat. 81. 3
'moribunda ab sede Pisauri'), i. 270 'ab sede Lauini', viii.
479 'urbis Agyllinae sedes'.

210. stellantis regia caeli: cf. *Geo*. i. 503 f. 'iam pridem nobis caeli te regia, Caesar, / inuidet'. *stellans* is a Lucretian epithet (iv. 212 'caelo stellante'): Cicero has it twice, at a few lines' interval (fr. 11 M. 19 'stellanti nocte', 36 'stellanti . . . Olympo').

211. accipit: the present indicates (as in the common *accipimus*, 'we have heard') that the effects of the action continue.

   numerum diuorum altaribus auget, the reading of the old manuscripts (FRMP¹: P² has *numero*), presents no difficulty: 'he increases the number of the gods by his altars'. For *augere numerum* in a similar context cf. Livy i. 7. 10 'te (Herculem) mihi mater . . . aucturum caelestium numerum cecinit': for the change of subject cf. xii. 351 f. 'illum . . . alio . . . / adfecit pretio nec equis aspirat Achilli'. Conington tried to defend *numerum . . . addit*, suggesting that it meant 'heaven adds his number' (or 'adds him as an item') 'to the altars of the gods', but there is no support for such a use of *numerus*.

212. dicta . . . uoce secutus: cf. ix. 636 'clamore sequuntur'.

213. genus egregium Fauni: cf. 556 'egregium Veneris genus' (where, however, *egregium* is ironical): for *genus* of an individual cf. vi. 792, xii. 127, 515.

214. subegit . . . succedere: for the construction cf. iii. 257, viii. 112 f.: so with *adigere* 112 f., with *agere* 239 f., 393. For the extended use of the infinitive in verse see on 35 f.

   uestris: i.e. of your people.

215. regione uiae: 'No star or shore has led us astray from the line of our journey', i.e. we have not gone off course by misreading stars or landmarks. For *regio* cf. ii. 737 'nota excedo regione uiarum', ix. 385 'fallitque timor regione uiarum', xi. 530. The original meaning of *regio* is 'line', which survives in the technical phrase *recta regione* (e.g. Caes. *B.G.* vii. 46. 1; cf. Caes. *B.C.* i. 69. 3 'superare regionem castrorum', 'pass the line of the camp') and in such metaphorical uses as Cic. *Verr.* ii. 5. 181 'nostrae rationis regio et uia' ('line of principle').

216. consilio, omnes, uolentibus all emphasize that their coming is no individual accident.

216 f. urbem adferimur: for the poetic use of the accusative of *terminus ad quem* without a preposition cf. i. 2 f. 'Lauiniaque uenit / litora'.

218. Olympo: 'the heavens', as in *Ecl*. 6. 86 'inuito processit Vesper Olympo', *Aen*. i. 374 'ante diem clauso componet Vesper Olympo', vi. 579 'quantus ad aetherium caeli suspectus Olympum', viii. 280 'deuexo interea propior fit Vesper Olympo', *Geo*. i. 450 '(sol) emenso cum iam decedit Olympo', iii. 223 'reboant siluaeque et longus Olympus'. The use is

already found in Greek: Soph. *Ajax* 1389 'Ολύμπου τοῦδ' ὁ
πρεσβεύων πατήρ ('the heavens that we see').

ueniens: cf. *Geo.* iv. 466 'te ueniente die, te decedente
canebat'; Ovid, *Met.* v. 440 f. 'illam non udis ueniens
Aurora capillis / cessantem uidit', *F.* iii. 877 'tres ubi Luciferos
ueniens praemiserit Eos'.

219. ab Ioue principium: Virgil had already used the phrase
in a different context in *Ecl.* 3. 60, translating ἐκ Διὸς ἀρχώμεσθα.

Dardana: for the proper name used adjectivally without
adjectival suffix see J. Wackernagel, *Vorlesungen*, ii. 59: so
ii. 618 'Dardana arma', vi. 57 'Dardana tela'; similarly 710
'Amiterna cohors', i. 686 'laticem Lyaeum', iii. 280 'Actia
litora', iv. 552 'cineri Sychaeo', vi. 118 'lucis Auernis', viii.
675 'Actia bella', x. 273 'Sirius ardor'.

pubes : see on 105.

220. Iouis de gente: the reference, as the emphatic *Troius*
shows, is to Aeneas' descent from Dardanus through the
Trojan royal house (see on 207): he could claim the same
descent through his mother Venus, but the emphasis is on
his patrilinear pedigree, as it is in Homer (*Il.* xx. 208 ff.).

suprema: cf. x. 350 'Boreae de gente suprema': presum-
ably 'exalted', as in Ennius, *Ann.* 178 V. 'nomine Burrus uti
memorant a stirpe supremo' (*stirps* masc.).

223. ierit: for *ire* used where a modern language would prefer
a more precise or colourful verb cf. xii. 283 f. 'it toto turbida
caelo / tempestas telorum', 451 f. 'ad terras abrupto sidere
nimbus / it mare per medium', ix. 433 f. 'pulchrosque per
artus / it cruor'; Prop. iv. 11. 60 'lacrimas uidimus ire deo'.
See also on viii. 557.

223 f. quibus actus . . . orbis: 'what were the destinies that
drove the two worlds of Europe and Asia to meet': cf. x. 90 f.
'quae causa fuit consurgere in arma / Europamque Asiam-
que'; Cat. 68. 89 'Troia (nefas!) commune sepulcrum Asiae
Europaeque'; Prop. ii. 3. 35 f. 'tanti ad Pergama belli /
Europae atque Asiae causa puella fuit'. As Conington points
out, the opposition of Europe and Asia is post-Homeric and
has its background in the Persian Wars. For *orbis* of a con-
tinent cf. Man. iv. 677 'ad Tanain Scythicis dirimentem fluc-
tibus orbes'.

225 ff. audiit . . . iniqui: the story of Troy is familiar to the
inhabitants of the remotest regions 'both one whom the
world's end where Ocean recoils keeps far away and one
whom the tract of the pitiless sun, that stretches midmost of
the four, severs from us'. The meaning of the descriptive
ablative *Oceano refuso* is best explained by *Geo.* ii. 163 'Iulia
qua ponto longe sonat unda refuso' (of the breakwater of the

Lucrine lake) and by Lucan's reminiscence, viii. 797 f. (the whole world is Pompey's tomb, even the ends of it) 'situs est qua terra extrema refuso / pendet in Oceano'. (In vi. 107 'Acheronte refuso' the participle seems to mean 'flooding over', as it does in Stat. *S*. iv. 3. 73; Sil. xi. 508, but the ocean does not overflow.) Virgil is thinking not of Homer's ἀψόρροος Ὠκεανός (*Il*. xviii. 399), the Ocean which encircles the world and flows back on itself, but of the sea thrown back from the edge of the land in the remote north.

The *plaga solis iniqui in medio quattuor plagarum extenta* is the torrid zone, the middle zone of the five on earth's surface corresponding to the zones in the heavens which Virgil describes in *Geo*. i. 233 ff.: the old poetic word *plaga* for a tract of the sky takes the place of the technical *zona*. For *iniqui* cf. Hor. *Od*. i. 22. 21 f. (with the same reference) 'sub curru nimium propinqui / solis in terra domibus negata'. For *summouet . . . dirimit* cf. *Ecl*. i. 66 'toto diuisos orbe Britannos'; Prop. ii. 10. 17 'si qua extremis tellus se subtrahit oris'.

226. Oceano et: for the hiatus see on 178.

228. diluuio: the 'cataclysm' continues the metaphor of the *tempestas effusa* (222 f.). The form *diluuium* occurs first in Virgil, here and at xii. 205: Lucretius had used *diluuies*.

uasta per aequora: see on 302.

230. innocuum, 'unharmed', i.e. where we shall be safe from molestation: for the rare 'passive' sense (which after Virgil does not reappear till Claudian) cf. x. 301 f. 'carinae . . . innocuae'.

231. indecores: a rare adjective, but Virgil uses it four times elsewhere.

231 f. nec . . . facti, 'not slight will be your renown current among men and gratitude for your great service will not wane': the negative modifies both clauses.

232. gratia facti: cf. iv. 539 'bene apud memores ueteris stat gratia facti'.

234. fata per Aenean, 'by the destiny of Aeneas': cf. ii. 554 'haec finis Priami fatorum'. Virgil (unlike Lucretius) rarely postpones a monosyllabic preposition, and only when it can stand between its noun and an accompanying genitive (as here and, e.g., vi. 58 'corpus in Aeacidae') or when other words also governed by the preposition follow it (e.g. v. 663 'transtra per et remos').

235. fide . . . armis: for the expression cf. Cic. *Fam*. vii. 5. 3 (of Caesar) 'manum tuam istam et uictoria et fide praestantem', *Deiot*. 8 'dextram non tam in bellis neque in proeliis quam in promissis et fide firmiorem'.

236. multi: Ilioneus overstates his case : Dido had proposed alliance with the Trojans (i. 572 'uultis et his mecum pariter considere regnis?') and Acestes in Sicily had been ready to receive those whom Aeneas left behind.

ultro, of an action which in some way goes beyond what was to be expected: the Trojans take the initiative in petition- ing instead of being petitioned, as Apollo in anticipating his answer to inquiry (iii. 155) or Dido in attacking Aeneas before he has time to defend himself (iv. 304; cf. ii. 279, 372). So ii. 145 (the Trojans not only spare Sinon's life but pity him), ii. 193 (the Trojans would not only defend themselves but attack Greece; cf. xi. 286), v. 55 (improbable as it seemed, Aeneas is able to honour his father's tomb), v. 446 (the boxer not only misses but falls), ix. 127 (far from losing confidence, Turnus rallies his men; cf. x. 830, xii. 3). The English idiomatic use of 'actually' conveys the same sense. (*ultro* has colloquially the implication of an action defying propriety or convention which 'actually' often has: e.g. Plaut. *Men.* 843 'insanire me aiunt ultro.quom ipsi insaniunt', *Aul.* 530; Cic. *Quinct.* 74.)

237. uittas: i.e. the strands of wool with which the olive- branch of the suppliant was wreathed, the στέμματα of *Il.* i. 14: see on 154 and cf. viii. 128 'uitta comptos uoluit prae- tendere ramos'. There is a mild zeugma in the combination of literal and metaphorical senses of *praeferimus*.

precantia: trisyllabic, the *-i-* being given consonantal value. Virgil uses this licence with the termination *-ia* only once elsewhere, vi. 33 'omnia': for other instances see on 175.

239. fata here has the old sense of 'oracular utterance', in which its origin as the participle of **fare* is still alive: cf. vi. 45 'poscere fata' ('ask for an oracle'), i. 382 'data fata secutus'. So in formal prose language, Cic. *Cat.* iii. 9 'ex fatis Sibyllinis', *Diu.* i. 100 'ex fatis quae Veientes scripta haberent'.

exquirere: for the infinitive after *agere* cf. 393 'agit . . . quaerere'; Hor. *Od.* i. 2. 7 f. 'Proteus pecus egit altos / uisere montes': so with *adigere* (112 f.) and *subigere* (214).

240. imperiis egere suis: Aeneas has used the same words in his defence to Dido, vi. 461 ff.

241. repetit: the subject must be Apollo, not Dardanus: his call has been clear (iii. 94 ff.; cf. iv. 345).

iussis ingentibus: cf. iii. 546 'praeceptis . . . dederat quae maxima'.

242. Tyrrhenum: the Tiber is Tuscan because it rises in Etruria (cf. *Geo.* i. 499 'Tuscum Tiberim', *Aen.* xi. 316 'Tusco . . . amni'; Hor. *Od.* iii. 7. 28 'Tusco . . . alueo': so *Aen.* ii. 781 f. 'Lydius . . . Thybris'), but the epithet has special point here since it was from Etruria that Dardanus had come (209). For *Thybris* see on 30.

fontis uada sacra Numici: cf. 797 f. 'sacrumque Numici / litus': but *sacer* is a general epithet of streams (83 f. 'sacro fonte', *Geo.* iv. 319 'sacrum caput . . . amnis', *Aen.* viii. 72).

243. dat: the omission of the subject—his leader, for whom he is acting—makes the sentence somewhat abrupt.

243 f. fortunae . . . prioris munera: so Dido is presented with 'munera . . . Iliacis erepta ruinis' (i. 647): the parallel (and *munera* in 261) shows that *munera fortunae prioris* here means 'gifts (from Aeneas to Latinus) belonging to his old estate'.

244. receptas, 'rescued', as in v. 80 f. 'recepti / nequiquam cineres', vi. 110 f. 'illum . . . / eripui . . . medioque ex hoste recepi'.

245. auro libabat: cf. i. 739 'pleno se proluit auro'.

246. hoc . . . gestamen erat: *gestare* can be used of what is worn as well as of what is carried in the hand and *gestamen* can include all three of the gifts which follow—the sceptre, the headdress, and the robe: Ilioneus hands them over one by one as he speaks.

247. tiaras: the τιάρας or τιάρα was an oriental headdress, a conical cap (of felt, Herod. vii. 61) which might be highly decorated (Xerxes' was χρυσόπαστος, Herod. viii. 120: Cyrus εἶχε . . . διάδημα περὶ τῇ τιάρᾳ, Xen. *Cyr.* viii. 3. 13): it and the *mitra* (iv. 216, ix. 616) are the only distinctive pieces of Oriental costume (besides the *manicae* of ix. 616) which Virgil gives his Trojans. Like the *mitra*, the *tiaras* had strings under the chin: an Oriental in Val. Flacc. vi. 700 'subligat extrema patrium ceruice tiaran'. Priam can actually be seen wearing a tiara with diadem on a S. Italian vase-painting (A. Baumeister, *Denkmäler des klassischen Altertums* [Leipzig, 1885–8], fig. 792).

248. labor, 'handiwork': the rare concrete sense is probably suggested by Hesiod's ἔργα γυναικῶν: the plural is used concretely in *Geo.* i. 325 'boum labores', *Aen.* viii. 439 (of the Cyclopes) 'coeptos auferte labores'. For the incomplete line see on 129.

249. talibus . . . dictis: for the ablative of attendant circumstances cf. 284, viii. 359.
   Ilionei is quadrisyllabic: see on 33.

249 f. defixa . . . tenet ora: cf. viii. 520 'defixique ora tenebant'.

250. obtutu, of an earnest gaze: so i. 495 'obtutuque haeret defixus in uno', xii. 666 'obtutu tacito'.

250 f. solo haeret repeats the idea of *defixus ora tenet*: his gaze is fixed on the ground but his straining eyes are restlessly moving (*uoluens*: 'rolling' gives the wrong suggestion) in thought as he reflects on the implications of the situation for himself; cf. xii. 939. *uoluere oculos* occurs twice elsewhere (iv. 363, viii. 618) but in these passages the phrase refers to shifting the eyes from point to point.

251 f. nec purpura regem . . . mouent: *regem* is emphatic—king though he was, he was not attracted by these trappings of royalty: his thoughts were elsewhere.

252. picta, 'embroidered': *pictus* often refers not to painted colour but to embellishment with gold or silver embroidery: so 277 'pictis tapetis', ix. 26 'diues pictai uestis et auri', 582 'pictus acu chlamydem', xi. 777 'pictus acu tunicas et barbara tegmina crurum'; Cic. *Tusc.* v. 61 'textili stragulo magnificis operibus picto'; Juv. 6. 482 'latum pictae uestis considerat aurum'.

253. moratur, 'dwells on': cf. ix. 439 'in solo Volcente moratur'. **conubio:** see on 96.

254. sortem, 'oracle', as *sortes* in 269 below: so iv. 346 'Lyciae . . . sortes'. The use comes from the practice of conveying the response of the oracle on tablets, *sortes* (cf. the story in Cic. *Diu.* i. 76, the *sortes* at Dodona upset by a pet monkey).

255. hunc illum: see on 128.

256. uocari: by destiny: cf. the striking phrase v. 656 'fatis uocantia regna', 'the kingdom which calls us by destiny'.

256 f. paribus . . . auspiciis: i.e. with equal authority, to be taken closely with *regna*: cf. iv. 102 f. (Dido's proposal for a joint sovereignty) 'communem hunc ergo populum paribusque regamus / auspiciis'. The background of the phrase is the distinctively Roman view which conceived of the right to take the auspices (*ius auspiciorum*) which were the preliminary to any important act, as an essential part and symbol of *imperium*.

259. secundent, 'bring to favourable issue': their *augurium* is the omens of 58 ff.; cf. *Geo.* iv. 397 'euentusque secundet', *Aen.* iii. 36 'rite secundarent uisus omenque leuarent'.

261. munera nec sperno, 'I welcome your gifts': an extreme *litotes*; there is no need to think that Latinus is apologizing for a seeming indifference.

rege Latino, 'while Latinus is king': for the emphatic ablative-absolute phrase cf. *Geo.* iv. 326 ff. 'ipsum uitae mortalis honorem / . . . te matre relinquo'.

262. uber agri: cf. i. 531 'potens armis atque ubere glaebae': a rendering of the Homeric οὖθαρ ἀρούρης. *uber* is the exact equivalent of its Greek cognate οὖθαρ, passing from the original meaning of 'udder' to that of fertility (first in *Geo.* ii. 234,

where *uber* by itself is richness of soil): its development into
an adjective is due to the analogy of such adjectives as *acer*.

deerit: disyllabic with the normal synizesis; so *deest* is
monosyllabic at x. 378.

263. si tanta cupido est: cf. vi. 133 'si tantus amor menti, si
tanta cupido est'.

264. iungi . . . properat: see on 56 f.

266. pars . . . pacis: i.e. an essential constituent; so Ovid, *Met.*
ix. 291 'parsque est meminisse doloris'. Tacitus borrows
the phrase, *Hist.* iii. 46. 3 'externo bello inligari pars con-
silii pacisque erat'.

tyranni: τύραννος, an Oriental word which came into
Greek from Asia Minor, is an early borrowing in Latin. In
Virgil's use the word has no suggestion of arbitrary or
despotic power: he does indeed apply it to Mezentius (viii.
483) and to the African princes (iv. 320), but it is also used
of Latinus himself (342), of Aeneas again (by Turnus) (xii.
75), and of Turnus (x. 448).

267. contra, 'in reply'.

268 ff. Servius has a pleasant note on this proposal, which he
thought needed some apology: 'male multi arguunt Vergi-
lium quod Latinum induxit ultro filiam pollicentem, nec
oraculum considerantes, quia Italo dari penitus non poterat,
nec Aeneae meritum, quem decebat rogari: nam antiquis
semper mos fuit meliores generos rogare'.

269. caelo, 'from heaven', going closely with *monstra*, which
here has its primary sense of 'warning', 'omen' (**mone-
strum*): see on 21.

270. generos: see on 98.

271. canunt, 'the prophets declare', with subject unexpressed
as in 79: Latinus repeats the words of the oracle in 98 ff.

272. hunc illum: see on 128.

poscere fata: cf. iv. 614 'et sic fata Iouis poscunt', viii.
11 f. 'Aenean . . . fatis regem se dicere posci', 477 'fatis huc
te poscentibus adfers', v. 707 'quae fatorum posceret ordo'.
At vi. 45 which ends with the same words, *fata* is object,
'seek a divine utterance'.

273. augurat: the archaic active form, used by Ennius, Pacu-
vius, and Accius, survives in formulas in Cicero and Livy.

opto, 'I choose, accept': for this old use cf. i. 425 'optare
locum tecto' (so iii. 109), i. 570 'Erycis finis regemque optatis
Acesten', viii. 503 'externos optate duces'.

274. numero . . . omni, as the passage stands, must mean 'from
his whole number' (cf. i. 170 f. 'septem . . . collectis nauibus
omni / ex numero'), explained by the following line, and not
'for the whole party', as Mackail takes it, comparing 573 f.

'omnis ... / pastorum ... numerus' (cf. also Ovid, *Met.* xi.
525 'miles numero praestantior omni'). But, as he points
out, the lines are overloaded and look like an unrevised
draft 'which would have been worked down'. Virgil might
have thought better of making Latinus part with a third of
his stud.

275. ter centum: the same indefinite large number in *Geo.* i. 15,
Aen. iv. 510, viii. 716.

nitidi: a technical term for animals with good, glossy
coats: cf. iii. 20 f. 'nitentem taurum'; Pliny, *Ep.* ii. 17. 3
'armenta quae ... herbis et tepore uerno nitescunt'.

praesepibus altis: for the 'enhancing' epithet cf. ix. 388,
x. 723 'stabula alta'.

276. ordine, 'in succession': i.e. he makes his presentation to
them one by one.

277. alipedes: Lucretius applies the epithet to stags (vi. 765),
Virgil to horses (xii. 484): the substantival use of *alipes* and
of *sonipes* (iv. 135) as poetic equivalents for *equus* becomes
conventional in later verse.

ostro pictisque tapetis: hendiadys, 'embroidered housings
of purple': see on 15. For *pictus* see on 252.

278 f. aurea ... auro ... aurum: they are caparisoned with
gold (i.e. embroidery on the purple cloths) and have gold
bits. For the pictorial repetition cf. viii. 659 ff. 'aurea ...
aurea ... auro', iv. 138 f. 'ex auro ... in aurum, / aurea':
similarly vii. 743 'aeratae ... aereus', i. 448 f. 'aerea ...
aere ... aënis'.

279. fuluum ... aurum: so Tib. i. 1. 1: for *fuluus* see on 76.

280. iugalis: the substantive is not found again till Silius.

281. spirantis naribus ignem: Lucretius has the phrase of
Diomede's horses (v. 29).

282. daedala Circe: *daedalus*, 'cunning', of the craftsman or of
his work, was an early borrowing from Greek δαίδαλος (En-
nius applied it to Minerva, *inc.* 46 V.), though in extant
Greek the personal use, which is the commoner in Latin,
is not found except in the proper name of the legendary arch-
craftsman Daedalus. It is a favourite word of Lucretius',
who has *daedala tellus* (i. 7, 228), *daedala carmina* (ii. 505 f.),
uerborum daedala lingua (iv. 549), *natura daedala rerum* (v.
234), *daedala signa* (v. 1451); Virgil has *daedala tecta* (of the
homes of the bees, *Geo.* iv. 179).

283. supposita ... creauit, 'bred, stealing them from her
father (the Sun) as bastards from a mother she mated (with
one of the Sun's horses)': the phrase is closely modelled on
Il. v. 268 f. (of the horses which Anchises got from those
of Laomedon) τῆς γενεῆς ἔκλεψεν ἄναξ ἀνδρῶν Ἀγχίσης, / λάθρῃ

Λαομέδοντος ὑποσχὼν θήλεας ἵππους. For the dative with *furata* cf. v. 845 'oculos furare labori'.

284. talibus . . . donis dictisque: for the ablative of attendant circumstances cf. 249.

285. sublimes in equis contrasts their triumphant return, after a successful mission, with their outward journey on foot.

> **pacem reportant:** cf. xi. 511 'fidem . . . reportant'.

286–340. *Juno sees Aeneas happily settled in Italy and her efforts to destroy his people thwarted. Determined to do her worst by delaying what she cannot now prevent, she summons the Fury Allecto to help her by stirring up strife in Italy.*

286. ecce autem: when all seems set in favour of the Trojans, there is a sudden reversal. As in Book I Juno was determined to keep Aeneas out of Italy and laid her plans accordingly (36 ff.), so now she is determined to destroy him in Italy. Again she calls a satellite to her aid, this time a more terrible one than Aeolus. *ecce autem* is a formula of common speech, frequent in comedy, to introduce an unexpected turn of events: for Virgil's dramatic use of it cf. ii. 203, iii. 687, vi. 255, viii. 81, xii. 672.

> **Inachiis . . . ab Argis:** Juno is moving round her favourite seats and making her way from Argos, presumably to Carthage, as in iv. 143 f. Apollo is on his way from his winter home in Lycia to Delos or as in *Od.* v. 282 Poseidon is on his way from the Ethiopians when he sees Odysseus.

> **Argis:** the masculine plural form is regular in Latin ('dicimus . . . oppidum graecanice *hoc Argos*, . . . latine *Argi*', Varro, *L.L.* ix. 89) and in the oblique cases invariable. Horace's use of the neuter singular, the only form which exists in Greek, in *Od.* i. 7. 9 is appropriate to lyric but exceptional. (The same curious change occurs in modern languages: English makes 'Lyon' and 'Marseille', and French 'London' and 'Dover', into plurals.) For Inachus see on 372.

287–9. tenebat et . . . prospexit: for the characteristically Virgilian paratactic expression, where prose and earlier poets would prefer subordination, see E. Norden, *Aeneis VI*, pp. 378 ff. A sentence like vii. 5–7, where the main verb is preceded by three subordinate temporal expressions (two ablatives absolute and a *postquam* clause), is rare in Virgil.

287. auras . . . tenebat: cf. iii. 192 'altum tenuere rates', v. 8 'pelagus tenuere rates'.

288 f. longe . . . prospexit: so xi. 909.

289. ab usque Pachyno, 'right from Pachynus', the promontory of SE. Sicily which Aeneas had passed at iii. 699. For

the position of the strengthening *usque* cf. xi. 262 f. 'Protei
... adusque columnas / exsulat', 317 'finis super usque
Sicanos'.

290. moliri tecta: see on 127.

    fidere terrae: cf. ix. 378 'fidere nocti'.

291. fixa, 'stabbed': the metaphor is perhaps suggested by *Il.*
v. 399 ὀδύνῃσι πεπαρμένος.

292. quassans caput: a gesture of anger or dejection as in xii.
894: cf. Caecilius 271 f. R. 'si quassante capite tristes in-
cedunt'; Plaut. *Merc.* 600 'tristis incedit ... quassat caput',
Asin. 403 'quassanti capite incedit'; Lucr. ii. 1164 'iamque
caput quassans grandis suspirat arator'. So in Homer, *Od.*
v. 285 κινήσας δὲ κάρη προτὶ ὃν μυθήσατο θυμόν.

293 ff. The thwarted Juno's outburst in these lines clearly re-
calls her soliloquy in i. 37 ff. Her indignant *ast ego* is repeated
from i. 46 and her *uincor* points back to *uictam* in i. 37. There
is the same bitter irony in *quippe* there (i. 39) and *credo* here,
the same comparison with more favoured divinities, there
Pallas, here Mars and Diana.

293 f. fatis contraria nostris / fata Phrygum: for the idea of
destinies independently working out and conflicting with
each other cf. i. 238 f. 'hoc equidem occasum Troiae tris-
tisque ruinas / solabar fatis contraria fata rependens' (com-
pensating the unhappy destiny of Troy with the happy
destiny promised to Aeneas). Cf. ix. 135 ff. and see refs.
cited on 313 ff.

294. Phrygum: emphatically placed, the name is no doubt
contemptuous: so it can be taken elsewhere when it is used
by Troy's enemies, e.g. by Juno herself (iv. 103), by Amata
(vii. 358), by Allecto (430), by Turnus (579, ix. 134, xii. 99),
by Numanus (ix. 599), by the Latin matrons (xi. 484). That
contemptuous colour is quite un-Homeric—Homer's Phry-
gians are a warlike race—and is a reflection of later associa-
tions with Cybele-worship and of the conventional Roman
attitude to Eastern peoples. But even in Virgil that colour is
not always to be found: see i. 468, v. 785, x. 255.

    Sigeis: i.e. the plains of Troy, from the promontory of
Sigeum in the Troad.

295. num capti potuere capi?, 'Let themselves be defeated in
defeat? Not they!'. The striking conceit is borrowed from
Ennius, *Ann.* 358 f. V. 'quae (sc. Pergama) neque Dardaniis
campis potuere perire / nec, cum capta, capi nec, cum com-
busta, cremari'. It appears in another form in Numanus'
taunt (ix. 599) 'bis capti Phryges'.

    potuere: see on 309.

296. per ignis: for the preposition with the second of a pair of

substantives cf. v. 512 'Notos atque atra . . . in nubila',
vi. 416 'informi limo glaucaque . . . in ulua', 692 'quas . . .
terras et quanta per aequora'.

297. at, credo: ironically, Juno offers the suggestion that her
powers have been failing, only to dismiss it with *quin etiam*.

298. odiis: i.e. hatred shown in a series of acts or on a series of
occasions: cf. iv. 623, v. 786. But see on 445.

299. patria excussos: for this vigorous phrase ('flung out of
their country') cf. Turnus' 'quae uia clausos / excutiat
Teucros uallo' (ix. 67 f.).

300. ausa continues the irony—'I did not lack courage: I pur-
sued them over the oceans'. Conington explains as 'τλᾶσα,
I who brought myself to follow them': but that common
meaning of τλῆναι is conveyed in Latin by *posse* (see on 309,
potui), not by *audere*.

While Virgil often omits *est*, omission of the first and second
persons is much rarer: *sum* is suppressed here and at ii. 792,
v. 414; *es* at i. 237, v. 687, x. 827; *sumus* at i. 558, ii. 25, 651;
estis at i. 202, v. 192. All these instances occur with de-
ponent or quasi-deponent verbs.

301. absumptae in Teucros, 'spent': cf. Cat. 64. 242 'anxia in
assiduos absumens lumina fletus'.

302. The line is a reminiscence of Catullus, 64. 156 'quae Syrtis,
quae Scylla rapax, quae uasta Charybdis': Lucretius also
has the phrase 'uasta Charybdis' (i. 722).

uastus is a favourite adjective of Virgil's: it is a cognate of
uacuus and *uanus*, and its basic implication is that of an
emptiness or desolation which appals or repels the beholder.
So he uses it of the sea (*uasta per aequora* vii. 228—cf. ii. 780,
iii. 191, x. 693; *uastos fluctus* i. 86, 333, iii. 421 f.; *gurgite
uasto* i. 118, iii. 197, vi. 741; *uasto ponto* iii. 605), of other
awe-inspiring phenomena of nature (*palus* xii. 745; *rupes* i.
162; *antrum* i. 52, iii. 431, 617, viii. 217, 424—cf. viii. 193,
vi. 237), sights (*uasti agri* of the stricken battle-field xi.
208 f.; *uasti campi* of the plains of Thrace iii. 13; *uasta ruina*
of an earthquake iii. 414; *uastum leonem* viii. 295) or sounds
(*uasto cum murmure montis* i. 245; *uasto clamore lacessunt*
x. 716 of a blood-curdling war-cry). *uastis uiribus* (v. 368),
uastis ictibus (v. 198) are not just 'vast strength', 'mighty
strokes': there too, and in *uasto certamine* (xii. 553), *uasta
caede* (vi. 503), the adjective has the same kind of emotional
content—as indeed it has in the usage of ordinary speech, in
contexts where there is no reference to size at all: so *uastus
homo* (Cic. *de Or.* i. 117) of an uncouth figure, *uasta littera*
(Cic. *Or.* 153) of the repulsive sound of *x*, *uasta oratio* (*ad Her.*
iv. 18) of a collocation of sounds abhorrent to the ear.

For the wrecking of Aeneas' ships on the Syrtes, quicksands off the African coast, see i. 110 ff.; for his escape from the sea-monster Scylla and the whirlpool Charybdis, twin hazards of the Sicilian straits, iii. 410 ff., 554 ff.

303. conduntur: cf. v. 243 'portu se condidit alto'.

alueo: for the synizesis see on 33.

304. securi pelagi atque mei, 'indifferent to the ocean and to me': for the genitive of reference cf. x. 326 'securus amorum'.

304 ff. Juno cites Mars and Diana here as she cites Pallas in i. 39. They were allowed to take vengeance on those who had offended them—and their enemies were a race of giants and an old-established city, her own a single man: the adjectives *immanem* and *antiquam* have point and *Aenea* is emphatically placed.

305. immanem: *immanis* (in origin the negative of the obsolete adjective *manis which survives in the euphemistic *manes* for the 'good' spirits: but the juxtaposition of *immanis* and *manes* at viii. 245 f. is probably only a curious accident) is a favourite adjective of Virgil's, usually with the implication of unnatural, terrifying, or forbidding size. He applies it to monstrous creatures (ii. 150 the Horse, v. 822 Neptune's seals, vi. 418 Cerberus, 576 the Hydra), to savage human beings (as here: viii. 330 the wild Thybris), to wild animals (v. 351 the lion, ix. 730 the tiger), to the Sibyl's cave (vi. 11), Ixion's wheel (*Geo.* iii. 39) and Aventinus' lion-skin (666 below), to a savage land (i. 616), a great rock (viii. 225, xii. 904), a whirlwind (vi. 594): occasionally he uses it with abstract nouns (v. 401 *pondus*, vi. 624 *nefas*, ix. 694 *ira*), and adverbially with participles (vii. 510 *spirans*, x. 726 *hians*, xii. 535 *frementi*).

Lapithum: for the genitive form in *-um* see on 189. The story of the quarrel between the Thessalian tribe of the Lapithae and their neighbours the Centaurs at the marriage-feast of the Thessalian hero Pirithous is told by Ovid, *Met.* xii. 210 ff. The provocation of it is usually represented as the doing of Bacchus (*Geo.* ii. 455 ff.; Hor. *Od.* i. 18. 7 ff.: so Homer, *Od.* xxi. 295 ff.) and Mars does not figure in the story elsewhere: Servius says that Mars was slighted when Pirithous did not invite him and took this revenge. For the story of Diana's revenge on Oeneus, King of Calydon in Arcadia, see Homer, *Il.* ix. 529 ff.; Ovid, *Met.* viii. 270 ff.; Oeneus' accidental neglect of the goddess at his harvest sacrifice was punished by the invasion of his country by a gigantic boar.

in iras, 'to satisfy her anger': for the plural see on 445.

306. Dianae: the usual prosody in dactylic verse; Virgil has

it ten times (always at the end of a line: cf. 764, 769), the
original -ī- once (i. 499).

307. quod scelus aut Lapithas tantum aut Calydona merentem? :
the conflict of the manuscripts represents an early variation
in the text. Priscian knows two readings, (a) *Lapithas . . .
Calydona merentem* and (b) *Lapithis . . . Calydone merente* (as
well as a third conflated one, *Lapithis . . . Calydona meren-
tem*): Servius reads (b) as the *uera lectio* and Macrobius
quotes it. Either is defensible, but (a), in which the accusa-
tives stand in a loose apposition to *gentem immanem Lapi-
thum . . . Calydona* in 304–6, is more in Virgil's manner than
the ablative absolute of (b): *merentem* miswritten or misread
as *merente* may have caused the 'correction' of the accusa-
tives to ablatives.

scelus . . . merentem: for *quod scelus* taking the place of
cuius sceleris poenas cf. ii. 229 'scelus expendisse' (and con-
versely vi. 569 'commissa piacula'). The shift from the
notion of crime to that of punishment is found even in
legal language: so Livy writes *noxam merere* (viii. 28. 8) as
well as *noxae reus* (v. 47. 10) and the Digest has *noxae dedere*
as well as *noxam committere*. For the idiomatic *quid tantum*
cf. Ter. *Heaut.* 83 'quid de te tantum meruisti?'; Prop. i. 18. 9
'quid tantum merui?'; Tac. *H.* iv. 72 'quid tantum Cre-
monam meruisse?'.

308. ast ego: *ast* was originally a continuative particle and is
found in early Latin continuing a conditional or relative
clause with a force similar to that of *autem*: so in the XII
Tables, 10. 9 'at cui auro dentes iuncti escunt ast im cum
illo sepeliet uretue, se fraude esto'; in a law cited by Festus
260 L. 'si parentem puer uerberit ast olle plorassit parens,
puer diuis parentum sacer esto'; and once in Plautus, *Capt.*
683 f. 'si ego hic peribo ast ille ut dixit non redit, / at erit mi
hoc factum mortuo memorabile'. Its occurrence in later
archaizing formulas, in Livy x. 19. 17, 'Bellona, si hodie
nobis uictoriam duis, ast ego tibi templum uoueo', where it
introduces an apodosis, and in some of the laws invented
by Cicero in his *de Legibus* (iii. 9, 11), where it appears to be
introducing, not continuing, a conditional clause, is probably
due to misunderstanding of an obsolete usage: see H. Nettle-
ship, *Contrib. to Lat. Lex.*, s.v.; J. S. Reid in *C.R.* xiii (1899),
311 f.

Virgil and Horace give the word a new currency as a con-
venient substitute for *at*, with which it has no demonstrable
connection (on the very doubtful earlier instances of this
use see Reid, loc. cit.). Horace has it only in his early work,
once in the *Epodes* (15. 24) and twice in the *Satires* (i. 6. 125,

8. 6). Virgil has it eighteen times in the *Aeneid*—always before a vowel (except x. 743 *ast de*) and usually before a pronominal form (*ille, ego, ipse, alius, ubi*: only twice before a substantive, x. 173 'ast Ilua', xi. 293 'ast armis').

inausum: a rare word which appears first here and in viii. 205.

309. potui, 'brought myself to': for this implication of the verb (corresponding to ἔτλην: cf. English 'How could you?') cf. *Geo.* iii. 453 f. 'si quis ferro potuit ('had the heart') rescindere summum / ulceris os', *Aen.* ix. 481 ff. 'tune ille senectae / sera meae requies, potuisti linquere solam, / crudelis?', xi. 307 'nec uicti possunt absistere ferro', xii. 151 'non pugnam aspicere hanc oculis, non foedera possum'; Cat. 62. 21 'qui natam possis complexu auellere matris', 68. 41 f. 'non possum reticere, deae, qua me Allius in re / iuuerit', 104. 1 'credis me potuisse meae maledicere uitae?'; Hor. *Od.* iii. 11. 31 f. 'impiae sponsos potuere duro / perdere ferro'; Prop. i. 8. 5 'tune audire potes uesani murmura ponti?'; Ovid, *Her.* 17. 97 'disce meo exemplo formosis posse carere'.

memet in omnia uerti, 'turned to any shift' (not 'changed' as in xii. 891 'uerte omnis tete in facies'): Virgil has the emphatic *-met* five times elsewhere, with *ego* (iii. 623, v. 650, vi. 505), *me* (iv. 606) and *uos* (i. 207). Norden is not justified in suggesting that it gives an archaic colour; it is common in Cicero's speeches and was clearly current in his time.

311. dubitem, 'I cannot hesitate': the weak use of the potential subjunctive is the same as that in the common idioms of *nolim, non ausim, credas, uideatur*, etc.

usquam is 'anywhere at all' and so naturally (like *quisquam*, 'any one at all') used in negative or (as here or in i. 603 f.) hypothetical sentences.

312. Acheronta mouebo: the force of *mouere* here is not 'make an impression on' (as in 252, *Geo.* iv. 505 'quae numina uoce moueret', and often elsewhere, e.g. Livy iii. 20 'mouerat plebem oratio consulis'), but 'set in motion' as in 603 *Martem mouent*.

313 ff. For the notion that a god may meet the declared decree of fate with an opposition which can delay its fulfilment but cannot reverse it cf. viii. 396 ff. (with Vulcan's aid Venus, had she chosen, could have postponed the fated fall of Troy by ten years more), xii. 676 (Turnus asks Juturna to abandon her attempt to delay fate), xii. 806 ff. (Juno, told by Jupiter that her opposition to fate must cease, asks to be allowed one concession against which fate has not provided). On the conception of *fatum* in Virgil and the difficulties inherent in the combination of epic convention with philosophical belief see C. Bailey, *Religion in Virgil*, 204 ff.; P. Boyancé, *La Religion de Virgile*, 39 ff.; J. MacInnes in *C.R.* xxiv (1910), 169 ff.; L. E. Matthaei in *C.Q.* xi (1917), 11 ff.

314. immota, 'unchangeable': see on 11 and cf. i. 257 f. 'manent immota tuorum / fata tibi'.

Lauinia coniunx, 'marriage with Lavinia': the use of a complex of substantive and adjective (*coniunx* being adjectival in function) to express a complex abstract notion is akin to the common participial idiom of *ab urbe condita*, 'from the foundation of the city': cf. v. 6 'notumque furens quid femina possit', 'the knowledge of what a distraught woman can do' (where the noun-clause takes the place of a substantive), viii. 132 'cognati patres', 'the kinship of our fathers', x. 320 'genitor Melampus'. (See K.–S. ii. 1. 770.)

315. at: for the use in apodosis ('still at any rate') cf. i. 542 f. 'si genus humanum et mortalia temnitis arma, / at sperate deos memores fandi atque nefandi', 557 ('at . . . saltem'), iv. 615, vi. 406, *Geo.* ii. 461–9, iv. 206 ff.

trahere: the object understood is presumably *res*.

316. exscindere: cf. iv. 425 f. 'non ego cum Danais Troianam exscindere gentem / Aulide iuraui', ix. 137 'ferro sceleratam exscindere gentem'.

317. gener atque socer: these words had a special significance in Virgil's youth as a catch-phrase referring to Caesar and Pompey: Catullus has it in 29. 24, Virgil himself in *Aen.* vi. 830 f., and the reappearance of the cliché in Lucan (i. 289 f., iv. 802, x. 417) and Martial (ix. 70. 3) shows the vogue it had acquired. But there is no need to suggest that Virgil had this application in mind here and meant his readers to be reminded of the horrors of the civil war or that *coeant* ('unite': as in xi. 292) carries an allusion to its other meaning of 'meet in war' (cf. xii. 709). (See E. Fraenkel, *J.R.S.* xxxv [1945], 4; W. A. Camps, *Intro. to Virgil's Aeneid*, 97). The emphasis on the relationship is point enough, as it is, e.g., in Livy i. 49. 1 'socerum gener sepultura prohibuit'; Ovid, *F.* vi. 600 'sceptra gener socero rapta Superbus habet', *Met.* i. 144 f. 'non hospes ab hospite tutus, / non socer a genero'.

atque: the use of *atque* before a consonant is generally avoided by the Augustan poets (except Horace) and their followers: the *Aeneid* has thirty-five examples (out of nearly 300 cases of *atque*) of which all but eight occur in the second half (or nine if *atque Charybdin* is read at iii. 684: Axelson includes this but has omitted i. 254 'atque deorum'): normally *atque* is elided. See B. Axelson, *Unpoetische Wörter*, 84; M. Platnauer in *C.Q.* xlii (1948), 91 ff.

hac . . . mercede suorum, 'at this price paid by their sub-
jects' or perhaps 'at this price consisting in their subjects'—
i.e. at the price of their subjects' lives.

318. sanguine . . . dotabere: the commentators quote Aeschy-
lus, *Agam.* 406 (of Helen) ἄγουσά τ' ἀντίφερνον Ἰλίῳ φθοράν.

319. Bellona was a primitive Italian war-goddess who appears
with Mars in Decius' formula of *deuotio* (Livy viii. 9. 6): her
temple in the Campus Martius, vowed by Appius Claudius
Caecus in 296 B.C. (Livy x. 19. 17), was used in later times
for the Senate when it wished to meet outside the *pomoerium*.
But by Virgil's time the name had become attached to the
Cappadocian goddess Ma, whose orgiastic worship came to
Rome from Asia in the Sullan period: she is the *gaudens
Bellona cruentis* of Horace, *Sat.* ii. 3. 223 whose fanatical
rites are described by Tibullus i. 6. 43 ff.; and *Aen.* viii. 703,
'cum sanguineo sequitur Bellona flagello', suggests that
there anyhow the later conception was in Virgil's mind.

pronuba: the matron who attended the bride at a Roman
wedding (cf. Cat. 61. 179 ff.); similarly Juno is represented
as acting as *pronuba* for Dido, iv. 166.

320. Cisseis: Hecuba, Priam's queen (the patronymic from
Cisseus comes from post-Homeric legend: in Homer her
father is Dymas). Before the birth of Paris she dreamed that
she was pregnant with a flaming torch and the prophets
interpreted the dream as meaning that her child would be
the ruin of Troy: cf. x. 704 f. Virgil plays on the image
further: Hecuba brought forth *ignis iugalis*, the marriage
torches of Paris and Helen which were to kindle the fires of
Troy.

321 f. Venus has in Aeneas a like progeny of her own, a second
Paris (*et* is explanatory), and the torches of Lavinia's mar-
riage will be torches ·to bring destruction on the resurgent
Italian Troy as Paris and his marriage did on the old Troy.
For the point of *iterum* cf. vi. 93 f. 'causa mali tanti coniunx
iterum hospita Teucris / externique iterum thalami'; but
here, as in x. 26 f. 'muris iterum imminet hostis / nascentis
Troiae' (and perhaps in *Geo.* i. 490), the word is elliptically
used—it is Troy, not the reborn Troy, that is threatened
with disaster a second time.

322. recidiua: in its literal use the word is a technical term for
new growth sprouting from a tree after cutting—so Servius
explains it on x. 58 ('tractus sermo est ab arboribus quae
taleis sectis repullulant') and so Tertullian uses it in an
elaborate arboricultural analogy (*de Pud.* 16 'siluam libi-
dinum caedat et eradicet et excaudicet, ne quicquam de
recidiuo fruticare permittat')—or for new growth from fallen

seed: so Mela iii. 47 'adeo agri fertiles ut cum semel sata
frumenta sint subinde recidiuis seminibus segetem nouanti-
bus septem minime . . . messes ferant'. The figurative use
first appears in Virgil (*recidiua Pergama* is repeated at iv.
344 and x. 58): in medical language the word was techni-
cally transferred to a recurrent fever (Pliny, *N.H.* xxx. 104;
Celsus iii. 4. 12).

324 ff. The *dirae deae* or *Dirae* (iv. 473, viii. 701, xii. 845) are
the Furies invented by Roman mythology as an equivalent
for the Greek Erinyes, supernatural beings belonging to a
very early stratum of Greek religion (though their significant
names of Allecto, Megaera (xii. 846), and Tisiphone (x. 761)
do not appear in Greek until after the classical age) whose
concern is the punishment of wrong-doing, especially within
the family, and who relentlessly pursue offenders in the
world of men and exact retribution in the underworld (Cic.
N.D. iii. 46 'speculatrices et uindices facinorum et sceleris').
In Virgil's Tartarus (vi. 571 ff., 605 ff., viii. 669) the Furies
appear in that role, but here the conception of them is quite
another one: their concern is provoking strife (335), not
punishing guilt: they do the mischievous work of that Dis-
cordia who appears in their company in vi. 280 and in viii.
702. Virgil's Allecto may have owed something to the figure
of Discordia in Ennius, who is probably the fiendish creature
described in *Ann.* 521 f. V. (with an allusion to Empedocles)
as 'corpore tartarino prognata Paluda uirago, / cui par imber
et ignis, spiritus et grauis terra' (E. Norden, *Ennius und
Vergilius* [Leipzig, 1912], 10 ff.), but we have no clue to the
context either of that fragment or of *Ann.* 266 f. V. in which
Discordia taetra is made to open the gates of war and from
which Virgil took a phrase in line 622: see E. Fraenkel, *J.R.S.*
xxxv (1945), 7, 12 ff. But there may also be a reminiscence of
Euripides' Lyssa (like Allecto an infernal creature, *sata
Nocte*) who as the instrument of Hera's spite drives Heracles
to madness (*Herc. Fur.* 822 ff.).

324. luctificam: Virgil is very sparing with the dactyl-produc-
ing verbal compounds which were a feature of the old epic
style: in *-ficus*, besides *luctificus* (which Cicero had used in
verse, *Tusc.* ii. 25) he has only *horrificus, terrificus, uulnificus*
(viii. 446) and the purely 'enhancing' *regificus* (vi. 605).

　　Allecto: the only certain instance of a Greek feminine ac-
cusative in *-o* in Virgil (in iv. 383 *Dido* may be vocative and
elsewhere Virgil does not use the name *Dido* in any oblique
case: for the genitive he substitutes *Elissae*): he has the
corresponding genitive form in *Mantus* (x. 199). The early
poets had given Latin inflexions to Greek feminines in *-o*

(Ennius has *Didone*, Pacuvius *Calypsonem*, Plautus *Ioni*):
Catullus' *Callisto* (66. 66) is the first and last instance of the
Greek dative form; in Prop. ii. 30. 29 *Io* is probably the
ablative.

dirarum . . . dearum: *dirus* is a word of religious usage,
'ill-omened' (Servius on iii. 235 may be right in saying that
it is of non-Latin origin): so *dirae* (*res*) are unfavourable
omens in the language of augury (Pliny, *N.H.* xxviii. 17, 26),
dirae (*precationes*) are curses (Hor. *Epod.* 5. 89; Tib. ii. 6. 53;
Prop. iii. 25. 17). Virgil puts the word to effective use many
times: so *dirus Ulixes* (ii. 261), *dira Celaeno* (iii. 211), *dira
bucina* (vii. 519 f.), *dira pugna* (x. 50), *dirae Belli portae*
(i. 293 f.), *dira fames* (iii. 256), *dira cupido* (vi. 373, 721,
ix. 185), *dirum nefas* (iv. 563), *religio dira loci* (viii. 349 f.).

326. cordi (sunt): cf. ix. 615, 776, x. 252, xi. 369: that the
idiom is a survival of a locative use is suggested by the
phrase *cordi habere* ('have by heart') which Gellius uses (e.g.
praef. 12).

327. odit et ipse . . . odere sorores: for *et* attached to the first
of two balancing clauses in asyndeton cf. 516 'audiit et
Triuiae longe lacus, audiit amnis', *Ecl.* 4. 6 'redit et uirgo,
redeunt Saturnia regna', 5. 29 f., *Aen.* viii. 91 f. 'mirantur
et undae, / miratur nemus'; so Prop. iv. 10. 19 'idem eques
et frenis, idem fuit aptus aratris'; Ovid, *F.* vi. 224 'utilis et
nuptis, utilis esse uiris'. For -*que* similarly used see on 75.

pater Pluton: her father, as *sorores* makes clear: in late
Greek mythology the Erinyes become the daughters of
Hades (*Orph. Hymn.* 69). In Aeschylus the Erinyes are
μισήματ' ἀνδρῶν καὶ θεῶν Ὀλυμπίων (*Eum.* 73): Virgil makes even
the powers of the underworld and her dreadful sisters recoil
from Allecto. Virgil uses the Greek Pluton only here: else-
where his name for the god of the underworld is the Italic Dis.

328. monstrum: see on 21.

328 f. ora . . . facies: cf. i. 658 'faciem mutatus et ora': for
facies see on 448.

329. atra: the tragedians make the Furies black-visaged
(μελάγχρωτες Eur. *Or.* 321, χρῶτα κελαιναί *El.* 1345) and their dress
is black (φαιοχίτωνες Aesch. *Cho.* 1049, ἁμετέραις ἐφόδοις μελανεί-
μοσιν *Eum.* 370). But *ater* is more than a colour-epithet in
Virgil's use: see on 525.

331. da proprium: the idiomatic sense of *proprium dare*, 'give
outright', 'give to someone as his own', is seen in Lucil.
701 M. 'cum sciam nihil esse in uita proprium mortali datum':
cf. *Bell. Afr.* 32 'uictoriam propriam se eis . . . daturum'.
Virgil has the phrase again in iii. 85 'da propriam, Thym-
braee, domum': and two similar uses in i. 73 'conubio iungam

stabili propriamque dicabo', vi. 870 f. 'nimium uobis Romana propago / uisa potens, superi, propria haec si dona fuissent'.

sata Nocte: the Furies are daughters of Night in Aeschylus (*Eum.* 416 Νυκτὸς αἰανῆ τέκνα).

332. honos: see on 3.

infracta: cf. v. 784 (Venus is speaking of Juno herself) 'nec Iouis imperio fatisque infracta quiescit': so ix. 499 'infractae . . . uires'.

333. conubiis: see on 96.

ambire: the metaphor is derived from political canvassing and usually conveys, as it does here, a suggestion of cajolery: that suggestion is not absent in iv. 283 f. 'quo nunc reginam ambire furentem / audeat adfatu' (Aeneas is wondering how to break his news to Dido) or even from Hor. *Od.* i. 35. 5 f. 'te pauper ambit sollicita prece / ruris colonus'.

335. tu potes: for the prayer formula, in which the speaker justifies his appeal to the person addressed, cf. i. 65 f., vi. 117, vii. 645; Hor. *Epod.* 17. 45, *Od.* iii. 11. 1 f.; Ovid, *A.A.* i. 204: see E. Norden, *Agnostos Theos* (Berlin, 1913), 150 ff.

unanimos . . . fratres: *unanimus* regularly refers to the sharing of affection, not of opinions: so iv. 8 'unanimam adloquitur male sana sororem'; Cat. 9. 4 'fratres unanimos', 30. 1 'unanimis sodalibus', 66. 80 'unanimis coniugibus'.

336. odiis: the word has a plural reference here: but see on 445.

337. nomina mille: the special title by which a deity is addressed represents a particular attribute of power: hence the common use of πολυώνυμος as an honorific epithet of a god, e.g. Soph. *Ant.* 1115 (Dionysus); Ar. *Thesm.* 320 (Artemis); Eur. *Hipp.* 1 (Aphrodite): in Callim. *Hymn.* 3. 7 Artemis asks Zeus for πολυωνυμίη in order to outdo her brother Apollo in prestige.

338. concute pectus: 'search', 'ransack', with the same metaphor from shaking out a garment (common with *excutere*) as in Hor. *Sat.* i. 3. 34 ff. 'te ipsum / concute num qua tibi uitiorum inseuerit olim / Natura'.

341–72. *Allecto carries out Juno's bidding, infecting her victims with her venom and implanting the 'insania' that leads to war. She begins with the queen and the women of Latium. Amata's first reaction is mild : she reproaches her husband for giving his daughter to a wandering stranger, another Paris, and urges the claims of Turnus, whose non-Latin origins will satisfy the oracle, but her reasoning has no effect.*

341. Gorgoneis . . . infecta uenenis: her snakes distil their poison into her. The Gorgon, a single monster in Homer, developed in legend into a sisterhood and acquired some of the attributes of the Erinyes: so in Aeschylus (*Eum.* 48) the Pythia describes the appearance of the Erinyes, οὔτοι γυναῖκας, ἀλλὰ Γοργόνας λέγω.

342. tyranni: see on 266.

343. tacitumque obsedit limen: the epithet points a contrast with the wild outbursts which are to follow. There is perhaps a kind of hypallage: Allecto takes up her position silently: cf. 505.

Amatae: the queen's name (which Dionysius gives as Amita) is perhaps to be connected with the title of *Amata* with which the new Vestal Virgin was addressed by the *pontifex maximus* at the ceremony of her admission (*captio*) in the formula preserved by Gellius i. 12. 14: 'sacerdotem Vestalem, quae sacra faciat, quae ius siet sacerdotem Vestalem facere pro populo Romano Quiritibus, uti quae optima lege fuit, ita te, Amata, capio'. The origin of the title is obscure: that it is the perfect participle is most unlikely and it (and the gentile name Amatius) may be Etruscan. See W. Schulze, *Lat. Eigennamen*, 121; A. C. Moorhouse in *C.R.* lxv (1951), 1 ff. refers both this *amata* and *amita*, 'aunt', to an I.E. root *am-, 'home'.

344. super, 'about', 'over': so 358, i. 750, x. 42, 839, *Geo.* iv. 560. This use of *super* belonged to familiar language (it is common in Plautus): it is rare in classical prose but the poets find it useful.

hymenaeis: for the 'Greek' rhythm of a final quadrisyllable cf. 358. Virgil has *hymenaei* fifteen times in this position, twice combining it with an irregular lengthening (see on 398) and once with hiatus (*Geo.* iii. 60), and *hyacinthus* five times.

345. iraeque: the plural can be explained as conveying the notion of repeated outbursts of passion but is no doubt also suggested by the combination with *curae*. See on 445.

coquebant: the metaphor from the seething pot is in Enn. *Ann.* 335 f. V. 'curamue leuasso / quae nunc te coquit et uersat in pectore fixa'; it seems to have belonged to popular language, sometimes combined with another verb from the kitchen, *macerare* (Plaut. *Trin.* 225 'egomet me coquo et macero et defetigo': so Quint. xii. 10. 77; Sen. *Ep.* 70. 4).

346. huic: for the dative cf. 456 'facem iuueni coniecit', xi. 194 'coniciunt igni': so with *iacere* ix. 712, x. 683, with *deicere* x. 319, with *proicere* xii. 256.

caeruleis: like other Latin colour-words, *caerul(e)us* is difficult to define. Virgil uses it of the sea and of sea- and river-deities (see on viii. 64) several times, never of the 'blue' sky, and generally it seems to connote for him a blackish blue or bluish black: he applies it to snakes again at ii. 381, v. 87, *Geo.* iv. 482, to a rain-storm *Aen.* iii. 194, v. 10 (cf. viii. 622), to mourning headbands iii. 64, to Charon's boat vi. 410, to a ship v. 123. See J. André, *Étude sur les termes de couleur* (Paris, 1949), 162 ff.

unum de crinibus anguem: according to Pausanias (i. 28. 6) Aeschylus was the first to give the Furies snaky hair (cf. *Cho.* 1049 f. πεπλεκτανημέναι / πυκνοῖς δράκουσιν) : in Euripides they are χειροδράκοντες (*El.* 1345) and δρακοντώδεις (*Or.* 256).

347. **subdit,** 'slipped it into her bosom to her very heart': what Conington calls Virgil's 'effort of ingenuity to sustain the physical probability' of his description is not altogether successful: it is difficult to reconcile *ad praecordia subdit* here with *inter uestis et pectora* in 349. The whole passage is imitated by Ovid (*Met.* iv. 490 ff.) in his description of the visitation of Ino and Athamas by the Fury.

348. **quo . . . monstro,** 'so that maddened by this horror': for the idiom by which the relative is accompanied by a noun defining the antecedent, cf. *Geo.* i. 329 f. 'fulmina molitur dextra, quo maxima motu / terra tremit', iv. 347 ff. 'diuum numerabat amores / carmine quo captae . . . pensa / deuoluunt'. See on 477.

monstro : see on 21.

350. **attactu :** a very rare noun : only the ablative is found and that elsewhere only in Varro discussing cows' skins.

350 f. **fallitque furentem . . . inspirans,** 'pours its snaky breath into her without her knowing' (λανθάνει εἰσπνέων): cf. i. 688 'occultum inspires ignem fallasque (eam) ueneno'. *furentem* seems to have a proleptic sense, 'to make her mad', as in the very similar i. 659 f. '(ut) . . . furentem / incendat reginam atque ossibus implicet ignem', though one would expect rather *furenti*.

351–3. Heyne's comment on the detail of these lines is not unjust: 'illa nescio an pro epica dignitate nimis ingeniosa sint: Ouidio forte ea condones'.

351 f. **tortile collo aurum :** *collo* may be ablative here (for the local ablative attached to a noun see on 140), but is probably dative as it is in i. 654 f. 'colloque monile / bacatum', 'a jewelled circlet for her neck', x. 135 'aut collo decus aut capiti'.

352. **taenia :** i.e. the hanging end of the ribbon of her headband ('uittarum extremitas', Servius; cf. Enn. *Sc.* 51 V. 'cum corona et taeniis').

uittae : see on 403.

354. **udo sublapsa ueneno :** to modern ears the 'clammy poison', mysteriously conveyed without contact, enhances the incongruity of the physical description. Ovid (*Met.* iv. 490 ff.),

after paraphrasing *attactu nullo* with the disarmingly matter-of-fact 'nec uulnera membris / ulla ferunt (angues): mens est quae diros sentiat ictus', goes on characteristically to give a list of the ingredients (noxious substances and abstractions fantastically compounded) of the hell-brew with which the Fury supplements her snake-venom and attacks (again directly) the *praecordia* of her victims—and makes her remember to put the snakes back in her hair.

355. pertemptat sensus, 'assails her senses': the verb is thus used three times elsewhere in Virgil—*Geo*. iii. 250 f. 'nonne uides ut tota tremor pertemptat equorum / corpora, si tantum notas odor attulit auras?', *Aen*. i. 502 'Latonae tacitum pertemptant gaudia pectus', v. 827 f. 'Aeneae suspensam blanda uicissim / gaudia pertemptant mentem'—and nowhere else in classical Latin. The simple *temptare* is common in this use, both in military and in other contexts: Virgil uses it in a very prosaic context at *Geo*. iii. 441.

ossibus implicat ignem: the words are repeated in i. 660. The bones, or the marrow, are represented as the seat of emotion because they are the innermost parts of the body: so *Geo*. iii. 258 f. 'magnum . . . uersat in ossibus ignem / durus amor', *Aen*. iv. 66 'est mollis flamma medullas', 101 'ardet amans Dido traxitque per ossa furorem', viii. 389 f. 'accepit solitam flammam, notusque medullas / intrauit calor et labefacta per ossa cucurrit'.

356. toto percepit pectore flammam: perhaps a reminiscence of Cat. 64. 92 'cuncto concepit corpore flammam': elsewhere Virgil uses *concipio* thus—iv. 474 'concepit furias', 501 f. 'furores concipit'—but Ovid, *Met*. xiv. 700 has 'totis perceperat ossibus aestum'.

358. super natae . . . Phrygiisque hymenaeis: so M; R's *nata* looks like a correction by someone who did not understand the combination of the genitive *natae* and the adjective *Phrygiis*, taking the place of the genitive *Phrygis*. For *super* see on 344.

359. datur, 'is she to be given?': for the vivid indicative replacing the deliberative subjunctive cf. iii. 88 'quem sequimur?', 367 'quae prima pericula uito?', x. 675 'quid ago?'.

Lauinia: in this name the -*a*- is short only here, ten times long elsewhere in Virgil; he has it long in the adjectival form *Lauin(i)a* (twice) but short in the name *Lauinium* (three times). For the variation cf. *Sīcănium* (viii. 416) and *Sĭcānos* (v. 24).

360. o genitor: the addition of *o* to a vocative (or to a wish or a command: viii. 579 'nunc, nunc o liceat') always marks a strongly emotional address.

363 f. at non sic: R reads *at*, M *an*; both readings were known
to Servius. With *at* the sense is 'Have you no compunction
about leaving your daughter and her mother at the mercy of
a freebooter? But, look, is not this the story of Paris and
Helen over again?'. This gives *at* a very weak force, since
there is no real opposition of ideas. Contrast Propertius' use
of the same formula, i. 15. 9 f. 'at non sic Ithaci digressu
mota Calypso / desertis olim fleuerat aequoribus', 'Your
behaviour shows that you do not really care about me: but
that is not how Calypso behaved' (similarly *at non* alone in
Prop. ii. 18. 7; Hor. *Od.* ii. 9. 13); and compare the question
introduced by *at non* in ix. 144 ff., 'Their defences are giving
the Trojans courage: but did they not once before see their
walls collapse?' *an non* gives better idiom and better rhetoric:
'he will carry off his bride without a thought for her people:
or can one think that this is not just Paris and Helen over
again?'.

363. Phrygius ... pastor: because of his mother's ominous
dream (see on 320) the infant Paris was exposed on Mount
Ida, but he was there found and brought up by a shepherd:
cf. Hor. *Od.* i. 15. 1 f. 'pastor cum traheret per freta nauibus /
Idaeis Helenen perfidus hospitam'. *Ledaeam* is not merely
ornamental: it serves to bring to mind Helen's birth and the
background of the story.

penetrat: for the present thus used of a past event vividly
recalled to mind cf. i. 97 ff. 'mene Iliacis occumbere campis /
non potuisse tuaque animam hanc effundere dextra / saeuus
ubi Aeacidae telo iacet Hector', ii. 274 f. 'qualis erat, quan-
tum mutatus ab illo / Hectore qui redit exuuias indutus
Achilli', 662 f. 'iamque aderit ... Pyrrhus, / natum ante ora
patris, patrem qui obtruncat ad aras', viii. 134 ff., 294 f.

365. quid tua sancta fides?, 'What of your pledge solemnly
given?': the verb understood in this elliptical phrase is not
easy to supply: for similar ellipses cf. x. 672 'quid manus illa
uirum, qui me meaque arma secuti?', *Geo.* iii. 258 ff. 'quid
iuuenis, magnum cui uersat in ossibus ignem / durus amor?
... quid lynces ... ? ... quid quae imbelles dant proelia
cerui?'.

366. consanguineo: Turnus was Lavinia's cousin, as Servius
explains: his mother, the nymph Venilia (x. 76), was Amata's
sister.

data dextera: there is an inconsistency between these lines
and 54 ff., where there is no suggestion of betrothal and
Turnus is only the suitor favoured by Amata.

367 ff. Amata offers two alternative loopholes by which the
obvious meaning of the oracle may be avoided: (1) by *ex-*

ternus the oracle means any nation separated from (*dissidet*), and independent of (*libera*), Latium—and Turnus is a Rutulian; (2) even if *externus* means not merely non-Latin but non-Italian, Turnus satisfies the description—by origin he is Greek.

368. idque sedet, 'and that is a firm resolve': so ii. 660 'sedet hoc animo', iv. 15 f. 'si mihi non animo fixum immotumque sederet / ne cui me . . . uellem sociare', v. 418 'idque pio sedet Aeneae', xi. 551 'subito uix haec sententia sedit'. *stat* is used in the same way in ii. 750.

370. sic dicere, 'that this is what they mean': cf. Hor. *Sat.* i. 3. 126 f. 'non nosti quid pater, inquit, / Chrysippus dicat'.

371. prima . . . origo: for the strengthening of a noun by the addition of an adjective of the same meaning, especially with words relating to beginning or end, see on 40.

372. From *patres* the notion of *patria* must be understood with *Mycenae*. Turnus could claim descent from the rulers of Argos, Acrisius, and before him, in the beginnings of Argive saga, the river-god Inachus, through Danae, Acrisius' daughter, who, in an Italian adaptation of Greek legend, when she was set adrift by her father, was cast up on the shore of Italy and there married Pilumnus, Turnus' ancestor (x. 619). See on 410.

mediae Mycenae, 'the heart of Mycenae' (cf. ix. 738 'media Ardea'), but *medius* seems to have the same intensive force here as it has in such phrases as 'mediis effusus in undis' (vi. 339), 'medio sub aequore mersit' (vi. 342), 'mediae per Elidis urbem' (vi. 588), 'mediis . . . / supplicia hausurum scopulis' (iv. 382 f.), 'medio puluere ferre rosam' (Prop. iv 2. 40): there is a close parallel in Juvenal 3. 79 f. 'non Maurus erat . . . mediis sed natus Athenis' (i.e. a true, genuine Athenian). The same intensive use is not uncommon where there is no local reference at all: e.g. *Geo.* i. 230 'ad medias sementem extende pruinas' ('right into the frosts'), *Aen.* ii. 533 'in media iam morte tenetur': similarly in prose *medius* is idiomatically applied to what is essential or genuine and not marginal: e.g. Cic. *Leg.* ii. 53 'hoc . . . e medio est iure ciuili', *Off.* i. 63 'quae sunt ex media laude iustitiae', *Tusc.* iii. 70 'in media stultitia . . . haerere'. For a similar use of *medius* see on 397.

373-405. *As the poison works, the queen goes raving through the city in a Bacchant's frenzy and carries the Latin matrons with her in her wild career.*

376. tum uero marks a climax or crisis: see on 519.
   excita: see on 623.
   monstris: see on 21.

377. sine more: without regard to convention, almost 'indecently': so in v. 694 (with a picturesque personification) 'tempestas sine more furit', viii. 635 'raptas sine more Sabinas'; Ovid, *A.A.* i. 119 'sic illae timuere uiros sine more ruentes'.

immensam . . . per urbem, 'through the length and breadth of the town': clearly the epithet cannot be taken literally but it heightens the picture of the queen's mad wandering.

lymphata: the word had already been used of Bacchic frenzy (cf. 385) by Pacuvius, 422 f. R. 'lymphata aut Bacchi sacris / commota', and by Catullus, 64. 254 'lymphata mente furebant'. It seems to have been a coinage made on the analogy of *laruatus* ('ghost-ridden') to render νυμφόληπτος, which represents the popular Greek belief that the anger of the nymphs caused madness. *lympha* itself, originally *lumpa*, an Italic word for 'water', probably owed its spelling to a popular etymology which connected it with νύμφη.

378 ff. The vivid image of the children's top owes nothing to the simile of Homer, *Il.* xiv. 413 ff., where Hector spins like a top under a blow. Unlike most of Virgil's similes, it seems to be drawn at first hand from life: for another example see ix. 710 ff. Tibullus applies the same simile to the lover, i. 5. 3 f. 'namque agor ut per plana citus sola uerbere turben / quem celer adsueta uersat ab arte puer'.

378. ceu quondam, 'as sometimes': for the archaic use (especially common in similes) of *quondam*, 'on occasion', cf. 699, *Geo.* iii. 99 f. 'ut quondam in stipulis magnus sine uiribus ignis, / incassum furit', iv. 260 f. 'tractimque susurrant, / frigidus ut quondam siluis immurmurat Auster', *Aen.* ii. 367 'quondam etiam uictis redit in praecordia uirtus', v. 448 f. 'concidit, ut quondam . . . radicibus eruta pinus', xii. 862 ff. 'alitis . . . / quae quondam in bustis aut culminibus desertis / nocte sedens serum canit': so occasionally in prose, e.g. Cic. *Diu.* i. 98 'saepe lapidum, sanguinis nonnumquam, terrae interdum, quondam etiam lactis imber affluxit'. For *olim* similarly used see *Geo.* iv. 421, *Aen.* v. 125, viii. 391.

torto, 'whirled': cf. *Geo.* iii. 106 'illi (the charioteers) instant uerbere torto', i. 309 'stuppea torquentem Balearis uerbera fundae'; Ovid, *Ibis* 161 'uerbera torta dabunt sonitum'.

380. ille: the pronoun enhances the pictorial effect of the epic simile either, as here, by taking up the subject (so iv. 69 ff., xi. 492 ff.; Cat. 64. 105 ff.) or by emphasizing a change of subject (as in ii. 628): Greek uses ὁ δέ similarly. See on 787.

381. stupet inscia supra: stand over it, fascinated by what they have never seen before: for this use of *inscius* cf. ii. 307 f.

'stupet inscius alto / accipiens sonitum saxi de uertice pastor', x. 249 f. (at the change of the ships into nymphs) 'stupet inscius ipse / Tros Anchisiades'; similarly *nescius*, Prop. i. 20. 41 'formosis incumbens nescius undis'.

382. buxum: being easily turned ('torno rasile', *Geo.* ii. 449) boxwood was adapted for making such small objects as a top (cf. Pers. 3. 51 'buxum torquere flagello'), a flute (Ovid, *Met.* xiv. 537 'inflati . . . murmure buxi'), a comb (Ovid, *F.* vi. 229 'crines depectere buxo') or a writing-tablet (Prop. iii. 23. 8).

383. dant animos, 'give it spirit', 'put life into it': for the personification cf. *Geo.* ii. 350 'animos tollent sata', 'the plants will take heart'.

cursu . . . illo: *illo* is to be taken with *cursu* (cf. viii. 414 'nec tempore segnior illo', though the ablative is there temporal), *illo cursu* being equivalent to *illius cursu*: cf., e.g., xii. 468 'hoc metu' (i.e. 'huius rei metu'): see on 595.

384. ferocis, 'proud peoples', as in 724 f., i. 263: the usual implication of *ferox* is defiant courage, 'pride' in the good sense of that word.

385. simulato numine Bacchi: if the Bacchic frenzy is being represented as a cover for removing Lavinia, then the deceitful intention is Allecto's (cf. 405 'Allecto stimulis agit undique Bacchi'), not the queen's. But *simulato* need not imply deceitful intention (cf. iii. 349 f. 'paruam Troiam simulataque magnis / Pergama', 'a replica of Pergamum'; Hor. *Ep.* ii. 1. 240 f. 'aera / fortis Alexandri uultum simulantia'): in the queen Bacchic possession is 'reproduced': so in the similar lines vi. 517 ff. Helen, on the night of the fall of Troy, 'chorum simulans euhantis orgia circum / ducebat Phrygias'. Virgil's conception in these lines, however, is far from clear: in 389 ff. the queen is making Lavinia a Bacchic votary while in 398 she is singing a mad song for her bridal. Perhaps the literal-minded Servius has come near the truth when he says on 398 'hic aperte expressit dementiam'. Ovid in his story of Procne (*Met.* vi. 587 ff.) turns the idea to more sophisticated effect, making Procne deliberately use the occasion of a Bacchic revel to disguise herself and rescue her sister: 'furiis agitata doloris, / Bacche, tuas simulat'.

388. thalamum . . . taedasque: cf. iv. 18 'si non pertaesum thalami taedaeque fuisset'. As Austin points out on that line, the metrical impossibility of *nuptiae* encourages the use of these metonymies. Catullus had already used *taedae* thus (64. 25, 302): the use of the singular in iv. 18 is unique.

389. euhoe Bacche fremens : the Bacchic cry is probably to be taken as standing parenthetically outside the construction

as it does in Cat. 64. 255 'euhoe bacchantes, euhoe capita inflectentes'.

fremere is a favourite verb of Virgil's, conveying the notion of inarticulate or confused sound: he uses it of the roaring of the lion (ix. 341) or the howling of the wolf (ix. 60), of cries of fury from man (ix. 703, x. 572, xii. 398) or monster (vii. 787), of the murmuring applause of a crowd (i. 559, v. 555, viii. 717, ix. 637, xi. 132) or the wailing of women (iv. 668), of the waves on the rocks (vii. 590), the wind in the trees (x. 98, xii. 702), the stones raining against the wall (xii. 922).

390. tibi, 'in your honour': cf. *Geo.* ii. 5 f. 'tibi (i.e. Baccho) pampineo grauidus autumno / floret ager', 388 f. 'tibique (Baccho) / oscilla ex alta suspendunt mollia pinu'; Stat. *Theb.* vii. 678 f. 'utinam ipse ueniret / cui furis'; Sen. *Oed.* 439 f. 'tibi commotae pectora matres / fudere comam'; Claud. *IV Cons. Hon.* 604 f. 'dubitassent orgia Bacchi / cui furerent'.

mollis ... thyrsos: i.e. wands wreathed with vine (the *pampineae hastae* of 396) or ivy; cf. *Ecl.* 5. 30 f. 'thiasos inducere Bacchi / et foliis lentas intexere mollibus hastas'. The suggestion of the word is the same in 488 'mollibus ... sertis', xi. 64 'molle feretrum' ('strewn with leaves'): cf. Prop. i. 20. 22 'mollia composita litora fronde tegit', iv. 6. 10 'pura nouum uati laurea mollit iter', 71 'candida nunc molli subeant conuiuia luco'. So *mollis umbra* is 'leafy shade' in *Geo.* iii. 464 'molli succedere ... umbrae'; Prop. iii. 3. 1 'molli ... Heliconis in umbra'.

391. te lustrare choro, 'move round you in the dance': cf. x. 224 '(nymphae) agnoscunt longe regem lustrantque choreis'. *lustrare* is originally a ritual term used of a purificatory rite which moved round, or from point to point in, its object: e.g. *Ecl.* 5. 75 'cum lustrabimus agros', *Aen.* vi. 229 ff. 'ter socios pura circumtulit unda / ... / lustrauitque uiros'. Hence it is extended first, as here (or in xi. 189 f. 'ter maestum funeris ignem / lustrauere in equis'), to other ritual movements of the same kind, and then to the more general meanings of (1) 'traverse' (e.g. 148 f. 'prima lustrabat lampade terras / orta dies', i. 577 'Libyae lustrare extrema iubebo', 607 f. 'montibus umbrae / lustrabunt conuexa', iii. 385 'salis Ausonii lustrandum nauibus aequor', ix. 57 f. 'huc turbidus atque huc / lustrat equo muros') and (2) 'traverse with the eye', 'survey', 'scan' (e.g. i. 453 'sub ingenti lustrat dum singula templo', ii. 564 'quae sit circum me copia lustro', viii. 153 'totum lustrabat lumine corpus', 228 f. 'omnemque / accessum lustrans huc ora ferebat et illuc', xi. 763 'tacitus uestigia lustrat'). The last two uses appear side by side in viii. 229–31.

pascere crinem, 'let her tresses grow': for the offering of a lock of hair cf. Eur. *Bacchae* 494 ἱερὸς ὁ πλόκαμος· τῷ θεῷ (i.e. Διονύσῳ) δ᾽ αὐτὸν τρέφω: Aesch. *Cho.* 6 πλόκαμον Ἰνάχῳ θρεπτήριον. For *pascere*, exactly corresponding to τρέφειν in this use, cf. Hor. *Sat.* ii. 3. 35 'sapientem pascere barbam', 'grow a philosopher's beard'.

393. idem . . . ardor: cf. iv. 581 'idem omnis simul ardor habet'. For the infinitive after *agere* see on 214.

394. deseruere: the perfect expressing instantaneous action (action which can be regarded as finished as soon as it is begun) is particularly common at this point in the line: cf. *Aen.* i. 84 'incubuere mari', 90 'intonuere poli', *Geo.* iv. 213 f. 'amisso (sc. rege) rupere fidem constructaque mella / diripuere ipsae', *Aen.* ix. 75 'diripuere focos', xii. 283 'diripuere aras'; so elsewhere in the line *Geo.* i. 330 'terra tremit, fugere ferae', *Aen.* iv. 164 'tecta metu petiere'.

uentis dant colla comasque: cf. i. 319 'dederatque comam diffundere uentis'.

The details of this description should be compared with Catullus' picture of the arrival of Bacchus and his train in Naxos (64. 251 ff.) and with the Messenger's account of the Bacchic rites on Cithaeron in Euripides, *Bacchae* 689 ff. (μήτηρ ὠλόλυξεν ἐν μέσαις (cf. 397) / σταθεῖσα βάκχαις . . . / καὶ πρῶτα μὲν καθεῖσαν εἰς ὤμους κόμας (cf. 394) / νεβρίδας δ᾽ ἀνεστείλανθ᾽ (cf. 396) ὅσαισιν ἀμμάτων / σύνδεσμ᾽ ἐλέλυτο, καὶ καταστίκτους δόρας / ὄφεσι κατεζώσαντο). Both passages must have been in Virgil's mind.

395. ast: see on 308.

396. incinctae pellibus: the phrase is repeated from *Geo.* iv. 342. For the fawnskins of the Bacchants cf. Eur. *Bacchae* 696 f. (quoted above), 137 νεβρίδος ἔχων ἱερὸν ἐνδυτόν.

397 f. The picture of these lines looks like a reminiscence of the Cassandra of Euripides' *Troades* who in her frenzy (307 μαινάς, 341 βακχεύουσαν) waves the pine-torch and, with the same irony, sings her own marriage-song (308 ff.).

397. inter medias: for the transferred use of *medius* ('right among them') cf. iv. 60 f. 'pateram . . . media inter cornua fundit' ('right between the horns'), v. 618 f. 'inter medias sese haud ignara nocendi / conicit', x. 761 'Tisiphone media inter milia saeuit', xi. 237 'sedet in mediis'; similarly Ovid, *F.* ii. 571 'anus in mediis residens annosa puellis'; Stat. *S.* i. 2. 10 'medias fallit permixta sorores'.

flagrantem feruida: Virgil has the same conceit in ix. 72 'manum pinu flagranti feruidus implet'.

398. canit hymenaeos: the lengthening of a short syllable

before a Greek quadrisyllable at the end of the line is an echo
of Greek rhythm (in such line-endings as *Od.* viii. 475 πλεῖον
ἐλέλειπτο, xi. 190 δμῶες ἐνὶ οἴκῳ: Call. *Hymn.* 4. 238 αἰφνίδιον
ἔπος εἴπῃ) which Catullus had already used (62. 4 'dicetur
hymenaeus', 64. 20 'despexit hymenaeos', 66. 11 'auctus
hymenaeo') and which Virgil repeats four times elsewhere (x.
720 'profugus hymenaeos', *Ecl.* 6. 53 'fultus hyacintho',
Geo. iv. 137 'tondebat hyacinthi', *Aen.* xi. 69 'languentis
hyacinthi'). See on 174, and for 'irrational' lengthening in this
position cf. also *Geo.* ii. 5, *Aen.* ix. 9.

399. sanguineam torquens aciem: cf. iv. 643 'sanguineam
uoluens aciem'. The transferred use of *acies* (properly the
sight) for the eye is common in Lucretius: Virgil has it again
at vi. 788, 'huc geminas nunc flecte acies'.

399 f. toruum . . . clamat: *toruus* is normally used of fierceness
of appearance, especially perhaps of the eye (hence A. Burger,
R.É.L. viii [1930], 222 ff., relates the word to *torqueo*: but
see M. Leumann, *Glotta* xxi [1933], 198): so 415 'toruam
faciem', iii. 677 'lumine toruo', vi. 467 f. 'torua tuentem . . .
animum', *Ecl.* 2. 63 'torua leaena', *Geo.* iii. 51 f. 'optima toruae
/ forma bouis'. For the transference to sound cf. Accius 223
R. 'tonitru . . . toruo'; Pers. 1. 99 'torua . . . cornua'.

400. io: the cry of jubilation occurs only here in Virgil.
ubi quaeque, 'wherever each of you is'.

401 f. piis . . . gratia, 'if you have regard for natural ties (*piis*)
and still cherish feelings of regard for poor Amata': for the
emotive effect of a speaker's use of his or her own name in
pathos or in pride, cf. xii. 56 f. (quoted below), ii. 778, 784
(Creusa), iv. 308 (Dido), viii. 73 (Aeneas), xii. 11, 74, 97, 645
(Turnus). For a similar pathetic use of words of relationship
see iv. 31 (*sorori*), ix. 484 (*matri*), xii. 872 (*germana*).

For *gratia* in this sense cf. Juv. 8. 64 f. 'nil ibi maiorum
respectus, gratia nulla / umbrarum': so in the common phrase
in gratiam alicuius. Amata uses *honos* in a similar appeal, xii.
56 f. 'si quis Amatae / tangit honos animum'.

402. iuris . . . remordet, 'if any concern for a mother's rights
bites into your hearts': *ius* is the code or system of rights and
duties which is recognized in some form of human relation-
ship: so 'pia iura parentum' (Ovid, *Met.* viii. 499), 'iure
sodalicii' (Ovid, *Tr.* iv. 10. 46), 'iura iugalia' (Ovid, *Met.*
vii. 715), 'iura summae necessitudinis' (Cic. *Fam.* xiii. 14. 1).
For *remordet* cf. i. 261 'haec te cura remordet'; Lucr. iv. 1135
'cum conscius ipse animus se forte remordet'.

403. soluite crinalis uittas: Ovid repeats the phrase in another
description of Bacchic rites, *Met.* iv. 4 ff. 'festum celebrare
sacerdos / immunesque operum famulas dominasque suo-

rum / pectora pelle tegi, crinales soluere uittas, / serta coma,
manibus frondentis sumere thyrsos / iusserat'. The *uitta* was
a linen headband, in the classical period part of the costume
of the Roman matron: cf. Plaut. *M.G.* 792 f. 'capite compto,
crinis uittasque habeat adsimuletque se / tuam esse uxorem';
Ovid, *Tr.* ii. 252 'stola . . . uittaque sumpta'. (Prop. iv.
11. 33 f. shows that the *uirgo ingenua* wore a *uitta* of another
kind: 'mox, ubi iam facibus cessit praetexta maritis, / uinxit
et acceptas altera uitta comas'.)

   orgia is used first of secret rites (ὄργια), especially those
of the mysteries and of Bacchic worship (*Geo.* iv. 521 'inter
sacra deum nocturnique orgia Bacchi', *Aen.* iv. 302 f.
'audito stimulant trieterica Baccho / orgia'; Cat. 64. 259
'pars obscura cauis celebrabant orgia cistis'). Later (in Latin:
this meaning is not found in Greek) the word is applied to the
sacred objects of such rites: Sen. *H.O.* 594 f. 'nos Cadmeis
orgia ferre / tecum solitae condita cistis'. Here the word has
its first meaning, *capere* being used, as in the phrase *rem
publicam capere*, in a sense for which prose would normally
use *suscipere*.

406–44. *Allecto's next victim is Turnus at Ardea. In the guise of
a priestess of Juno carrying a message from the goddess she ap-
pears to him in sleep and invites him to avenge the affront put
upon him by attacking the Trojans and calling on Latinus to
give him satisfaction. Turnus treats her and her message with
scorn.*

406. uisa: i.e. *sibi uisa*.

407. consilium . . . uertisse, 'had overturned both his purpose
and his home'. ('Upset' corresponds closely to *uertisse* but
is too much weakened by usage to represent it here.)

408. tristis dea, 'the grim goddess': so ii. 337 'tristis Erinys'.

409. audacis Rutuli: i.e. Turnus: he has the same epithet, with
its suggestion of presumptuous and ill-starred gallantry, in
ix. 3, 126, x. 276. See on viii. 110.

409 f. muros, quam dicitur urbem . . . fundasse: see on 477.

410. Acrisioneis: the adjective is formed from *Acrision*, a con-
venient by-form of Acrisius. In the Greek legend Acrisius,
alarmed by a prophecy that the son of his daughter Danae
would kill him, sent her out to sea, with the infant Perseus,
in an open chest which carried them to the island of Seriphus.
The Italian version of the story which Virgil favours does
not mention the cause of Danae's voyage but makes her
land on the coast of Italy and establish a settlement for her
crew at Ardea in Rutulian territory, where she married the
king, the ancestor of Turnus. (Servius, noting that 'sola

uenerat, non cum colonis', tries to keep the usual form of the legend with the desperate suggestion that *Acrisioneis* is a feminine patronymic!)

411. praecipiti . . . Noto: cf. Hor. *Od.* i. 3. 12 'nec timuit praecipitem Africum'.

   delata, 'carried to shore': cf. 22 'delati', v. 57.

412. auis: for the dative of the agent after a passive verb cf. 507 'quod cuique repertum', i. 326 'audita mihi', iii. 14 'regnata Lycurgo', viii. 169 'iuncta est mihi', ix. 565 'quaesitum . . . matri': the construction, in prose usage severely restricted (and generally confined to gerundial phrases and perfect participles), is freely employed in verse. *a* or *ab* with the ablative of the agent is rare in Virgil: the only examples seem to be ii. 429, iv. 356 (= 377), vii. 310, x. 375.

   nunc: for the shift of perspective to the poet's own time cf. 3 'et nunc', viii. 339 'quam memorant'.

   magnum manet Ardea nomen: so MV; M²R have *tenet*, which Servius reads, perhaps a reminiscence of vi. 234 f. 'qui nunc Misenus ab illo / dicitur aeternumque tenet per saecula nomen'. 'bene adlusit' says Servius: 'nam Ardea quasi ardua dicta est, id est magna et nobilis, licet Hyginus in Italicis urbibus ab augurio auis ardeae dictam uelit'. Virgil plays on the meaning of place-names elsewhere (see on 3, 4, and 684) and this may be an instance of the same trick: Servius' etymology may indeed be true. The alternative one, out of which Ovid (*Met.* xiv. 573 ff.) makes a story of a heron rising out of the ashes of the city when it was destroyed, is fanciful.

   The legendary foundation of Ardea is an anachronism: archaeological evidence shows that the settlement of the site, on a hill seven miles inland from the sea, by the Rutulians, a Latin people, was more or less contemporary with the settlement of Rome. (See A. Boëthius in *Boll. dell'Ass. Internaz. degli Studi Mediterranei*, June–July 1931.) In the sixth century Ardea was a powerful member of the league of Latin towns which challenged the supremacy of Rome: in the fifth it found itself involved in the wars of Rome with the Volsci to the south of it and a Romany colony, an outpost against Volscian attack, was established in it in 434 B.C. (Diod. xii. 34; Livy iv. 11. 3). By the time of the second Punic War it had already declined (Livy xxvii. 9. 7), and in the Augustan period it was no more than ἴχνη πόλεως (Strabo v. 3. 5), one of the deserted towns of Latium, unhealthy and insignificant except for the ancient cults which were maintained in it (see on 419: cf. Cic. *N.D.* iii. 47 'cum fana circuimus in agro Ardeati').

413. fortuna fuit, 'is no more', 'is a thing of the past', as in ii. 325 'fuimus Troes, fuit Ilium'. So Tib. iii. 5. 32 'siue erimus seu nos fata fuisse uelint'; Ovid, *Her.* 17. 192 'cumque nihil speres firmius esse (amore), fuit'; *El. in Maec.* 2. 14 'cum dicar subita uoce fuisse tibi'.

414. carpebat . . . quietem: for this peculiarly Virgilian use cf. *Geo.* iii. 435 'mollis sub diuo carpere somnos', *Aen.* iv. 522 f. 'placidum carpebant fessa soporem / corpora', 555 'carpebat somnos'.

415. toruam: see on 399 f.

faciem: see on 448.

417. obscenam: *obscenus* is properly a term of religious practice, 'ill-omened', 'sinister': Virgil has it of howling dogs (*Geo.* i. 470), of the Harpies (*Aen.* iii. 241), of an omen of blood (iv. 455), of the Furies (xii. 876).

rugis arat: so Ovid, *Met.* iii. 275 f. has 'simulauit anum . . . / sulcauitque cutem rugis'.

418. ramum innectit oliuae: the badge of the priestly function: cf. 750 f. 'sacerdos / fronde super galeam et felici comptus oliua', vi. 808 f. 'quis procul ille autem ramis insignis oliuae / sacra ferens?'; so Aeneas, making an offering, is 'caput tonsae foliis euinctus oliuae' (v. 774).

419. Calybe: Virgil does not hesitate to give his Italian priestess a Greek name (*Καλύβη*): it is not uncommon, probably as a slave-name, in Italian inscriptions.

Iunonis . . . templique: for the combination cf. ii. 319 'arcis Phoebique sacerdos'.

anus . . . sacerdos : *anus* is regularly used as an adjective with feminine nouns as *senex* is with masculine: so Cat. 68. 46 'carta anus'; Ovid, *A.A.* i. 766 'cerua anus'; Mart. i. 105. 4 'testa anus'; Suet. *Nero* 11 'anus matronas'.

The temple of Juno at Ardea, with old paintings on its walls, was an object of interest in Pliny's time (*N.H.* xxxv. 115). Recent excavation on the arx has brought to light the remains of a temple which show work extending over a long period, from the sixth century B.C. to the first; it may well be the temple of Juno but no inscription has been found and it cannot be certainly identified.

421. fusos . . . labores: cf. *Geo.* iv. 491 f. 'omnis / effusus labor'.

422. tua . . . sceptra: i.e. the sceptre that is yours by right. For the plural see on 445.

transcribi, 'be made over': *transcribere* is a technical term of law for the transference or assignment of property by one person to another (e.g. *Dig.* 19. 5. 12 'conuenisse . . . ut eos fundos . . . mulier transcriberet uiro': so *nomina transcripticia* are transferred debts). In v. 750 'transcribunt urbi matres'

Virgil uses another technical sense of the verb, that of trans-
ferring a name from one register to another (cf. Val. Max.
ii. 7. 15 'ut . . . qui pedites fuerant in funditorum auxilia
transcriberentur ').

423. quaesitas sanguine is difficult to reconcile with 46, 'longa
. . . in pace' (but cf. viii. 55 'hi [the Arcadians settled on the
site of Rome] bellum adsidue ducunt cum gente Latina'),
and the juxtaposition of *quaesitas* (*a te*) and *quaeritur* (*ab eo*),
with different reference, is extremely awkward: see on 491.

425. i nunc . . . offer: '*Now* go and face danger, if you like';
for the sarcastic formula cf. Hor. *Ep*. i. 6. 17 f. 'i nunc,
argentum et marmor uetus . . . / suspice'; Ovid, *Her*. 9. 105
'i nunc, tolle animos et fortia gesta recense'. More often the
imperatives are connected by *et*; so Hor. *Ep*. ii. 2. 76 'i nunc
et uersus tecum meditare canoros'; Ovid, *Her*. 3. 26 'i nunc
et cupidi nomen amantis habe'; Juv. 12. 57 'i nunc et uentis
animam committe'. *nunc* is omitted at ix. 634 'i, uerbis
uirtutem inlude superbis'.

ingratis: i.e. bringing no return: cf. *Geo*. iii. 97 f. 'fru-
straque laborem / ingratum trahit'.

inrise: for the literary artifice by which a predicative ad-
jective or participle which would normally agree with the
subject in the nominative is attracted into agreement with
a vocative expressed or implied cf. ii. 282 f. 'quibus, Hector,
ab oris / exspectate uenis?', x. 327 'miserande iaceres', 811
'quo moriture ruis?', xi. 856 'huc periture ueni', xii. 947 f.
'tune hinc spoliis indute meorum / eripiare mihi?'. It ap-
pears first in the Augustan poets and was no doubt suggested
by Greek precedents: cf. Aesch. *Pers*. 674 ὦ πολύκλαυτε φίλοισι
θανών: Soph. *Phil*. 759 f. δύστηνε σύ, / δύστηνε δῆτα διὰ πόνων πάντων
φανείς: Theoc. 17. 66 ὄλβιε κοῦρε γένοιο. In Virgil's use it can be
felt to enhance pathetic effect, but it has an obvious metrical
advantage which poets exploit: for other examples cf. Hor.
Od. i. 2. 37; Tib. i. 7. 53; Ovid, *Her* 5. 59; Lucan v. 231; Pers.
3. 28. See E. Löfstedt, *Synt*. i². 103; K.–S. ii. 1. 255 f.

427. haec adeo, 'this very message': *adeo* emphasizes the word
which it follows—often a pronoun as here (cf. xi. 275 f. 'haec
adeo ex illo mihi iam speranda fuerunt / tempore', iv. 96
'nec me adeo fallit', *Ecl*. 4. 11 'teque adeo', *Geo*. i. 24 'tuque
adeo'), sometimes an emphatic adverb (*nunc adeo Aen*. ix. 156,
xi. 314; *iamque adeo* ii. 567, v. 268, 864, viii. 585, xi. 487; *sic
adeo* iv. 533; *uix adeo* vi. 498; *usque adeo Ecl*. 1. 12, *Geo*.
iv. 84, *Aen*. xii. 646) or a numeral (vii. 629 *quinque adeo*,
iii. 203 *tris adeo*).

iaceres: Henry pours scorn on the idea that Allecto-Calybe
should explain to Turnus that her message was to be delivered

to him in his sleep—'the whole verisimilitude of the vision destroyed in one word by the apparition itself!'—and accepts the anonymous correction *iacerem*, comparing the case of Beroe (v. 636 ff.) who reveals a message given to her in her sleep by Cassandra. But Virgil is simply following a Homeric pattern: when Oniros appears to Agamemnon in the guise of Nestor, announcing himself as a messenger sent by Zeus with a call to arms, he begins (*Il.* ii. 23) εὕδεις, Ἀτρέος υἱέ: when the εἴδωλον of her sister Iphthime is sent to the sleeping Penelope by Athena she begins (*Od.* iv. 804) εὕδεις, Πηνελόπεια; and Penelope (like Turnus here) replies to her before she wakes.

428. Saturnia: the Ennian title (Enn. *Ann.* 64 V.) associates Juno with the legendary past of Italy, the *Saturnia arua* (i. 569) of the Golden Age (see on 47 ff.).

429 f. moueri . . . in arua para: *in arma* of the manuscripts (cf. vi. 813 f. 'residesque mouebit / Tullus in arma uiros') does not fit *portis* and the repetition *armari . . . in arma* is intolerable: Peerlkamp's *arua* removes both faults. (Bentley detected the same corruption at xi. 173.) The accusative and infinitive as object of *para* is unparalleled (but cf. 56 f. 'quem . . . adiungi . . . properabat'): M's *iube* is a simplification borrowed from x. 242 and ill placed between *iussit* (428) and *iubet* (432).

429. pubem: see on 105.

430. laetus: of ready compliance as in 130 above, iii. 169.

Phrygios: see on 294.

431. consedere: cf. i. 572 'uultis et his mecum pariter considere regnis?'.

pictas: a stock epithet (like Homer's more particular μιλτοπάρῃος, φοινικοπάρῃος): so *Geo.* iv. 289, *Aen.* v. 663, viii. 93; Ovid, *Met.* iii. 639, vi. 511. For references to the painting of ships see C. Torr, *Ancient Ships* (Cambridge, 1894; repr. Chicago, 1964), 35 ff.: it is an inessential ornament for Horace (*Od.* i. 14. 14 f. 'nil pictis timidus nauita puppibus / fidit'), and Seneca (*Ep.* 76. 13 'nauis bona dicitur non quae pretiosis coloribus picta est . . . sed stabilis et firma').

432. caelestum uis magna, 'the mighty power of heaven': cf. i. 4 'ui superum', xii. 199 'uimque deum infernam'.

caelestum: for the form see on 189.

433. dicto parere, 'obey orders': Virgil has the same common phrase in i. 695, iii. 189, xi. 242 (cf. xii. 568 'ni frenum accipere et uicti parere fatentur'). There is no evidence for the meaning 'keep his word' (Heyne); for that the appropriate verb would be *manere*: cf. viii. 643 'dictis . . . maneres', ii. 160 'promissis maneas'.

parere fatetur, 'agrees to obey', perhaps: the present in-finitive in place of the future is not uncommon with such verbs: e.g. with *sperare* iv. 305 f., 337 f., v. 18; with *iurare* iv. 425 f.; with *promittere* iv. 487, xi. 503 (Caesar regularly uses the present infinitive with *polliceri*). But the present here and in the similar xii. 568 (quoted above) should prob-ably be strictly taken, 'admits that he allows the wedding and accepts orders': cf. Stat. *Ach.* i. 483 'cedit turba ducum uincique haud maesta fatetur', *Theb.* vi. 660 f. 'absistunt procul attonitique fatentur / cedere'.

ni . . . fatetur: the use of the present in the protasis of conditional sentences in future time is not uncommon (especially in comedy and Cicero's letters), in admonitions, threats or promises, when the verb refers to the immediate future: cf. ix. 194, 240; Plaut. *Merc.* 510 'bona si esse uis, bene erit tibi'; Cat. 55. 18 f. 'si linguam clauso tenes in ore, / fructus proicies amoris omnes', 13. 1 f. 'cenabis bene . . . apud me / paucis, si tibi di fauent, diebus'; Cic. *Phil.* vii. 19 'si bellum omittimus, pace numquam fruemur', *Fam.* xvi. 1. 2 'si statim nauigas, nos Leucade consequēre', *Acad.* ii. 93 'erunt (molesti) nisi cauetis'; Tib. i. 8. 77 'te poena manet ni desinis esse superba'. For the omission of *se* cf. iii. 603, xii. 568, 794, and see on viii. 534.

434. sentiat, 'let him feel it to his cost', is best taken absolutely as in Ter. *Ad.* 139 f. 'iste tuos ipse sentiet / posterius': so in Greek γνώσῃ (Aesch. *Agam.* 1649; Eur. *Heracl.* 65) and εἴσεται (Aesch. *Cho.* 305; Eur. *I.A.* 970). For this meaning of *sentire* with an object cf., e.g., Hor. *Od.* iv. 6. 1 ff. 'quem proles Niobaea magnae / uindicem linguae . . . / sensit', ii. 7. 9 f. 'tecum Philippos et celerem fugam / sensi'.

experiatur in armis: cf. 235.

435. hic, 'thereupon'.

uatem: she has claimed to be a seer by reporting her vision to Juno.

435 f. orsa . . . refert: again in xi. 124: the substantival use of the participle, 'beginnings', is very rare, and this meaning, 'first words', is found only in Virgil: in x. 632 he uses it more generally as equivalent to *incepta* ('in melius tua . . . orsa reflectas').

437. rere: apart from the convenient participle *ratus*, the forms of *reor* have an archaic colour, as Cicero (*de Or.* iii. 153) and Quintilian (viii. 3. 26) recognized. In Cicero's speeches and Caesar they are not found: in classical verse they are rare (once in Tibullus, Propertius, and Juvenal: not in Horace) except in Virgil and Ovid. See A. Yon, *Ratio et les mots de la famille de reor* (Paris, 1933), 52.

nuntius: for the accusative and infinitive noun-clause depending on the noun *nuntius* cf. vi. 456 f.

438. mihi: ethic dative—'pray do not invent these alarms'. *ne finge* (see on 96) is parenthetical: I know just what has happened, Turnus says, and Juno will take care of me.

439. For the incomplete line see on 129.

440. uicta situ, 'overcome by decay': cf. *Geo.* i. 180 'puluere uicta fatiscat'. *situs,* 'disuse', 'neglectedness'—sometimes concretely used of the physical effects of disuse, mould, rust, or dirt—is here metaphorically used of mental 'rusting': cf. Livy xxxiii. 45. 7 'marcescere otii situ queri ciuitatem'.

uerique effeta, 'past bearing truth': the genitive may be explained as one of the sphere within which the epithet is applied or as an extension of the usage with adjectives signifying want: similarly Virgil has *ueri uana,* x. 630 f. Persius' *ueri steriles* (5. 75) is perhaps a reminiscence of Virgil's phrase. For the metaphor of *effeta* cf. viii. 508 'saeclisque effeta senectus'.

441. o mater: for the emotional address cf. 360.

exercet, 'harasses': cf. v. 779 'exercita curis', *Geo.* iv. 453 'non te nullius exercent numinis irae'.

442. inter: for *inter* following its objects cf. *Geo.* ii. 344 f. 'frigusque caloremque / inter'.

443 f. The adjuration is Homeric: *Il.* vi. 490 ff. (Hector to Andromache) ἀλλ' εἰς οἶκον ἰοῦσα τὰ σ' αὐτῆς ἔργα κόμιζε / . . . πόλεμος δ' ἄνδρεσσι μελήσει / πᾶσι, μάλιστα δ' ἐμοί (cf. xx. 137: μελήσει in both passages confirms the future *gerent*).

445–74. *Allecto throws off her disguise and uses her own weapons on the sleeping Turnus: he wakes to an infatuated passion for war and calls on his Rutulians to take up arms.*

445. exarsit in iras: Ovid borrows the expression, *Met.* v. 41 'ardescit uulgus in iras'. Servius here has the curious note 'est specialis Cornelii elocutio': if the reference is to Tacitus, the name is surprising, but the use of *in* 'de consilio et effectu actionum' is in fact common in Tacitus (J. N. Madvig, *Opusc. Acad.* i. 168 f.). For other adverbial phrases in which *in* indicates result or intention cf. ii. 347 'ardere in proelia', x. 455 'meditantem in proelia', xii. 71 'ardet in arma', 854 'in omen . . . occurrere iussit': see also on vii. 13 and viii. 260.

iras: Virgil uses the plural of both *ira* and *odium* oftener than the singular and shows a preference for the plural even where there is neither plural implication (as there is, e.g., in 15, 336, 755) nor obvious metrical convenience to account for his preference. Sometimes, as here and in 305, the plural

of an abstract noun may be felt to give the notion more con-
creteness: so perhaps *amores* in iv. 292, *furias* in iv. 474. It is
difficult to establish generalizations on the principles which
Virgil, and Latin poets in general, observed in their use of the
'poetic' plural: considerations of metre and euphony play
an important part, but the idiom, whatever its origin, is re-
cognized and cultivated as a matter of technique, as a dis-
tinctive mannerism of poetic language. See E. Löfstedt, *Synt.*
i². 27 ff.; P. Maas in *A.L.L.* xii. 479 ff.; G. Landgraf in *A.L.L.*
xiv. 63 ff.; E. Norden, *Aeneis VI*, pp. 408 f.; W. Schink,
De Romanorum plurali poetico (diss. Jena, 1911); M. Leu-
mann, *Kl. Schr.* 145, who quotes the extreme example,
uocabula used of a single word in Ovid, *Met.* xiv. 621.

446. oranti: here (and perhaps in x. 96 'talibus orabat Iuno')
orare has the archaic sense of 'speak' which survived in *orator*.

448. facies, 'shape', 'form', 'figure' (it is a verbal noun cor-
responding to *facio*: compare English 'make'): so vi. 575
(of the Fury) 'facies quae limina seruet', viii. 194 'Caci
facies . . . dira', xii. 416 'faciem circumdata nimbo', v. 619
'faciemque deae uestemque reponit', ii. 601 'Tyndaridis
facies', iii. 310 'uerane te facies, uerus mihi nuntius adfers?',
i. 658 'faciem mutatus et ora', *Geo.* iii. 58 '(bos) faciem tauro
propior'.

449. cunctantem: cf. iv. 390 f. 'multa metu cunctantem et
multa parantem / dicere'.

451. uerbera insonuit: the internal accusative is unparalleled:
Virgil has the normal ablative in v. 579 'insonuitque flagello'.

454. respice ad haec: she displays her snakes and her whip as
she speaks: for the parenthetical *respice* cf. ii. 615.

455. For the incomplete line see on 129.

456. iuueni: for the dative cf. 346.

456 f. atro lumine: cf. iv. 384 'sequar atris ignibus absens',
viii. 198 f. 'atros / ore uomens ignis', xi. 186 'subiectisque
ignibus atris'. The suggestion is of smoky flame, but *ater*, as
always in Virgil, has its sinister overtone: see on 525.

457. fixit sub pectore taedas: for the attempt to convey mental
phenomena in physical terms cf. 347 ff. *sub* is not 'beneath'
but 'in the depths of': so iv. 332 'sub corde', x. 464 f. 'sub
imo corde', iii. 431 'uasto . . . sub antro', 443 'rupe sub ima',
ix. 244 'sub uallibus', xi. 23 'Acheronte sub imo': similarly
with the accusative xi. 397 'sub Tartara', 'into the depths of
Tartarus': for a corresponding use of *ante* see on 531.

458. olli: *ollus* or *olle* is an archaic doublet of *ille* (the first
syllable of the adverbs *olim* and *ultra* represents the same
stem); it is used by Ennius but was already out of currency
by Plautus' time, though it was preserved in a few fixed

formulas (e.g. *olla centuria* at the comitia: see Varro, *L.L.*
vii. 42). Virgil uses three forms of it—dative singular (four-
teen times), nominative plural (line 505: and six other times),
and dative plural (twice). These forms almost always stand
in an emphatic position at the beginning of a line or a sen-
tence: they occur oftener in Book XII than in any other
book (six times: five times in V, thrice in VIII, twice each
in VI and VII, once in I, IV, IX, X, XI). This is one of the
Virgilian archaisms mentioned with admiration by Quin-
tilian (viii. 3. 24): 'propriis (uerbis) dignitatem dat anti-
quitas. namque et sanctiorem et magis admirabilem faciunt
orationem quibus non quilibet fuerit usurus: eoque orna-
mento accerimi iudicii P. Vergilius unice est usus. olli enim
et quianam et moerus et pone et porricerent aspergunt illam,
quae etiam in picturis est gratissima, uetustatis inimitabilem
arti auctoritatem'. Virgil's choice of the archaism seems to
have been suggested by considerations of sound, for (1) he
confines it to those forms which avoid a repeated *i*, and (2)
he tends to use it in a context of *o*-sounds: so here and in
i. 252 ff., vi. 729 ff., x. 744 ff., xii. 308 ff. See F. Glöckner,
A.L.L. xiv. 185 ff.; J. Kvičala, *Neue Beiträge zur Erklärung
der Aeneis* (Prague, 1881), 410; N. I. Herescu, *La Poésie
latine* (Paris, 1960), 100.

459. proruptus, 'breaking out': cf. i. 246 'mare proruptum',
vii. 569 'rupto . . . Acheronte': the use of the participle with
active meaning represents the same reflexive use, correspond-
ing to the Greek middle voice, which survives in so-called
deponent and semi-deponent verbs and in a number of other
active participles of passive form from intransitive verbs
(e.g. *cenatus, pransus*: see on 503). For the collocation *pro-
ruptus . . . rumpit*, awkward to a modern ear, see on 491.

460. arma . . . requirit: cf. xi. 453 'arma manu trepidi poscunt,
fremit arma iuuentus'. For *fremere* see on 389: *arma* seems
to be an internal limiting accusative ('raises a cry of arms'):
cf. Accius, *trag.* 288 R. 'fremere bellum'. The repetition *arma
. . . arma* is traditional in the call to arms: cf. ii. 668 'arma,
uiri, ferte arma'; Hor. *Od.* i. 35. 15 f. 'ad arma cessantis
ad arma / concitet'; Ovid, *Met.* xi. 377 f. 'arma, / arma
capessamus', xii. 241 'certatimque omnes uno ore arma,
arma loquuntur'; so Aesch. fr. 140 N². ὅπλων ὅπλων δεῖ: see
E. Fraenkel in *J.R.S.* xxxv (1945), 6 n. 9.

    toro: his sword is beneath his pillow: cf. vi. 523 f. 'arma
omnia tectis / emouet et fidum capiti subduxerat ensem'.

461. insania belli is equivalent to *insana cupido belli* (cf. *Ecl.*
10. 44 'insanus amor duri . . . Martis'): similarly viii. 327
'belli rabies'.

462. ira super, 'to crown all, personal resentment': as Conington observes, the analysis of feeling which represents personal resentment as supervening on an infatuate desire for fighting is hardly plausible. For the adverbial *super* in the sense of *insuper* cf. i. 29, ii. 71; Lucr. iii. 672, 901, v. 763.

462 ff. Virgil elaborates into a simile (suggested, no doubt, by *Il.* xxi. 362 ff.) the common metaphor of *aestuare* or *feruere*, but the comparison of the surging passions in Turnus' breast to the heaving and bubbling of water in a pot over a roaring fire is not a very happy one: as in the description of the eating of the tables (see on 110 ff.), Virgil sets himself to invest commonplace things with epic dignity by enhancement of language—the extravagant *amnis* and *unda*, the poetic *latices,* the archaic *aquai*.

462 f. flamma . . . uirgea: cf. viii. 694 'stuppea flamma'.

464. exsultant: cf. iii. 557 'exsultant uada'.

latices : *latex* is a word of unknown origin (the suggested derivation from λάταξ is very doubtful), almost entirely confined to verse (though Livy has it in a purple passage, xliv. 33. 2): Virgil, like Lucretius before him, uses it of any liquid.

aquai: only M reads *aquai*; F and R have *aquae uis* (as has the quotation in Macrobius v. 11. 23). Servius read *aquai* and Quintilian's reference (i. 7. 18 'pictai uestis et aquai Vergilius amantissimus uetustatis carminibus inseruit') must (if it is true) be to this line, since the form does not occur elsewhere in Virgil: *aquae uis* was presumably introduced to make the construction easier. Servius' statement that in Virgil's own manuscript the line ended *aquae amnis* and that, because the ending of two consecutive lines with the same word was 'satis asperum', Varius and Tucca substituted *aquai* cannot be taken seriously: Varius can have taken no such liberty (see F. Leo, *Plautinische Forschungen*² [Berlin, 1912], 40 ff.).

Virgil uses the archaic genitive form *-ai* (which is common in Lucretius) three times elsewhere—iii. 354 *aulai*, vi. 747 *aurai*, ix. 26 *pictai*.

465 f. amnis . . . unda: Virgil uses both words elsewhere in similar contexts: *Geo.* i. 296 'foliis undam trepidi despumat aëni', *Aen.* xii. 417 (of a healing preparation poured from a jar) 'fusum labris splendentibus amnem'.

466. nec iam se capit, 'has not now room for itself': cf. ix. 644 'nec te Troia capit'.

467. polluta pace must refer to Turnus' act: 'desecrates the peace and orders his men to march'. For *polluere* of the violation of a solemn obligation cf. iii. 61 'pollutum hospitium', v. 5 f. 'amore . . . polluto'.

468 f. parari . . . tutari . . . detrudere: for the shift from passive to active cf. iii. 60 f. 'omnibus idem animus, scelerata excedere terra, / linqui pollutum hospitium et dare classibus Austros', v. 772 f. 'agnam / caedere deinde iubet soluique ex ordine funem', xi. 83 f. 'indutosque iubet truncos hostilibus armis / ipsos ferre duces inimicaque nomina figi'.

470. satis ambobus, 'a match for both parties': cf. Prop. iv. 8. 32 'potae non satis unus erit'; Sil. vii. 62 f. 'nec tamen occisos est cur laetere: supersunt / quot tibi sint Libyaeque satis'; Gell. v. 5. 4 'putasne . . . satis esse Romanis haec omnia?'.

ambobus : for the rare use of *ambo* as a 'double plural' cf. x. 758 f. 'di . . . iram miserantur inanem / amborum' (i.e. of both armies).

uenire: for this emphatic use of the verb to mark the impact of someone or something appearing in an unexpected or striking guise see D. R. Shackleton Bailey, *Propertiana*, 31: cf. viii. 365 'rebusque ueni non asper egenis'; Prop. i. 10. 25 'irritata uenit, quando contemnitur illa'; Man. v. 620 'immitis ueniet': so with impersonal subject *Aen.* v. 344 'gratior et pulchro ueniens ('presenting itself') in corpore uirtus'; Prop. ii. 34. 81 'non tamen haec ulli uenient ingrata legenti'. For a similar use of ἐλθεῖν see Jebb on Soph. *O.T.* 1357.

Teucrisque . . . Latinisque: for the repeated *-que* see on 186: for the hypermetric line see on 160.

471. Turnus calls the gods to witness his vow that he will repay them if they grant him victory: cf. v. 234, xii. 780. Note the alliteration on *d* and *u*, and see Appendix.

474. claris . . . factis: ablative of description with *dextera*.

475–510. *Allecto now moves to the other side. Finding Iulus hunting, she puts his hounds on the scent of a tame stag belonging to Silvia, the daughter of Latinus' chief herdsman, and makes Iulus innocently shoot it down. Silvia's distress rouses her brothers and they and their neighbours seize weapons to avenge the injury.*

477 ff. The incident of the tame stag is Virgil's own addition to the story (perhaps based on a Hellenistic motive) which enables him to make the Trojans (thanks to Allecto) the innocent cause of offence. Ovid's account of the accidental killing of the tame stag by Cyparissus (*Met.* x. 109 ff.) owes some of its details to Virgil—'ingens ceruus erat'; 'celebrare domos mulcendaque colla / quamlibet ignotis manibus praebere solebat'; 'texebas uarios per cornua flores'. (Unwilling, as often, *quod bene cessit relinquere,* Ovid makes Cyparissus take rides on the stag.)

477. locum, quo litore: a development of the idiom, common
in early Latin and occasionally found in classical prose,
especially with *locus* and *dies*, by which the antecedent is
repeated in a relative clause (e.g. Plaut. *Epid.* 41 'est caussa
qua caussa simul mecum ire ueritust'; Ter. *Heaut.* 20 'habet
bonorum exemplum quo exemplo...'; Caes. *B.G.* i. 49
'ultra eum locum quo in loco Germani consederant'). Here
the repeated antecedent is replaced by a word of similar
sense: so 409 f. 'ad muros quam dicitur urbem / ... Danae
fundasse' (cf. 348), i. 187 f. 'sagittas / corripuit fidus quae
tela gerebat Achates'; Cat. 64. 204 f. 'annuit inuicto caele-
stum numine rector; / quo motu ...', 96. 1 ff. 'si quicquam
... / accidere a nostro, Calue, dolore potest, / quo desiderio
ueteres renouamus amores'.

478. insidiis cursuque: i.e. by setting snares and by coursing.
agitare (cf. xi. 686, *Geo.* iii. 372, 409) is the technical term for
hunting game (e.g. Cic. *Off.* iii. 68; Livy xli. 9. 6; Hor. *Od.*
ii. 13. 40, iii. 12. 10; Ovid, *Met.* x. 539).

479. rabiem: see on 493.
 Note the unusual rhythm produced by three successive
anapaestic words: Virgil has sixteen such lines (see L. P.
Wilkinson, *Golden Latin Artistry*, 82). It might be thought to
convey a notion of breathless hurry here (and perhaps in,
e.g., *Geo.* i. 361 or *Aen.* iv. 403), but no such suggestion is
obvious in, e.g., *Aen.* v. 822 'tum uariae comitum facies'
or iii. 259 f. 'at sociis subita gelidus formidine sanguis /
deriguit'.

480. noto: see on 491.
481. laborum, 'trials', 'sufferings': see on 559.
482. bello, 'for war': for the dative of purpose cf. 536, 637, 642.
483. forma praestanti: the ablative forms an adjective parallel
to *cornibus ingens*.
485. nutribant: so xi. 572 *nutribat*: cf. 790 *insignibat*, viii. 160
uestibat, x. 538 *redimibat*; in these words the -ie- form is
metrically impossible, but that consideration does not apply
to *polibant* (viii. 436).
 Tyrrhus: the patronymic *Tyrrhidae* (484), which should
point to *Tyrrheus*, is dictated by metrical necessity, as
Belīdae (from *Belus*) is in ii. 82. In Dion. Hal. (i. 70. 2) the
herdsman is Τυρρηνός.
486. late is supported by Servius and *lati* is an obvious sim-
plification: Donatus knew both readings.
487. Siluia: 'bonum puellae rusticae nomen formauit', says
Servius: on the other hand it is perhaps surprising that
Virgil should have used for a minor character a name so
prominent in the legendary pedigree of the Kings of Rome.

488. mollibus ... sertis: i.e. wreaths of leaves: see on 390.

489. ferum, 'the wild creature': not so 'inappropriate' as Conington thinks. It contrasts the stag's natural state with its submission to handling, and *ferus* need not imply savagery: Neptune's team are *feri* in v. 818, Hercules' cattle in Ovid, *F*. i. 556.

490. manum patiens: i.e. *mansuetus*. Henry follows Servius in taking *patiens* as adjectival (comparing *patiens laborum*, *patiens Phoebi* and the like) and *manum* as a contracted genitive plural (for which there is a parallel in vi. 653 'quae gratia currum'). But there is no reason why *manum* should not be accusative and *patiens* participial (cf. Lucan iv. 239 'hominem didicere pati'): Henry's objection that the singular *manum* could only 'refer to a particular occasion' is ill-founded.

mensae ... erili: see on 1.

491. limina nota, 'the familiar door': Virgil likes the 'affective' use of the adjective, which he has here repeated (unconsciously, no doubt: see below) three times in twenty lines (cf. 480, 500): so ii. 256 'litora nota petens' (again iii. 657), v. 34 'laeti notae aduertuntur harenae', vi. 221 'uelamina nota', ix. 471 f. 'ora uirum praefixa mouebant / nota nimis', xi. 195 'munera nota', ('uelamina', 'ora' and 'munera' are the 'familiar' reminders of dead comrades).

It is natural for a writer unconsciously to repeat (in the same sense or even in a different sense) a word or phrase which is in his mind: so one finds Virgil writing *somno uinoque soluti* at ix. 189 and again at ix. 236 and using the rare *incita* (which occurs nowhere else in the poem) at xii. 492 and again at xii. 534. But Latin writers in general (Horace is a notable exception, as Housman points out, Lucan, p. xxxiii [see, however, W. C. Helmbold, *C.P.* lv (1960), 173 f. J. D. C.]) are remarkably insensitive to such fortuitous repetitions and much less concerned to avoid them than modern taste demands: their indifference in this matter is the more striking in view of the use which they make of deliberate repetition as a stylistic device. Virgil has many such repetitions, some, as here, at a few lines' interval (e.g. *Ecl*. I. 20-25 'solemus ... solebam ... solent', *Geo*. iv. 122-44 'sera ... sera ... seram ... seras', *Aen*. i. 103-16 'fluctus ... fluctu ... fluctus ... fluctibus ... fluctus'), some in successive lines (e.g. i. 614-15 'casu ... casus', ii. 470-1 'luce ... lucem', v. 780-1 'pectore ... pectus', vi. 684-5 'tendentem ... tetendit', vii. 423-4 'quaesitas ... quaeritur', 458-9 'rumpit ... proruptus', ix. 193-4 'exposcunt ... posco', x. 444-5 'iusso ... iussa', xi. 618-19 'uersi ...

uertunt'). On non-significant repetitions see J. Vahlen, *Opusc. Acad.* i. 355 ff.; J. Marouzeau, *Traité de stylistique latine*, 261 ff.; A. B. Cook in *C.R.* xvi (1902), 146 ff., 256 ff.; A. Poutsma in *Mnem.* xli (1913), 397 ff.; for Propertius, D. R. Shackleton Bailey, *Propertiana*, 9; for Ovid, E. J. Kenney in *C.Q.* liii (1959), 248.

With repetition may be considered another phenomenon which is equally at variance with later taste—the 'jingles' produced by placing at a short distance apart unrelated words which have some similarity of form. At vi. 204 'auri per ramos aura refulsit', the mannered originality of the phrase *auri aura* makes it impossible to think that the assonance was the result of inadvertence: that it was not is confirmed on the one hand by Horace, *Od.* i. 5. 9 ff. 'qui nunc te fruitur credulus aurea, / qui semper uacuam, semper amabilem / sperat, nescius aurae / fallacis', on the other by Pacuvius 363 R. 'terra exhalat auram ad auroram umidam'. At i. 399 'puppesque tuae pubesque tuorum', the jingle might be taken to be accidental, but Quintilian (ix. 3. 75) accepts it as a deliberately contrived effect. These examples suggest that other 'echoes' of this kind in Virgil are deliberate and calculated to appeal to the ear: such are vii. 164 'aut acris tendunt arcus' (repeated at ix. 665), iv. 238 'parere parabat', x. 99 'murmura uenturos nautis prodentia uentos', 191 f. 'canit . . . canentem' (repeated at 417 f. 'canens . . . canentia'), xi. 644 'tantus in arma patet: latos huic hasta per armos', xii. 389 'lato . . . latebram'.

492. ipse, 'of his own will': cf. *Ecl.* 4. 21 f. 'ipsae lacte domum referent distenta capellae / ubera', 7. 11 'ipsi potum uenient per prata iuuenci', *Geo.* iii. 316 '(oues) ipsae memores redeunt in tecta'; Varro, *R.R.* iii. 7. 6. 'ipsae (columbae) propter pullos quos habent utique redeunt'; Prop. iii. 13. 40 'dux aries saturas ipse reduxit ouis'.

493. rabidae: the regular term for hounds in cry: cf. Ovid, *A.A.* ii. 373 f. 'neque fuluus aper media tam saeuus in ira est, / fulmineo rabidos cum rotat ore canes'; Sen. *Oed.* 931 f. 'Cithaeron, uel feras in me tuas / emitte siluis, mitte uel rabidos canes', *Dial.* iii. 1. 6 'rabidarum canum tristis aspectus est'.

494. commouere, 'started': cf. v. 213 'spelunca subito commota columba'.

494 f. fluuio . . . leuaret: most editors have taken the meaning to be that when the dogs startled him, the stag was unsuspectingly taking his ease, floating with the stream, or (as we should say: Latin prefers to express the alternation by -*que*: see on 131) resting on the bank: Virgil amplifies the description, as Page says, to emphasize the animal's sense of security. But Henry may be right in taking the clauses to refer to the same act and picturing the stag as floating with the stream and at the same time enjoying the coolness of the shade of the greenery on the bank. *forte*, as usual, emphasizes the coincidence: *cum forte* is 'just when' (see on 509).

fluuio . . . deflueret: for the ablative of space cf. viii. 549 'secundo defluit amni'; Prop. ii. 4. 19 'tranquillo . . . descendis flumine'.

497. curuo . . . cornu is here a bow but in 513 *cornu recuruo* is a bugle: see on 509.

498. erranti cannot stand for (*alioquin*) *erraturae*, 'which was going to miss': it must be proleptic, 'did not fail his hand so that it missed'. The proleptic (or anticipatory) use of an adjective or a participle to express the result of the action of a verb is common in Virgil (e.g. 509 f. 'quadrifidam quercum . . . scindebat', 626 'spicula lucida tergent', i. 659 f. 'furentem / incendat reginam', iii. 141 'sterilis exurere . . . agros', 237 'scuta latentia condunt', x. 103 'premit placida aequora pontus', 331 '(tela) deflexit . . . stringentia corpus'), and the objections which have been made to such proleptic use in a negative sentence are due to failure to realize that *nec* negatives the whole sentence ('it was not the case that the god failed his hand so that it missed').

deus: there is no need to refer this to Allecto: the reference to divine power is formal and general, as it is, if the reading is sound, in ii. 632 'ducente deo', 'under divine guidance' (the guide is in fact Venus). So in Homer σὺν θεῷ, οὐκ ἄνευ θεοῦ: *Il.* vii. 4 f. ὡς δὲ θεὸς ναύτῃσιν ἐελδομένοισιν ἔδωκεν / οὖρον, *Od.* ix. 158 ἔδωκε θεὸς μενοεικέα θήρην.

499. perque . . . perque: for the expressive repetition cf. xi. 696 'perque arma . . . perque ossa'.

501. stabulis: i.e. the steading, farm-buildings.

502. imploranti similis: Dryden's 'beseeching eyes' of the hunted hare (*Annus Mirabilis*, 132) was perhaps suggested by this passage: cf. ii. 679 'gemitu tectum omne replebat'.

503. palmis percussa lacertos: this gesture of grief, striking the upper part of the arm with the other hand, appears elsewhere only in Claudian, *R.P.* ii. 248 f. 'planctuque lacertos / uerberat'.

percussa lacertos: a 'middle' or reflexive voice, indicating an action in which the agent has a concern beyond the action itself, was indigenous in Latin: it coincided in form with the passive (historically indeed in I.E. the passive had developed out of it). It survives in ordinary usage in the so-called deponent verbs (*laetor, mentior, miror, utor, fruor, uescor*, etc., in which the 'middle' force is not difficult to discern) and in the participles of some other verbs, such as *gauisus* and *ausus* (the so-called semi-deponents), *pransus* and *cenatus*. As in Greek, a 'middle' verb could govern a direct object and there are early examples of *indutus* so used: so Plautus has (*Men.* 511 f.) 'non ego te indutum tunica / exire uidi pallam?', (*Epid.* 223) 'quid erat induta? an regillam induculam an mendiculam?'. That use Virgil often follows with *induor* (640 'loricam induitur': for his other uses of the verb see note there). He also extends it to verbs of similar meaning (as Ennius had done in *Ann.* 400 V. 'succincti corda machaeris' and Catullus in 64. 64 f. 'non contecta leui uelatum pectus amictu, / non tereti strophio lactentis uincta papillas'), the direct object being either (*a*) what is put on or (*b*) the part of the body which is clothed: so (*a*) ii. 510 f. 'inutile ferrum / cingitur', iv. 137 'chlamydem circumdata', 493 'magicas . . . accingier artis', (*b*) ii. 721 f. 'umeros . . . insternor pelle leonis', iii. 545 'capita . . . Phrygio uelamur amictu', v. 309 'caput nectentur oliua', viii. 457 'tunicaque inducitur artus', xii. 120 'uerbena tempora uincti'. A development of the same usage, perhaps under Greek influence, can be seen in a number of participial phrases in which a 'middle' sense is obvious: so here ('striking her arms with her hands'), i. 481 'tunsae pectora palmis', xi. 877 'percussae pectora matres', xii. 606 'laniata genas', iii. 65 'crinem de more solutae' ('having loosed their hair'), ix. 478 'scissa comam', ix. 659 'os impressa toro', i. 561 'uultum demissa', vi. 156 'defixus lumina', x. 133 'caput . . . detectus honestum' ('uncovering his head'), xi. 480 'oculos deiecta', xii. 224 'formam adsimulata Camerti' ('making her appearance like C.'), vii. 806 'adsueta manus', v. 608 'saturata dolorem'. See also on 796. The same use is found, rarely, in other forms of the verb: so viii. 265 'nequeunt expleri corda'.

But Virgil uses a large number of other phrases in which a participle which is clearly not 'middle' but passive, since the subject's will is not concerned at all, is accompanied by an accusative which cannot be a direct object (e.g. *Geo.* iv. 357 'percussa noua mentem formidine': cf. *Cat.* 64. 296 'restrictus membra catena'; Lucr. v. 1223 'percussi membra timore'). In these one must recognize the influence of a purely Greek construction, the so-called 'accusative of respect' (or 'of part affected'), a particular form of the internal or limiting accusative. That construction is in Latin found also with intransitive active verbs (with a finite verb in Lucr. iii. 489 'tremit artus', repeated in *Geo.* iii. 84: often with participles, e.g. *Aen.* ii. 381 'colla tumentem', v. 97

'nigrantis terga') and with adjectives (e.g. i. 320 'nuda genu',
v. 285 'Cressa genus', vii. 59 f. 'laurus . . . sacra comam',
ix. 650 f. 'omnia longaeuo similis uocemque coloremque / et
crinis albos', Geo. iii. 58 'faciem tauro propior', iv. 181
'(apes) crura thymo plenae': the existence of the 'middle'
construction, which afforded a Latin 'frame' (L. R. Palmer,
The Latin Language [London, 1954], 288) for this Greek con-
struction, probably accounts for its frequency with past
participles: some of the many Virgilian instances are iii. 47
'mentem formidine pressus', v. 869 'animum concussus',
viii. 29 'turbatus pectora', ix. 543 f. 'pectora . . . transfossi'.
(See K.-S. ii. 1. 288 ff.; G. Landgraf in A.L.L. x. 209 ff.)

There are a few instances in which Virgil seems to have
experimented beyond these patterns and in which another
Greek construction, the so-called retained accusative after a
passive verb, may have influenced his expression: Ecl. 3. 106 f.
'inscripti nomina regum / . . . flores', Aen. ii. 273 'traiectus
lora', iii. 428 'delphinum caudas utero commissa luporum',
x. 156 f. 'puppis / . . . Phrygios subiuncta leones'.

504. conclamat: conclamare in the sense of conuocare is only
here in Virgil (and later in Ovid, Met. xiii. 73 and Claudian,
R.P. iii. 4): elsewhere the con- is intensive (e.g. ii. 233, iii.
523, vi. 259, xii. 426).

505. olli: see on 458.

pestis: i.e. the Fury who is standing by to watch the pro-
gress of her handiwork and prompt further mischief.

tacitis: see on 343.

aspera: 'savage' perhaps comes near to the force of the
word in Virgil: Juno herself is aspera in i. 279, Mezentius
in 647 below: cf. i. 14 '(urbs) studiis asperrima belli', v. 730
'gens dura atque aspera cultu', vi. 882 'fata aspera', vii. 729
'Saticulus asper', ix. 667 (xii. 124 f.) 'pugna aspera', x. 87
'grauidam bellis urbem et corda aspera'.

506. improuisi: i.e. before Silvia looked for them.

torre . . . obusto: the sudibus praeustis of 524: cf. xi. 894
'stipitibus ferrum sudibusque imitantur obustis'.

507. stipitis . . . grauidi nodis : cf. viii. 220 f. 'nodisque graua-
tum / robur'.

cuique: for the dative of the agent see on 412.

508. rimanti: the verb is rare before the Silver Age, but Virgil
has it four times elsewhere: Geo. i. 384 '(uolucres) rimantur
prata Caystri', iii. 534 'rastris terram rimantur', Aen. vi.
597 ff. 'uultur . . . / uiscera rimaturque epulis', xi. 748 f.
'partis rimatur apertas, / qua uulnus letale ferat'.

509. quadrifidam . . . scindebat: for the proleptic use of the ad-
jective ('was cleaving to split it into four') see on 498.

ut forte: cf. xii. 270: so *cum forte* ('just when'), vii. 494, iii. 301, vi. 190, *tum forte* ('just then') ix. 3, 638: the force of *forte* is to emphasize coincidence.

cuneis ... coactis, 'driven home': Virgil repeats the phrase in a quite different sense in xii. 457, of 'massed wedges' of troops. Conington on x. 396 gives a list of such repetitions: e.g. 'cessere magistri' (*Geo.* iii. 549, *Aen.* xii. 717), 'per uarios casus' (i. 204, x. 352), 'securus amorum' (i. 350, x. 326), 'arma quiescunt/-ant' (x. 836, xii. 78); *discrimina dare* is used in two senses in twelve lines (x. 382 f., 393); *alta petens* occurs three times with three different meanings of *alta* (*Geo.* i. 142, *Aen.* v. 508, vii. 362).

510. spirans immane: cf. x. 726 'hians immane', xii. 535 'immane frementi'; the phrase is perhaps suggested by μέγα πνέων. For *immanis* see on 305.

511–39. *Exploiting her success, Allecto raises a general alarm: the countryside gathers to attack the strangers and the Trojans muster in defence of Iulus: the struggle begins and the first victims fall.*

512. ardua tecta ... culmine summo: Henry explains by the supposition (probably true) that ancient farm-buildings had high conical straw roofs like those of barns and byres in the modern Campagna (cf. *Ecl.* 1. 68 'pauperis et tuguri congestum caespite culmen', of a turf-roofed hut). But Virgil is probably thinking here (as in *Ecl.* 1. 82 'summa procul uillarum culmina fumant') of a rural *uilla* of his own day, like Varro's (*R.R.* iii. 7. 1), whose *turres* and *culmina* provided lofts for the pigeons.

513. pastorale ... signum: the herdsman's signal, given by the horn, *bucina* (519): Columella repeats the phrase of calling the cattle home, vi. 23. 2 'pastorali signo quasi receptui canitur' (cf. Varro, *R.R.* ii. 4. 20, iii. 13. 3). *signum canere* is the regular military phrase. The use of the *bucina* as a meeting-signal in later times in the summoning of the *comitia centuriata* to which Gellius draws attention is the less remarkable since it was also used for such sophisticated purposes as the 'striking' of a clock (Vitr. ix. 8. 5; Sen. *Contr.* vii. *pr.* 1).

recuruo: both this compound and *procuruus* (v. 765) occur first in Virgil.

514. intendit uocem: 'sounded a loud note': for the use of the verb cf. Cic. *Or.* 59 'omnis sonorum tum intendens tum remittens (orator) persequetur gradus'. For a different and more difficult use of *intendere* cf. ix. 776 'numerosque intendere neruis'.

514 ff. Cf. iii. 672 ff. 'clamorem immensum tollit, quo pontus et omnes / intremuere undae, penitusque exterrita tellus / Italiae curuisque immugiit Aetna cauernis'. The lines were clearly suggested by Ap. Rhod. iv. 129 ff.: (at the dragon's hiss) ἀμφὶ δὲ μακραὶ / ἠιόνες ποταμοῖο καὶ ἄσπετον ἴαχεν ἄλσος· / ἔκλυον οἳ καὶ πολλὸν ἑκὰς Τιτηνίδος Αἴης / Κολχίδα γῆν ἐνέμοντο παρὰ προχοῇσι Λύκοιο.

Virgil exploits both the 'pathetic fallacy', attributing personal feeling to inanimate nature, which was a piece of Alexandrian technique (cf. 722, 760), and the romantic value of Italian names. The call goes North and South. To the South, *Triuiae lacus* is the woodland lake in the Alban Hills, near Aricia, which adjoined the precinct of Diana Nemorensis (cf. 762 ff.); Triuia (Τριοδῖτις, the goddess of the crossroads) is an epithet of the chthonic goddess Hecate, who had early become identified with Artemis (cf. Eur. *Phoen.* 109 f. παῖ Λατοῦς Ἑκάτα), and, like other attributes of Artemis, passed to the Italian wood-spirit Diana when Artemis was conflated with her. Northwards, the *Nar* flows down from the Umbrian Apennines to join the Tiber some thirty miles north of Rome: its name (according to Servius) was a Sabine word for sulphur (cf. Enn. *Ann.* 260 V. 'sulphureas posuit spiramina Naris ad undas') and its whiteness, due to sulphate of lime produced by the release of sulphuretted hydrogen, is noted by Pliny, *N.H.* iii. 109. The *fontes* or *lacus Velini* were in the Sabine uplands north of Reate, in a basin (the *Rosea rura* of 712) which in Virgil's time had been made fertile by cutting through the deposits of lime a short channel which released the imprisoned floodwaters of the Velinus into the Nar (Cic. *Att.* iv. 15. 5).

515. contremuit, 'fell a-shivering': as often, *con-* stresses the immediacy of the action.

siluae profundae : so Lucr. v. 41; cf. Hom. *Il.* v. 555 βαθείης ὕλης.

517 f. The repetition of *a*-sounds is noticeable.

518. pressere ad pectora: cf. Ap. Rhod. iv. 136 ff. δείματι δ' ἐξέγροντο λεχωίδες, ἀμφὶ δὲ παισὶν / νηπιάχοις, οἵ τέ σφιν ὑπ' ἀγκαλίδεσσιν ἴαυον, / ῥοίζῳ παλλομένοις χεῖρας βάλον ἀσχαλόωσαι.

519. tum uero: cf. 376: a favourite Virgilian connective in vivid narrative: so i. 485, ii. 309, iii. 47, iv. 397, 450, 571, v. 172, 720, ix. 424, xi. 633, xii. 494.

ad uocem, 'at the sound': cf. iii. 669 'ad sonitum uocis uestigia torsit'.

520. concurrunt undique telis: an Ennian half-line (*Ann.* 154 V.).

521. nec non et, 'and also', 'as well': an emphatic formula of familiar style which Virgil first brings into poetry; he has it fifteen times, usually at the beginning of the line but in the middle again at *Geo.* ii. 452, *Aen.* ix. 310. He has also the variations *nec non etiam* (*Geo.* ii. 413: several times in Varro) and *nec minus et* (xi. 203). The simple *nec non* (viii. 646, ix. 169, x. 27, xii. 23), which is not uncommon in Cicero (but always with a separating word), is rare in Virgil. See J. B. Hofmann, *Lat. Umgangsspr.* 97; J. Wackernagel, *Vorlesungen* ii. 303 f.; E. Löfstedt, *Per. Aeth.* 95; B. Kübler in *A.L.L.* viii. 181.

pubes: see on 105.

523. derexere acies: a formal military phrase; cf. *Geo.* ii. 281 'derectaeque acies'.

524. praeustis : the diphthong is shortened before a vowel here and at v. 186 *praeeunte*, the only two examples in Virgil: at Stat. *Theb.* vi. 519 *praeiret* retains the normal quantity.

525. ferro . . . decernunt : an Ennian phrase (*Ann.* 133 V.).

ancipiti: the two-edged sword here probably, like the ξίφος ἄμφηκες of Homer, *Od.* xxi. 341, rather than the double axe as it is in Lucr. vi. 168.

atra connotes much more than colour (if indeed it refers to colour here at all): in Virgil it is a word of strongly emotional content—'deadly', 'ghastly', 'dreadful'—and that implication is present even when there is a colour reference: so 456 f. 'atro / lumine', 565 f. 'atrum / . . . latus nemoris', 801 'atra palus', iv. 472 'serpentibus atris', ix. 239 'ater . . . fumus', xi. 186 'ignibus atris'; *Geo.* i. 323 'imbribus atris', ii. 308 f. 'atram / . . . nubem'. W. Warde Fowler (*The Death of Turnus* [Oxford, 1919], 93 n. 2) draws attention to the contrast in ix. 33–6, where the *niger puluis* of simple description becomes for the excited observer *atra caligo*.

526. horrescit strictis seges ensibus: *seges* is the crop consisting of the drawn swords as in the similar lines xii. 663 'strictisque seges mucronibus horret', *Geo.* ii. 142 'densisque uirum seges horruit hastis' (cf. *Aen.* iii. 45 f. 'confixum ferrea texit / telorum seges').

527. lacessita, 'assailed by the sun': Lucretius perhaps points the way to the metaphor with his (iv. 217) 'corpora quae feriant oculos uisumque lacessant'.

lucem . . . iactant: a Lucretian phrase, v. 576 '(luna) suam proprio iactat de corpore lucem'.

528 ff. The simile of *Il.* iv. 422 ff. may have been vaguely in Virgil's mind, but Virgil's image is quite different: Homer is comparing an embattled army to waves breaking on the shore (as Virgil does in *Geo.* iii. 237 ff.), Virgil to waves swelling under a gale.

528. primo . . . uento must be right: *ponto* of MR, supported by

Macrobius' quotation, is probably due to a reminiscence of *Geo*. iii. 237 'fluctus uti medio coepit cum albescere ponto'. If *primo* is taken as an adverb, *ponto* is awkwardly bare: if as an adjective, *primo ponto*, 'at the edge of the sea' (if the words can mean that on the analogy of i. 541 'prima ... terra'), has no point here.

530. imo ... fundo: cf. ii. 419 'imo Nereus ciet aequora fundo'.

531. primam ante aciem: apparently 'in the front line' (as in 673, ix. 595), Homer's ἐν προμάχοις. With *ante* meaning not 'in front of' but 'in the front of' (so perhaps *uestibulum ante ipsum* is to be taken in vi. 273) compare the regular use of *pro* in *pro ripa, pro rostris*, etc. and the use of *sub* to mean not 'beneath' but 'in the depths of' (see on 457). *ante* and *primam* reinforce each other here (as *sub* and *imo* do in xi. 23 'Acheronte sub imo').

532. fuerat: for the force of the pluperfect, 'had been (before he was killed)', see on viii. 358.

Almo: Virgil draws on the names of Italian rivers for several of his heroes: the Almo was a small tributary of the Tiber running down from the Alban hills, and Galaesus (535), Ufens (745), Umbro (752), Liris (xi. 670) are all Italian rivers. (Similarly on the Trojan side Caicus (i. 183), Hypanis, (ii. 340) and Thymbris (x. 124) are river-names.) But with curious implausibility he attaches his geographically named heroes to parts of the country remote from those to which the names belong: Umbro is a Marsian named from an Etrurian river: Massicus (x. 166) is not a Campanian but an Etruscan and Ufens is not a Volscian but an Aequian.

It is noticeable that while a few of the Italian heroes have names which are known in history (e.g. Arruns, Herminius) and others have names which are recognizably Italic (e.g. Aquiculus, Camers, Fadus, Hisbo, Privernus, Quercens, Tolumnius, Volusus), many have pure Greek names (e.g. Antaeus, Cisseus, Haemon, Idmon, Lichas, Sthenius, Theron). The Greek names Alcanor and Gyas are shared by a Trojan and a Latin; Sthenelus is a Greek concealed in the horse in Book II and a Trojan victim of Turnus in Book XII; Abas is a Trojan in Book I (and in Homer) but a Greek in Book III and an Etruscan in Book X. An Italian bears the name of Ilus (x. 400) which belongs to the Trojan royal pedigree. What may look like carelessness or onomastic insensitivity is a reminder that for Virgil the prehistory of Italy and the Greek and Trojan background which is attached to it form a single legendary complex (cf. E. Norden, *Kleine Schriften* [Berlin, 1966], 411 ff.).

533. haesit ... uulnus: a striking variation of the usual expression, in which the wound-dealing weapon *haeret*: cf. iv. 689 'infixum stridit . . . uulnus'.

533 f. udae uocis iter: the epithet is 'transferred'—speech needs a moist channel: cf. Ovid, *Met*. vi. 354 f. 'caret os umore loquentis / et fauces arent uixque est uia uocis in illis'.

534. tenuem . . . uitam: the insubstantial vital spirit: so *Geo*. iv. 223 f. 'hinc (i.e. ex deo) . . . / quemque sibi tenuis nascentem arcessere uitas'.

inclusit, 'imprisoned', a variation on the usual *interclusit*: so Livy ii. 2. 8 'consuli . . . admiratio incluserat uocem'. (In Cic. *Rab. Post*. 48 'dolor . . . includit uocem' Lambinus' *intercludit* may be unnecessary.)

535. circa: Virgil uses *circa* as an adverb in preference to his normal *circum* (which he uses some forty times) only to avoid a repeated -*um*: the other instances are vi. 865 'circa comitum', xi. 197 'boum circa', xii. 757 'circa et caelum'.

seniorque Galaesus : for -*que* introducing a particular name after a general expression cf. viii. 330 'reges asperque . . . Thybris'.

536. medium: for *medius* used of a mediator or go-between cf. Ovid, *Met*. v. 564 'medius fratrisque sui maestaeque sororis'; Prop. ii. 9. 50 'media non sine matre': similarly Sen. *Contr*. i. 1. 3 'me foedere medium pignus addite'.

paci: a dative of purpose, *ad pacem faciendam*, 'for peace': cf. 482, 637, 642.

536 ff. The pathetic effect of the descriptive characterization is already a part of Homeric technique: cf. *Il*. vi. 12 ff. Ἄξυλον δ' ἄρ' ἔπεφνε βοὴν ἀγαθὸς Διομήδης / Τευθρανίδην, ὃς ἔναιεν ἐϋκτιμένῃ ἐν Ἀρίσβῃ / ἀφνειὸς βιότοιο, φίλος δ' ἦν ἀνθρώποισι· / πάντας γὰρ φιλέεσκεν ὁδῷ ἔπι οἰκία ναίων. So ii. 426 f. 'Rhipeus, iustissimus unus / qui fuit in Teucris et seruantissimus aequi', xii. 517–20.

iustissimus unus : for the common use of *unus* ('uniquely') emphasizing a superlative cf. ii. 426 (quoted above).

538. balantum: the substantival use (cf. *Geo*. i. 272), a poetic descriptive substitute for *ouium*, like *uolantes* for *aues* (vi. 239, 728), *sonipes* for *equus* (e.g. iv. 135), is already in Ennius (*Ann*. 186 V. 'balantum pecudes quatit') and Lucretius (vi. 1132).

quinque . . . quina: the basic meaning of the so-called 'distributive' numeral adjectives is 'a set of *x*' and Virgil has examples both of that regular use (v. 306, vii. 687 f. *bina spicula* 'a pair of spears' (for each man), v. 557 *bina hastilia*, v. 247 *ternos iuuencos* (three to a ship), vi. 21 f. *septena corpora*, 'a set of seven persons' (each year): similarly, without 'distributive' sense, in v. 120 *terno ordine* is a set of three banks of oars, the *triplici uersu* of 119, in x. 207 *centena arbore* is a complement of a hundred oars) and of the idiomatic uses in periphrastic numerals (ii. 126 *bis quinos*: so i. 381, viii. 47, x. 213, xi. 326) and with '*pluralia tantum*' (viii. 168 *bina frena*). But elsewhere the 'distributive' implication is not '*x* each' but 'one to each of *x*', 'a corresponding *x*'. So here each of the five flocks of sheep is matched by a herd of cattle: similarly in v. 560 f., 'tres equitum numero turmae ternique uagantur / ductores', *terni* is 'a corresponding three' and in x. 329 f., 'septem numero septenaque tela / coniciunt', *septena* is 'a corresponding seven'; in x. 565 f., 'centum cui bracchia dicunt / centenasque manus', each of a hundred hands corresponds to one of a hundred arms, and in v. 85, 'septem ingens gyros septena uolumina traxit', each *uolumen* corresponds to (being in fact identical with) one of the seven *gyri*. The point is the same in i. 265 f. 'tertia . . . regnantem uiderit aestas / ternaque transierint . . . hiberna' (each of three winters matching a summer), and in viii. 564 f. 'tris animas . . . mater / . . . dederat, terna arma mouenda' (arms to be taken up once for each life), though in these two cases the nouns are '*pluralia tantum*'. See also on viii. 448 f.

redibant : came home at night to the steading: cf. *Geo.* iii. 316 'ipsae memores redeunt in tecta'.

540–71. *Allecto reports to Juno the successful performance of her mission; her offer to do further mischief is refused and, dismissed, she returns to the underworld through the valley of Amsanctus.*

540. atque: for this formula of transition cf. ix. 1 'atque ea diuersa penitus dum parte geruntur'.

aequo . . . Marte is not a poetic turn: it is found in Caesar's prose (*B.G.* vii. 19. 3).

541. promissi . . . potens, 'having secured what she promised': for this use of *potens* in the sense of *compos* cf. Plaut. *Poen.* 1182 'pacis potentes'; Livy viii. 13. 14 'di immortales ita uos potentes huius consilii fecerunt', xxii. 42. 12 'imperii potentes'; Ovid, *Met.* iv. 510 'uictrix iussique potens'.

541 f. sanguine bellum imbuit: 'inaugurated', 'handselled' ('initiauit', Servius rightly), as in Prop. iv. 10. 5 'imbuis exemplum primae tu, Romule, palmae'; Ovid, *A.A.* i. 654 'imbuit . . . opus'; Val. Fl. i. 69 f. 'uomere terras/imbuit', but the primary sense of 'stained' is clearly present here as in 554 below.

542. primae commisit funera pugnae, 'set on the deadly opening of the fight': an extension of *commisit pugnam*.

543. caeli conuersa per auras: *conuersa*, 'changing her course', preserved by M¹, has been displaced elsewhere by an echo of the Virgilian phrase *caeli conuexa* (iv. 451: cf. vi. 241, 750 'supera conuexa'). The explanation of *conuexa* which Servius offers, on the authority of Probus and Asper, that the words stand for 'per caeli conuexa et per auras', is impossible: a preposition expressed with the second of a pair of substantives can be understood with the first (for examples see on 296) only if the substantives are coupled by a conjunction.

546. dic is sarcastic defiance (*uoce superba*): 'now go and tell them'.

547. quandoquidem is a conjunction of ordinary speech (as its form shows, with the quantity of the -o- reduced by iambic shortening), common in comedy, but rare in classical prose: in Virgil (who uses it twice again in speeches: x. 105, xi. 587), as already in Catullus (33. 6, 40. 7, 64. 218, 101. 5) and later in Livy (who has it nine times, always in speeches) it has a solemn, dramatic, or pathetic effect, stressing the finality of a situation.

548. tua si mihi certa uoluntas, 'if I can rely on your compliance': the phrase is repeated from iv. 125, where Juno herself is seeking to be assured of Venus' co-operation.

550. insani Martis amore: a variation on *Ecl.* 10. 44 'insanus amor . . . Martis'.

552. fraudis abunde est: in origin a neuter form (like *pote* and *necesse*), *abunde* is normally used adverbially (with adjectives, e.g. Sall. *Jug.* 14. 18 'abunde magna'; or with verbs, e.g. Ovid, *Tr.* i. 7. 31 'laudatus abunde'). Sallust has the substantival use (*Jug.* 63. 2 'alia omnia abunde erant', *Cat.* 21. 1): with a dependent genitive, as here, it does not appear till Quintilian (x. i. 94 'abunde salis'). A characteristic 'Silver' development is the use with a dependent *si*-clause (*abunde est si* . . ., 'it is more than enough if . . .': Sen. *Contr.* x. 5. 15; Pliny, *Ep.* iv. 30. 11, vii. 2. 3; Tac. *Hist.* ii. 95).

553 f. armis . . . arma: for the repetition, see on viii. 271 f.

553. stant, 'are there, unalterably': cf. Hor. *Od.* i. 16. 17 ff. 'irae . . . altis urbibus ultimae / stetere causae cur perirent': the force of the verb is similar in x. 467 'stat sua cuique dies' and in ii. 750 'stat ('it is my fixed purpose') casus renouare omnis'.

554. prima: it is difficult to know whether *prima* is to be taken with *fors* (cf. ii. 387 f. 'qua prima . . . Fortuna salutis / monstrat iter') or with *arma*.

nouus: see on viii. 637.

555. hymenaeos: see on 344.

556. The honorific *genus* (cf. vi. 792 'Augustus Caesar, diui genus', 839 'genus armipotentis Achilli', xii. 198 'Latonae genus': so Cat. 61. 2 'Uraniae genus', 64. 23 'deum genus') is effectively coupled with *egregium*, here ironical and emphatically placed at the beginning of the line (as it is in iv. 93 'egregiam uero laudem', vi. 523 'egregia . . . coniunx'): contrast vii. 213 'genus egregium Fauni'.

557. aetherias . . . auras: i.e. the upper air, the light of day, as opposed to her proper home. The phrase is Lucretian: iii. 405 'aetherias uitalis suscipit auras'. *super auras* is not 'above the air' but 'in the air above', as *Acheronte sub imo* (xi. 23) is 'in Acheron beneath': see on 531.

558. pater ille: see on 110.

559. cede locis, 'leave the scene': the plural (cf. vi. 445, viii. 311, 604) avoids the suggestion of the usual *cedere loco*, 'abandon one's place'.

    si qua super fortuna laborum est, 'whatever issue of sorrow is still to come': *labores* is nearly always a word of pathos in Virgil's use (cf. 481 f. 'quae prima laborum / causa fuit', i. 597 'infandos Troiae miserata labores', ii. 284 'post uarios hominumque urbisque labores', 362 '(quis) possit lacrimis aequare labores') and *si quis*, as often, is equivalent to *quicumque*, not implying any doubt that there is some *fortuna laborum* in store. Virgil had already used the phrase at *Geo.* iii. 452 f. (of sick animals) 'non tamen ulla magis praesens fortuna laborum est / quam si . . .', 'no issue for their sufferings is of such avail as when . . .'. For the division *super . . . est* cf. ii. 567 'iamque adeo super unus eram'.

561. The snakes in her wings are an addition to the Fury's horror which does not appear elsewhere.

562. supera ardua: cf. vi. 787 'supera alta', vi. 241, 750 'supera conuexa'.

563 ff. est locus . . . hic: the abrupt introduction of a short piece of local description which is later picked up and related to the narrative in a following clause is a piece of epic technique inherited from Homer: cf., e.g., *Od.* iv. 844 ff. ἔστι δέ τις νῆσος . . . τῇ, *Il.* ii. 811 ff. ἔστι δέ τις προπάροιθε πόλιος αἰπεῖα κολώνη . . . ἔνθα, xiii. 32 ff. ἔστι δέ τι σπέος . . . ἔνθα. (So also Aesch. *Pers.* 447 ff.: Hellenistic epic continued the device, e.g. Ap. Rhod. i. 936, iii. 927.) Virgil uses the 'Homeric' opening with *est* again in i. 159 ff. 'est in secessu longo locus . . . huc', ii. 21 ff. 'est in conspectu Tenedos . . . huc', 713 ff. 'est urbe egressis tumulus . . . hanc . . . sedem', v. 124 ff. 'est procul in pelago saxum . . . hic', viii. 597 ff. 'est ingens gelidum lucus prope Caeritis amnem . . . haud procul hinc', xi. 522 ff. 'est curuo anfractu ualles. . . . hanc super' *Geo.* iv. 418 ff. 'est specus ingens . . . his . . . in latebris': similarly in this book 59 ff., 170 ff., 607 ff. He has variations of the formula in iii. 13 ff. 'terra procul uastis colitur Mauortia campis . . .

huc', 73 ff. 'sacra mari colitur medio gratissima tellus . . .
huc', 210 ff. 'Strophades Graio stant nomine dictae . . . huc',
533 ff., viii. 416 ff. Ovid uses the device often, e.g. *Met.* xi.
592 ff., *F.* iv. 337 ff., vi. 9 ff., *Her.* 16. 53 ff., *Am.* iii. 1. 1 ff.;
so Propertius, iv. 4. 3 ff., 6. 15 ff. For a prose example cf.
Livy. i. 21. 3 'lucus erat, quem . . . eum lucum'. On the
device see E. Fraenkel, *De Media et Noua Comoedia Quaes-
tiones Selectae* (Göttingen, 1912): but he does not distinguish
clearly between examples of a deliberate device of literary
narrative and those of a casual conversational manner
of speech (e.g. Plaut. *Aul.* 674 ff.; Ter. *Ad.* 576) which is
natural in any language.

563. Italiae medio: see on 59.

564. nobilis, 'renowned': cf. Cat. 4. 8 'Rhodum nobilem'.

oris, 'regions', as in 660 'sub luminis . . . oras', iii. 97
'cunctis dominabitur oris': cf. Cat. 66. 43 f. 'mons . . . quem
maximum in oris / progenies Thiae clara superuehitur'.

565. ualles: nominative singular as at xi. 522, where Servius
guarantees it: Caesar twice uses this form (*B.G.* vi. 34. 2,
vii. 47. 2). The same variation is found with *aedis, felis, uulpis,*
and (in early Latin) *canis.*

Amsanctus, where the Fury goes to ground, was a sul-
phurous lake in the hills of South Samnium, in the volcanic
belt which extends eastwards from Vesuvius: Pliny includes
it in his account of exhalations (ii. 208), 'ut in Sinuessano
agro et Puteolano quae spiracula uocant, alii Charonea,
scrobes mortiferum spiritum exhalantes, item in Hirpinis
Amsancti ad Mephitis aedem locum quem qui intrauere
moriuntur'. (For Mephitis see on 84: her shrine has been
displaced by one of S. Felicità, but she survives in the
modern name of the place, Le Mefite.)

565 f. atrum . . . latus nemoris, 'a black wooded hillside closes
in on it all round': Virgil's 'realistic' description of the
scene, as usual, is the realism not of observation but of
literary convention. At Amsanctus the hills are several miles
away: the pools lie in a wooded defile between limestone
rocks but there is no raging torrent and they are only a few
feet deep: and the whole phrase *densis . . . latus* is repeated
in a description of another place, the pass where Turnus
sets his trap for Aeneas (xi. 523 f.).

566. medio: see on 59.

566 f. fragosus . . . torrens, 'a broken torrent utters a roar
with its rocks and whirling eddies': Virgil uses *fragosus* only
here, probably with the meaning 'broken' (as we use that
word of water): in Lucr. ii. 860 *fragosa* is 'broken' or 'brittle';
Grattius (527) applies the word to a mountain and Quintilian

(ix. 4. 7) to 'broken' speech. But Virgil may have given it the reference to sound ('crashing') which the noun *fragor* usually has: there is the same uncertainty about Ovid's use, *Met.* iv. 778 'siluis horrentia saxa fragosis'. *torto uertice* is a Lucretian phrase (i. 293, of the winds).

567. dat sonitum: see on viii. 570 f.
Note the alliteration on *s* and *t*.

568. specus horrendum: in the other six Virgilian instances the gender of *specus* is indeterminable: it is normally masculine (in the early poets sometimes feminine), but Silius uses the neuter once (in a similar context, xiii. 425) as well as the masculine.

    spiracula Ditis: *spiracula* are 'vents', 'air-holes', but Virgil's phrase gives a new vividness to an everyday expression (cf. Pliny quoted on 565), as Lucretius had already done with his *spiracula mundi* (vi. 493).

569. monstrantur: cf. vi. 440 f. 'nec procul hinc partem fusi monstrantur in omnem / Lugentes campi; sic illos nomine dicunt'.

    rupto . . . Acheronte, 'where Acheron bursts forth': the participle has 'middle' force (so 459 'proruptus', i. 246 'it mare proruptum'); cf. *Geo.* iii. 428 'amnes . . . rumpuntur fontibus'.

571. leuabat: the imperfect is surprising: its force may be to emphasize the gradual relief which Allecto's disappearance brought: cf. xi. 827 (of the dying Camilla) 'simul his dictis linquebat habenas'.

572–600. *Enraged by the death of their friends and stimulated by Turnus and Amata, the Latins call on the king to declare war. He stands firm in his refusal to comply but, unable to control his angry people, he gives up the struggle and retires into his palace.*

572. nec minus interea: a Lucretian formula of transition: so *Geo.* ii. 429, *Aen.* i. 633, vi. 212, xii. 107.

572 f. extremam . . . manum, 'put the finishing touch': *extrema, summa,* and *ultima manus* are all used in this metaphor from a piece of handiwork: cf. Cic. *Brut.* 126 'manus extrema non accessit operibus eius'; Ovid, *Tr.* ii. 555 f. 'manus ultima coeptis / defuit'; Sen. *Ep.* 12. 4 '(potio) ebrietati summam manum imponit'. Ovid perhaps has Virgil's phrase in mind when he writes, *Met.* xiii. 403, 'imposita est sero tandem manus ultima bello': cf. Lucan v. 483 f. 'summam . . . belli / te poscit fortuna manum'; Val. Max. vii. 5. 4 '(bello) summam manum . . . adiecit'.

575. foedatique ora Galaesi: the variation, as Conington points

out, fixes the reader's attention on Galaesus' disfigured face.
foedare of wounding belongs to the heroic vocabulary: so
ii. 55 'ferro Argolicas foedare latebras', 285 f. 'quae causa
indigna serenos / foedauit uultus? aut cur haec uulnera
cerno?', iii. 241 'obscenas pelagi ferro foedare uolucris' (on
which Servius quotes from Ennius 'ferro foedati iacent'),
iv. 673 'unguibus ora . . . foedans et pectora pugnis', xi. 86,
xii. 99: similarly Plaut. *Amph.* 246 (a mock-heroic passage)
'foedant et proterunt hostium copias'; Lucr. iv. 844 'lacerare
artus foedareque membra cruore'; Cic. *Tusc.* ii. 24 (quoting
his own lines on Prometheus) 'quae me perenni uiuum foedat
miseria'.

576. **obtestantur:** call him to witness the breach of the treaty,
says Servius: but probably the verb has its more general
sense of 'appeal to' here as in ix. 260, xi. 358, xii. 820.

577. **medio in crimine caedis et igni,** 'in the midst of the outcry
at bloodshed and the blaze of passion'. The *crimen caedis* is
provoked by the victims of 574 f.: *igni* must be meta-
phorical (cf. ii. 575 'exarsere ignes animo'): *medio in igni* is
the equivalent of xi. 225 'medio in flagrante tumultu'.

578. **in regna:** i.e. to share the kingdom: cf. 313.

579. **Phrygiam:** the name has the same contemptuous or dis-
paraging suggestion as it has elsewhere on the lips of Troy's
enemies: see on 294.

580. **attonitae:** perhaps an Ennian word, as E. Wölfflin (*A.L.L.*
xiii. 449) suggests: Virgil has it ten times but it is rare in
prose.

580 f. **nemora . . . insultant,** 'dance through the woods': for
the accusative of space travelled cf. iii. 191 'currimus
aequor', v. 235 'aequora curro', *Geo.* iii. 260 'natat . . .
freta'. For *insultare* in this context cf. Enn. *Sc.* 127 V.
'alacris Bacchico insultans modo'.

581. **neque enim:** Virgil has this combination a score of times,
usually introducing a parenthesis. In two cases both particles
can be given their normal force, *neque* being followed by
a corresponding *nec* (iv. 170) or a corresponding -*que* (vii. 195).
In most other cases, as here, *enim* can be given its explanatory
force but *neque* has no connective function and the idiom has
been seen as a survival of the archaic use of *neque/nec* as
a simple negative which is found in the XII Tables and sur-
vives elsewhere in some compounds (e.g. *necopinatus*) and a
few fixed formulas (*nec recte, nec mancipi, nec manifestum*):
see E. Löfstedt, *Synt.* i². 338. But in two cases (*Geo.* ii. 104,
Aen. ii. 100), while *neque* is connective, *enim* is clearly not
explanatory and must be given its archaic asseverative force
('indeed': see on viii. 84), and this must have been its

original function in the idiom; later the connective force of *neque* was weakened to vanishing point (as it has been in *neque uero*) and *enim* came to assume its usual explanatory function. *etenim* has developed in exactly the same way.

582. Martemque fatigant: *fatigare* is a favourite word of Virgil's: he sometimes uses it in a literal sense, e.g. i. 316 f. 'equos Threissa fatigat / Harpalyce', vi. 79 f. 'fatigat / os rabidum', ix. 609 f. 'iuuencum / terga fatigamus hasta' xi. 306 f. 'quos nulla fatigant / proelia', 714 'quadripedemque . . . ferrata calce fatigat', sometimes in a striking metaphor, e.g. i. 280 'terrasque metu caelumque fatigat' ('gives earth and heaven no peace'), viii. 94 'remigio noctemque diemque fatigant', ix. 605 'uenatu inuigilant pueri siluasque fatigant'. So here the meaning is 'weary Mars, give him no peace, with their demands for war': the word is similarly used of importunate prayer, Lucr. iv. 1239 'nequiquam diuum numen sortisque fatigant'; Hor. *Od.* i. 2. 26 ff. 'prece qua fatigant / uirgines sanctae . . . Vestam'.

583. ilicet: *ilicet* and *ilico* are two old words which had no connection with each other and nothing in common except that they went out of use. *ilico* is **enstlocōd*, 'on the spot': from the local sense, as in the English phrase, a temporal sense develops. Plautus has examples of both the local sense (e.g. *Bacc.* 24 'qui ilico errat intra muros ciuicos'), and the temporal (e.g. *Curc.* 81 'de odore adesse me scit: aperit ilico'), the latter being the more numerous; Terence has 33, nearly all temporal; there are a dozen examples in the fragments of tragedy and comedy. Thereafter the word is rare; it is found once in Sallust, fourteen times in Cicero (speeches, philosophical works, and letters), and once in a speech in Livy (xxxix. 15. 8), always with the temporal sense of 'immediately'. *ilicet*, on the other hand, was an expression of dismissal, in which the first syllable represented either the imperative or the infinitive of *ire* (*scilicet* and *uidelicet* are parallel or analogical formations). In Plautus its equivalence to *ire licet* is made clear when it is accompanied by a dative and an accusative of *terminus ad quem*, *Capt.* 469 'ilicet parasiticae arti maxumam malam crucem'. It was the formula used to close meetings of the Senate or proceedings of a court and it followed the *conclamatio* at a funeral (Servius on vi. 216, quoting Varro), and it had a familiar use as an expression of despair or resignation: so it is used in Plautus (e.g. *Amph.* 338 'ilicet: mandata eri perierunt una et Sosia', *Cist.* 685 'actum est, ilicet: me infelicem et scelestam', *Epid.* 685 'ilicet: uadimonium ultro mihi hic facit') and in Terence

(e.g. *Eun.* 54 f. 'actumst, ilicet, / peristi'). After the come-
dians *ilicet* disappears from literature (it fell into disuse
earlier than *ilico*) until it is revived by Virgil, who uses it
five times in the *Aeneid* and, what is even more remarkable,
appears to use it adverbially, in the sense of *ilico*, 'im-
mediately'. So here, and so in ii. 424 'ilicet obruimur
numero', 758 f. 'ilicet ignis edax summa ad fastigia uento /
uoluitur', viii. 223 f. 'fugit ilicet ocior Euro / speluncamque
petit', xi. 468 'ilicet in muros tota discurritur urbe'. Both
words were archaic: *ilico* does not suit dactylic verse and
Virgil boldly substitutes the accommodating *ilicet* with no
more than a vestige of the colour of despair belonging to its
earlier use. His successors follow his example. See A. Ernout
in *Mélanges Paul Thomas* (Bruges, 1930), 229 ff.

583 f. omina . . . fata: i.e. the omens of 64 ff. and the oracle of
96 ff.

584. peruerso numine repeats the sense of *contra omina . . .
contra fata deum*, 'overturning the will of heaven' (cf. Cic.
Off. i. 26 'omnia iura diuina atque humana peruertit'). To
interpret the phrase as *peruerso studio*, 'with misguided im-
pulse' (a common enough adjectival use of *peruersus*), is
to give *numen* a meaning which would be unique in Virgil,
who uses the word many times but always with reference
to divine powers: the only examples of any other reference
are in Lucretius iii. 144 'ad numen mentis momenque
mouetur', and iv. 179 'in quem quaeque locum (simulacra)
diuerso numine tendunt'.

586 ff. The image is an elaboration of Homer's simple simile,
Il. xv. 618 ff. ἴσχον γὰρ πυργηδὸν ἀρηρότες, ἠύτε πέτρη / ἠλίβατος
μεγάλη, πολιῆς ἁλὸς ἐγγὺς ἐοῦσα, / ἥ τε μένει λιγέων ἀνέμων λαιψηρὰ
κέλευθα / κύματά τε τροφόεντα, τά τε προσερεύγεται αὐτήν.

uelut pelago rupes . . . ut pelagi rupes: the device of
epanalepsis is as old as Homer (*Il.* xx. 371 f. τοῦ δ' ἐγὼ ἀντίος
εἶμι, καὶ εἰ πυρὶ χεῖρας ἔοικεν, / εἰ πυρὶ χεῖρας ἔοικε, μένος δ' αἴθωνι
σιδήρῳ, xxii. 127 f. ἅτε παρθένος ἠΐθεός τε, / παρθένος ἠΐθεός τ' ὀαρίζετον
ἀλλήλοισιν) and was taken up by the Hellenistic poets. In Latin
Lucretius had made considerable use of it, e.g. iv. 789 f.
'mollia membra mouere, / mollia', v. 950 f. 'lauere umida
saxa, / umida saxa super uiridi stillantia musco': so ii. 955 f.,
iii. 12 f., vi. 528 f., 1168 f. In the Alexandrians it is an orna-
ment lavishly applied: Catullus has seven examples in his
epyllion (64. 26, 61, 132, 259, 285, 321, 403: cf. 68. 88 ff.) and
the *Culex* as many (124, 132, 134, 231, 275, 311, 337): Pro-
pertius makes effective use of it in i. 3. 31, 11. 28, iv. 1. 63
(cf. ii. 34. 85). In Virgil it is introduced, sparingly, to heighten
pathetic or dramatic effect: so ii. 405 f. 'ad caelum tendens

ardentia lumina frustra, / lumina, nam teneras arcebant uin-
cula palmas', vi. 495 f. 'lacerum crudeliter ora, / ora manus-
que ambas', x. 821 f. 'uultum uidit morientis et ora, / ora
modis Anchisiades pallentia miris', xii. 546 f. 'domus alta sub
Ida, / Lyrnesi domus alta, solo Laurente sepulcrum', 673 f.
'turrimque tenebat, / turrim compactis trabibus quam edux-
erat ipse', 896 f. 'saxum circumspicit ingens, / saxum anti-
quum ingens, campo quod forte iacebat': sometimes the
repetition of a personal name (which had Homeric precedent:
Il. vi. 395 f. θυγάτηρ μεγαλήτορος Ἠετίωνος, / Ἠετίων ὅς ἔναιεν ὑπὸ
Πλάκῳ ὑληέσσῃ) serves to give body to a minor figure: e.g. ii.
318 f. 'telis Panthus elapsus Achiuum, / Panthus Othryades',
ix. 774 f. 'amicum Crethea Musis, / Crethea Musarum comi-
tem', x. 180 f. 'pulcherrimus Astyr, / Astyr equo fidens'. See
Norden on vi. 164.

588. latrantibus: the waves are like a pack of barking hounds
round their quarry: Statius (*Ach.* i. 450 f.) and Silius (iii. 471,
v. 397) borrow the idea in commonplace imitation.

588 f. sese . . . mole tenet: cf. x. 771 'mole sua stat': observe
the heavily spondaic line emphasizing the idea of solidity.

589. nequiquam, 'without effect': the cliff remains unshaken
for all the din and fury.

590. refunditur: the seaweed is dashed against the rock and
swept off again.

591. datur . . . exsuperare potestas: cf. iii. 670 'nulla datur
dextra adfectare potestas', ix. 739 'nulla hinc exire potestas
(est)', 813 'nec respirare potestas (est)'. Virgil has a liking
for extending the use of the prolative infinitive with verbs
(see on 35 f.) to its use with phrases which are in sense
equivalent to verbs: so, e.g., ii. 10 'tantus amor (est) casus
cognoscere', xii. 282 'omnis amor unus habet decernere
ferro', ii. 575 f. 'subit ira . . . / ulcisci', v. 183 f. 'spes est
accensa . . . superare', ix. 484 'adfari . . . data (est) copia',
x. 276 f. 'haud . . . fiducia cessit / litora praecipere'.

591 f. caecum . . . consilium: 'their blind purpose' (*caecus* is
common of mental blindness) rather than the 'secret pur-
pose' of Juno.

592. eunt res: the phrase is perhaps colloquial: cf. Cic. *Att.* xiv.
20. 4 'prorsus ibat res', 15. 2 'incipit res melius ire quam
putaram'. Lucan iv. 143 f. 'omnia fatis / Caesaris ire uidet'
may be an echo of this line.

The monosyllabic ending, which by producing a conflict
between ictus and accent disturbs the characteristic pattern
of the Virgilian hexameter, in which (as Bentley first ob-
served) conflict of ictus and accent in the first four feet is
contrasted with coincidence in the last two, appears more

than thirty times in Virgil. (This figure does not include
lines ending in a monosyllable preceded by another mono-
syllable, e.g. 310, 643, or in an enclitic monosyllable, e.g.
x. 259 'parent se': these endings, of course, do not produce
conflict.) In some instances one may be able to diagnose with
some plausibility an attempt to reflect sense in sound with
an effect expressive of suddenness, abruptness, or decisive
action: so in the *Georgics* 'ruit imbriferum uer' (i. 313), in the
Aeneid 'praeruptus aquae mons' (i. 105), 'ruit Oceano nox'
(ii. 250: cf. *Geo.* i. 247 'intempesta silet nox'), 'procumbit
humi bos' (v. 481). But the purpose is not simply expressive
but literary, not mere onomatopoeia but allusion or re-
miniscence: Virgil is echoing familiar rhythms of earlier
poetry. So 'lupi ceu' (ii. 355) is a simple echo (perhaps
through Ennius) of Homer's λύκοι ὣς (*Il.* xi. 72, xvi. 156).
'diuum pater atque hominum rex' (i. 65, x. 2), 'et magnis dis'
(iii. 12, viii. 679), 'restituis rem' (vi. 846) and 'nituntur opum
ui' (xii. 552) are all borrowings from Ennius (*Ann.* 175, 201,
370, 161 V.): with the third of these one may group not only
this line but also 'iam tempus agi res' (v. 638), 'ipsa uocat
res' (ix. 320), 'qui casus agat res' (ix. 723), with the fourth
'nulla uiam uis' (x. 864), 'si qua tibi uis' (xi. 373). 'densusque
uiro uir' (x. 361: cf. xi. 632 'legitque uirum uir') repeats a
line-ending of Furius Bibaculus, which may have first ap-
peared in an Ennian battle-scene. 'odora canum uis' (iv. 132)
is a Lucretian phrase which may have gone back beyond
Lucretius: 'auersa deae mens' (ii. 170) and 'praesaga mali
mens' (x. 843) repeat a Lucretian rhythm (iii. 152, 453): the
final *sus* which Virgil has four times (*Geo.* iii. 255 'dentesque
Sabellicus exacuit sus', *Aen.* iii. 390 'inuenta sub ilicibus
sus', viii. 43, 83) has its prototype in Lucr. v. 25 'Arcadius
sus'. Even of those endings in which an onomatopoetic in-
tention can be most plausibly presumed some are literary
reminiscences (and all may be): 'ruit Oceano nox' echoes
Homer's thrice-repeated ὀρώρει δ' οὐρανόθεν νύξ (*Od.* v. 294 etc.),
'procumbit humi bos' his ἦλθε μὲν ἄρ βοῦς (*Od.* iii. 430), and the
mus which in *Geo.* i. 181, as in Hor. *A.P.* 139, has been
recognized as stressing a comic incongruity may have its
origin in a Greek μῦς.

593. **deos aurasque . . . inanis :** a compressed phrase: he
launches his appeals to the gods into the air (cf. ix. 24
'onerauitque aethera uotis') which carries them away.

595. **has . . . poenas:** 'the penalty for this', we say: for the
same idiom cf. xii. 468 'hoc . . . metu' ('fear of this'), ii. 171
'ea signa' ('signs of that'), viii. 705 'eo terrore', and see on
383 above.

596. o miseri: *o* as usual marks an emotional address: 'my poor people'.

596 f. nefas . . . supplicium, 'your sin and its grim punishment will dog you'.

    triste supplicium: cf. Livy vii. 28. 9 'iudicia . . . tristia', xxv. 6. 2 'triste senatus consultum'.

597. seris: emphatically placed at the end of the line.

598. nam mihi: the thought is 'It is *you* who will suffer: for I am an old man'.

    omnisque in limine portus: the metaphorical use of *portus* for a haven of rest is common (so, e.g., Enn. *Sc.* 364 f. V. 'neque sepulchrum quo recipiat habeat portum corporis, / ubi remissa humana uita corpus requiescat malis'; Cic. *de Or.* i. 255, *Tusc.* i. 118, v. 117, *Sen.* 71) and so is the metaphorical use of *limen* with a genitive (so *in limine belli, uictoriae, mortis*), but the relation of the words here is far from clear. Servius' paraphrase 'securitas omnis in promptu est' does not help; *portus* may well mean *securitas* (though what of *omnis*?), but there is no evidence that *in limine* can mean *in promptu* ('on the doorstep' in our colloquial phrase) and, if it could, the mixture of metaphor would be absurd. Taking *portus* as genitive and punctuating at the end of the line, Heyne interprets 'totus sum in aditu portus': *in limine portus* is no doubt a possible equivalent of *in aditu* or *in ostio portus*, but the omission of *sum* with a change of subject is very awkward. With the punctuation of the Oxford text *omnis . . . portus* is attached to *spolior*: taking the words so, Conington translates 'it is only when just on the harbour's verge that I am robbed of a happy death'. In either case the use of the predicative *omnis* for *omnino* where there is no notion of quantity (as there is in Hor. *Od.* iii. 30. 6 'non omnis moriar', *Ep.* i. 1. 11 'omnis in hoc sum') is noteworthy.

600. rerumque reliquit habenas, 'abandoned the reins of state': Virgil uses the literal sense at xi. 827 'linquebat habenas'.

601–40. *When Latinus refuses to perform the ceremonial act of opening the gates of War, Juno bursts them open herself. War is inevitable and the Latin towns make their preparations.*

601. Hesperio in Latio: the adjective (see on 4) colours the phrase with the romantic associations of legend.

    protinus: 'thenceforward', of a continuous onward movement.

601 f. urbes Albanae implies the succession which is explicitly set out in i. 267 ff. (cf. i. 7, xii. 826 f.): Alba succeeds to Lavinium and Rome to Alba. Livy (i. 19. 2) attributes the custom here described to King Numa in Rome itself.

602. maxima rerum: cf. *Geo.* ii. 534 'rerum . . . pulcherrima Roma'.

603. prima . . . proelia, 'the beginning of the battle': cf. xii. 103, 735.

604 ff. A series of complimentary anticipatory references to the campaigns of Augustus' principate. The Getae on the lower Danube, a constant threat to the NE. frontier, were the objective of an expedition under M. Licinius Crassus in 29 B.C.: in 24 B.C. the Arabs of the Yemen saw a show of force under Aelius Gallus which was Augustus' furthest penetration of the East. The appearance of the Hyrcanians, whose country lay on the southern shores of the Caspian, reflects the propagandist wishful thinking which represents Augustus' Oriental progress after Actium in 30–29 B.C., which was confined to Egypt, Syria, and Asia, as promising the conquest of the whole of the East. In fact Augustus showed himself extremely reluctant to undertake military commitments in the further East and preferred to maintain Roman prestige and secure the frontier by diplomatic means, especially by the use of client kingdoms and the exploitation of local rivalries. In particular he declined *reposcere signa* with the military measures against the Parthians which public opinion, conscious of the disgrace of Carrhae, demanded (cf. Hor. *Od.* i. 12. 53 ff., iii. 5. 1 ff.; Prop. iv. 6. 77 ff.): the recovery of Crassus' standards was secured on Augustus' behalf by Tiberius, not by force but by negotiation, when he was in Syria in 20 B.C. For the imaginary picture of Augustus' activities in the East compare *Geo.* ii. 170 ff. 'te, maxime Caesar, / qui nunc extremis Asiae iam uictor in oris / imbellem auertis Romanis arcibus Indum', iii. 30 ff. 'addam urbes Asiae domitas pulsumque Niphaten / fidentemque fuga Parthum uersisque sagittis', *Aen.* vi. 794 ff. 'super et Garamantas et Indos / proferet imperium . . . / huius in aduentum iam nunc et Caspia regna / responsis horrent diuum et Maeotia tellus'; Hor. *Od.* i. 12. 53 ff. 'ille (Caesar) seu Parthos Latio imminentis / egerit iusto domitos triumpho / siue subiectos Orientis orae / Seras et Indos'.

604. manu: see on 127, 621.

lacrimabile bellum: an echo of Homer's πόλεμον δακρυόεντα (*Il.* v. 737), πολύδακρυν Ἄρηα (*Il.* iii. 132), which Horace also uses (*Od.* i. 21. 13 'bellum lacrimosum').

606. Auroramque sequi: 'sequi dicimur etiam quae non fugiunt' (Housman on Man. iv. 880): so iv. 361 'Italiam non sponte sequor', viii. 333 'pulsum patria pelagique extrema sequentem', x. 193 'sidera uoce sequentem', xii. 892 f. 'ardua pennis / astra sequi'; Cic. *Att.* iii. 16 'si spes erit, Epirum,

si minus, Cyzicum aut aliud aliquid sequemur'; Prop. ii. 27.
5 'seu pedibus Parthos sequimur seu classe Britannos'.

607 ff. geminae Belli portae . . . Ianus. The *Belli portae* of this
passage and i. 293 ff. are the structure elsewhere called *Ianus
Quirinus* (Suet. *Aug.* 22: Horace has the variant *Ianus
Quirini, Od.* iv. 15. 9: on the significance of the epithet see
Koch in *Zeit. f. Relig. u. Geistesgesch.* v [1953], 6 ff.), an arched
passage with gates at either end standing in the Argiletum
near the point where it entered the Forum on the north-east.
It is sometimes described as a temple (Plut. *Numa* 20. 1
νεὼς δίθυρος: cf. Ovid, *F.* i. 257 f.) and it is so represented on
coins of Nero: that it had a statue of Janus is stated by
Varro (*L.L.* v. 165) and implied by Ovid. No trace of the
structure has been found. There were other *iani* in Rome
(cf. Suet. *Aug.* 31. 5, *Dom.* 13. 2; Cic. *N.D.* ii. 67 'Ianum . . .
ab eundo . . . ex quo transitiones peruiae iani . . . nominan-
tur': if, as is probable, Janus, the god of the door and the
passage, is a personified *ianus*, Cicero has the facts the wrong
way round, but his derivation from the root of *ire* may be
right), either free-standing (such presumably was the *Ianus
medius* of commercial dealings) or forming part of a city-gate
(Livy ii. 49. 8 'infelici uia, dextro iano portae Carmentalis,
profecti'): Livy ascribes the origin of this one and its tradi-
tional use to Numa (i. 19. 2 'ianum ad infimum Argiletum
indicem pacis bellique fecit, apertus ut in armis esse ciuita-
tem, clausus pacatos circa omnes populos significaret'). It
probably acquired importance only in Virgils' own time
with the exploitation of it by Augustan propaganda: the
gates were closed after Actium, having been open since 235
B.C., when they were closed after the Punic War and opened
again in the same year (Varro, *L.L.* v. 165; Livy i. 19. 3),
and they were twice again closed under Augustus, as he
proudly records in the Monumentum Ancyranum (*Res
Gestae* 13), once in 25 B.C. after the Cantabrian War (Dio
liii. 26. 5) and once later. In the imagery of this passage
(which may be based on Ennius: see on 622 below) Bellum
is conceived as imprisoned within the gates under the
custody of Janus, as Furor is in i. 293 ff., a prophecy of the
Augustan peace: 'claudentur Belli portae: Furor impius
intus / saeua sedens super arma et centum uinctus aenis /
post tergum nodis fremet': Horace reverses the image and
makes peace the prisoner (*Ep.* ii. 1. 255 'claustraque custo-
dem pacis cohibentia Ianum': similarly Ovid makes Janus
say, *F.* i. 281, 'pace fores obdo ne qua discedere possit').

607-11. sunt . . . has: for this narrative formula see on 563 ff.:
stridentia limina (613) can perhaps be taken as an amplifica-

tion of *has* (for the apposition cf. ii. 438 ff. 'hic uero ingentem pugnam . . . Martem indomitum Danaosque ad tecta ruentis / cernimus') rather than an anacoluthon.

607. sic nomine dicunt: for this Hellenistic turn cf. vi. 441 'Lugentes campi: sic illos nomine dicunt', *Geo.* iii. 280 'hippomanes uero quod nomine dicunt'.

608. religione sacrae . . . formidine: cf. viii. 598 '(lucus) religione patrum late sacer', *Geo.* iv. 468 'caligantem nigra formidine lucum'. For *religio* see on 172.

609. aerei: for the synizesis see on 33.

611. sedet: cf. 368, v. 418 ('id sedet'), ii. 660 ('sedet hoc'), xi. 551 ('haec sententia sedit').

   pugnae is probably genitive with *sententia*, but it may be a dative of purpose attached to the phrase *sedet sententia*.

611 ff. No doubt Virgil derived this impressive picture of the ceremony of opening the gates from antiquarian sources: it can hardly have been a reality, as he represents it, at the time of writing, when all our evidence shows the emphasis to have been on the closing of the gates, not on the opening of them, and they had been almost continuously open for centuries.

612. Quirinali trabea: see on 187 f.

   cinctu Gabino: this archaic ceremonial style of wearing the *toga*, associated with certain ritual occasions, is defined by Servius 'toga sic in tergum reiecta ut ima eius lacinia ('fringe') a tergo reuocata hominem cingat'. The origin of the name is obscure. For its use cf. Livy v. 46. 2, viii. 9. 9, x. 7. 3.

614. uocat pugnas: i.e. calls out the war that is imprisoned behind the gates.

   pubes: see on 105.

616. et tum : as in 92, of a regular practice followed in a particular case.

   Aeneadis: epic convention extends the metrically useful patronymic, properly applied to a tribe in respect of descent from a common ancestor, to the followers of a hero: *Aeneadae* is 'Aeneas' people' (as here) or even the Romans (as in viii. 648 or Lucr. 1. 1). Similarly *Romulidae* is 'Romulus' people' in viii. 638 (and Lucr. iv. 683), *Thesidae* the Athenians in *Geo.* ii. 383.

617. iubebatur: i.e. by the *patres* (611): there is some inconsistency, for elsewhere Latinus is no constitutional monarch, like the kings of Rome, governing with a senate of elders, but an autocrat who has made an alliance with the Trojans (266) on his own authority.

618. pater: the title emphasizes his fatherly concern for his people.

620 f. morantis . . . portas: Servius takes the verb actively, 'bellum differentes', but it need mean no more than 'slow to move'.

621. impulit: struck them open with a blow: cf. i. 81 f. 'cuspide montem / impulit in latus'.

 manu reinforces *ipsa*: cf. 143 '(pater) ipse manu quatiens . . . nubem', iii. 372 'ipse manu . . . ducit'. The colourful addition of *manu* to emphasize personal effort is a mannerism of Virgil's which amounts to a cliché, especially in the second half of the poem: cf., e.g., 604, 664, 688, viii. 220 'rapit arma manu', ix. 758 'rumpere claustra manu', xi. 453 'arma manu trepidi poscunt', 650 'lenta manu spargens hastilia', 799 'missa manu . . . hasta', xii. 629 'saeua manu mittamus funera Teucris', 901 ff. 'manu raptum . . . / tollentemue manu'.

622. Belli ferratos . . . postis: the phrase comes from Ennius (*Ann.* 266 f. V.) 'postquam Discordia taetra / Belli ferratos postes portasque refregit'. See on 324 ff.

623. ardet: note the emphatic position, 'up blazed Italy'.

 inexcita : Virgil has both *excĭtus* (642, iii. 676, x. 38) and *excītus* (376, iv. 301, xii. 445): the negative is taken up by Statius (*Ach.* ii. 67).

624. pedes ire parat campis: cf. x. 453 f. 'pedes apparat ire / comminus', iv. 404 'it nigrum campis agmen'. Cf. also vii. 223 on *ire*.

 pars pedes . . . pars arduus : the masculine form of the collective singular in the first phrase seems to have suggested the illogical masculine in the second. Note the alliteration on *p*.

 arduus : of proud bearing, here of the chariot-borne warrior but of an admiral in viii. 683 ('arduus agmen agens'), of Turnus on foot in ix. 53 ('campo sese arduus infert') and, in the same phrase, of the war-horse itself in *Geo.* ii. 145.

625. omnes arma requirunt: a half-line from Ennius (*Ann.* 196 V.) 'balantum pecudes quatit, omnes arma requirunt'. For the break after the third foot cf. x. 545 (again after *furit*).

626. leuis . . . tergent, 'rub their shields smooth and their spears bright': for the proleptic (or anticipatory) use of the adjective see on 498.

627. subigunt, 'grind down': the verb may have been technically used in this connection as it is for breaking up soil (*Geo.* i. 125; Cato 161), kneading dough (Cato 74; *Moretum* 46) and massaging animals (Col. vi. 30. 1).

629. quinque adeo, 'five cities, no less': see on 427.

629 f. urbes . . . tela nouant: the same personification at viii. 385 f. 'quae moenia . . . / ferrum acuant': cf. viii. 497.

630 f. The place-names cover the whole of Latium. Three towns are in the north of the country, in the Tiber and Anio valleys, Crustumerium on the Tiber on the fringes of the Sabine territory, Antemnae at the confluence of Tiber and Anio, and Tibur itself on the Anio; Ardea is in the lowlands of the Rutulian country near the coast, Atina in the south among the Volscian hills.

Atina, *monte niuoso descendens* (Sil. viii. 398 f.), was a Samnite town in historical times; unlike some of its neighbours, it maintained its importance and was a thriving place when Cicero's client Plancius came from it (Cic. *Planc.* 19). *superbum* no doubt refers primarily to Tibur's pride in her commanding situation crowning the cliff above a loop in the river, but perhaps it has an oblique anachronistic reference to the prosperity she enjoyed in Virgil's own time as the resort of well-to-do Romans. For *Ardea* see on 412. The plural *Crustumeri* (i.e. *Crustumerii*: for the syncopated form cf. Prop. iv. 1. 34 *Gabi*; Man. i. 789 *Deci*) is unique: the usual name of the town is *Crustumerium* (with the variants *Crustumeria* and, in verse, *Crustumium*), that of its inhabitants *Crustumini*: it was in a fertile region (Cic. *Flacc.* 71; Livy i. 11. 4), particularly famous for its pears (*Geo.* ii. 88; Col. v. 10. 18). *Antemnae* disappeared from history early: it does not appear among the thirty cities of the Latin League and it was decayed in Varro's time (*L.L.* v. 28).

631. turrigerae: cf. x. 253 'turrigeraeque urbes'.

turrigerae Antemnae: the spondaic hexameter (σπον-δειάζων), i.e. a hexameter with a spondee in the fifth foot, which had been a not uncommon but apparently accidental variation in Homer, became in Alexandrian narrative verse an effect deliberately pursued for its own sake. In the *Iliad* about one line in 25 is a σπονδειάζων, but in Callimachus the proportion is one in eleven and in Aratus one in six. The mannerism was taken up by the Latin *neoterici* (cf. Cic. *Att.* vii. 2. 1) and in Catullus' epyllion the incidence of spondaic lines is almost as high as in Callimachus. Virgil uses the effect much more sparingly: the *Aeneid* has thirty-three instances, hardly more than Catullus has in the 408 lines of poem 64. Often the spondaic ending is associated with the presence in the line of Greek words, especially Greek names (the exploitation of the emotive value of the name was itself a piece of Alexandrian technique), usually in the ending itself—so i. 617 'Dardanio Anchisae' (cf. v. 761, ix. 647), iii. 74 'Neptuno Aegaeo', 517 'circumspicit Oriona', viii. 54 'nomine Pallanteum' (cf. 341, ix. 196, 241), ix. 9 'petit Euandri' (cf. xi. 31), xi. 659 'flumina Thermodontis', xii. 83

'decus dedit Orithyia'—but once earlier in the line (*Geo.* i. 221 'Atlantides abscondantur'): with these lines may be reckoned two, this line and viii. 345 'nemus Argileti', with names belonging to Graeco-Italian legend. More rarely the spondaic line contains Greek words other than a name: so *Ecl.* 5. 38 'purpureo narcisso', *Geo.* iv. 270 'graue olentia centaurea', *Aen.* viii. 167 'chlamydemque auro dedit intertextam', 402 'potest electro'. Sometimes the spondaic ending is combined with another 'Greek' effect—hiatus (see on 178) in this line and in *Ecl.* 7. 53, *Aen.* i. 617, iii. 74, ix. 647, xi. 31, irregular lengthening (see on 174, 398) in *Geo.* ii. 5, *Aen.* ix. 9. In a few lines the effect seems to be a rhythmical echo of the sense: so 634 below 'leuis ocreas lento ducunt argento', *Aen.* ii. 68 'constitit atque oculis Phrygia agmina circumspexit', xii. 863 'in bustis aut culminibus desertis'; perhaps *Ecl.* 4. 49 'magnum Iouis incrementum', *Geo.* ii. 5 'grauidus autumno', *Aen.* iii. 549 'cornua uelatarum obuertimus antemnarum', v. 320 'longo sed proximus interuallo' may be similarly intended. Some spondaic endings may be verbal echoes of Greek lines: one (viii. 679 'et magnis dis') is an echo of Ennius.

632. Note the alliteration on *t*, representing here (one may guess) the beating of hammers, as in Lucr. ii. 618, 'tympana tenta tonant palmis', it represents the tattoo of the tambourine.

tegmina ... cauant: i.e. make *tegmina caua*, 'encircling coverings': for this use of *cauus* see on viii. 598 f. 'colles caui'.
633. umbonum cratis: *umbo*, the boss (which was of metal) stands (as in ix. 810, x. 884) for the shield itself, which was made on a wicker framework (*crates*: cf. Caes. *B.G.* ii. 33. 2 'scutis ex cortice factis aut uiminibus intextis, quae subito, ut temporis exiguitas postulabat, pellibus induxerant').

634. The spondaic line (see on 631) echoes the slow and laborious process: Virgil has a spondaic fifth foot preceded by a spondaic fourth only here and in *Geo.* iii. 276, *Aen.* iii. 74.
lento: here of molten metal: see on 28.

ducunt: *ducere* of shaping, moulding, or beating out soft material is a technical term of the bronzesmith (as here: so Lucr. v. 1264 f. 'quamuis in acuta ac tenuia posse / mucronum duci fastigia procudendo'; Tib. i. 3. 47 f. 'nec ensem / immiti saeuus duxerat arte faber'), the statuary in bronze (Hor. *Ep.* ii. 1. 240; Pliny, *N.H.* vii. 125), the brickmaker (Vitr. ii. 3. 1), the potter (Quint. ii. 17. 3), the maker of wax figures (Juv. 7. 237).

635. honos: see on 3.
635 f. huc ... cessit, 'come to this', 'taken this turn': the

nearest parallel seems to be the more obvious viii. 395 f.
'fiducia cessit / quo tibi, diua, mei?'. For the thought cf.
Geo. i. 506 ff. 'non ullus aratro / dignus honos . . . / et curuae
rigidum falces conflantur in ensem'.

636. recoquunt: they retemper their fathers' swords: for
patrios cf. 653 and see on 1.

637. iamque: see on 25: *iamque* stands in the second place
again at iii. 588, v. 225, vi. 81, x. 813.

   it: see on 223, viii. 557.

   bello: for the dative cf. 482, 536, 642.

   tessera was originally the tablet passed round from com-
pany to company or man to man giving a pass-word: in
later military usage the word was applied to a message
conveying orders (so, e.g., Livy vii. 35. 1, ix. 32. 4, xxvii.
46. 1): Virgil goes even further when he extends it to a
mobilization order.

638. trementis: so in *Geo.* iii. 84 the war-horse 'stare loco
nescit, micat auribus et tremit artus'.

639. ad iuga cogit: cf. *Moretum* 121 (the ploughman) 'sub iuga
. . . cogit lorata iuuencos'.

   -que . . . -que: see on 186.

639 f. auro trilicem loricam: the same phrase at v. 259 f.: for
the Virgilian complex of adjective and descriptive ablative
cf. ii. 765 'crateresque auro solidi', iv. 504 f. 'pyra . . . ingenti
taedis', v. 663 'pictas abiete puppis', vi. 593 f. 'fumea taedis /
lumina', viii. 694 'telisque uolatile ferrum', ix. 359 f. 'aurea
bullis / cingula', x. 783 f. 'orbem / aere cauum triplici', xi.
890 'duros obice postis', xii. 522 'uirgulta sonantia lauro'.
See E. Löfstedt, *Synt.* i². 301.

   trilicem: *licia* were loops (μίτοι, 'heddles') attached to the
vertical threads of a warp so that, in plain weaving, by
fastening alternate loops to a rod (*liciatorium, arundo, κανών*)
one set of alternate threads could be lifted apart from the
other ('shed') and a thread of weft passed through between
them with the shuttle. In weaving of more complicated pat-
tern two, three, or more rods with sets of loops appropriately
attached to them were manipulated so that, as the pattern
required, the weft-thread could be passed, say, under one
warp-thread and over two or three. Such a piece of weaving
is *bilix* or *trilix*, in Greek δίμιτος or τρίμιτος (or even πολύμιτος).
Some of these terms have survived in English names of cloth,
trilix in 'drill' (through German 'drillich': 'twill' is a hybrid
analogical formation), δίμιτος in 'dimity', and ἐξάμιτος in
'samite'. Here, and elsewhere where Virgil applies *bilix* or
trilix to a *lorica* (*bilix* xii. 375; *trilix* iii. 467, v. 259), it is
extended from cloth-weaving to the mesh of chain armour.

640. loricam induitur: Virgil's use of the verb shows a remarkable variety of construction: (*a*) active with accusative *rei* (e.g. ix. 180 'induit arma', 365 f. 'galeam . . . / induit', xi. 439), (*b*) active with accusative *personae* and ablative *rei* (*Geo.* iv. 142 f. 'quot . . . pomis se fertilis arbos / induerat'), (*c*) active with accusative *personae* followed by *in* with accusative *rei* (vii. 19 f. 'quos . . . / induerat Circe in uultus ac terga ferarum' [see note there], *Geo.* i. 187 f. 'se nux . . . / induet in florem'), (*d*) active with accusative *rei* and dative *personae* (xi. 76 f. 'harum unam iuueni . . . / induit'), (*e*) (as here) 'middle' (see on 503) with accusative *rei* (ii. 275 'exuuias indutus', 392 f. galeam . . . / induitur', xi. 487), (*f*) 'middle' with accusative *rei* and dative (666 ff. 'tegimen . . . leonis, / . . . / indutus capiti'), (*g*) 'middle' with ablative *rei* (v. 674 'qua (galea) indutus', xii. 947 'spoliis indute').

641 ff. The 'Gathering of the Clans' (in Warde Fowler's happy phrase), with which Virgil sets the scene for the story of the fighting, is inspired by Homer's 'Catalogue' of the Greek forces in *Il.* ii. 484 ff. Virgil makes that clear to his reader when, invoking the Muses to assist the poet in a task demanding detailed memory, he uses Homer's formula: ὑμεῖς γὰρ θεαί ἐστε, πάρεστέ τε, ἴστέ τε πάντα, / ἡμεῖς δὲ κλέος οἶον ἀκούομεν οὐδέ τι ἴδμεν (*Il.* ii. 485 f.) But Virgil's 'Catalogue' (as Macrobius already observed in his own pedantic way, v. 15. 14 ff.) is very differently conceived from Homer's. Homer's is for the most part a bare list of contingents; there is comparatively little individual characterization or descriptive digression and the same formulas are used over and over again. Virgil gives his 'Catalogue' life, and turns it into poetry, with imaginative realism and skilfully contrived variation, bringing the figures of the leaders, the traditions of their regions, and the accoutrements of their men before the reader's eye in a series of romantic pictures—Aventinus parading his team on the grass, the snake-charmer Umbro, Halaesus yoking his horses, the legends of Caeculus and Virbius—and vivid similes, the Centaurs descending from the snows and the swans flying over the Cayster. Even in the rapid enumeration of lines 797 ff., the variety and the colour of his phrases contrast sharply with the ναῖον, ἔχον, and ἐνέμοντο of Homer. And the whole passage is made relevant to his conception of his theme: the Catalogue gives him his opportunity to survey the greatness of the old Italy and the unsophisticated virtues of her people as a background to the new greatness and the new civilization of which they would be part.

There is no obvious geographical arrangement in the list:

as Macrobius noted (v. 15. 4) 'nullum in commemorandis regionibus ordinem seruat sed locorum seriem saltibus lacerat'. Virgil begins with Caere in Etruria, Tibur, Praeneste: then he passes to more distant contingents—Faliscans and Sabines from the north-east, Auruncans and Campanians from the south, Aequiculans and Marsians from the central Apennines: he returns to Aricia in Latium before closing with the Rutulian Turnus and the Volscian Camilla. On the other hand, the significance of the beginning and the end is unmistakable: the list is framed by outstanding figures—Mezentius with Lausus at the beginning, Turnus and Camilla at the end—whose appearance foreshadows the most dramatic scenes in the later books. Between, there is a sequence of an unexpected kind: the eleven names appear (with the exception of Messapus) in an alphabetical order. If that order is accidental, the accident is remarkable: on the other hand it is not easy to believe that the order is that in which Virgil found his heroes listed in an antiquarian source. Alphabetical lists of names existed in Virgil's time (see L. W. Daly in *A.J.P.* lxxxiv [1963], 68 ff.): a list of twenty-nine Latin peoples (signatories to a treaty) in Dionysius (v. 61) is shown to have been taken from a Latin source by the imposition of Latin alphabetical order on names written in Greek, and there is one of thirty (partakers in the Latin Festival) in Pliny (*N.H.* iii. 69), but these are bare documentary lists relating to historical times and presumably first made for a practical purpose. The great lexicon of Virgil's contemporary Verrius Flaccus was alphabetically arranged and occasional traces of alphabetical arrangement in Book VII of Varro's *De Lingua Latina* suggest that he was using alphabetical glossaries. But an alphabetical handbook of legendary Italian heroes would be another thing. Besides, some of the heroes look as if they were Virgil's own invention (see on 745 Ufens, 750 ff. Umbro, 761 ff. Virbius), and it is to be observed that in the 'Catalogue' of Etruscan heroes in x. 166 ff. the arrangement is largely, though not so strikingly, alphabetical. (In literature the only other example is in Plautus, *Asin.* 865 f.: the eight names of Demaenetus' alleged dinner-hosts are fitted into two *octonarii* in a roughly alphabetical order which is no doubt part of the joke.)

On the Catalogue see B. Brotherton, *T.A.P.A.* lxii (1931), 192 ff.; E. A. Hahn, *T.A.P.A.* lxiii (1932), lxii; B. Rehm, *Philol.* Supp. xxiv. 2 (1932), 91 ff.; R. D. Williams, *C.Q.* lv (1961), 146 ff.; E. Fraenkel, *J.R.S.* xxxv (1945), 8 ff.; A. Lesky, *Festschrift Büchner* (Wiesbaden, 1970), 189 ff.

641. pandite ... mouete: i.e. give me free access to Helicon

and inspire my song: cf. Ovid, *Met.* x. 149 f. 'Musa parens
... / carmina nostra moue'.

642. exciti: see on 623.

bello : for the dative see on 482.

643. iam tum: even then, in those remote times, before the
great days of the later Italy that we know: similarly viii. 349
'iam tum' (even in those early times, before the great temple
of our day) 'religio pauidos terrebat agrestis'.

644. alma retains its etymological sense of 'quae alit': cf.
Geo. ii. 330 'parturit almus ager'.

645. meministis ... memorare: see on 41: for the prayer-
formula with *enim* see on 335.

647. asper: see on 505.

ab oris is to be taken closely with *Mezentius* and not with
the verbs; for Mezentius had not come directly from Etruria
—his Etruscan subjects had revolted and dethroned him
and he had taken refuge with the Rutulians (viii. 481 ff.).
For the descriptive local phrase attached to the name cf.
x. 345 'Curibus ... Clausus', *Geo.* iii. 2 'pastor ab Amphryso';
Prop. iv. 6. 37 'Longa mundi seruator ab Alba'. The attribu-
tive use of an ablative of place is regular even in prose with
names of persons: e.g. Caes. *B.C.* i. 24. 4 'N. Magius Cre-
mona', *B.G.* v. 27. 1 'Q. Iunius ex Hispania quidam'; Cic.
Clu. 36 'Auillius quidam Larino'; Livy i. 50. 3 'Turnus Her-
donius ab Aricia': so in comedy Plaut. *Asin.* 499 'Peri-
phanes Rhodo'.

oris : see on 564.

648. contemptor diuum: according to the legend in Cato (*ap.*
Macr. iii. 5. 10) Mezentius had arrogated divine honours by
claiming for himself first fruits offered by the Rutulians to
the gods. Virgil conveys his hybris in more subtle ways—
the flippancy of x. 743 f. (which he utters 'subridens' over his
victim Orodes) 'nunc morere. ast de me diuum pater atque
hominum rex / uiderit', the blasphemous self-sufficiency
of x. 773 f. 'dextra mihi deus et telum ... adsint', the ar-
rogant defiance of his last words x. 880 'nec mortem hor-
remus nec diuum parcimus ulli'. In x. 689, when he enters
the battle 'Iouis monitis', these words may be taken to
imply that he is made the instrument of heaven for his own
destruction. Servius is right in the reason he suggests for the
appearance of Mezentius at the head of the catalogue of
Aeneas' enemies: the *contemptor diuum* who has no respect
for divine law is the counterpart of the *pietas* of Aeneas whose
mission is to fulfil it.

649. iuxta 'he had his son beside him, leading ...': for the
dative cf. viii. 104 'Pallas huic filius una'. (*iuxta* with the

dative is used first by Livy, but only in a transferred sense, xxiv. 19. 6 'rem paruam ac iuxta magnis difficilem'.)

quo pulchrior alter: for the formula cf. i. 544 f. 'quo iustior alter / nec pietate fuit, nec bello maior et armis'. For the 'pathetic' description see on 536 ff.: there is a reminiscence of *Il*. ii. 673 f. Νιρεύς, ὃς κάλλιστος ἀνὴρ ὑπὸ ῎Ιλιον ἦλθε / τῶν ἄλλων Δαναῶν μετ' ἀμύμονα Πηλείωνα. For the repetition of the name see on 586 ff.

650. corpore Turni: the periphrasis has the effect of stressing the picture of physical beauty: for similar periphrases cf. 18 'formae . . . luporum', viii. 194 'Caci facies'.

651. equum domitor: see on 189.

debellator: the noun occurs first here and again in Statius, *Theb*. ix. 545.

652. Agyllina: Agylla was the earlier name (cf. Herod. i. 167) of Caere in Etruria: cf. viii. 479 f.

nequiquam : the pathetic adverb looks forward to the death (x. 789 ff.) from which his men could not save him: cf. xi. 536 '(Camilla) nostris nequiquam cingitur armis', xii. 517 'iuuenem exosum nequiquam bella Menoeten'. *nequiquam*, which in Plautus is as common as *frustra*, was later supplanted by it in general use: see the statistics given in *T.L.L.* s.v. *frustra*. Virgil has a marked preference for *nequiquam* (forty-one examples against twenty-nine of *frustra*) and so has Livy: after Livy it disappears almost entirely from prose. See E. Wölfflin, *A.L.L.* ii. 1 ff., 614 ff.; B. Axelson, *Unpoetische Wörter*, 128 n. 22.

653. mille uiros: one may wonder how Lausus was able to bring a contingent of a thousand from the city from which his father had been expelled by popular revolt. The accounts of Cato (fr. 10, 11 P.) and Dionysius (i. 64. 3–4) make either Turnus or the Rutulians after Turnus' death call in Mezentius and his Etruscans to support them. Virgil, representing the Etruscans as Aeneas' allies (in compliment, perhaps, to Maecenas' Etruscan connections), makes Mezentius a refugee playing a lone hand and attaching himself to Turnus: this reference to a large Etruscan contingent on the Italian side seems to be a survival from the other version.

653 f. dignus . . . qui . . . esset, 'worthy to have had a father in whose rule he could find more happiness, worthy of a father who was not Mezentius': cf. Ovid, *Met*. viii. 847 'filia restabat non illo digna parente'. For *patriis* see on 1.

esset . . . esset: the repetition is awkward and, unlike those in viii. 271 f., 396 f., seems to serve no rhetorical point. See on viii. 271 f.

655 ff. Auentinus appears in Livy (i. 3. 9: cf. Varro, *L.L.* v. 43;

Dion. Hal. i. 71. 4) as a king of Alba who gave his name to the Roman hill where he was buried, and Rhea is there the name of his granddaughter, daughter of Numitor, the Vestal mother of Romulus and Remus (who in the tradition followed by Virgil is Ilia). This account of Aventinus' birth and the connection with the story of Hercules' visit to Italy (cf. viii. 200 ff., where, however, the hill on which he encounters Cacus already has the name of Aventine) seem to be Virgil's own. One cannot guess where Virgil means to place him and his following (see on 664 ff.).

656. uictores: so *Geo.* iii. 499 'uictor equus'; cf. x. 891 'bellatoris equi'.

656 f. pulchro pulcher: for other Virgilian examples of the favourite Latin stylistic device of 'polyptoton' cf. i. 684 'pueri puer indue uultus', iii. 159 f. 'moenia magnis / magna para', 329 'me famulo famulamque Heleno transmisit habendam', iv. 83 'absens absentem auditque uidetque', v. 569 'pueroque puer dilectus Iulo', xii. 138 f. 'adfata sororem / diua deam'.

657 f. insigne paternum ... Hydram: for the device commemorating his father's exploit cf. Eur. *Phoen.* 1135 ff. where Adrastus bears it (not as *paternum*): ἑκατὸν ἐχίδναις ἀσπίδ' ἐκπληρῶν γραφῇ, / ὕδρας ἔχων λαιοῖσιν ἐν βραχίοσιν / Ἀργεῖον αὔχημα: the curious hendiadys—the *centum angues* are the *serpentes* which encircle the Hydra—was perhaps suggested by Euripides' form of words. For *insigne* cf. ii. 389 f. 'mutemus clipeos Danaumque insignia nobis / aptemus', 392 f. 'galeam clipeique insigne decorum / induitur', vii. 789 f. 'clipeum sublatis cornibus Io / auro insignibat'. On distinguishing badges on ancient shields see L. Wickert, *Philol.* lxxxv (1930), 299 ff.

660. sub luminis ... oras, 'into the regions of light' (see on 564): an Ennian phrase (*Ann.* 114, 131 V.) taken up by Lucretius, who has it nine times.

661. mixta deo mulier: a reminiscence of *Il.* xvi. 176 γυνὴ θεῷ εὐνηθεῖσα.

Laurentia: the adjective is loosely used (cf. 47 'nympha genitum Laurente Marica') to include the site of Rome on the Tiber which when Hercules came there, according to Virgil's own account, was in the possession of Evander and his Arcadians.

662 f. Tirynthius: Hercules has the same epithet in viii. 228, derived either from his birth at Tiryns or from his service under Eurystheus there: the accounts vary. The *boues Hiberae* are the cattle of Geryon which Hercules had driven from Spain and which Cacus stole from him. Servius already

noted the effect of the two names *Tyrrheno* ... *Hiberas*
framing the line in suggesting the distance traversed by
Hercules and his herd.

664 ff. These lines show signs either of lack of finish or of dis-
placement: (1) The transition from the leader Aventinus to
his people, the unexpressed subject of *gerunt*, is extremely
abrupt, and there is no indication, as there is for the other
contingents, of the region from which the people came (unless
ueru Sabello can be taken to be one). (2) At the beginning of
the passage Aventinus appears in proud possession of a war-
chariot and a prize team which he is exercising (like Virbius
in 781 f.): at the end he is on foot. And, even to secure variety,
it is surprising that he should be represented as paying a call
on Latinus (if that is what 'regia tecta subibat' means) while
his fellow captains Catillus and Coras 'densa inter tela
feruntur' (673). (3) There is some awkwardness in the con-
struction of 665-7, where the object for *indutus* has to be
found in that of *torquens*. Warde Fowler neatly removes the
first two difficulties by transposing 664-9 to follow 744-9,
the account of the Sabine Ufens, which as it stands is short,
suggesting that the phrase 'Herculeo amictu' caused the
lines to be attached to Aventinus, Hercules' son.

664. in bella: cf. 13 'in lumina'.

dolones: Servius offers two meanings for *dolo*: (*a*) a kind
of sword-stick, 'flagellum intra cuius uirgam latet pugio'
(cf. Hesych. δόλωνες· . . . ξιφίδια ἐν ξύλοις ἀποκεκρυμμένα): that
appears to be the meaning of the word in *Dig.* 9. 2. 52 (an
opinion of Alfenus on a case of assault) 'flagello quod in
manu habebat in quo dolo inerat uerberare tabernarium
coeperat' (Suet. *Claud.* 13. 1 'cum dolone ac uenatorio cultro
praestolantes' throws no light on the meaning); (*b*) a pole
with a short iron head, 'ingens contus cum ferro breuissimo',
for which he cites Varro.

665. It is not certain whether Virgil has one weapon or two in
mind here, but 'tereti . . . mucrone ueruque Sabello' is prob-
ably a hendiadys—'the tapering point of the Sabellian spit'.
The *ueru* is presumably the *uerutum* of Festus 514 L., a *pilum*
headed with a *ueru* or spit-point. The Volscians are armed
with the *ueru* in *Geo.* ii. 168: in Livy (i. 43. 6, xxi. 55. 11) the
uerutum is a throwing-spear carried by light-armed troops.
teres, which combines the ideas of rounded and tapering,
might be expected to refer to the shaft, as it expressly does
in Livy's description of another throwing-weapon, the
phalarica (xxi. 8. 10), 'hastili abiegno et cetera tereti prae-
terquam ad extremum . . .; id, sicut in pilo, quadratum': so
Virgil uses the adjective of a staff (*Ecl.* 8. 16) and of a tree-

trunk (*Aen.* vi. 207). Here, however, with *mucrone*, it perhaps describes a tapering metal head; cf. Ovid, *A.A.* i. 622 where it is used of the fingers.

666. torquens, 'flinging about him': cf. viii. 460 'demissa ab laeua pantherae terga retorquens'. The construction is awkward, the object of *torquens* being also understood with *indutus*: he flings the skin about his shoulders and draws the head, teeth and all, over his own head: so in xi. 680 f. Ornytus wears a wolf's skin with its head, 'caput ingens oris hiatus / et malae texere lupi cum dentibus albis'. For *immane* see on 305.

667. saeta: a collective singular such as is regular with *crinis* and *capillus*.

668. indutus capiti: see on 640.

sic is used, like οὕτως, to sum up a description ('like that') or a situation ('that being so', 'then'): so i. 223 ff. 'aethere summo / despiciens mare ueliuolum terrasque iacentis / litoraque et latos populos, sic uertice caeli / constitit', v. 622, viii. 488, xii. 304.

669. horridus: cf. v. 37 'horridus in iaculis et pelle Libystidis ursae': the adjective has point in reference to his shaggy ('impexum') accoutrements: but the adjective may have its wider sense; see on 746.

Herculeo . . . amictu repeats the description in a new form, relating it (if the lines are not misplaced) to his father's familiar costume.

innexus: having tied the skin about his shoulders: cf. vi. 281 'crinem uittis innexa'. See on 503.

671. cognomine: Virgil uses the word especially of the significant name, the ἔτυμον or αἴτιον: so iii. 163, 334, 350, 702, vi. 383, viii. 331, xi. 246. See on 3.

672. The founder of Tibur is usually Catillus (so Hor. *Od.* i. 18. 2, ii. 6. 5; Stat. *S.* i. 3. 100) who in Cato's account (fr. 56 P.), as here, is the father of another Catillus, Coras, and Tiburtus: but in Pliny, *N.H.* xvi. 237 he is Tiburnus (cf. Hor. *Od.* i. 7. 13). He is himself represented as the son of Amphiaraus, the prophet-king of Argos: hence *Argiua iuuentus* (cf. Hor. *Od.* ii. 6. 5. 'Tibur Argeo positum colono'). Virgil's *Cătillus* is *Cātĭlus* in Horace (*Od.* i. 18. 2), *Cătillus* in Statius.

673. primam ante aciem: see on 531.

674 ff. nubigenae: the Centaurs are *nubigenae* as the offspring of Ixion and a cloud to which Zeus, to tempt him, had given the form of Hera (Pindar, *P.* 2. 21–48), and the epithet is a convention of poetry (so viii. 293; Ovid, *Met.* xii. 211, 541; Stat. *Theb.* v. 263): but here it is given fresh meaning in the picture of the Centaurs as wild denizens of the cloud-wrapped mountain-tops of Thessaly, Homole (associated with the Centaurs in Eur. *H.F.* 371), and Othrys.

In this vivid image the phrases *dat . . . locum* and *magno . . . fragore* express the same idea. Warde Fowler tries to give precision to the picture by distinguishing them as two successive stages in the Centaurs' descent to the valleys: leaving the snowy crests, they first cross the belt of high pinewoods which make way before them and then crash through the underwoods of the lower slopes. But there is no justification for distinguishing between *dat locum* and *cedunt* or between *silua* and *uirgulta*, which are similarly coupled in xii. 522 'arentem in siluam et uirgulta sonantia lauro'.

678 ff. To this account of Caeculus Servius and the Verona scholia add, from Cato, that he was the miraculous child of a virgin by a spark leaping up from the hearth; that he was exposed and found by girls fetching water; and that, when after a career of *latrocinium* he founded Praeneste with his robber band, his claim to be Vulcan's son was spectacularly confirmed by a fire-prodigy. On this folk-tale, which appears in variant versions attached to other figures, see H. J. Rose, *Mnem.* liii (1925), 410 ff., *J.R.S.* xxiii (1933), 54 f. The name suggests a connection with Cacus, who in Virgil's story is also a son of Vulcan and a robber (see on viii. 184–279).

681. legio: in its original use of a muster or levy as in viii. 605, ix. 174, 368, x. 120.

682 ff. Caeculus' territory runs from his capital of Praeneste on its steep hill-top westwards to the fertile lowlands of Gabii and the Anio valley behind it, eastwards to Anagnia in the hill-country of the Hernici, and southwards as far as the Amasenus, running down from the Volscian hills above Privernum to the sea by Terracina.

682. Gabinae: the cult of Juno was widespread in Latium, but this is the only evidence for her worship at Gabii.

683. Anienem: while *Anio* supersedes *Anien* as the nominative (though Statius finds *Anien* convenient, *S.* i. 5. 25), the forms in *-en-* are normal in the oblique cases (though, if Servius on this line is to be believed, Ennius used *Anionem*).

684. Hernica saxa: *herna* was a Sabine word for rocks (Marsian, according to Festus, 89 L.) and the phrase looks like a piece of verbal play. In other examples of such etymological play in Virgil the roles are reversed, a Latin adjective explaining a non-Latin name: so i. 298 'nouae . . . Karthaginis arces', iii. 402 'parua . . . Petelia', 516 'pluuiasque Hyadas', 693 'Plemyrium undosum', 698 'stagnantis Helori', 703 'arduus

... Acragas'. (See also on 713.) See J. Marouzeau, *Quelques aspects de la formation du latin littéraire* (Paris, 1949), 71 ff.; J. S. T. Hanssen, *Symbolae Osloenses* xxvi (1948), 113 ff.

684 f. quos ... pascis ... Amasene pater : for the apostrophe see on 49.

685. pater: for the title of honour for a river-god cf. *Geo.* iv. 369 'pater Tiberinus', *Aen.* viii. 540 'Thybri pater'.

687. liuentis : the colour denoted by *liuere* (*liuidus*) is the dull dark blue or bluish grey of plums (Ovid, *Met.* xiii. 817), of grapes (Hor. *Od.* ii. 5. 10), of decayed teeth (Ovid, *Met.* ii. 776), of bruises (Hor. *Od.* i. 8. 10 and often elsewhere).

688. galeros, skin caps: the primitive warrior wears a *galerus* in Prop. iv. 1. 29 'prima galeritus posuit praetoria Lycmon'. The accoutrements of these rustic levies are those which they wear in peace: the ploughman has his *galerus* in *Moretum* 120 and his *perones* in Persius 5. 102.

689 f. uestigia ... instituere : i.e. they plant their left feet: *uestigia*, as *tegit altera* shows, refers to the foot itself, as in v. 566 f. 'uestigia primi / alba pedis'; Cat. 64. 162 'candida permulcens liquidis uestigia lymphis'. There are similar expressions in xi. 573 f. 'pedum primis infans uestigia plantis / institerat' and Lucr. i. 406 'cum semel institerunt uestigia certa uiai', but in these *uestigia* has the sense of footmarks and the verb is *insisto*: the use of *instituo* is unparalleled. The perfect is 'gnomic', 'they have the custom of treading . . .'.

Why do these warriors have the right foot booted and the left bare? When Roman infantry wore only one greave, they wore it on the right leg because when it was advanced the right leg was not protected by the shield as the left was (Veg. i. 20): but these light-armed troops have no such protection. Macrobius (v. 18. 17 ff.) noted the question but did not solve it, contenting himself with quoting Euripides, *Meleager* (fr. 534 N.), for the Aetolian custom, τὸ λαιὸν ἴχνος ἀνάρβυλοι ποδός, / τὸ δ' ἐν πεδίλοις, ὡς ἐλαφρίζον γόνυ / ἔχοιεν ὃς δὴ πᾶσιν Αἰτωλοῖς νόμος, and Aristotle's comment that Aetolian practice was in fact the reverse, and rightly so: δεῖ γὰρ, οἶμαι, τὸν ἡγούμενον ἔχειν ἐλαφρόν, ἀλλ' οὐ τὸν ἐμμένοντα. The idea may be that a man using his right arm to throw plants his left foot firmly (so in x. 587 Lucagus puts his left forward to get into a 'ready' position) and a bare foot gives a better grip (cf. Thuc. iii. 22. 2 τὸν ἀριστερὸν μόνον πόδα ὑποδεδεμένοι—i.e. leaving off the right boot —ἀσφαλείας ἕνεκα τῆς πρὸς τὸν πηλόν). But Virgil may merely have been using a reminiscence of Euripides' lines; it may be observed that *uestigia pedis* exactly translates ἴχνος ποδός.

691. Messapus was the eponymous hero of Messapia, the country in the heel of Italy to which he was said to have

migrated from Boeotia (Strabo ix. 2. 13): Virgil has trans-
ferred him to another part of Italy and now moves north from
Latium to the country beyond the Tiber, the southern
fringes of Etruria.

Neptunia proles: Messapus has this pedigree only in Virgil.

693. Virgil uses the line (with *animos* for *populos* and *corda* for
bello) at i. 722 in a very different context, of Dido's heart
unmoved by love since Sychaeus' death. For the combination
of adjectives cf. also vi. 813 ff. 'residesque mouebit / Tullus
in arma uiros et iam desueta triumphis / agmina'.

695. If *acies* has its usual meaning, *habent* goes awkwardly with
it. Hence D. A. Slater (*C.R.* xix [1905], 38) suggested that
acies is here used in a sense like that of the English 'edge'
in its geographical use and Warde Fowler made the further
suggestion (*Virgil's 'Gathering of the Clans'*, 64–5) that *acies*
and *arces* should be transposed. A. W. Van Buren's objection
(*C.R.* xxxiv [1920], 26 ff.) that the commonness of *acies* in
Virgil in its military sense (so, in this passage, in 643, 703,
796) makes such a meaning unlikely loses some of its force
in view of Virgil's habit of using a word in quite different
senses even at only a few lines' interval (see on 509). But
there is no evidence for this use of *acies* and the awkwardness
of *habent* may well be another sign of lack of revision.

Aequosque Faliscos: Falisci is the name of the people whose
country, the *ager Faliscus*, on the west side of the Tiber
formed a bridge between Etruscan and Latin cultures. It
contained the neighbouring towns of Fescennium and Falerii:
Ovid uses *Falisci* for the latter place (*Am.* iii. 13. 1 'pomi-
feris . . . Faliscis') and Virgil may have done the same: but
what of *aequos*? Strabo's mention (v. 2. 9) of a place which
he calls Αἰκονουμφαλίσκον on the via Flaminia points to a
town-name, Aequum Faliscum; when the town of Falerii
was destroyed in 241 B.C. the population was resettled on
a new site on lower ground and Hülsen (P.–W. vi. 2. 1971)
supposes that this new settlement was Aequum Faliscum,
though it was not on the via Flaminia. If this identification is
right, and Virgil chose to substitute *Aequi Falisci* for the
neuter form, he committed a glaring anachronism. Servius,
glossing *aequos* with 'iustos', offers the explanation that the
Romans derived certain fetial and other laws from the
Faliscans.

696. Soractis . . . arces, 'the high places of Soracte': for *arx* or
arces used of a mountain-top without the implication of an
inhabited stronghold cf. *Geo.* i. 240 'Riphaeas . . . arces',
iv. 461 'Rhodopeiae arces', *Aen.* ix. 86 (of Ida) 'lucus in arce
fuit summa'. Soracte, a detached outlier of the Sabine hills

across the Tiber, some 26 miles north of Rome, is not very
high (2420 ft.) but its sudden emergence from the river-basin
makes it conspicuous.

Flauinia: the name appears elsewhere only in Silius' imita-
tion of this passage (viii. 492).

697. Cimini cum monte lacum : the *mons Ciminius* was the
forest-clad range running down to the sea near Tarquinii
and separating the Tiber basin from the Etruscan plain, the
lacus a volcanic crater in the heart of it. For the defining
genitive see on viii. 231.

lucos Capenos : the Faliscan town of Capena, just south of
Soracte, had a sacred grove of Feronia (see on 800).

698. aequati numero, 'in even ranks', 'dressed': cf. xi. 599
'compositi numero in turmas'.

regem . . . canebant : cf. Hor. *Epod.* 9. 17 f. 'ad hunc fre-
mentes uerterunt bis mille equos / Galli, canentes Caesarem';
Tac. *Germ.* 3. 1 'Herculem . . . ituri in proelia canunt'.

699–705. Of the two bird-similes, the first, that of the swans on
the Cayster, is a Homeric reminiscence, suggested by the
vivid picture in the introduction to the Catalogue, *Il.* ii.
459 ff.: τῶν δ', ὥς τ' ὀρνίθων πετεηνῶν ἔθνεα πολλά, / χηνῶν ἢ γεράνων ἢ
κύκνων δουλιχοδείρων, / Ἀσίῳ ἐν λειμῶνι, Καϋστρίου ἀμφὶ ῥέεθρα, / ἔνθα
καὶ ἔνθα ποτῶνται ἀγαλλόμενα πτερύγεσσι, / κλαγγηδὸν προκαθιζόντων,
σμαραγεῖ δέ τε λειμών, / ὣς τῶν ἔθνεα πολλὰ νεῶν ἄπο καὶ κλισιάων / ἐς
πεδίον προχέοντο Σκαμάνδριον. The second is based on Ap. Rhod.
iv. 238 ff.: οὐδέ κε φαίης / τόσσον νηίτην στόλον ἔμμεναι, ἀλλ' οἰωνῶν /
ἰλαδὸν ἄσπετον ἔθνος ἐπιβρομέειν πελάγεσσιν. That Virgil intended the
two to stand together it is difficult to believe, even if sound
may be said to be the main point of the first (as Virgil has
used it: in Homer the sound is only a picturesque incidental
detail) and number the second; the broken line 702 (see on
129) suggests that they may have been alternative versions,
the first unfinished.

699. quondam: for the use in a simile see on 378.

liquida inter nubila: cf. v. 525 'liquidis in nubibus'.

701 f. Asia . . . palus : Homer's Ἄσιος λειμών, the *Asia prata*
of *Geo.* i. 383 f., the alluvial coastlands of Lydia round the
mouths of the Cayster and the Maeander, from which the
name was extended to the whole land-mass. In the restricted
reference Virgil follows Homer in making the first vowel long;
in the extended reference it is always short in *Asia* (though
Ovid twice uses the Alexandrian alternative *Āsis*) and *Asius*.

702. pulsa : for this use describing an echo cf. *Ecl.* 6. 84 'ille
canit, pulsae referunt ad sidera ualles', *Geo.* iv. 49 f. 'con-
caua pulsu / saxa sonant'. For the incomplete line see on
129.

703 f. examine tanto misceri, 'are massed in so great a swarm':
examine not only restores logic to the sentence—as A. E.
Housman observed (*C.R.* v [1891], 294 f.), there is no dif-
ficulty in believing that armed ranks are massed out of
a great multitude (*ex agmine tanto*): what may be difficult
to believe is that a great multitude consists of armed ranks—
but agrees with the sense of the words of Apollonius (iv.
238 f.) which Virgil clearly has in mind. Housman further
argued that Virgil used *exagmen*, an archaic form of *examen*,
and wrote *exagmine* both here and at ii. 727 '(aduerso
glomerati examine Grai'), where the same corruption has
occurred, and at the four places in *Ecl.* and *Geo.* where the
word has its literal sense, at all of which M's reading either
shows or points to *-agm-*. The assumption of a form **exagmen*
is not without difficulty, since *examen* might be expected to
represent not **exagmen* but *exagsmen* (see A. Ernout, *R. de
Ph.* lvii [1931], 403; cf. W. Lindsay, *The Latin Language*
(Oxford, 1894), 292), but has support from the form *subteg-
men* for *subtemen* (which certainly represents **subtexmen*)
transmitted by GM[1] at *Aen.* iii. 483 and by all the manu-
scripts twelve times in Cat. 64. 327–81. But the change of
examine to *ex agmine* can readily be explained without that
hypothesis.

For the metaphorical use of *examen* cf. Hor. *Od.* i. 35. 30 ff.
'iuuenum recens / examen Eois timendum / partibus': simi-
larly Aesch. *Pers.* 126 ff. πᾶς γὰρ ἱππηλάτας / καὶ πεδοστιβὴς λεὼς
/ σμῆνος ὣς ἐκλέλοιπεν μελισσᾶν σὺν ὀρχάμῳ στρατοῦ.

704. gurgite ab alto : *gurges* (a cognate of *uorare*) is properly
used of an enveloping body of water which swallows or
sweeps away, but the poets regularly use it generally of open
water: cf. vi. 310, ix. 23, xi. 913, xii. 114 and see Henry's
note on i. 118.

705. uolucrum . . . nubem : cf. 793 'nimbus peditum'.

707. Clausus, the Sabine leader, is an ancestor of that Clausus
or Claudius from whom the patrician *gens Claudia* claimed
descent (as the Emperor proudly declared, Tac. *Ann.* xi.
24. 1) and from whose settlers on the Anio the *tribus Claudia*
was formed. According to Livy's account (ii. 16. 4; so also
Dion. Hal. v. 40) Clausus left Regillum with his Sabine fol-
lowers and threw in his fortunes with Rome not when the
συνοικισμός with Tatius' Sabines, to which line 709 clearly
refers, took place under Romulus, but in 504 B.C. after the
foundation of the Republic; but the dating of the settlement
of the Claudii in the period of the monarchy (so Suet. *Tib.* 1;
App. *Reg.* 12) must be the true one. (See R. M. Ogilvie,
Comm. on Livy 1–5, p. 273.) Clausus' country extends from

Cures in the Tiber valley, 24 miles north of Rome, northward
to Nursia, and westwards to Amiternum in the heart of the
central Apennines 60 miles away, beyond the watershed
of Italy.

agminis instar, 'as good as an army': *instar* in classical
Latin always conveys the notion of equivalence either (*a*)
literally of size or quantity (so ii. 15 f. 'instar montis equum
... / aedificant', iii. 635 ff. 'lumen ... / Argolici clipei aut
Phoebeae lampadis instar') or (*b*) metaphorically of effect,
importance, or worth (so here and in xii. 923 f. 'uolat atri
turbinis instar / exitium dirum hasta ferens': cf. Livy
xxxviii. 7. 5 'armati ... instar munimenti erant'). The word
is used attributively, as in these four Virgilian examples (so,
e.g., Ovid, *Her.* 7. 19 'ut condas instar Carthaginis urbem'),
as predicate with *esse* (e.g. Cic. *Fam.* xv. 4. 8 'quae fuit non
uici instar sed urbis', *Pis.* 52 'unus ille dies ... immortalitatis
instar fuit', *Rab. Perd.* 24 'latere mortis erat instar turpis-
simae'; Ovid, *Met.* xiv. 124 "numinis instar eris semper
mihi'), or as object of *habere* or *obtinere* (e.g. Ovid, *Her.*
16. 368 'unus is innumeri militis instar habet'). Virgil makes
an unparalleled use of the word in vi. 865, 'quantum instar
in ipso', where no comparison is expressed. For an analysis
of the usage of the word see H. Nettleship, *Contrib. to Lat.
Lex.* 487-9.

709. in partem data, 'shared'.

710. Amiterna : for the adjective without adjectival suffix see
on 219.

Quirites: i.e. the people of the Sabine town of Cures: an
allusion to the fanciful theory of Roman etymologists (Varro,
L.L. vi. 68; Fest. 304 L.; Ovid, *F.* ii. 475 ff.) which made
Quirites equivalent to *Curenses* and derived the use of the
name for the people of Rome from the incorporation of
Tatius' Sabines in the time of Romulus.

711 f. Eretum and Nomentum were both near river-crossings
between Rome and Cures: Virgil appears to have forgotten
that in vi. 773 ff. he made Nomentum one of the places,
nunc sine nomine terrae, which were to be founded by Aeneas'
descendants. Mutusca, or Trebula Mutusca (Pliny, *N.H.* iii.
107) lay in the Sabine hills behind.

712. Rosea rura Velini: the *Rosei campi* were the alluvial basin
of the Velinus (see on 514 ff.) just north of Reate: their
fabulous fertility (*sumen Italiae*, they were called: Pliny,
N.H. xvii. 32; and Varro, himself a farmer at Reate, alleges,
in *R.R.* i. 7. 10, that a pole left lying on the ground at night
would be overgrown with grass in the morning) was achieved
in 275 B.C. when a short channel was cut to carry the

flood-waters of the Velinus, imprisoned by limestone deposits, into the Nar.

713. Tetrica (so the mountain is called also by Varro, *R.R.* ii. 1. 5) was part of the rugged central massif which separated the Sabine country from Picenum. *Seuerum* is understood by Servius as a proper name but it is otherwise unknown and that two Sabine mountains should have names coinciding with Latin adjectives would be a remarkable coincidence: it may be the adjective, *montem seuerum* repeating the sense of *Tetricae horrentis rupes* and playing (as *horrentis* itself may do) on the meaning of *tetricus* in Latin. (For etymological play on names in Virgil see on 684.) For *seuerus* used of cold or forbidding physical objects cf. Lucr. v. 1190 'noctis signa seuera', iv. 460 'seuera silentia noctis'; *Geo.* iii. 37 f. 'amnemque seuerum / Cocyti', *Aen.* vi. 374 f. 'amnemque seuerum / Eumenidum'.

714. Casperia, otherwise unknown, is identified with the modern Aspra: Foruli, a hill-village near Amiternum, was seen by Strabo, or one of his informants, who thought (v. 3. 1) it was a more suitable home for brigand outlaws than for men of peace.

715. qui . . . bibunt reproduces one of the few vivid touches in the Homeric Catalogue, *Il.* ii. 825 πίνοντες ὕδωρ μέλαν Αἰσήποιο: cf. *Ecl.* 1. 62, 10. 65; Hor. *Od.* ii. 20. 20 'Hiber Rhodanique potor', iii. 10. 1 'Tanain si biberes', iv. 15. 21 'qui profundum Danubium bibunt'.

Tiberim Fabarimque: Fabaris is identified by Servius with Ovid's *opacae Farfarus umbrae* (*Met.* xiv. 330) and that must be the modern Farfa, a small stream running down from the Sabine Hills to join the Tiber above the site of Cures: for the forms of the name see A. Ernout, *Philologica* ii (Paris, 1957), 210 ff. *Tiberis* is surprising, not so much because elsewhere in the *Aeneid* the Tiber is given its romantic Hellenized name of *Thybris* (see on 30) as because, though the Tiber has indeed Sabine territory on its left bank, the great river of Italy is here incongruously paired with one of its own minor tributaries and because it is to appear again later in the Catalogue, personified as its god *Tiberinus*, when Virgil comes to Turnus' contingent (797). But Mackail's suggestion that *Tiberis* is, or conceals, the name of another Sabine tributary is hardly plausible.

716. Ortinae classes populique Latini: if (*H*)*ortini* represents the *Horta* we know (the regular adjective for which would be *Hortanus*), its inclusion here is unexpected, since that Horta is on the right or Etruscan bank of the river, and, if *Latini* has its usual sense, the general *populi Latini* seems out of

place in a detailed list of Sabine communities. Pliny's list
(*N.H.* iii. 69) of extinct communities in Latium contains
as successive items 'Hortenses, Latinienses' and Nettleship
suggested that Virgil's two peoples might be identified with
these and represent a Horta and a Latinium otherwise un-
known.

  classes, 'levies'. As *classicum* survived to bear witness,
classis is not originally a naval term: it is a muster of men
(from the root *kal-*). *classis* was the archaic term for the
citizen army, which Livy curiously failed to recognize (iv.
34. 6) when he thought that *classi* in one of his authorities
implied a naval engagement on the upper Tiber.

717. infaustum . . . nomen: on 18 July 390 B.C. (the traditional
Roman date) the Gauls, advancing down the Tiber, met and
defeated a Roman army on the Allia, a stream running into
the Tiber eleven miles from Rome (Livy v. 37). The day
was a *dies ater* in the Roman calendar: Cic. *Att.* ix. 5. 2
'maiores nostri funestiorem diem esse uoluerunt Alliensis
pugnae quam urbis captae': Lucan vii. 409 'damnata diu
Romanis Allia fastis'. For the slight irregularity of the ap-
position cf. i. 288 'Iulius, a magno demissum nomen Iulo',
vi. 763 'Siluius, Albanum nomen'; Lucan vi. 795 'uidi ego
laetantis, popularia nomina, Drusos'.

719. saeuus . . . undis : the line is a reminiscence of Ap. Rhod.
i. 1201 f. εὖτε μάλιστα / χειμερίη ὀλοοῖο δύσις πέλει Ὠρίωνος. The set-
ting of Orion in early November marked a stormy season:
cf. Hor. *Od.* i. 28. 21 f. 'me quoque deuexi rapidus comes
Orionis / Illyricis Notus obruit undis', iii. 27. 17 f. 'sed uides
quanto trepidet tumultu / pronus Orion', *Epod.* 10. 10 'tristis
Orion cadit', 15. 7 f. 'dum . . . nautis infestus Orion / turbaret
hibernum mare'.

720. uel cum . . . aristae : the two similes are loosely co-
ordinated: strict grammar would demand *uel quam multae
sole nouo torrentur aristae*; for a similar irregularity cf. Prop.
ii. 2. 6 f. 'incedit uel Ioue digna soror, / aut cum Dulichias
Pallas spatiatur ad aras'.

  sole nouo : elsewhere *sol nouus* means either 'the early
morning' (*Geo.* i. 288) or 'the beginning of the warm weather',
in spring (*Geo.* ii. 332). The second meaning provides an
artificial contrast to the preceding line but is as inappropriate
here as the first: in Asia, as in Italy, it is the *maturi soles*
(*Geo.* i. 66) that bake the corn, not the *sol nouus*.

721. Hermi . . . Lyciae : the Hermus was the chief river of
Lydia, whose alluvial seaboard, volcanic hinterland, and
great river-valleys combined with a temperate climate (the
best in all the Greek lands, says Herodotus, i. 142. 1) to

make it highly fertile. Lycia has little title to be in this
company and the mention of it reflects the vagueness of
Latin poets about the geography of not very distant lands.
It was a rugged country with a meagre extent of cultivable
land and its timber was more important than its crops.

722. scuta sonant: they strike their spears on their shields: cf.
viii. 3 '(Turnus) impulit arma', xii. 332 'Mauors clipeo in-
crepat'.

conterrita: for the 'pathetic fallacy' cf. 514 ff.: for the
alliterative effect cf. xii. 445.

723 ff. The Campanians come in two bodies, the northern
peoples under Halaesus, the southern under Oebalus: both
names are elsewhere connected with other regions of Italy.
Halaesus appears elsewhere in legend as the eponymous
founder of Falerii, an Argive who fled to Italy after the
murder of Agamemnon (Ovid, *F.* iv. 73 f., *Am.* iii. 13. 31 ff.):
Virgil transfers him from the Faliscan country to northern
Campania. *Agamemnonius* seems to mean no more than that
he was of Agamemnon's following: Servius is the only
authority for the alternative story which makes him Agamem-
non's son and in the account of his death in x. 417 ff. he
is given an unnamed prophetic father (a motive drawn from
Il. ii. 831 ff.) who had vainly tried to keep him from harm.

723. Troiani nominis, 'all that was called Trojan': like the
regular *nomen Romanum, nomen Latinum* (e.g. Sall. *Cat.*
52. 24 'gentem infestissimam nomini Romano').

724. Note the rare rhythm of a feminine caesura in the second
and third feet which Virgil has only here, where Scaliger
fancifully took it to represent the time taken to harness.

ferocis: see on 384.

725. rapit, 'sweeps with him': cf. x. 178 'mille rapit densos acie
atque horrentibus hastis', 308 f., xii. 450.

felicia, 'fruitful', the original meaning of the word: cf.
Geo. ii. 81 'exiit ad caelum ramis felicibus arbos', iv. 329
'ipsa manu felicis erue siluas'. *Baccho* is probably ablative
(for the metonymy see on 113) but it may be dative ('for
Bacchus'). The *mons Massicus* and the adjoining country
of the *ager Falernus* were the most famous wine-growing
region of Italy: cf. *Geo.* ii. 143 'Bacchi Massicus umor',
iii. 526 f. 'Massica Bacchi / munera'.

726. Massica: for the neuter plural see on 91.

727. Aurunci: see on 39 and 730: the towns of Cales (which
also was a centre of wine-growing: cf. Hor. *Od.* i. 20. 9, 31. 9,
iv. 12. 14) and Teanum Sidicinum lay in the high lands
bordering the Campanian plain between the valleys of Liris
and Volturnus, Saticula to the south of the Volturnus.

727 f. Sidicinaque iuxta aequora: the construction of the words is difficult and ambiguous. It is possible (1) to take *Sidicina iuxta aequora* as parallel to *de collibus altis*, (2) to take *Sidicina aequora* as parallel to *patres*, a second subject for *misere*, *iuxta* being adverbial, (3) to regard *Sidicina iuxta aequora* as a noun-phrase, 'those adjacent to the plains of Sidicinum', parallel to the preceding relative clauses. (1) is most probable, (3) least, but the awkwardness suggests lack of revision, as do the nominative nouns in 729 f. and the nominative adjective in 741, which have no construction, and the ellipse of a verb in 732.

[J. Delz in *Mus. Helv.* xxxii (1975), 155 ff. argues that *aequora* is accusative case, object of *linquunt*, and that *qui* is to be taken ἀπὸ κοινοῦ, the *-que* linking *aequora* and *Cales*. With this interpretation the Oxford Text's comma after *aequora* would be omitted and commas might be inserted after *patres* and *linquunt*. J. D. C.]

729. Saticulus: for the absence of adjectival suffix (elsewhere the people are *Saticulani*) cf. 710 *Amiterna*: see on 219.

asper: see on 505.

730. Oscorum: The name of the Osci, here applied to the inhabitants of northern Campania, occurs rarely in Latin except as a linguistic term for the language which was spoken in southern Italy. Ancient tradition identified them, under their Greek name of Ὀπικοί, with the Ausones (see on 39: so Arist. *Pol.* vi. 1329ᵇ; Strabo v. 4. 3) and ascribed a large territory to them (Thuc. vi. 2. 4; Dion. Hal. i. 72. 3), but in historical times the Ausones, under their Latin name of Aurunci, inhabited the region between the Liris and the Volturnus and it is from that country that they come (727) to join Turnus here.

aclydes: Servius quotes a definition of the *aclys* as a club (*claua*) a cubit and a half long, pointed at the ends (*eminentibus hinc et hinc acuminibus*) and having a leash (*lorum uel linum*) attached for recovery when it was thrown. *teretes*, rounded and tapering, fits that description. Silius and Valerius Flaccus take the word over from Virgil and reveal their ignorance about the weapon when one makes it Spanish and the other Oriental. The origin of the word is unknown: Virgil gives it a Greek plural in *-ĕs*, but the only Greek derivation which has been suggested for it—from ἀγκύλη, 'javelin-thong', perhaps through Etruscan—is very precarious.

731. sed: for *sed* with a weak sense like that of *autem* adding a further detail cf. x. 576: see K.–S. ii. 2, p. 77.

732. caetra is a round leather targe, not peculiar to Italy:

Spaniards and Britons, Africans and Greeks are armed with it in Caesar and the historians.

falcati comminus enses: an elliptical phrase; the sense seems to be 'falcati sunt enses comminus pugnantibus'.

733. nec tu . . . abibis: for the formula cf. x. 185 f. 'non ego te . . . / transierim, Cunare', 793 'non equidem nec te, iuvenis memorande, silebo'; Hor. *Od.* i. 12. 21 f., iv. 9. 30 f.: for the use of apostrophe see on 49.

734. The leader of the Southern Campanians is Oebalus, who has extended his kingdom from Capreae to the opposite mainland: the Sebethus, his mother's stream, is there. Elsewhere the name belongs to a legendary king of Sparta: Virgil gives the epithet *Oebalius* to Tarentum in honour of its Spartan foundation (*Geo.* iv. 125), Ovid to Tatius (*F.* i. 260) in recognition of a mythical connection of Sparta with the Sabines.

735. Teleboum: the Teleboae gave their name to the Taphian islands off the coast of Acarnania (Pliny, *N.H.* iv. 53; Strabo x. 2. 20): their legendary association with the Campanian island of Capreae appears again in Tac. *Ann.* iv. 67.

736. non et filius: 'the son, not content as his father had been'.

738. The Sarnus is in the far south of the Campanian plain (*aequora*), running into the sea below Pompeii. The Sarrastes, whom Servius associates with the river, are otherwise unknown.

739. Batulum and Celemna are unknown. Rufrae appears in Silius (viii. 566) as a Samnite town.

740. maliferae . . . Abellae: Servius tells a curious story that Virgil originally wrote *maliferae . . . Nolae* but was offended by the people of Nola 'propter sibi negatum hospitium' and in retaliation removed the name of this town and substituted *Abellae* (or *Bellae*, which the manuscripts read here). Servius knew both readings and preferred *Bellae*, no doubt wrongly: Abella was an old town only a few miles from Nola which had a reputation for its nuts (Cato 8. 2; Col. v. 10. 14; Pliny, *N.H.* xv. 88), but Bella is unknown. To increase perplexity, Gellius (vi. 20. 1) tells the same story (which he says he found 'in quodam commentario') about another passage, *Geo.* ii. 224 f., alleging that there Virgil, having first written 'uicina Vesaeuo Nola iugo', substituted *ora* for *Nola*, and adding that the cause of the quarrel was that Nola had refused Virgil its water-supply. The strange tale is made even stranger by the fact that Paulinus, Bishop of Nola from 409 to 431, makes exactly the same complaint on his own behalf against his fellow townsmen and uses Servius' phrase: *Carm.* 21. 758 ff. 'nam mihi, Nola, tui consortia iusta petenti / fontis quo turbata metu quasi dura negabas / hospitium communis aquae?'.

The implausibility of Servius' story, whatever its origin may be, is not the only reason for believing that *maliferae* ... *Abellae* was what Virgil wrote. There is ground for thinking that the name *Abella* preserves an Italic word for 'apple', a cognate of those existing in the Northern groups of I.G. languages (Teutonic, Celtic, and Baltic), which was supplanted in Latin by *malum*, borrowed from Greek. If Abella was 'apple-town', *maliferae Abellae* is another Virgilian etymological play like those noted on 684.

741. soliti: another piece of loose writing; the structure of the sentence demands *solitos*: cf. 787.

cateias: we know as little about the *cateia* (which Silius and Valerius Flaccus take over from Virgil) as about the *aclys* of 730 to which Servius likens it: Isidore (*Orig.* xviii. 7. 7) makes it a kind of boomerang.

742. subere: for the use of cork cf. xi. 554, where Metabus wraps the infant Camilla in cork-bark.

743. aeratae ... aereus: for the pictorial repetition see on 278 f.

744 ff. From Campania Virgil goes north again to the central Apennines—to the Aequi and their southern neighbours the Marsi.

744. Nersae: the Aequi or Aequiculi were even in historical times hardy mountaineers whose descents from the upper Anio were a constant threat to the towns of Latium until their subjection in 304 B.C. They were not town-dwellers and their country had no settlements of any importance: Virgil's Nersae, otherwise unknown, may be identical with the Aequiculan 'uicus Neruesiae' which is casually mentioned in Pliny, *N.H.* xxv. 86.

745. Ufens: on Virgil's use of river-names for his heroes see on 532; the Volscian river itself appears in 802.

746. horrida ... gens: *horridus* is regularly used of a primitive habit of life: so Ovid, *Met.* i. 513 f. 'non ego sum pastor, non hic armenta gregesque / horridus obseruo'; Juv. 10. 298 f. 'sanctos licet horrida mores / tradiderit domus ac ueteres imitata Sabinos'; Cic. *Quinct.* 59 'uixit enim semper inculte atque horride', 93 'sibi ait officium, fidem, diligentiam, uitam omnino semper horridam atque aridam cordi fuisse', *Brut.* 117 'ut uita sic oratione durus incultus horridus' (cf. *Leg.* i. 6 'habuit uires agrestis ille quidem atque horridas').

747. uenatu: dative as in ix. 605: Virgil has the *u*-form in *uictu* (*Geo.* iv. 158), *concubitu* (*Geo.* iv. 198), *metu* (*Aen.* i. 257), *curru* (i. 476, iii. 541), *aspectu* (vi. 465).

duris . . . glaebis: the character of the land is reflected in that of the people.

748. exercent: cf. 798 'exercent uomere collis', *Geo.* i. 99.

748 f. semper . . . rapto: the words are repeated at ix. 612 f. (with the change of *comportare* for *convectare*), where the Italian Remulus uses them of his own people.

750 ff. The Marsi, here called by the name of their town of Marruvium on the Lacus Fucinus, set in a basin of hills in the very centre of Italy, are headed by the figure of the medicine-man Umbro (a river-name—see on 532—and presumably Virgil's invention). The name of King Archippus does not appear elsewhere but he is obviously an eponym of the Marsian town of Archippe, which according to the annalist Cn. Gellius (Pliny, *N.H.* iii. 108) was inundated by the lake (though by a fantastic piece of etymology he makes Marsyas its founder), and may be the unnamed son of Circe whom Pliny (vii. 15, xxv. 11) and Aulus Gellius (xvi. 11. 1–2) make the founder of the nation. Magic was indigenous to the region (for Marsian spells see Hor. *Epod.* 5. 76, 17. 29; Ovid, *F.* vi. 142, *A.A.* ii. 102): its snake-charmers were proverbial (Lucil. 575 f. M. 'ut Marsus colubras / disrumpit cantu'; Pomponius 118 R. 'mirum ni haec Marsa est: in colubras callet cantiunculam': cf. Pliny and Gellius cited above) and their tradition is said to have survived, in connection with popular religious ceremonies, to the present day (see W. Warde Fowler, *Virgil's 'Gathering of the Clans'*, 75 f.).

751. fronde . . . et felici . . . oliua: the olive wreath marks the priest as with Calybe (418) or the priest-king Numa (vi. 808). For the hendiadys see on 15.

755. iras: the word has a plural reference here (cf. 15); but see on 445.

756. sed non: cf. ix. 327 f. 'rex idem et regi Turno gratissimus augur, / sed non augurio potuit depellere pestem'. The pathetic formula was suggested by *Il.* ii. 858 ff. Ἔννομος οἰωνιστής· / ἀλλ' οὐκ οἰωνοῖσιν ἐρύσατο κῆρα μέλαιναν, / ἀλλ' ἐδάμη ὑπὸ χερσὶ ποδώκεος Αἰακίδαο.

757. eum: see on 63.

759. Angitiae: the name of the goddess appears in inscriptions of the region in various forms, sometimes in the plural (see A. Ernout, *R. de Ph.* xci [1965], 195 ff.; G. Radke, *Die Götter Altitaliens* [Münster, 1965], 65 f.). In Hellenizing legend the local tradition of magic turned her into a sister of Medea and Circe (Sil. viii. 498). Her *lucus* on the south shore of the Lacus Fucinus is perpetuated in the modern village of Luco.

760. te . . . fleuere lacus: for this form of the Alexandrian 'pathetic fallacy' (see on 514 ff.) cf. *Ecl.* 10. 13 'illum etiam lauri, etiam fleuere myricae', *Geo.* iv. 461 f. 'flerunt Rhodopeiae arces / altaque Pangaea et Rhesi Mauortia tellus': so Moschus 3. 1 f. αἴλινά μοι στοναχεῖτε, νάπαι καὶ Δώριον ὕδωρ, / καὶ ποταμοὶ κλαίοιτε τὸν ἱμερόεντα Βίωνα. For the pathetic apostrophe see on 49. For the incomplete line see on 129.

761 ff. With Virbius Virgil returns to Latium. The sequel to the Euripidean story of Hippolytus, that when he had been killed by his runaway horses, scared by a sea-monster sent by Poseidon in fulfilment of his father's curse, he was restored to life by Asclepius at the behest of his patroness Artemis, conveyed by her to Italy and hidden away in her sanctuary at Aricia, had probably been told by Callimachus in the *Aitia* (see Pfeiffer on Call. fr. 190): for Ovid's version see *Met.* xv. 542 ff. (cf. *F.* iii. 263 ff., vi. 737 ff.). Behind this legend lies an indigenous local *numen* Virbius associated with Diana in her cult at Aricia, which had a taboo on horses attached to it (see J. G. Frazer, *The Golden Bough* [London, 1914], v. 45 ff., who compares the taboo on the riding of a horse by the *flamen dialis*). When Diana became identified with Artemis, Hellenizing ingenuity turned Virbius into her votary Hippolytus, miraculously restored to life: the taboo on horses and an etymology of the name as *bis uir* both gave support to the identification. A younger Virbius, the son of Hippolytus-Virbius, appears only here: there is a flagrant incongruity, which did not escape Servius, in crediting Hippolytus, whose obdurate celibacy was notoriously the cause of his disaster, with having a son, and another in giving the son the same name as his father.

762. mater Aricia: the resemblance between 763 and the formula in ix. 673 (see below) suggests that Aricia is not a personification of the town (like *mater Populonia* in x. 172) but an eponymous nymph. For *educere* in the sense of *parere* cf. vi. 764 f. 'quem tibi longaeuo serum Lauinia coniunx / educet siluis', 778 f. 'Romulus, Assaraci quem sanguinis Ilia mater / educet', ix. 673 'quos Iouis eduxit luco siluestris Iaera'. Elsewhere Virgil (like other writers) uses *educere* as a synonym of *educare*, 'bring up': so viii. 412 f. 'ut . . . possit paruos educere natos' (and see note there).

763. Egeriae lucis: i.e. the grove of Diana beside the Lacus Nemorensis in a fold of the Alban Hills below Aricia. Egeria was a spring-goddess associated with a stream in Diana's precinct. When the Latin cult of Diana was transplanted for political reasons to the Aventine about 540 B.C., Egeria came with her to Rome, where another sacred spring outside the Porta Capena had her name and where the legend connecting her with Numa became attached to her (see Ogilvie on Livy i. 45).

764. pinguis . . . et placabilis: the phrase, which is repeated at ix. 585, seems to have been suggested by lines in the Homeric Catalogue, *Il.* ii. 540 ff. ἐῷ ἐν πίονι νηῷ· / ἔνθα δέ μιν ταύροισι καὶ ἀρνειοῖς ἱλάονται / κοῦροι Ἀθηναίων. The *ara* is *pinguis* with the blood and fat of sacrifice (cf. iv. 62 'pinguis spatiatur ad aras'), *placabilis* since sacrifice can secure divine favour (for *aram placare* cf. Ovid, *Met.* xv. 574 'placat odoratis herbosas ignibus aras').

Dianae: see on 306.

765. ferunt fama: see on 48.

nouercae: see on viii. 288.

766. patrias . . . poenas, 'satisfied the penalty demanded by his father': cf. vi. 565 'deum poenas'.

767. turbatis . . . equis : again at ix. 124; for Virgil's use of *turbatus* see on viii. 435.

769. Paeoniis: trisyllabic, as xii. 401 'Paeonium in morem': see on 175. Paeon (Παιών) is the title of Apollo as the healer.

771. lumina . . . uitae: cf. vi. 828 f. 'si lumina uitae / attigerint'.

772 f. repertorem . . . Phoebigenam : i.e. Asclepius. The patronymic, emphatically placed, has its point: 'for all that Apollo was his father'.

774. Triuia: i.e. Diana: see on 514 ff.

recondit : cf. i. 681 'sacrata sede recondam'.

776 f. ignobilis aeuum exigeret: so in a similar context (where Venus proposes to remove Iulus to Paphos), x. 52 f. 'positis inglorius armis / exigat hic aeuum'.

779. cornipedes . . . equi: again in vi. 591; the compound is not found before Virgil, but *sonipes, plumipes,* and *pinnipes* are and there is no reason to suppose that he invented it.

780. effudere : the technical term for throwing a rider or a driver (cf. x. 574 '(equi) . . . effunduntque ducem').

781. haud setius: i.e. just like his father, in spite of his father's fate.

783 ff. The Catalogue is closed by the heroic figure of Turnus, at the head of his Rutulians, supernatural in his savage splendour, with the Chimaera as his crest and the story of Io on his shield, and by the romantic picture of Camilla among her Volscians.

784. uertitur, 'moves to and fro', a more vivid equivalent of the commonplace *uersatur*.

toto uertice supra est: like Ajax in *Il.* iii. 227 ἔξοχος Ἀργείων κεφαλήν τε καὶ εὐρέας ὤμους.

785. Chimaeram: Turnus' crest is the fire-breathing monster of *Il.* vi. 181 ff., πρόσθε λέων, ὄπιθεν δὲ δράκων, μέσση δὲ χίμαιρα, / δεινὸν ἀποπνείουσα πυρὸς μένος αἰθομένοιο: imagination sees the terrible figure (pictured, no doubt, as it appears in the famous fifth–fourth century Etruscan bronze of Arretium, now in Florence) flaming (cf. viii. 620 of Aeneas' helmet) and taking life in the heat of battle. The Chimaera is a creature of the primitive underworld and she is among the terrors of Virgil's Tartarus (vi. 288), but there is no need to think that the emblem is meant to have a dramatic significance in representing Turnus as the unconscious agent of infernal powers, the Acheron to which Juno appealed (312): it is the symbol of savage strength. In the battle scenes themselves there is no word of this marvellous device: Turnus wears a golden helmet with a red plume (ix. 50: cf. xii. 89).

787. illa: for the resumptive use of *ille*, emphasizing the subject, and corresponding to the Homeric ὅ γε, cf., e.g., i. 3, v. 457, x. 274, xi. 494: so often with *non*, e.g. 805, v. 334, vi. 593, ix. 479, xii. 414. To recognize that the insertion of the pronoun has its metrical convenience, as it obviously has, is not to say (with Henry) that it is a mere stopgap: its deictic or pictorial effect in seizing the reader's attention is also unmistakable. For a similar use, not resumptive but anticipatory, in similes see on 380 and cf. x. 707, xi. 809, xii. 5.

The phrase is loosely attached in the nominative and not brought into agreement with *Chimaeram*: cf. 741.

fremens: see on 389.

787 f. tam magis ... quam magis is quoted as an archaism by Quintilian (ix. 3. 15): Plautus has two examples and Lucretius such variations as *quam plurima ... tam magis* and *quam magis ... tanto magis*. Virgil himself has *quam magis ... magis* at *Geo.* iii. 309 f.

788. crudescunt, 'grow bloodier': the word keeps its original sense, as *crudus* (the adjective corresponding to *cruor*) does in the phrase *crudum uulnus*: cf. xi. 833.

789 ff. The figure of Io, daughter of Inachus, King of Argos, whom Juno's jealousy transformed into a heifer and placed under the charge of the hundred-eyed Argus, commemorates Turnus' Argive ancestry: cf. 372 and *Argiva* in 794 below. Moschus had used the same motif in the description of Europa's basket, *Eur.* 44 f. ἐν μὲν ἔην χρυσοῖο τετυγμένη Ἰναχὶς Ἰώ, / εἰσέτι πόρτις ἐοῦσα, φυὴν δ' οὐκ εἶχε γυναίην, and Virgil clearly has these lines in mind.

790. auro insignibat: i.e. an emblema of gold figures in relief was attached to the shield. For the form -*ibat* see on 485.

iam: the repetition stresses the completeness of the metamorphosis. For the monosyllabic ending see on 592.

791. argumentum: the technical term for the theme of a work

of art: cf. Cic. *Verr.* ii. 4. 124 'ex ebore diligentissime per-
fecta argumenta erant in ualuis'; Ovid, *Met.* vi. 69 'uetus in
tela deducitur argumentum', xiii. 683 f. (of a decorated cup)
'fabricauerat Alcon / . . . et longo caelauerat argumento'.

792. caelata . . . urna: the Argive king is the god of the Argive
river Inachus, who is represented with the urn which is a
river-god's regular attribute in art.

793. insequitur nimbus peditum : from *Il.* iv. 274 νέφος εἵπετο
πεζῶν.

794. Argiuaque pubes: i.e. Turnus' own people from Ardea:
see on 372, 412.

795. Auruncaque manus: the Aurunci have already appeared
with Halaesus' contingent in 727. One can suppose that
Turnus' Aurunci are the tribes on the north or Rutulian side
of the Liris, Halaesus' those on the south or Campanian side.
But it is more likely that the double mention is an accident,
as the repetition of *Rutuli* (795) and *Rutulos* (798) must be
supposed to be.

Sicani: in xi. 317 the Sicani appear as neighbours of
Aurunci and Rutuli in a geographically perplexing passage in
which *fines super usque Sicanos* defines a hilly region near the
Tiber, west of Latinus' kingdom, inhabited by Aurunci and
Rutuli; in viii. 328 in Evander's sketch of history the *gentes
Sicanae*, with the *manus Ausonia*, are the first settlers in
Latium after the Golden Age of Saturn.

The Siculi, a people of Illyrian stock, were established in
prehistoric times in South Italy as well as in Sicily and there
is some evidence that they penetrated northwards from
there: there is no evidence that the Sicani who shared Sicily
with them, a people of Libyan–Iberian origin, were ever in
Italy. But there was a Latin community of Sicani (presum-
ably inhabitants of Sica), one of the thirty members of the
Alban League in Pliny's list (*N.H.* iii. 69) which had dis-
appeared in historical times. This coincidence of name com-
bined with a tradition of settlements of Siculi in Italy may
have served to give the 'Sicani' their prominence in Virgil's
ethnology. See Schulten in P.–W. s.v. Sikaner.

796. Sacranae acies are unknown: the connections with the
cult of the Magna Mater (Servius) and with a migration of
Sabines in a *uer sacrum* (Festus 424 L.) look like guesses
from the name.

Labici: the town of Labici was in north Latium, a member of
the Latin league at one time important enough to give its
name to the *uia Labicana*. The appearance of its people (else-
where *Labicani*: for the absence of adjectival suffix see on
219) is surprising since it lay far from Turnus' coastal terri-

tory, separated from it by the Alban hills, and might have been expected to have its place in Caeculus' domain.

  picti scuta: here and in ix. 582 'pictus acu chlamydem', xi. 777 'pictus acu tunicas et barbara tegmina crurum', the participle may be explained as a 'middle' use (see on 503) referring to an action effected by the subject in his own interest through another agent—a regular use of the middle in Greek (e.g. τὸν υἱὸν διδάσκομαι, 'I have my son taught'): so 'having had their shields painted'. *pictus* used of a shield probably refers to gold and silver ornamentation.

797. Tiberine: see on 30.

   Numici: see on 150.

798. exercent uomere collis: repeated at xi. 318 f. (again of the Rutulians).

799. Circaeumque iugum: i.e. the promontory of Circei: see on 10.

  Iuppiter Anxurus: Anxur was the Volscian name of the coast town, at the south end of the Pomptine marshes, which later reverted in common usage to the earlier Greek (perhaps Etruscan) name of Tarracina. The adjective is found nowhere else: in *C.I.L.* x. 6483 the local cult-title is 'Iuppiter A⟨n⟩xoranus'. See K. Latte, *Röm. Rel.* 176.

800. The goddess **Feronia** was probably of Sabine provenance (as Varro believed, *L.L.* v. 74: but some scholars have suggested an Etruscan origin): a *lucus* at Capena under Soracte (the *luci Capeni* of 697) was a flourishing centre of her worship. Her festival was observed in the Roman calendar and her cult is found at various places in central Italy: for this shrine at Anxur cf. Hor. *Sat.* i. 5. 24 ff. In viii. 564 she appears as the mother of the monstrous Erulus, king of Praeneste. See K. Latte, *Röm. Rel.* 189 f.; G. Radke, *Die Götter Altitaliens* (Münster, 1965), 124 ff.

801. Saturae palus is presumably part of the Pomptine marshes through which the Ufens runs to sea.

802. quaerit iter: for the personification cf. v. 807 f. 'nec reperire uiam atque euoluere posset / in mare sua Xanthus'. The description is romantic rather than realistic: there is more realism in Silius' catalogue, viii. 380 ff. 'atro / liuentis caeno per squalida turbidus arua / cogit aquas Ufens atque inficit aequora limo'.

803 ff. Virgil has made his Camilla one of the most memorable figures in the poem, but she is a mysterious figure, unique among his major characters in that she is otherwise entirely unknown. Whether Virgil's picture of her had some basis in native legend, or whether he gave a name charged with local associations (see below) to a figure drawn from his own

romantic imagination, no one can say. There is a curious
inconsistency in the picture. In xi. 535 ff., where Diana tells
the story of her childhood, her father Metabus has been de-
posed by his subjects and driven from his kingdom in the
Volscian town of Privernum: sharing his escape and his exile,
she is reared in the woods and spends her life as a huntress,
a single-minded votary of Diana, skin-clad and with hair
unadorned. Here, on the other hand, she appears at the
head of a company of the very Volscians who had exiled her
father, a princess drawing all eyes with the purple of her
mantle and the gold in her hair. Diana laments her turning
from the pursuits of the chase to those of war, but the
change of fortune is unexplained. She seems to be a confla-
tion of the dedicated huntress and the Amazon queen: here,
and again in xi. 648 ff., the resplendent leader of a band of
Italian Amazons experienced in fighting, she is the Pen-
thesilea of cyclic saga to whom Virgil compares her (xi. 662);
in xi. 535 ff. she is an Italian replica of the Harpalyce of i. 317,
whose story Servius tells on that passage, the exiled Thracian
king's motherless daughter who took to the forests with her
father and provided for him by her skill in hunting. Perhaps
Virgil's use of Harpalyce's father's name, Harpalycus, for
one of Camilla's victims (xi. 675) confirms that that story
was in his mind, but the inconsistency between the picture
of Camilla in xi. 535 ff. with that given here, and the way in
which Diana, telling the story of Camilla's upbringing, is
made to refer to herself in the third person (xi. 537, 566, 582)
has suggested that Virgil had a draft of the Camilla/Har-
palyce story which he worked into the narrative of Book XI
without adjusting it to the context.

The name as a common noun is an ancient ritual term at
Rome which provided a Roman cognomen. A *camillus* or
camilla was a boy or girl attendant at a religious ceremony
(Varro, *L.L.* vii. 34; Macr. iii. 8. 6; Fest. 82 L.): in Pacuvius'
Medus Medea disguised as a priestess was addressed as
caelitum camilla (232 R.). But the origin of the word is
obscure. Varro connected it with Κασμῖλος (or Καδμῖλος), the
name of a deity, identified with Hermes, in the mysteries
of Samothrace, and Camillus or Κασμῖλος is alleged to be an
Etruscan name for Hermes/Mercury (Servius on xi. 558;
Macr. iii. 8. 6; Schol. on Lycophron 162): for the collected
evidence see Pfeiffer on Callimachus fr. 723; Goetz–Schoell
on Varro, *L.L.* vii. 34. It seems likely that the word came to
Rome from Etruria: the Latin cognomen Camillus has an
Etruscan counterpart 'Camithlas' (see W. Schulze, *Lat.
Eigennamen*, 290). Virgil's romantic derivation of Camilla's

name 'from her mother's name of Casmilla' may have some linguistic foundation. The equally mysterious word Camena, which is alleged to have had an earlier form Casmena (Varro, *L.L.* vii. 26; Fest. 59 L.) and was believed to have been derived from Etruria (Macr. *Somn.* ii. 3. 4) may have had a similar history. But in both words, if an -s- has been lost, the quantity of the -ă- is inexplicable.

804. The line is used again of Camilla in xi. 433. For *florere* used of radiant light cf. Lucr. i. 900 'flammai fulserunt flore coorto', iv. 450 'bina lucernarum florentia lumina flammis'; Accius 631 f. R. 'aere atque ferro feruere ⟨?⟩ / insignibus florere'. So in Greek ἄνθος, ἀνθεῖν: e.g. Aesch. *P.V.* 7 f. τὸ σὸν γὰρ ἄνθος, παντέχνου πυρὸς σέλας, / θνητοῖσι κλέψας ὤπασεν.: Eur. *I.A.* 73 ἀνθηρὸς μὲν εἱμάτων στολῇ.: Xen. *Cyr.* vi. 4. 1 ἤστραπτε μὲν χαλκῷ, ἤνθει δὲ φοινικίσι πᾶσα ἡ στρατιά.

805. non illa sharpens the contrast: see on 787.

806. adsueta manus: for the 'middle' use of the participle governing an object see on 503.

807. dura is to be taken with *proelia*, the infinitives depending on *adsueta* carried on with a slight change of construction— 'but accustomed, maiden though she was, to endure grim fighting': *bellatrix* and *uirgo* have the same emphatic positions as in the description of Penthesilea in i. 493 'bellatrix, audetque uiris concurrere uirgo'. This picture of Camilla hardly matches Diana's words in xi. 581 ff., which seem to imply that she has taken to war for the first time: see on 803 ff. above.

808–11. The lines are a reminiscence of Homer's description of the magic horses of Erichthonius, *Il.* xx. 226 ff. αἱ δ' ὅτε μὲν σκιρτῷεν ἐπὶ ζείδωρον ἄρουραν, / ἄκρον ἐπ' ἀνθερίκων καρπὸν θέον οὐδὲ κατέκλων· / ἀλλ' ὅτε δὴ σκιρτῷεν ἐπ' εὐρέα νῶτα θαλάσσης, / ἄκρον ἐπὶ ῥηγμῖνος ἁλὸς πολιοῖο θέεσκον, and Apollonius' of Euphemus, i. 182 ff. κεῖνος ἀνὴρ καὶ πόντου ἐπὶ γλαυκοῖο θέεσκεν / οἴδματος, οὐδὲ θοοὺς βάπτεν πόδας, ἀλλ' ὅσον ἄκροις / ἴχνεσι τεγγόμενος διερῇ πεφόρητο κελεύθῳ.

808. intactae segetis: the *stans seges* of Ovid's variation, *Met.* x. 654 f. 'posse putes illos sicco freta radere passu / et segetis canae stantes percurrere aristas': cf. *Pont.* iii. 4. 61 f. 'nec minimum refert intacta rosaria primus / an sera carpas paene relicta manu'.

808 ff. uolaret . . . laesisset . . . ferret: the subjunctives are potential and the pluperfect may be given its full force, 'she might fly over the corn and not be found to have crushed the ears'.

810. fluctu suspensa tumenti, 'poised on the swelling waves': cf. Cic. *Tusc.* ii. 67 'equi Pelopis . . . qui per undas currus suspensos rapuisse dicuntur'.

813. prospectat, follow her with their eyes: cf. *Od.* ii. 13 τὸν δ' ἄρα πάντες λαοὶ ἐπερχόμενον θηεῦντο.

814 f. ut ... uelet: for the indirect exclamation dependent on *inhians* cf. the indirect question in ii. 120 f. 'obstipuere animi gelidusque per ima cucurrit / ossa tremor, cui fata parent, quem poscat Apollo'.

815. honos, 'splendour': for the form see on 3; and see also Austin on i. 591.

816. internectat: a rare compound, found elsewhere only in Statius and Boethius.

   Lyciam: for the conventional epithet cf. viii. 166 f. (Evander speaks) 'ille (Anchises) mihi insignem pharetram Lyciasque sagittas / ... dedit', xi. 773 (the Trojan Chloreus) 'spicula torquebat Lycio Gortynia cornu'.

   ipsa turns the reader from the details of her costume to herself: cf. xi. 772.

817. myrtum: cf. *Geo.* ii. 447 f. 'at myrtus ualidis hastilibus et bona bello / cornus'.

COMMENTARY ON BOOK VIII

1–17. *Turnus collects his forces for war and sends an appeal for help to Diomede.*

1 f. signum . . . ab arce extulit, 'displayed 'the signal for war': Virgil is no doubt thinking of the military custom of later days when a *vexillum* was displayed on the general's quarters before a battle (Plut. *Fab.* 15; Caes. *B.G.* ii. 20. 1) or on the Janiculum before a meeting of the *comitia centuriata*, a muster of the people under arms (Livy xxxix. 15. 11). Turnus has now taken command in Latinus' own citadel.

2. rauco . . . cantu: cf. Lucr. ii. 619 'raucisonoque minantur cornua cantu'.

3. acris concussit equos, 'threw his mettlesome horses into violent motion': similarly *Geo.* iii. 132 'saepe etiam cursu quatiunt' (of putting horses to the gallop in exercise), *Aen.* xii. 337 f. 'equos . . . / fumantis sudore quatit'. Elsewhere Virgil uses the verb of the reins, literally in v. 146 f. 'immissis aurigae undantia lora / concussere iugis', metaphorically in vi. 100 f. 'frena furenti / concutit'.

    impulit arma : i.e. struck his shield with his spear: cf. x. 568 'tot paribus streperet clipeis', xii. 332 f. 'sanguineus Mauors clipeo increpat, atque furentis / bella mouens immittit equos', 700 'horrendumque intonat armis': so more explicitly Call. *Hymn.* 4. 136 f. ὑψόθε δ' ἐσμαράγησε (Ἄρης) καὶ ἀσπίδα τύψεν ἀκωκῇ / δούρατος.

5. coniurat . . . iuuentus : the verb is probably suggested by the later technical use of taking the military oath (*sacramentum*), 'signing on' for a campaign: cf. Caes. *B.G.* vii. 1. 1 'de senatusque consulto certior factus, ut omnes iuniores Italiae coniurarent'.

    trepido : of the excitement of 'war hysteria' (C. Day-Lewis): cf. xi. 453 'arma manu trepidi poscunt'.

6 f. primi : the first to move their forces are Messapus, leading the clans from the upper Tiber valley (vii. 691 ff.), Ufens (vii. 745) with his Aequians, and Mezentius, the expelled ruler of Caere in Etruria (vii. 648: cf. 479 f. below).

8. uastant cultoribus, 'empty the broad lands of their husbandmen': *uastus* (a cognate of *uacuus*) is 'empty', 'desolate' (see on vii. 302): for that sense cf., e.g., Cic. *Sest.* 53 'lex erat lata uasto ac relicto foro', *Leg. Agr.* 70 'genus agrorum . . .

uastum atque desertum'; Livy iii. 7. 3 'uasto ac deserto
agro': in Livy iii. 32. 2 'uastati agri' are lands depopulated
by pestilence. The construction of *uastare* with an ablative
is natural: cf. Caes. *B.G.* viii. 24. 4 'finis eius uastare ciuibus,
aedificiis, pecore'; Stat. *Theb.* iii. 576 f. 'agrosque uiris an-
nosaque uastant / oppida'.

9. et: i.e. they look for foreign aid besides their own forces.

Diomedis ad urbem: Argyripa, the Arpi of historical times,
in Apulia, which was said to have been founded after the
Trojan War by Diomede, and to have taken its name from
his kingdom of Argos (xi. 246 f.). As Servius points out,
Venulus is from Tibur (xi. 757), which also claimed Argive
origin (vii. 672 ff.), and so makes a suitable ambassador. The
mission returns unsuccessful at xi. 226.

11 f. uictosque penatis inferre: the taunting *uictos*, which Juno
uses at i. 68, 'Ilium in Italiam portans uictosque penatis', is
calculated to tell with Diomede, who had been one of the
conquerors: Servius finds the same point in *inferre* ('hic
inuidiam facit'), but that word is used without any dis-
paraging suggestion at i. 6 'inferretque deos Latio'.

12. fatis . . . posci: so Latinus himself had been the first to
say, vii. 272 f. 'hunc illum poscere fata / . . . reor'. Virgil
makes *poscere* a keyword of Aeneas' destiny: cf. 512 'quem
numina poscunt', 533 'ego poscor Olympo'.

13 f. multas . . . gentis: a diplomatic misrepresentation like
that which Ilioneus offers at vii. 238: Aeneas has no Italian
allies yet. But *Dardanio uiro* emphasizes his ancestral con-
nection with Italy, which Latinus had recognized in his
speech of welcome (vii. 195, 205 ff.).

14. late Latio: the difference in quantity does not preclude
a play on words and Virgil may intend that (cf. 322 f.).

15. quid struat, 'what he is planning': cf. ii. 60 'hoc ipsum ut
strueret', iv. 235 'quid struit?'. The verb often implies mis-
chief-making, with such objects as *mendacium, insidiae,
odium, nefas, crimen*.

si fortuna sequatur, 'if luck attends him': cf. iv. 109 'si
modo quod memoras factum fortuna sequatur'.

16. ipsi: i.e. to Diomede himself, who could judge from his
own knowledge of the Trojans.

17. regi . . . regi: for the formal expression (as it were 'their
majesties Turnus and Latinus') cf. xi. 294 f. 'responsa simul
quae sint, rex optime, regis / audisti'.

18–65. *The river-god Tiber appears to Aeneas in his troubled
sleep, assures him that he has reached his destined home, pro-
mises the confirming omen of the white sow, and tells him to seek*

help from the neighbouring king Evander, an incomer from Arcadia, who is at war with the Latins.

18. **talia per Latium:** for the ellipse cf. xii. 154 'uix ea (dicta sunt), cum lacrimas oculis Iuturna profundit'.

   Laomedontius heros : for the periphrasis cf. xii. 456 (also of Aeneas) 'Rhoeteius hostis': on Virgil's use of the adjective see on vii. 105.

19. **fluctuat aestu:** for the metaphor from a surging sea to express distracted thought cf. iv. 532 'magnoque irarum fluctuat aestu', xii. 486 'uario nequiquam fluctuat aestu'.

20 f. The lines are repeated from iv. 285 f.

22 ff. The simile comes from Apollonius, who applies it to Medea's fluttering heart (iii. 755 ff.) : πύκνα δέ οἱ κραδίη στηθέων ἐντοσθεν ἔθυιεν, / ἠελίου ὥς τίς τε δόμοις ἐνιπάλλεται αἴγλη / ὕδατος ἐξανιοῦσα, τὸ δὴ νέον ἠὲ λέβητι / ἠέ που ἐν γαυλῷ κέχυται· ἡ δ' ἔνθα καὶ ἔνθα / ὠκείῃ στροφάλιγγι τινάσσεται ἀίσσουσα, but Virgil may also have had Lucretius' lines in mind (iv. 211 ff.) : 'simul ac primum sub diu splendor aquai / ponitur, extemplo caelo stellante serena / sidera respondent in aqua *radiantia* mundi. / iamne uides igitur quam puncto tempore *imago* / aetheris ex oris in terrarum accidat oras ? '. The light is struck back, thrown off, from the water by the sun or the moon's reflection, *imagine lunae* being parallel to *sole*. There is no need to take *imagine* of the face of the moon: in the instances of that use which are cited *imago* has an epithet (Ovid, *Met.* vii. 181 'solida terras spectauit imagine luna', xiv. 768 'nitidissima solis imago', xv. 785 'solis quoque tristis imago').

22. **tremulum . . . lumen:** an Ennian phrase; cf. vii. 9.

24 f. **sub auras erigitur:** cf. iii. 422 f. ' (Charybdis) fluctus . . . sub auras / erigit'.

26. **nox erat:** for the opening cf. iii. 147 'nox erat et terris animalia somnus habebat', iv. 522 ff. 'nox erat et placidum carpebant fessa soporem / corpora per terras, siluaeque et saeua quierant / aequora'.

27. **alituum . . . genus:** Lucretius has five examples of the heteroclite genitive form, four of them with *genus*: the invention of it to take the place of the metrically inconvenient *alitum* may go back to Ennius.

28. **pater** stresses Aeneas' concern for the people in his charge: cf. 115, iii. 716, v. 700.

29. **turbatus:** see on 435.

30. **dedit per membra quietem,** 'let sleep come over his limbs': cf. 405 f. 'petiuit / . . . per membra soporem': for *dare* cf. xii. 69 'talis uirgo dabat ore colores', 'let colours show on her face', and see on 570 f.

31. ipse: i.e. in bodily presence.

Tiberinus: see on vii. 30 where the same descriptive phrase is used.

The water-god is by convention old (*senior*: cf. v. 823 'senior Glauci chorus') and his linen dress is greenish-blue, *glaucus*, like that of the water-nymph Juturna (xii. 885)—the colour of water itself (Lucr. i. 719 'glaucis . . . ab undis') and of the reeds with which he is crowned (cf. x. 205, of Mincius represented on a figure-head, 'uelatus harundine glauca'; Ovid, *A.A.* i. 223 'hic est Euphrates, praecinctus harundine frontem')—or *caeruleus* (cf. 64).

34. harundo: the use of the collective singular with names of plants, flowers, and trees is normal idiom: cf. 599 'abiete': so, e.g., *Geo.* iv. 134 'primus uere rosam . . . carpere'; Cic. *Verr.* ii. 5. 27 'puluinus . . . rosa fartus'; Sen. *Ep.* 36. 9 'ut . . . in rosa iaceat'; Varro, *R.R.* i. 35. 1 'serere lilium et crocum'. See K.–S. ii. 1, p. 68, *c*.

For the rhythm, with trochaic caesura in both fourth and fifth foot, see on vii. 27.

35. The line is repeated at ii. 775, iii. 153: for Virgil's use of the 'historic' infinitive see on vii. 15.

36 f. sate gente deum: the reference is to the descent of the Trojan royal house from Zeus through Dardanus and *reuehis nobis* again recalls the Italian origin of Dardanus (vii. 219, 240).

37. Pergama: the metrically convenient plural form is invariable in Virgil.

39. ne absiste: see on vii. 96.

40. tumor . . . et irae : cf. vi. 407 'tumida ex ira tum corda residunt'. For the plural *irae* see on vii. 445.

41. concessere: this assurance is not borne out in the rest of the poem; the heavenly anger that pursues the Trojans is Juno's and her hostility continues unabated. Hence, says Servius, a would-be improver absurdly completed the line with *profugis noua moenia Teucris*, giving consistency to Virgil at the cost of ignoring *omnis*. On Virgil's incomplete lines see on vii. 129.

42 ff. The episode of the sow and her young was part of the traditional legend. In Dionysius' version (i. 55. 4 ff.) the incident is prepared for by a prophecy—given according to one account by the oracle at Dodona (cf. i. 51. 1), where Aeneas met Helenus, according to another by a 'sibyl' at Erythrae—which, after predicting the eating of the tables (see on vii. 116), tells the Trojans that a four-footed beast will then lead them to their new home. After their first meal on Italian soil a sow escaping from sacrifice leads Aeneas to

the unpromising site of the future Lavinium, where a super-
natural voice encourages him with the assurance of a second
city—that is, Alba—which will be founded from Lavinium
after a number of years corresponding to the number of the
litter: he sacrifices the mother and young to the local deities
and proceeds to found his city. Varro, according to Servius
(on iii. 256), also ascribed the prophecy to Dodona, and in two
passing references (*L.L.* v. 144, *R.R.* ii. 4. 18) shows that he
agreed with Dionysius on the places of Lavinium and Alba
in the story: he mentions that bronzes of the sow and her
young were to be seen (at Lavinium, it seems) in his day.

To the traditional account Virgil gives turns of his own:
he keeps the prophecies but puts them into new contexts.
The prophecy of the tables he gives to the Harpy Celaeno (iii.
255 ff.), who utters it as a threat. The prophecy of the white
sow, which here is put into the mouth of Tiberinus, appears
also at an earlier point in the poem, when it is delivered in
Greece, not by the oracle at Dodona but by Helenus himself
at Buthrotum. Here Tiberinus offers the portent in confirma-
tion of the reality of Aeneas' vision and the promise is im-
mediately fulfilled where Aeneas is encamped on the river
bank. At iii. 389 ff. Helenus promises it as a sign which will
assure the Trojans that they have reached the end of their
journey: *is locus urbis erit*, he says, and that must mean
Italy or Latium—there is no question of a settlement on
the river bank. Tiberinus adds a brief oracular reference to
the foundation of Alba by Ascanius in later days and to the
significance of its name and the symbolism of the number
thirty: Helenus says nothing of these things. Lavinium does
not appear in either place—naturally, since in Virgil's
handling of the main story its foundation is postponed to fall
outside the narrative of the *Aeneid*.

What is even more remarkable than the repetition of the
prophecy is that it is repeated in the same words: the lines
viii. 43–6 are identical with iii. 390–3, apart from the varia-
tion of *hic* in 46 and *is* in 393. Line 46 is suspect since it is
absent from MP, and R, which gives it, is prone to inter-
polation: the line has been introduced from Book III with
a change of pronoun to adapt it to 39. But the other three
lines are tied in to each context by the line preceding:
line 42 in particular is put above suspicion by the evidence of
Silius, who borrowed most of it (viii. 179), and by its position
after the incomplete line 41 ; an inventive interpolator operat-
ing at that point would have completed it, with words that
might have provided a smoother connection than *iamque tibi*.
Verbatim repetition on this scale is rare in the poem and this

repetition is the more striking since the point of the prophecy is different in the two passages. Relating it to what we know of Virgil's piecemeal method of composition, we must suppose that he used a second time a block of lines which he had in his mind. At which place he used it first we can only guess: the argument that the passage in VIII must have been written first since the Tiber-context there must have suggested *secreti ad fluminis undam* in III is ingenious but not decisive.

43. litoreis: see on 83.

sus: for the monosyllabic ending cf. 83 and see on vii. 592.

47. ex quo: probably 'from that time': cf. 268 'ex illo'.

48. clari . . . cognominis : for *cognomen* used of a significant name see on vii. 3, 671.

49. haud incerta: i.e. *certissima*: for the litotes cf. vii. 261 'munera nec sperno', ix. 552 'haud nescia', xi. 238 'haud laeta fronte', 725 f. 'non . . . nullis . . . oculis', xii. 50 'ferrum haud debile'. For *cano* of prophetic utterance see on vii. 79.

50. expedias: 'triumphantly unravel what lies before you'.

paucis (aduerte) docebo : cf. iv. 116.

51. profectum: the metaphorical use of *proficisci*, 'originate', is not uncommon in prose: it is first used here of descent by birth.

51 ff. The story of the Arcadian settlement on the Palatine hill, which Virgil (followed by Propertius and Ovid) shares with Livy (i. 5) and Dionysius (i. 31), was a figment of early Hellenizing antiquarianism: its basis was the resemblance between the name *Palatium* and that of the place in Arcadia called Παλλάντιον or Παλλαντεῖον (Paus. viii. 43. 1–2). Other 'meaningful' origins for *Palatium* (which probably goes back to an I.E. root meaning 'hill': see Walde–Hofmann, s.v.) were offered by the ingenuity of Roman etymologists— *balare*, *palari*, *Pales* (see Varro, *L.L.* v. 53; Festus 245 L.; cf. Vell. i. 8. 4): these Dionysius dismisses (i. 31 4) as ἄτοποι ἐτυμολογίαι. The Arcadian derivation found support in another etymological fancy which connected the name of the primitive ceremony of the Lupercalia, centred on the Palatine, with that of Mount Lycaeum in Arcadia and the cults associated with it (see on 343), and it was firmly established in the literary tradition. Two centuries after Virgil it even justified Antoninus Pius in elevating the Arcadian Pallantion to the status of a free town exempt from taxation (Paus. viii. 43. 1). Evander, who seems to have been a minor δαίμων associated with Pan in Arcadia (in Virgil's account he is a son of Mercury, 138), was transferred to find a new importance as a key-figure of Roman pre-history, associated on the one hand with the legend of Aeneas, on the other with the myth of Hercules' visit to Italy (that connection may have been the occasion of Stesichorus' mention of Pallantion in his *Geryoneis*: fr. 5 P.) and was provided with a new pedigree (see on 335 f.) to equip him for that role. See J. Bayet, 'Les Origines de l'arcadisme romain' in *Mél. d'Arch. et d' Hist.* 38 (1920), 63 ff.

54. **Pallanteum:** for the spondaic ending (repeated in 341) see on vii. 631.

55. **bellum adsidue ducunt:** the statement is hardly consistent with the *longa pax* of vii. 46.

56. **foedera iunge:** failure to recognize this common use of the verb (as in *pontem iungere*: cf. 641, iv. 112, vii. 546, xii. 822) has produced the variant *foedere*, which was known to Servius.

57. **ripis et recto flumine,** 'along the banks and right up the stream': cf. vi. 900 'recto . . . limite' and the common *recta uia, recto itinere*.

58. **aduersum . . . superes . . . amnem:** the verb can have its general meaning here ('surmount the current') but the nautical use was perhaps in Virgil's mind: see on 95.

   subuectus : for *subuehi* of rowing upstream cf., e.g., Livy xxiv. 40. 2 'lembis biremibus . . . flumine aduerso subuectum', xlv. 35. 3 'aduerso Tiberi ad urbem est subuectus'; Tac. *Ann.* ii. 60. 1 'Germanicus . . . Nilo subuehebatur'.

59. **cadentibus:** as the stars begin to set, i.e. at break of day: cf. ii. 9 (iv. 81) 'suadentque cadentia sidera somnos'; so of nightfall iv. 352 'astra ignea surgunt'.

60 f. **Iunoni . . . uotis:** so Helenus had already prescribed in almost the same words, iii. 438 f. 'Iunoni cane uota libens dominamque potentem / supplicibus supera donis'.

61. **honorem,** 'offering': cf. 76, 102, 189, 617.

63. **stringentem ripas:** cf. Lucr. v. 256 'ripas radentia flumina'.

64. **caeruleus:** the Tiber is notoriously *flauus* (see on vii. 31 f.), but *caeruleus* (or *glaucus*: see on 31) is the conventional epithet of a water-god: cf. 713 'caeruleum in gremium' (of the figure of Nile on the shield), *Geo.* iv. 388 'caeruleus Proteus'.

   caeruleus . . . caelo gratissimus looks like a play on words: the implied etymology is probably true. On Virgil's use of *caeruleus* see on vii. 346.

65. **hic mihi magna domus, celsis caput urbibus exit:** 'here, where I stand, is my great habitation: my source issues among lofty cities.' *caput*, both in literary and in technical language, is the source of a spring or the head-waters of a

river (*Geo.* iv. 319 'ad extremi sacrum caput astitit amnis', 368 'caput unde altus primum se erumpit Enipeus'; *Dig.* 43. 20. 1. 8 'caput aquae illud est unde aqua nascitur') and that meaning is confirmed by the combination with *exit* (for *exire* of a source cf., e.g., 75 'quocumque solo pulcherrimus exis'; Ovid, *Met.* xi. 140 f. 'fonti qua plurimus exit / subde caput'; Lucan vii. 193 'Aponus terris ubi fumifer exit'). *urbibus*, whether it is a local ablative ('among lofty cities') or a dative of advantage ('to provide for lofty cities'), will refer to the Etruscan towns of Tiber's upper course.

W. Warde Fowler (*C.R.* xxx [1916], 219 ff.) takes *caput* as being in apposition to *domus* and interprets 'This is the place where my great palace, the head of waters which gives life and power to Italian cities, breaks to sea', supporting this interpretation with *Geo.* iv. 363 ff. But (1) there, while Cyrene's *domus* is pictured as a subterranean water-system which is a reservoir for the rivers of the world, *caput* has its usual sense of 'source', without any implication of 'source of life and power'; (2) while *exire* can mean 'break to sea' (e.g. Ovid, *Am.* ii. 13. 10 'per septem portus in maris exit aquas'), it is natural to give *exit* here the meaning which it clearly has a few lines below in 75. Even less likely is the interpretation, as old as Servius, which makes the words refer to Rome —'Here my great home, head over lofty cities, rises' (i.e. shall rise, a prophetic present): *caput urbibus* would be exactly paralleled by x. 203 *ipsa* (Mantua) *caput populis*, but the god's *domus* is the river and a prophecy of Rome's future greatness is out of place here.

66–101. *Aeneas wakes and after prayer to Tiber sails up the stream, finds the promised omen and reaches Evander's town.*

66. lacu fluuius se condidit: the river-god *is* the river: cf. 711–13.

67. nox ... reliquit: i.e. it is day and he wakes.

68. aetherii ... solis: a Lucretian phrase (e.g. iii. 1044).

68 ff. spectans ... undam ... sustinet: for the attitude cf. xii. 172 f. 'ad surgentem conuersi lumina solem / dant fruges manibus'; for the ceremonial washing or sprinkling of the hands before prayer cf. ix. 22 ff. 'ad undam / processit sum-moque hausit de gurgite lymphas / multa deos orans': so Ovid, *F.* iv. 777 f. (of prayer to Pales) 'haec tu conuersus ad ortus / dic quater et uiuo perlue rore manus'; Soph. *O.C.* (of prayer to the local deities) χοὰς χέασθαι στάντα πρὸς πρώτην ἕω.

71. genus ... est: cf. i. 6 'genus unde Latinum'.

72. The line is Ennian: *Ann.* 54 V. 'teque, pater Tiberine, tuo cum flumine sancto'; Servius quotes a prayer-formula 'adesto, Tiberine, cum tuis undis'. The combination of the possessive with another adjective and the use of *cum* with the adjectival phrase are archaic: cf. 522 'suo tristi cum corde', ix. 816 'ille suo cum gurgite flauo', *Geo.* ii. 147 'tuo (sc. Clitumni) perfusi flumine sacro'; so Enn. *Ann.* 51 V. 'aegro cum corde meo'; Lucr. i. 38 'tuo recubantem corpore sancto', 413 'meo . . . diti de pectore', iv. 394, vi. 618.

Thybri : see on vii. 30.

73. **Aenean:** for the emotive effect of the speaker's use of his own name see on vii. 401 f.

arcete periclis: *arcere* is 'to keep at a distance' and so *arcere alicui* (or *ab aliquo*) *pericula* and *arcere aliquem periculis* (or *a periculis*) are equally possible constructions: the latter is much the less frequent but cf. Hor. *Ep.* i. 8. 10 'me funesto properent arcere ueterno', *A.P.* 64 'Neptunus classis aquilonibus arcet', and in prose Cic. *Off.* i. 122 'haec aetas a libidinibus arcenda est'. (Similarly *prohibere*, with the same sense, is sometimes construed with an accusative of the person, e.g. Cic. *Leg. Man.* 18 'magnum numerum ciuium calamitate prohibere'; Hor. *Ep.* i. 1. 31 'corpus . . . prohibere cheragra'; and conversely *defendere* with an accusative *rei*, e.g. *Ecl.* 7. 47 'solstitium pecori defendite', *Aen.* x. 905 'hunc, oro, defende furorem'; Cic. *Sen.* 53; Prop. i. 20. 11; Hor. *Od.* i. 17. 3.)

75. **quocumque solo pulcherrimus exis,** 'in whatever ground you rise in beauty', repeats *quo . . . fonte tenent*, 'wherever is the basin of your source': for *exis* see on 65. Warde Fowler's interpretation '(wherever you rise and) wherever you break to sea' is impossible here, where Aeneas must know quite well where Tiber breaks to sea, having just rowed up from its mouth.

76. **honore meo,** 'worship (cf. 61) from me': cf. Hor. *Od.* i. 26. 9 f. 'nil sine te mei / prosunt honores'.

77. **corniger:** river-gods are regularly represented in bull shape or with bull's horns: cf. 727 'Rhenusque bicornis', *Geo.* iv. 371 f. 'auratus taurino cornua uultu / Eridanus'; Hor. *Od.* iv. 14. 25 'tauriformis . . . Aufidus': so in Greek, Soph. *Tr.* 507 ff. ὑψίκερω τετραόρου φάσμα ταύρου, Ἀχελῷος: Eur. *Ion.* 1261 ὦ ταυρόμορφον ὄμμα Κηφισοῦ πατρός.

Hesperidum: i.e. *Italarum* (see on vii. 4): the adjective is so used only here.

regnator aquarum: cf. *Geo.* i. 482 'fluuiorum rex Eridanus'. Ennius had called the Tiber 'fluuius qui est omnibus princeps' (*Ann.* 67 V.)—a line which Fronto quotes (p. 153 van den Hout) in comment on an orator's phrase 'Tiber amnis et dominus et fluentium circa regnator amnium'.

78. adsis . . . firmes, 'only be with me and by thy presence (i.e. by direct intervention) confirm thy will'—i.e. confirm the revelation of it by its fulfilment: cf. ii. 691 'omina firma'; Cic. fr. 7 M. 13 'sic aquilae clarum firmauit Iuppiter omen', where the reference is to the confirmation of one sign by another. For *numen* thus used of revealed will cf. vii. 119 'stupefactus numine', ii. 123 f. 'quae sint ea numina diuum / flagitat', iii. 363 f. 'cuncti suaserunt numine diui / Italiam petere'. For *propius* cf. i. 526 'propius res aspice nostras': the sense is that of *praesentius* in xii. 152 (Juno to Juturna) 'pro germano si quid praesentius audes'.

80. remigio here and in iii. 471 ('remigium supplet, socios simul instruit armis') may refer either to oarage or to oarsmen: in 94 it is abstract, 'rowing'.

81. ecce autem: see on vii. 286.

    mirabile monstrum: so Cicero, fr. 22 M. 20—perhaps an Ennian reminiscence. For *monstrum* see on vii. 21.

83. litore: for *litus* used of a river-bank, cf. *Ecl.* 6. 44; Hor. *Od.* i. 2. 14; Cic. *de Inu.* ii. 97: so *litoreus* xii. 248.

    sus : for the monosyllabic ending cf. 43 and see on vii. 592.

84. tibi enim, tibi: this archaic use of *enim* as an asseverative particle ('indeed', 'in fact'), which is common in Plautus, is revived by Virgil in three other places—*Geo.* ii. 509, iii. 70, *Aen.* x. 874. The asseverative force, otherwise obsolete, maintained itself in combination in the common *at enim* ('but indeed') and the rarer *sed enim* (which Virgil uses four times), and it probably explains the origin of the combinations *etenim* and the characteristically Virgilian *neque enim* (see on vii. 581), in which the first particle has come to lose its connective force and *enim* to be felt as having its usual explanatory function. Here the emphatic particle stresses the fact that it is to his bitter enemy Juno that Aeneas, following the urgent instruction of Helenus (iii. 435 ff.), makes his first sacrifice.

85. mactat: see on vii. 93.

    mactat . . . et . . . sistit ad aram: for Virgil's practice of conveying a complex action under two aspects in two clauses connected by *et* or *-que* without regard to the order in which these aspects present themselves in time see on vii. 7.

86. quam longa est, 'through all its length': Virgil uses this idiom once elsewhere, at iv. 193 'hiemem inter se luxu, quam longa, fovere', where the verb (which would be subjunctive) is omitted, as it is in Ovid's one use, *Am.* i. 2. 3 'noctem, quam longa, peregi'. The present *est* is probably to be explained as a durative historic, i.e. a-temporal, present like that which is regular in *dum*-clauses. Ovid has a similar use of *quanta*, but with a perfect: *Her*. 12. 58 'acta est per lacrimas nox mihi, quanta fuit'.

Aeneas has his vision in the small hours and Tiber tells him to make his offering to Juno at dawn, *primis cadentibus astris* (59); he does so, *spectans orientia solis / lumina* (68 f.), and then sets out when he has manned his ships. He arrives at the site of Rome at mid-day (97)—one might suppose after a morning's journey. *ea quam longa est nocte* and *noctemque diemque* (94) are inconsistent with that supposition and Conington and Heinze (following Servius) conclude that he starts his journey on the following night, having spent the intervening day on preparations. Either Virgil used these romantic clichés (cf. v. 766 'noctemque diemque', *Geo*. iii. 341 'diem noctemque', *Aen*. vi. 556 'noctesque diesque', ix. 488 'noctes . . . diesque') without thinking of their implications or else, dealing with the immediate neighbourhood of Rome, he was so indifferent to geography as to make Aeneas spend a night and a morning on a miraculously assisted passage of some twelve miles.

87. **ita:** Virgil does not use correlative *ita . . . ut* elsewhere and *ita* should perhaps be taken independently with the resumptive function in which it picks up a description or a situation, 'like that', 'that being so', 'then': for *sic* so used see on vii. 668.

88. **mitis . . . stagni placidaeque paludis:** a striking example of Virgil's technique of conveying the same notion in two coordinated phrases.

89. **aquis:** this extension of the instrumental ablative is repeated in v. 821 'sternitur aequor aquis'.

   luctamen: when Virgil uses the same metaphor at vii. 28, it is calm water, not rough, that causes the oars *luctari*.

90. **rumore secundo,** 'amid murmurs of applause', the parting cheers of their companions: that this is the meaning is shown both by the other occurrences of the phrase (Enn. *Ann*. 255 V. 'mox auferre domos populi rumore secundo'; Sueius fr. 7 M. 'redeunt referunt rumore petita secundo'; *trag. inc.* 89 R.[2] 'soluere imperat secundo rumore aduersaque aui'; Hor. *Ep*. i. 10. 8 f. 'ista . . . / quae uos ad caelum fertis rumore secundo'; Tacitus revives it, *Ann*. iii. 29) and by similar phrases in Virgil (v. 338 'plausuque uolat fremituque secundo', 491 f. 'primus clamore secundo / . . . exit locus Hippocoontis', x. 265 f. '(grues) aethera tranant / cum sonitu, fugiuntque Notos clamore secundo': cf. Ovid, *Met*. viii. 419 'gaudia testantur socii clamore secundo'). The latter suggest that Virgil has in mind the original meaning of *secundus* as the verbal adjective of *sequi* ('attendant cries',

'cries in their train'): compare v. 338 (quoted above) with
ix. 54, 'clamorem excipiunt socii fremituque sequuntur', and
observe how in x. 266 (above), where the *clamor* is that of the
cranes themselves, the cliché is turned into a realistic touch
of description.

91. labitur uncta . . . abies: like iv. 398 'natat uncta carina',
an Ennian reminiscence (*Ann.* 386 and 478 V. 'labitur uncta
carina'). The metonymy of *abies* (with which cf. x. 206 *pinu*)
appears first here, but may well be older.

uncta: i.e. caulked with pitch or wax: for this technical
use of the verb cf. Vegetius iv. 37 'cera qua unguere solent
naues', 44 'unctas cera et pice et resina tabulas (nauium)':
see C. Torr, *Ancient Ships* (Cambridge, 1894; repr. Chicago,
1964), 34 f.

uadis: see on vii. 24.

91 f. mirantur et undae, miratur nemus insuetum: for the
structure see on vii. 327: for the Alexandrian device of the
'pathetic fallacy', attributing human emotions to objects of
nature, see on vii. 514 ff.

93. scuta: hung along the sides of the ship, as in Viking galleys:
cf. i. 183, x. 80.

pictas: see on vii. 431.

94. olli: see on vii. 458.

fatigant, 'give night and day no rest': cf. Prop. iv. 11. 81
'noctes quas de me, Paulle, fatiges'; Virgil has a somewhat
similar use of *exercere* in x. 808 'exercere diem'. See also on
vii. 582.

95. superant flexus, 'they round the bends': for the nautical
sense of 'make' cf. *Ecl.* 8. 6 'magni superas iam saxa Timaui',
Aen. i. 244 (of Antenor's journey) 'regna Liburnorum et
fontem superare Timaui' (cf. iii. 698 'exsupero praepingue
solum stagnantis Helori'); so Livy xxvi. 26. 1 'superato
Leucata promuntorio', xxxi. 22. 7 'Sunium superare'. See on
58.

uariis: probably 'all manner of trees' (see on vii. 32 f.)
rather than a picturesque epithet which makes the trees, in
the play of light and shade, 'mottled' or 'dappled', like the
lynces uariae of *Geo.* iii. 264 or the *uariae columnae* of Hor.
Ep. i. 10. 22.

96. uiridisque secant . . . aequore siluas: cleave the reflections
of the woods in the water, says Servius, enhancing the pic-
torial effect, but probably Virgil's idea is simpler—they
have trees on either side of them and above them.

97. sol . . . orbem: cf. *Geo.* iv. 426 f. 'medium sol igneus orbem /
hauserat',

98. procul: for the lengthening see on vii. 174.

98 f. rara domorum tecta, 'scattered houses': cf. *Geo.* iii. 340 'raris habitata mapalia tectis'.

100. 'and (where) then Evander had his poor possessions': for the suppression of a second relative see on vii. 61 ff.

Euandrus: the form which Virgil always uses except at x. 515, where he has *Euander*. (At x. 391–4 the alternative forms *Thymber* and *Thymbrus* are used only three lines apart.) For Evander see on 51 ff. above.

102–25. *Aeneas and his men approach Evander's town, where he is conducting a sacrificial rite in honour of Hercules: his son meets and welcomes the strangers.*

The situation is clearly reminiscent of the opening passage of *Odyssey* iii, where Telemachus on landing at Pylos finds Nestor sacrificing, is greeted by Nestor's sons, and is invited to join the rite. See also on 157 ff.

102. forte: as usual emphasizing coincidence, 'as luck would have it': see on vii. 509.

sollemnem: a regular, appointed act of worship, contrasted with the unexpected incident which is to follow: there is a similar point in ii. 202 'sollemnis . . . ad aras', iii. 301 'sollemnis . . . dapes'. For *honorem* cf. 61, 76.

103. Amphitryoniadae: the limitations on the use of the name of Hercules in hexameters are met by the use of the patronymics *Amphitryoniades* (from his mortal father: already in Catullus) and *Alcides* (203: from his mortal father's father) and of the epithet *Tirynthius* (228): the adjective *Herculeus* also supplies a convenient alternative (270, 288).

diuisque : a general invocation is added to the particular as in iii. 19 f. 'sacra Dionaeae matri diuisque ferebam / auspicibus coeptorum operum'.

104. Pallās: note the quantity: the name of the goddess is *Pallăs*.

huic filius una (*tura dabat*), 'he had his son along with him sacrificing': for the dative cf. vii. 649 'filius huic iuxta'. There is no need to construe the dative with *una* or *iuxta*.

105. pauperque senatus: the primitive simplicity of the community is emphasized again.

107 f. uidere has as object first the noun *rates* and then the noun-clause *adlabi et incumbere*, and *tacitos* of the manuscripts implies a subject (*Aeneadas*) for the infinitives. But the variant *tacitis* which Servius knew and preferred cannot be dismissed: *rates* as the subject of both verbs, although *incumbere* is appropriate only to the crews, is not more bold than 385 f. 'quae moenia clausis / ferrum acuant portis': the oars are *taciti* because the water is still.

110. audax: here Pallas is fearless in confronting possible danger, but the word presages his later story. Servius is right when he says that the implication of *audax* in Virgi'ls use is *uirtus sine fortuna*, 'ill-starred gallantry' (or, as he puts it on ix. 3, *fortis sine felicitate*): it is so applied to Turnus four times (vii. 409, ix. 3, 126, x. 276).

112 f. subegit . . . temptare: see on vii. 214.

114. The questioning of the stranger is Homeric: *Od.* i. 170 τίς πόθεν εἰς ἀνδρῶν; πόθι τοι πόλις ἠδὲ τοκῆες;: and for the present theme cf. *Od.* iii. 71 ff.

    qui genus?: for the limiting accusative cf. v. 285 'Cressa genus', and see on vii. 60.

    unde domo?, 'whence in respect of home?': for the formula (corresponding to πόθεν οἰκόθεν) cf. Hor. *Ep.* i. 7. 53 f. 'quaere et refer unde domo, quis, / cuius fortunae': similarly Plaut. *Cist.* 658 'haec cistella numnam hinc ab nobis domo est?'.

115. puppi . . . ab alta: the stern is the captain's place (cf. 680, v. 132), but Aeneas' ship has presumably been beached with bows to the water, ready to put out again—the usual ancient practice: cf. vi. 3 'obuertunt pelago proras'.

116. ramum praetendit oliuae: see on vii. 154.

117. Troiugenas: the compound, made for convenience in hexameters, is already used by Lucretius and Catullus, the corresponding *Graiugenae* (127) by Pacuvius and Lucretius.

118. profugos egere is a striking piece of diplomatic exaggeration and *superbo bello* is hardly justified by the fact that Latinus had allowed his pledge to be broken: *superbia* is that insolent disregard of the rights of others which is most conspicuous in the tyrant. (For the phrase cf. Livy iii. 9. 12 'crudeli superboque nobis bello institere'.) In 146 ff. Aeneas goes even further in misrepresentation.

119. ferte haec, 'carry this message': cf. i. 645 'Ascanio ferat haec' and the similar use of *reportare*, vii. 167.

121. tanto . . . nomine: i.e. the name Dardania. Here, as at *Geo.* ii. 476 and *Aen.* i. 513 the manuscripts are divided between *percussus* and *perculsus*: *perculsus* is perhaps too strong for this context.

124. excepitque manu, 'welcomed him with outstretched hand': cf. *Od.* iii. 35 χερσίν τ' ἠσπάζοντο.

    amplexus inhaesit: i.e. took Aeneas' right hand in both of his and held it there: cf. *Il.* vi. 406 ἔν τ' ἄρα οἱ φῦ χειρί.

125. For the structure of the line see on vii. 7. For *subire* cf. Prop. iv. 6. 71 'molli subeant conuiuia luco', and see on vii. 161.

126–51. *Aeneas tells Evander that they are descended from a common stock and that he seeks help against a common enemy.*

127. Graiugenum: for the genitive form see on vii. 189.

   cui ... precari: a dative of the person addressed with *precari* occurs only here, but Plautus has the dative with *comprecari* (*Amph.* 739 f.).

128. uitta comptos: see on vii. 154.

130. quod ... fores: 'I was not dismayed at the thought that you were ...' is the force of the subjunctive.

   a stirpe ... coniunctus Atridis, 'in lineage akin to the two sons of Atreus', i.e., probably, being of the same Greek stock as the hated Atridae: Aeneas is less likely to be thinking of the descent of both Evander and the Atridae from Jupiter, since he shared that descent himself. The repetition *coniunctus ... (133) coniunxere* perhaps stresses the fact that while one connection is being disregarded there are others which must count.

131. sed mea me uirtus: a verbal reminiscence of Lucretius' dedication, i. 140 ff. 'sed tua me uirtus tamen et sperata uoluptas ...', which perhaps accounts for the choice of *sed* as connective. The unashamed self-commendation is in line with the Homeric hero's behaviour: cf. *Od.* ix. 19 f. εἴμ' Ὀδυσεὺς Λαερτιάδης, ... καί μευ κλέος οὐρανὸν ἵκει, which Virgil adapts in i. 378 f. 'sum pius Aeneas, ... fama super aethera notus'.

131 ff. sed ... uolentem: the expression is compressed: for while *egere* fits all the subjects *uirtus, oracula, cognati patres, didita fama,* the ablative *fatis* fits only *oracula*.

132. cognati patres, 'the kinship of our fathers': see on vii. 314 and cf. x. 320.

   didita: cf. vii. 144 'diditur ... rumor': a Lucretian verb, rare elsewhere.

134. Dardanus: the story of Dardanus, founder of the royal house of Troy, is told in vii. 206 ff.

135 ff. ut Grai perhibent: for the appeal to tradition see on vii. 48: there is a certain *naïveté* in Aeneas' quoting the authority of Greek legend to the Greek Evander. Since Virgil is a poet and not a mythographer, the emphasis on the heroes' descent from the Pleiad sisters and on Atlas four times appearing as the central figure of the joint pedigree, though they also had Jupiter as a common ancestor, is not surprising; the repetition of *aetherios ... qui sustinet orbis* (137) in *caeli qui sidera tollit* (141) is less happy.

135. Grai: in poetry *Graius* is the normal form of the adjective, 'Greek', and *Grai* the name of the people. (On the adoption by the Romans, for the people who called themselves *Ἕλ-ληνες*, of what appears to have been a local name belonging to a region of Boeotia, see J. Miller in P.–W. vii. 1693 ff.) Virgil uses only *Graius* and never the commonplace *Graecus*: the poets before him show the same preference (apart from Ennius, *Ann.* 356 V., Cicero, *Arat.* 317, and Catullus, 68. 102, *Graecus* is confined in earlier verse to comedy) and so do Horace in the *Odes*, Ovid in the *Metamorphoses*, and Propertius. In the writers of verse who use both forms, and in prose, *Graius*, as opposed to the matter-of-fact *Graecus*, generally has a nuance of historical association, which is well illustrated by Cic. *Rep.* i. 58 'ut Graeci dicunt omnes aut Graios esse aut barbaros' (cf., e.g., Hor. *Ep.* ii. 2. 42; Juv. 8. 226; Cic. *de Inu.* ii. 69; Sen. *Dial.* xii. 7. 8). See J. Bérard in *R.E.A.* liv (1952), 5 ff.; A. Ernout in *R. de Ph.* lxxxviii (1962), 209 ff.

136. aduehitur Teucros: cf. vii. 216 f. 'urbem adferimur'. For the present used of a past event vividly called to mind see on vii. 363.

137. edidit: a word of epic style, which Horace uses in his highflown opening address, *Od.* i. 1. 1 'Maecenas atauis edite regibus'.

138. uobis: i.e. Evander and Pallas or, more generally, Evander's house.

139. gelido: a conventional epithet for a mountain in Arcadia: cf. 159.

    fudit : the only parallel to this use of the verb for human birth seems to be Cicero's contemptuous use of *effundere*, *Pis.* fr. 14 'te tua . . . mater pecudem ex aluo, non hominem effuderit' (where one might suppose it to be suggested by *pecudem*). Catullus has a similarly rare use of *deponere* at 34. 7 f. '(Latonia) quam mater prope Deliam / deposiuit oliuam'.

140. at: for *at* with a sense like that of *autem* but more vivid, adding a corroborative fact or a descriptive detail, cf. Hor. *Sat.* i. 5. 60.

140 f. Atlas, idem Atlas: for the dramatic or pathetic use of epanalepsis with a proper name see on vii. 586 ff. Here, reinforced by *idem*, it intensifies the appeal to common blood.

141. generat: for the present expressing a past action whose effect continues into the present cf. ix. 266 'dat'. The usage is particularly associated (as here) with verbs relating to birth or nurture: so *Ecl.* 8. 45 'edunt', *Geo.* i. 279; Prop. iv. 1. 77 'creat'; *Aen.* x. 518 'educat'; Prop. iv. 4. 54 'nutrit'; and in Greek, Eur. *Bacch.* 2 ὃν τίκτει ποθ' ἡ Κάδμου κόρη: Soph. *O.T.* 1247 τὴν τίκτουσαν, 'the mother'.

144. temptamenta . . . pepigi is an extension of the common *foedus pangere*: *legatos* (143), with which another verb (such as *misi*) would be appropriate, is included by a kind of zeugma.

me, me: for the emotional repetition cf. ix. 427 'me, me, adsum qui feci, in me conuertite ferrum', xii. 260 f. 'me, me duce ferrum / corripite'.

145. obieci caput: cf. ii. 751 'caput obiectare periclis', xii. 229 f. 'pro cunctis talibus unam / obiectare animam': so in prose, e.g. Cic. *Dom.* 145 'obieci meum caput . . . perditissimorum ciuium furori'.

146. gens . . . Daunia: i.e. the Rutulians, whose eponymous king was Turnus' father Daunus (x. 616). In these lines Aeneas' diplomacy rests its case on total misrepresentation: for the Italians have done no more than repel the Trojan incomers and there has been no suggestion that they even have designs on anything that is not their own. See on 118 and for *crudeli bello* cf. Livy iii. 9. 12 there quoted.

149. The line is adapted from the 'laudes Italiae', *Geo.* ii. 158.

150. accipe daque fidem: an Ennian phrase (*Ann.* 32 V. 'accipe daque fidem foedusque feri bene firmum').

fortia bello: as in x. 185 ('fortissime bello'), *bello* may be local ablative or dative of purpose (cf. vii. 482).

151. rebus spectata, 'tested in action'.

152–83. *Evander's reply recalls an old friendship with Anchises: he readily promises assistance and invites Aeneas and his men to join the sacrificial feast.*

153. lustrabat lumine, 'let his gaze pass over' (cf. ii. 753 f. 'uestigia . . . lumine lustro'): for *lustrare* see on vii. 391.

155. accipio agnoscoque: cf. xii. 260 'accipio agnoscoque deos'.

157 ff. The visit of distinguished strangers remembered in later days has its precedent in *Il.* iii. 205 ff., where Antenor recalls entertaining Odysseus and Menelaus; the recognition of Aeneas from his likeness to his father recalls *Od.* iv. 140 ff., where Telemachus is similarly recognized. So Dido recollects a visit of Teucer to her native Sidon (i. 619 ff.).

157. uisentem, 'going to see': cf. Cat. 11. 10; Hor. *Od.* iii. 4. 33 ff.

158. Salamina: Hesione, Priam's sister and Anchises' cousin, was the wife of Telamon, king of Salamis.

159. protinus . . . inuisere, 'went on to visit'; the collocation of *uisentem . . . inuisere* is awkward. For Virgil's preference for the present infinitive after *memini* see on vii. 206.

gelidos: cf. 139.

160. uestibat flore iuuentas: cf. Lucr. v. 888 f. 'puerili aeuo

florente iuuentas / occipit et molli uestit lanugine malas';
Pacuv. 362 R. 'nunc primum opacat flora lanugo genas'. For
the imperfect in -*ibam* see on vii. 485.

163. amore, 'desire', as often elsewhere (e.g. ii. 10, vii. 57):
the parallel of iii. 298 suggests that the following infinitive
is to be taken with *amore* (cf. vi. 133 f., xii. 282): see on vii.
591.

165. Phenei: Pheneus was a town in northern Arcadia.

166 ff. The exchange of gifts between guest-friends is an epic
commonplace: so *Il.* vi. 219 ff., x. 266 ff.; *Aen.* iii. 464 ff.,
ix. 359 ff.

166. Lycias: for the conventional epithet cf. vii. 816.

167. For the spondaic ending see on vii. 631.

168. aurea: the placing of *aurea* in the relative clause avoids
attaching two epithets to *frena*.

169. Evander acts as he speaks: 'my right hand that you ask
for (at line 150) has clasped yours in alliance'. *mihi* is dative
of the agent (see on vii. 412): for *foedere* cf. iii. 83 'iungimus
hospitio dextras'.

171. The line is repeated from i. 571 with the change of *tutos* to
laetos.

173. celebrate fauentes, 'attend our rites with good will' (cf.
i. 735): *fauentes* may perhaps carry a suggestion of the
technical meaning of ceremonial silence conveyed by *ore
fauete* (v. 71), *fauete linguis* (Hor. *Od.* iii. 1. 2).

174. iam nunc, 'from this moment, without loss of time': there
is a curious verbal echo of the address to Octavian in *Geo.* i. 42
'uotis iam nunc adsuesce uocari'.

175. reponi: the materials of the meal, put away at the inter-
ruption by the strangers, are to be served again. But in
similar contexts elsewhere *reponere* is 'duly place' (see on
vii. 134).

176. sedili: Macrobius (iii. 6. 16) notes the appropriateness of
the word to a rite of Hercules at which the worshippers sat
and did not recline, but that may be reading too much into it.
There are no chairs here for any but the chief participants—
Aeneas is singled out for special honour (*praecipuum*)—and in
any case sitting to eat was the general practice of the heroic
age (see on vii. 176).

177. toro et . . . pelle: a hendiadys (see on vii. 15); the 'cushion'
is the lion-skin.

178. solioque inuitat: in its earlier usage *inuitare*, 'entertain',
'treat' (in comedy *sese inuitare* is 'do oneself well': e.g.
Plaut. *Amph.* 283), is almost a synonym of *accipere* (cf.
Lucil. 1269 M. 'pulchre inuitati ⟨sumus⟩ acceptique benigne')
and is naturally accompanied, like *accipere* (cf. vii. 210 f.

'solio ... / accipit'), by an ablative; though the case-form is usually ambiguous, it is certain in, e.g., Cic. *Verr*. ii. 4. 25 'ecquis est qui senatorem ... tecto ac domo non inuitet?'. So here *solio* is to be taken as an ablative parallel to *toro*. But Virgil also uses the verb in its later meaning 'invite', with an infinitive in *Geo*. iv. 23, *Aen*. v. 485 f., perhaps with a dative at ix. 676, but without either at v. 292 'inuitat pretiis animos' (*pretiis* is ablative).

180. **uiscera**: the flesh, 'quicquid sub corio est' (Servius on i. 211): cf. i. 211, x. 727.

180 f. **onerant canistris dona**: the same variation on the normal construction *onerant canistra donis* is used in i. 185 'uina ... ... quae ... cadis onerant'.

181. **dona laboratae Cereris**: i.e. bread: for the combination of the literal use of *Ceres* (the goddess) and the metonymic use ('corn') implied in the epithet see on vii. 113. For the rare transitive use of *laboro* cf. i. 639 'laboratae uestes'.

183. **perpetui tergo bouis** translates the νῶτα διηνεκῆ of the Homeric feast (*Od*. xiv. 437, *Il*. vii. 321). For *perpetuus*, 'undivided', cf. vii. 176 'perpetuis ... mensis'.

lustralibus, 'sacrificial', in a general sense, probably: there is no reference here to any *lustratio*. Livy says (i. 7. 13) that the *exta*, usually burned on the altar, were at sacrifices to Hercules eaten at the beginning of the meal: Virgil may be alluding to this practice.

184–279. *Evander explains the origin of the rite in which he is engaged and recounts the story of Hercules' visit to the place and his fight with Cacus.*

This cult, Evander tells his guest (187), is no foreign importation unrelated to traditional belief: it arose on their own soil out of their own experience. Virgil is throwing back into primitive times an attitude of his own day (reflected again in the picture of the Egyptian pantheon on the shield, 696 ff.), when the infiltration of ecstatic Eastern cults was a threat to the traditional native worship. Some of these (like the cult of the Magna Mater) had already been tolerated and allowed to establish themselves under conditions; the spread of others was a matter of concern to Augustus. But there is a certain incongruity in imputing these nationalistic sentiments to Evander, himself an incomer from a foreign land.

In fact the cult was neither indigenous nor primitive. Ovid (*F*. i. 543 ff.) and Propertius' aetiological poem on the Ara Maxima (iv. 9), in accounts based on Virgil, attribute the establishment of the cult to Hercules himself (so too Livy ix. 34. 18), Livy (i. 7. 11), and Dionysius (i. 40) (with Strabo

v. 3. 3, and Tacitus, *Ann*. xv. 41) to Evander. But the worship of Hercules was an importation from Greece (Roman antiquarians themselves recognized some of its features as characteristically Greek: so Varro, quoted by Macrobius, iii. 6. 17) and it was widely diffused, as inscriptions show, in central Italy and in Etruria (cf. Dion. Hal. i. 40. 6 σπανίως ἂν εὕροι τις Ἰταλίας χῶρον ἔνθα μὴ τυγχάνει τιμώμενος ὁ θεός). That it spread from the Greek cities of the South, where Hercules had a natural place as the patron of trade and financial dealings, is not unlikely: the same connection may be reflected in the position of the Ara Maxima at Rome in the cattle-market (*forum boarium*). Virgil contrives to combine some truth with legend when he credits the *gentes* Potitia and Pinaria with the establishment of the Ara Maxima cult (269 ff.): for the tradition makes it clear that it originated as a family cult, though there is no knowing from where the two *gentes* imported it, with themselves, into Rome and the title is unexplained. The superintendence of the cult remained with the two *gentes* until 312 B.C., when it was transferred to the state (Livy ix. 29. 9; cf. Dion. Hal. i. 40. 5), but it maintained its individuality alongside other cults of Hercules: in historical times the Potitii have disappeared and the extinction of the family may have been the cause of the transference, of which Livy, Dionysius, and Festus (270 L.) give a fanciful account. The alleged distinction of function between the two families, the Potitii having the superior status, which appears in Dionysius, Livy (i. 7. 13), and Macrobius (iii. 6. 14) was no doubt based on popular etymology of the two names: it seems unlikely that Virgil is hinting at it in using *auctor* and *custos* to describe them.

Whatever were the actual origins of the Ara Maxima cult, it found an aetiology in a myth which itself seems to represent a fusion of Italian and Greek legend—the story of Cacus. Cacus was a local deity associated with the Palatine (where the *scalae Caci* preserved his name in historical times), a member of a divine pair Cacus–Caca (i.e. a bi-sexual deity); a local legend made him the victim of deception by a guest who stole his cattle. This folk-tale seems to have been combined with a Greek story of the theft of the cattle which Hercules was driving to Greece after taking them from Geryon in the far West, and in the conflated version the name of Cacus, interpreted as κακός, reversed his role and made him into the villain of the story. Virgil is alone (with Ovid following him) in representing Cacus (who in Livy i. 7. 5 is only a local herdsman, in Dionysius i. 39. 2 λῃστὴς ἐπιχώριος) as a supernatural being, the fire-breathing son of Vulcan: that description suggests that he was originally a fire-god

and, combined with his name, points to a connection between
him and Caeculus, the hero of Praeneste (vii. 678 ff.: see note
there), who is also a son of Vulcan and a robber.

On the Hercules cult, see J. Bayet, *Les Origines de l'Hercule
romain* (Paris, 1926); G. Wissowa, *Rel. u. Kult.*[2] 271 ff.;
K. Latte, *Röm. Rel.* 213 ff.; J. G. Winter, *The Myth of
Hercules at Rome* (Univ. of Michigan Stud. 4: New York,
1910); G. H. Hallam in *J.R.S.* xxi (1931), 276 ff.: on Cacus,
F. Münzer, *Cacus der Rinderdieb* (Basel, 1911); J. Fontenrose,
Python (Berkeley, 1959), 339 ff.; Ogilvie on Livy i. 7.

Virgil's purpose in introducing the story of the Ara
Maxima and the Cacus legend within it has been the subject
of much discussion. Has he an ulterior dramatic purpose in
mind? Or a political one? In Hercules, the pattern of the
θεῖος ἀνήρ, the deliverer of men (here in Italy, as elsewhere
before) from oppression and wrong, is the perceptive reader
to see an image of Aeneas, who is to give a new order to
a troubled Italy, or of Augustus himself, who brings peace to
a disordered world?

Dramatic purpose has been elaborated in the theory that
the desperate fight with Cacus symbolizes the struggle with
Turnus, who like Cacus represents the infernal powers of
which he is the instrument, and that his defeat foreshadows
the inevitable end of the war in Italy. To see that symbolism
is to take a superficial view of Virgil's argument: if Turnus
is an instrument, he is Juno's instrument. That Virgil has
a political reference in mind—and even that Evander's in-
sistence on the indigenousness of the Hercules cult is a veiled
apologia for the ascription of divine honours to Augustus,
the *praesens diuus* of Hor. *Od.* iii. 5. 2—has been argued from
the association of Hercules with Augustus elsewhere in
Augustan poetry. But in Virgil himself that association is
confined to vi. 801 ff. where Hercules is paired with Bacchus,
a very different figure, and the point of comparison is the
range of his beneficent progress. In Horace the association
occurs five times, but in *Od.* iii. 14 the explicit point is that
Spain has been the scene of Augustus' activities, as it once
was the scene of those of Hercules; in three places Hercules
is not alone—he appears with Pollux, Bacchus, and Romulus,
deified benefactors of mankind with whom Augustus invites
comparison (*Od.* iii. 3. 9 ff.) but who received recognition only
after death (*Ep.* ii. 1. 1 ff.), and with Castor as a demigod who
is honoured in Greece as Augustus will be in Rome (*Od.* iv.
5. 35); in *Od.* ii. 12. 1 ff. the exploits of Hercules are linked,
as a theme of poetry, on the one hand to those of Augustus
but on the other to the triumphs of early Rome. If a political

purpose was to be made effective here, one might expect the reader to be given a pointer to assist his thoughts in that direction. Hercules comes to Evander's people as a deliverer (189 'seruati') and Augustus could be said to have come as a deliverer to his world (Prop. iv. 6. 37 'mundi seruator'): would a tale of Hercules be expected by itself to make the reader think of Augustus?

To suppose that beneath the *monstrum* Cacus the reader would have seen the *monstrum* of Augustan propaganda, Cleopatra, and that Cacus' anonymous victims of lines 196 f. would have reminded him of the murder of Cicero, is fantasy. More seriously to be considered are two possible contemporary allusions which have been detected in the details of the Evander episode: Virgil's introduction of the Salii (285 ff.) to sing a hymn in praise of Hercules and his emphasis (269, 281) on the place of a Potitius (or the Potitii) in the ceremonies might allude to the honours paid to Octavian in 29 B.C., when the Senate decreed that his name should be 'inserted among the gods' in the traditional hymn of the Salii of Mars (*Res Gestae* 10: Dio li. 20. 1) and when the public sacrifice of thanksgiving for his safe return was offered by a consul who happened to bear the name of Valerius Potitus (Dio li. 21. 1). As for the first, a hymn devoted to a hero's praises and the insertion of a name in a well-known existing hymn are rather different compliments and Salii may have been (or Virgil may have believed that they were) a traditional part of the Hercules cult (see on 285): as for the second, in an account of the Ara Maxima Virgil could hardly avoid giving the Potitii a prominent place (see above: it is to be observed that he does not omit to mention the Pinarii as well) and there is no evidence that Potitus was a figure of such note that his name might be expected to be lingering in a reader's mind. These may be coincidences. Virgil's details are a natural part (one at least an almost inevitable part) of his description: the detailed resemblance of the picture of Latinus' palace (vii. 17 ff.) to the Capitoline temple of Virgil's own day is much more striking, for there he was free to make his fanciful description what he pleased. But even if they are not and Virgil is deliberately making points for his reader to take, that does not mean that his design in incorporating the whole episode was to compliment Augustus.

Political allusion need not be looked for here any more than in the Aristaeus episode of *Geo*. iv. In both places artistic purpose is justification enough. Virgil's introduction of this aetiological epyllion, appropriate to the scene, is a piece of literary technique, diversifying his narrative with an artful digression in which colourful realism and antiquarian appeal combine to hold his interest and the Cacus story is given life by the device of putting it into the mouth of an eyewitness.

See B. Otis, *Virgil*, 334 ff.; W. A. Camps, *Intro. to Virgil's Aeneid*, 98 ff.; V. Pöschl, *Die Dichtkunst Virgils*, 276 ff.; F. J. Worstbrock, *Elemente einer Poetik der Aeneis* (Münster, 1963), 103 ff.; V. Buchheit, *Vergil über die Sendung Roms* (Heidelberg, 1963), 116 ff.; P. Grimal in *R.E.A.* liii (1951), 51 ff.; H. Schnepf in *Gymn.* lxvi (1959), 250 ff.; H. Bellen in *Rh. Mus.* cvi (1963), 23 ff.

184. The formula is a common Homeric cliché: αὐτὰρ ἐπεὶ πόσιος καὶ ἐδητύος ἐξ ἔρον ἕντο.

187. uana superstitio: here *superstitio* carries the meaning which, though the term is often vaguely used, seems to be basic to it—that of religious practice and belief which goes beyond accepted tradition and is accordingly extravagant (*nimia*) and irrational (*uana*, as here, or *inanis*): so Cicero defines it (*N.D.* i. 117, ii. 71 f., *Diu.* ii. 148), opposing it to *religio*, and so it is applied to imported foreign cults like that of the Bacchanalia (Livy xxxix. 16). Virgil's other use of the word at xii. 817 where the oath by Styx is 'una superstitio superis quae reddita diuis' is unique. See Pease on Cic. *Diu.* ii. 148, *N.D.* i. 45, and literature there cited.

189. facimus . . . honores, 'we perform and renew (from year to year: cf. 173) our due worship': *facere* can be used absolutely for 'sacrifice' (cf. *Ecl.* 3. 77 'cum faciam uitula'; Cic. *Att.* i. 13. 3 'cum . . . populo fieret') but here it is more naturally taken with *honores*. For *honores* cf. 61, 76, 102.

190. iam primum: a lively conversational opening to Evander's story.

suspensam . . . rupem, 'vaulted': *suspendere* (with its nouns *suspensio* and *suspensura*) is the builder's technical term for vaulting, here applied to the natural cavern-roof: for the characteristically Virgilian use of the ablative of material in a complex of noun and adjective see on vii. 639 f.

190 ff. hanc aspice rupem . . . ut . . . stat domus: the paratactic usage in which *aspice* (here with an object, elsewhere without) is combined with an exclamation in the indicative occurs again at *Ecl.* 4. 52 'aspice uenturo laetantur ut omnia saeclo', 5. 6 f. 'aspice ut antrum / siluestris raris sparsit labrusca racemis', *Aen.* vi. 855 f. 'aspice ut insignis spoliis Marcellus opimis / ingreditur': Catullus has the same use, 62. 12 'aspicite innuptae secum ut meditata requirunt'. It must

be taken in connection with the similar use of *uiden*, a col-
loquial idiom which appears in early Latin (Plaut. *Curc.* 311
'uiden ut expalluit?', *Most.* 1172 'uiden ut astat furcifer?';
Accius 303 R. 'uiden ut te impietas stimulat?'; Turpilius
103 R. 'uiden ut fastidit mei?') and which also in classical
poetry is confined to Catullus and Virgil (preserving evidence
of its origin in the 'iambic shortening' of the second syllable):
Cat. 61. 77 f. 'uiden ut faces / splendidas quatiunt comas?',
62. 8 'uiden ut perniciter exsiluere?'; *Aen.* vi. 779 'uiden
ut geminae stant uertice cristae?'. Virgil has also the variant
nonne uides, *Geo.* i. 56 f. 'nonne uides . . . ut . . . / India mittit
ebur?'.

191 f. montis . . . domus: Cacus' lair on the hillside.

192. traxere ruinam: cf. ii. 465 f. 'ea (turris) lapsa repente
ruinam / cum sonitu trahit', 631 '(ornus) congemuit tra-
xitque iugis auulsa ruinam'.

193. uasto : the word implies more than size; here, as often in
Virgil's use, it connotes a desolation that appals or repels:
see on vii. 302.

194. semihominis: quadrisyllabic: in compounds of *semi-* the
-i- is regularly treated as consonantal; so 297 *sem(i)esa*, xi.
200 *sem(i)usta*, x. 396, 404, xi. 635 *semianimis*. Cacus, here
semihomo, is *semiferus* at 267.

   Caci facies: for *facies*, 'figure', 'shape', see on vii. 448: for
the force of the periphrasis see on vii. 18, 650.

195. inaccessam: see on vii. 11.

196. foribus . . . superbis: 'proud portals' (as we say) appear
elsewhere as a symbol of sovereignty and conquest: 721 f.
'(Augustus) dona recognoscit populorum aptatque superbis /
postibus', ii. 504 (of Priam's palace) 'barbarico postes auro
spoliisque superbi' (cf. viii. 202, of Hercules himself, 'spoliis
superbus'). But here *superbus* has its common implication
of insolent ruthlessness: see on 118.

197. tristi . . . pallida tabo: for the complex of adjective and
ablatival phrase see on vii. 639. On *pallidus* see on 244 f.

198. illius, following on *huic*, is emphatic: it is to his parent
that Cacus owes his terrifying appearance. For *monstrum*
see on vii. 21.

198 f. atros . . . ignis: cf. iv. 384 'sequar atris ignibus absens'.
The adjective no doubt has a literal reference to smoky
flame (cf. vii. 456 f. 'atro / lumine fumantis') but, as usual
in Virgil, it has an emotional colour and carries the sugges-
tion of 'ghastly', 'deadly': see on vii. 525.

199. magna se mole ferebat: cf. iii. 656 (of the Cyclops) 'uasta
se mole mouentem'. *se ferre* is used to imply an impressive
carriage (cf. i. 503 f. '(Dido) talem se laeta ferebat / per

medios', iv. 11 '(Aeneas) quem sese ore ferens!') or bulk (cf.
ix. 597 '(Remulus) ingentem sese clamore ferebat'): for com-
pounds similarly used, ix. 53 'campo sese arduus infert', x.
768 'talis se uastis infert Mezentius armis', xi. 36 'Aeneas
foribus sese intulit altis', xii. 441 '(Aeneas) portis sese ex-
tulit ingens'.

200. et nobis: we too, like others, have at last (*aliquando*) had
our prayers answered by a divine deliverance.

201. aduentumque dei: Hercules is called *deus* by anticipation:
for *aduentus* of the epiphany of a god cf. Lucr. i. 6 f. 'te, dea,
te fugiunt uenti, te nubila caeli / aduentumque tuum'; Ovid,
F. i. 239 f. 'posteritas . . . / hospitis aduentum testificata
dei': the word carries the same suggestion in vi. 798 f.
'huius (i.e. Augusti) in aduentum iam nunc et Caspia regna /
responsis horrent diuum . . .'.

   maximus ultor: the great redresser of wrong.

202. tergemini . . . Geryonae: the phrase is Lucretian, v. 28
'tripectora tergemini uis Geryonai'.

205. furis is confirmed by Prop. iv. 9. 13 f. 'furem sonuere
iuuenci, / furis et implacidas diruit ira fores'. Cf. 211.

205 f. ne quid . . . fuisset, 'to ensure that no crime or deceit
would have been (i.e. would be found to have been) left
unattempted': *fuisset* corresponds to *fuerit*, 'will be found
to have been', of direct speech.

   inausum: see on vii. 308.

207. stabulis: 'halting-place', as in 213, without the usual
implication of permanent quarters (as in vii. 501, 512, ix.
388): similarly in vi. 179, x. 723 'stabula alta' are lairs in
the forest (so Cat. 63. 53 'gelida stabula').

208. auertit: the regular word for driving or carrying off spoil:
cf. i. 472 'auertit equos in castra', x. 78 'auertere praedas';
Cat. 64. 5 'auratam . . . auertere pellem'; Caes. *B.G.* iii. 59. 3
'praedam omnem domum auertebant'.

   superante: this adjectival use of *superans* as equivalent to
praestans seems to be unique.

209. The trick is a reminiscence of Hermes' exploit in the
Homeric *Hymn to Hermes*, 75 ff.

   pedibus . . . rectis: an attributive ablative with *uestigia*,
'marks of feet pointing forward'.

211. raptor: Wakefield's correction is confirmed by Propertius'
reminiscence (cf. 205), iv. 9. 9 'incola Cacus erat, metuendo
raptor ab antro'.

212. quaerenti, 'in the eyes of a searcher': a common use of
the dative in prose to express either a positional (*descendenti,
instantibus, egressis*) or a mental (*aestimanti, reputanti*)
standpoint (K.–S. ii. 1, pp. 321 f.).

Wakefield's objection to the line as 'superuacuus' is re-
vived by M. D. Reeve (*C.R.* lxxxiv [1970], 134 f.), who adds
the objection that it is the only self-contained line in the
passage: but the parataxis, taking the place of *ita occultabat
ut quaerenti ferrent*, is thoroughly Virgilian.

213. interea makes a loose temporal connection, indicating
a succession in time and not simultaneity: so, e.g., xi. 1 and
182 (where it marks the opening of a new day), xii. 842. See
R. Heinze, *Virgils Epische Technik*, 388 n. 2; O. W. Rein-
muth in *A.J.P.* liv (1933), 323 ff.

215. discessu: for the ablative cf. x. 445 'Rutulum abscessu', *Ecl.* 7. 59 'Phyllidis aduentu'; Cat. 65. 22 'aduentu
matris'.

215 f. querelis impleri: perhaps a reminiscence of Lucr. ii.
358 f. 'completque querelis / frondiferum nemus'.

216. clamore is naturally taken as a modal ablative, *colles
clamore* (*a bubus*) *relinqui* being equivalent to *colles clamore
boues relinquebant*, which is exactly parallel to i. 519 'templum clamore petebant' (cf. ix. 597 'ingentem sese clamore
ferebat', xii. 252 'conuertunt clamore fugam'). There is no
ground for removing a striking phrase in favour of the banal
propinqui as A. Y. Campbell, anticipated by Peerlkamp,
proposed (*C.R.* lxix [1955], 137; lxxii [1958], 15 f.). Some
commentators have objected to the three-fold repetition
of the same notion in different words (though the tricolon is
by no means un-Virgilian) and looked for a reference to echo
in the final phrase: and G. Watson (*C.R.* lxviii [1954], 99 f.)
ingeniously found it by taking *clamore* to be an instrumental
ablative and the phrase to mean 'the hills were left behind
by the sound', i.e. the sound came back from the hills in
echo. But, while it is true that Virgil twice brings the notion
into a similar context (305 'consonat omne nemus strepitu
collesque resultant', v. 149 f. 'consonat omne nemus . . .
pulsati colles clamore resultant'), that is no reason why he
should have used the same pattern here. To argue that the
imprisoned cow (217) would not have delayed its answering
bellow until the herd had got so far as to be leaving the hills
behind, or that Hercules would not have had to pick up his
club after the move had begun, is to take a piece of romantic
description (in which the Aventine, a hundred feet high, is
aerius mons) too literally. The herd had been grazing in the
hollow under the hills: they now get under way.

219. hic, 'thereupon'.

exarserat: the use of the pluperfect in past narrative cor-
responds to the use of the perfect in present time to express
instantaneous action; see on vii. 394.

219 f. furiis . . . atro felle: for the combination of two ablatives modifying the verb in different ways cf. *Geo.* iii. 439 'linguis micat ore trisulcis' and see 226, 387 f. For the plural *furiis* cf. 494 'furiis surrexit Etruria iustis', i. 41 'ob . . . furias Aiacis Oilei', iv. 474 'concepit furias euicta dolore' and see on vii. 445 'iras'.

220. manu: see on vii. 621.

nodis grauatum: cf. vii. 507 'stipitis . . . grauidi nodis'.

221. ardua montis: cf. xi. 513 f. 'ardua montis / per deserta'. The combination of a neuter plural adjective with a partitive genitive is a form of expression which already appears in Ennius (*Ann.* 89 V. 'infera noctis') and becomes a mannerism in Lucretius (e.g. i. 86 'prima uirorum', v. 35 'pelagi seuera', vi. 96 'caerula caeli'). As the idiom develops the partitive notion fades or disappears and the formula serves to throw emphasis on the adjective. It is common in Augustan poetry (cf. Hor. *Od.* ii. 1. 23 'cuncta terrarum', iv. 4. 76 'acuta belli', iv. 12. 19 f. 'amara . . . curarum'): in prose it is affected by the historians Sallust, Livy, and especially Tacitus. For other Virgilian examples cf. i. 422 'strata uiarum', ii. 332 'angusta uiarum', 725 'opaca locorum', v. 695 'ardua terrarum', vi. 633 'opaca uiarum', xi. 310 'cetera . . . rerum', 882 'tuta domorum'.

223. oculis: the order of words is perhaps in favour of taking *oculis* with *turbatum*, 'with consternation in his eyes' (cf. Aesch. *Pers.* 168 ἀμφὶ δ' ὀφθαλμοῖς φόβος): the phrase is used by Livy, vii. 26. 5 '(Gallum) oculis simul ac mente turbatum Valerius obtruncat'. But it may belong to *uidere*: *oculis uidere* is idiomatic as a strengthening of *uidere*, 'set eyes on': cf. Cat. 64. 16 f. 'illa . . . uiderunt luce marinas / mortales oculis nudato corpore Nymphas'. For *turbatus* see on 435.

ilicet: see on vii. 583.

224. addidit alas: this metaphor for speed does not seem to be found before Virgil.

225 ff. Cacus has a rock hung on iron chains which he lets down like a portcullis.

226. ferro . . . et arte paterna: the two ablatives stand in different relations to the subject, the first an ablative of material, the second modal: the co-ordinating *et* makes the construction less simple than in 219.

227. fultos . . . obice postis: cf. Ovid, *A.A.* ii. 244 'ianua fulta sera'. The *obex* here is the suspended rock.

228. animis, 'with anger', probably: cf. 256 'non tulit Alcides animis'.

Tirynthius: see on vii. 662 f.

omnemque: for the hypermetric line see on vii. 160.

229, 231. lustrans . . . lustrat: the verb seems to be used here in two different ways, first of ranging with the eye and then of ranging on foot: for the development of the word see on vii. 391.

229. ora ferebat: cf. 310 'oculos fert omnia circum', ii. 570 'oculos per cuncta ferenti'. For the rare rhythm cf. vii. 45.

231. Auentini: for the defining genitive cf. vii. 697 'Cimini cum monte lacum', vi. 659 'Eridani . . . amnis', i. 270 'sede Lauini', iii. 687 'sede Pelori', iii. 477 'Ausoniae tellus': see K.–S. ii. 1, p. 419.

233 ff. A jagged pinnacle of rock rises from the steep side of the hill above the cave, of the roof of which (*dorsum*) it forms part, leaning towards the river below to the left of it and on Hercules' left as he approaches it from behind. Attacking it from the right (*dexter*) he pushes full against it (*in aduersum nitens*): dislodged, it crashes over into the river below, leaving a gap through which Hercules first attacks Cacus with stones and branches and then leaps down to tackle him at close quarters.

233. praecisis, 'precipitous': cf. Sall. *Jug.* 92. 7 'iter . . . praecisum'.

235. dirarum, 'ill-omened': see on vii. 324.

  opportuna: for the adjective ('fit', 'favourable': in origin a nautical metaphor) cf. *Geo.* iv. 129 'nec pecori opportuna seges nec commoda Baccho'.

239. impulit: cf. ii. 460 ff. 'turrim . . . conuellimus altis / sedibus impulimusque'. The emphatic position of *impulit* (cf. vii. 621) is enhanced by the pause and by the repetition *impulit, impulsu*: note also the unusual rhythm, with dactylic words forming the fourth and fifth feet.

240. An imaginative picture of the effect of the plunging of the rock in the river: the wash floods the banks—and they seem to be starting back; it checks the current—and the river seems to be retreating in fear.

  exterritus: for the 'pathetic fallacy' cf. vii. 514 f., 722.

241 f. ingens regia: a heroic description of Cacus' gruesome cave.

242 f. penitus . . . penitus: the repetition at the same place in the line points the comparison.

243 ff. The earthquake of *Il.* xx. 59 ff.—πάντες δ' ἐσσείοντο πόδες πολυπίδακος Ἴδης / καὶ κορυφαί... / ἔδεισεν δ' ὑπένερθεν ἄναξ ἐνέρων Ἀϊδωνεύς, / δείσας δ' ἐκ θρόνου ἆλτο καὶ ἴαχε, μή οἱ ὕπερθε / γαῖαν ἀναρρήξειε Ποσειδάων ἐνοσίχθων, / οἰκία δὲ θνητοῖσι καὶ ἀθανάτοισι φανείη / σμερδαλέ' εὐρώεντα, τά τε στυγέουσι θεοί περ—is behind Virgil's picture of the opening of Hell, as *pallida dis inuisa* clearly shows.

244 f. regna . . . pallida: cf. iv. 26 'pallentis umbras'; Enn. *Sc.* 109 f. V. 'pallida leti nubila tenebris / loca'; Tib. i. 10. 38

'pallida turba'. *pallidus* is 'dim' rather than 'pale', implying discoloration rather than lightness of colour, and is often applied to objects abnormally dark (cf., e.g., Prop. iv. 7. 36 'pallida uina', 82 'numquam ... pallet ebur'; Pliny, *N.H.* x. 144 'ouorum alia sunt candida ... alia pallida').

245. immane barathrum: for *immanis* see on vii. 305. (The juxtaposition of *immane* and *manes* here is a curious accident.) *barathrum*: an old borrowing from Greek and already a familiar word in Plautus: Virgil uses it of Charybdis in iii. 421 in a phrase adapted from Catullus, 68. 108.

248. insueta rudentem, 'uttering strange roars': see on vii. 16.

249. telis: clearly here not Hercules' usual armament of arrows but generally 'missiles' (as the *Digest* defines the word, 50. 16. 233: 'omne significatur quod mittitur mann: itaque sequitur ut et lapis et lignum et ferrum hoc nomine contineatur'): the *tela* are the *arma*, the *rami*, and *molares* of the following clause. So in ii. 447 the *tela* of the defending Trojans are pinnacles torn from a roof.

250. molaribus: i.e. *lapides* as large as millstones, the μύλακες of *Il.* xii. 160 f. κόρυθες ... / βαλλομένων μυλάκεσσι.

251. neque enim: see on 84.

254. prospectum eripiens: cf. i. 88 f. 'eripiunt ... nubes caelumque diemque / Teucrorum ex oculis': the phrase is perhaps suggested by Enn. *Sc.* 182 V. 'caligo oborta est, omnem prospectum abstulit'.

256. animis: cf. 228.

257 f. undam fumus agit: cf. *Geo.* iii. 203 'spumas aget'.

260. in nodum, 'knotwise', 'in a knot': for the modal use of *in* cf. *in orbem* ('in a ring', 673), *in numerum* ('in rhythm', 453, *Geo.* iv. 175), *in uersum* ('in rows', *Geo.* iv. 144), *in plumam* ('featherwise', xi. 771), *in obliquum* ('aslant', *Geo.* i. 98), *in morem* ('ritually', 282) and such common phrases as *in uicem*, *in modum*.

260 f. angit ... elisos oculos: a compressed phrase, *angit* being more appropriate to *guttur* than to *oculos*, 'throttles him till his eyes start out and his throat is dry of blood'; *elisos* (cf. 289) and *siccum* are proleptic. For *oculos elidere*, 'squeeze out the eyes' cf. Plaut. *Rud.* 659 'oculos elidere itidem ut sepiis faciunt coqui.' For *siccus* with the ablative on the analogy of *uacuus* or *inanis* cf. ix. 64 'siccae sanguine fauces' (though there *sanguis* is not the wolf's own blood but that of his victims).

263. abiuratae, 'denied on oath' (cf. Plaut. *Rud.* 14 'abiurant pecuniam', 'denied that they had the money'): i.e. Hercules had challenged Cacus with the theft. Such references by implication to a previous element in the story which has not been mentioned (as this one is in Dionysius' prose account, i. 39. 3) is characteristic of the selective technique of Alexandrian narrative poetry.

265. expleri corda, 'glut their hearts': cf. i. 713 'expleri mentem nequit ardescitque tuendo': the passive form is used with the reflexive 'middle' force (see on vii. 503) which is commonest with participles.

268. ex illo, 'from that time', as in ii. 169: cf. 47 'ex quo'.

celebratus honos: cf. v. 58 'ergo agite et laetum cuncti celebremus honorem', xii. 840 'nec gens ulla tuos aeque celebrabit honores'. For the form *honos* see on vii. 3.

minores : a later generation, one must suppose, than those who had witnessed the events: while the expression would be natural if it were the poet's own proleptic aside (like 339 'memorant', 348 'aurea nunc', vii. 602 'nunc'), it is surprising to find it put into the mouth of Evander, who is himself a surviving witness (cf. 361). But in other respects also these lines look like an unfinished draft. *statuit* (271) is awkward whether its subject is the plural *Potitius et domus Pinaria* or (with a stop after 270) the unexpressed *Hercules*: the Potitii are given an unexpected role (see below): and the unparalleled repetition of 271–2 can perhaps be explained more readily than it can be condoned.

269 f. Potitius . . . Pinaria : see on 184–279.

269. primus . . . auctor, 'first originator': for the adjective reinforcing the noun see on vii. 371. Both *primus auctor* and *statuit* (with the punctuation of the Oxford Text) are difficult: while the establishment of the cult at Rome was probably in fact due to the two families, that is not how it is represented in the traditional legend, which makes the founder of the cult Hercules himself or Evander (see on 184–279). To stop after *sacri* and make the subject of *statuit* Hercules (for the introduction of a new subject which is not expressed cf. 546) removes the difficulty of *statuit* but makes that of *primus auctor* the more obvious.

271 f. quae maxima semper . . . quae maxima semper : the repetition (which Markland on Stat. *S.* iii. 1. 9 roundly condemned as un-Virgilian)[1] may be supposed to emphasize the

---

[1] The other Virgilian examples of repetition at the end of successive lines are all of a single word: *Geo.* i. 407 f. *auras*, iv. 341 f. *ambae*, *Aen.* vii. 653 f. *esset*, viii. 396 f. *fuisset*, ix. 544 f. *Helenor*, xi. 204 f. *partim*. (There are also examples of the repetition of the same word in a different case at i. 349 f., v. 569 f., vii. 553 f., viii. 330 f., xii. 617 f.) For a parallel to the repetition of a phrase one must go to Ovid, e.g. *Met.* i. 325 f., 361 f.

correspondence of the name with the reality: the altar will be what its title declares.

273. tantarum in munere laudum, 'by the way of honour to such glorious achievements': for *laudes* in the sense of *res laude dignae* cf. ix. 252 f. 'quae digna . . . pro laudibus istis / praemia posse rear solui', x. 825 f.: for the 'objective' genitive cf. vi. 637 'perfecto munere diuae' ('the offering to the goddess'); Prop. i. 10. 12 'accipe commissae munera laetitiae' ('recompense for'): for *in munere* cf. v. 536 ff. '(cratera) quem . . . / Anchisae . . . in magno munere Cisseus / ferre . . . dederat'.

274. fronde: for the wearing of a wreath in the performance of a ritual act see on vii. 135.

porgite: i.e. hold out in libation; the sense is repeated in *date uina.* The archaic syncopated form occurs only here in Virgil.

275. communem: Hercules has become *communis* to Evander's people and the Trojans by virtue of the new alliance.

276 ff. dixerat . . . cum . . . : no sooner had he spoken than a wreath was on his head and a cup in his hand. For the association of the poplar (*bicolor* because the under-side of its leaf is white) with Hercules cf. Theoc. 2. 121 λεύκαν, Ἡρακλέος ἱερὸν ἔρνος: *Ecl.* 7. 61 'populus Alcidae gratissima', *Geo.* ii. 66 'Herculeaeque arbos umbrosa coronae'; Prop. iv. 9. 29. The mention of the *scyphus*—the deep wooden drinking-cup (*impleuit* has its point) which belongs to simple rustic life (cf. Tib. i. 10. 8)—may also have a ritual reason, though perhaps not the reason which Macrobius offers (v. 21. 16), that the use of the capacious σκύφος was a regular attribute of Hercules—as indeed it was: cf. Stesich. 4 P.; σκύφος Ἡρακλέους was proverbial (Plut. *Alex.* 75. 3; Sen. *Ep.* 83. 23)—and that he brought one with him to Italy.

277. For *-que . . . -que* see on vii. 186.

279. in mensam . . . libant: cf. i. 736 (Dido at her banquet) 'in mensam laticum libauit honorem'.

280–369. *The ceremony is continued with sacrifice and feasting and a ritual dance and hymn. Then Evander conducts Aeneas to his home, telling him the history of the place and pointing out features of the scene which were to be famous in later days.*

280. deuexo . . . Olympo, 'as the heavens rolled down': *Olympus* is *caelum* (as in *Geo.* i. 450 'emenso . . . Olympo', iii. 223 'longus Olympus', *Aen.* x. 216 'medium pulsabat Olympum'; cf. Cat. 62. 1: so in Greek, Soph. *Ajax* 1389) and the notion is that of two hemispheres, one light and one dark, which succeed each other in revolution: cf. ii. 250 'uertitur interea caelum' (from Ennius), xi. 201 f. 'nox umida ... / inuertit caelum'; as the dark rolls into place, the evening star comes into sight.

282. in morem, 'ritually': cf. v. 556 'in morem tonsa coma pressa corona' and see on 260.

283. instaurant: they resume the ceremony: see on vii. 146. Servius' statement that the ritual had two parts, one in the morning and one in the evening, may be no more than an invention based on this account.

mensae grata secundae: the resemblance of the phrase to *Geo.* ii. 101 'mensis accepta secundis', where it is used in the special sense of a second course of fruit and wine which it had in Virgil's own time (cf. Cic. *Att.* xiv. 6. 2), suggests that the words have the same reference here: for the ana-chronism cf., e.g., i. 427 ff. (theatres in Dido's Carthage).

285. Salii: elsewhere the title belongs to the dancing priests who played a prominent part in the cult of Mars. Its ap-pearance here in a rite of Hercules puzzled Macrobius (iii. 12. 7): but Salii were associated, he says, with the cult of Hercules Victor at Tibur (he cites a work by Octavius Her-sennius *De sacris Saliaribus Tiburtium*). The Salii of Mars were divided into two groups of twelve, *palatini* and *collini*, but there is no evidence elsewhere for a division between *iuniores* and *seniores*.

ad cantus: 'appear to the sound of music', perhaps, rather than 'arrive to sing': cf. Liv. And. *trag.* 5 f. R. 'lasciuum Nerei simum pecus / ludens ad cantum' and the common *ad tibiam*, *ad numeros*.

287 f. laudes Herculeas: see on vii. 1.

288. prima is adverbial in sense: 'throttled as his first act the creatures sent by his stepmother, a pair of snakes'.

nouercae: Juno, as Jupiter's consort, is Hercules' step-mother, his mother being the mortal Alcmena, and *nouerca* has its usual implication of spitefulness: cf. *Ecl.* 3. 33, *Geo.* ii. 128, iii. 282, *Aen.* vii. 765.

290. disiecerit: cf. 355 'disiectis oppida muris', ii. 608 'disiectas moles' (of the ruins of Troy); Hor. *Od.* ii. 19. 14 f. 'tectaque Penthei / disiecta'.

291. Troiamque Oechaliamque: the reference to Hercules' destruction of Troy in punishment for the bad faith of Laomedon (*Il.* v. 638 ff.) is somewhat tactless in the presence of a Trojan guest: it is another matter when Anchises refers pathetically to the first destruction of Troy (ii. 642 f.) or when Turnus and Remulus contemptuously call their enemies *gens bis uicta* (xi. 402) and *bis capti Phryges* (ix. 599). Oechalia was destroyed because its king Eurytus, having offered his daughter

Iole to anyone who could defeat him in archery, cheated Hercules of his promise. For *-que . . . -que* see on vii. 186.

292. Eurystheo : for the synizesis of *-eo* cf. ix. 716 *Typhoeo*, x. 129 *Menestheo*, and see on vii. 33. That Hercules was condemned by Juno's spite to serve Eurystheus is Homer's story (*Il.* xviii. 119), but there were others.

fatis Iunonis: see on vii. 293 f., 313 ff.

293. tu . . . inuicte: the apostrophe, itself a poetic device to secure variety (see on vii. 49), involves an abrupt transition from reported speech to direct quotation of the hymn. Apollonius had used the same unusual technique in a hymn to Apollo (ii. 708): Conington cites a curious imitation of it by Milton, *P.L.* iv. 724. The anaphora of *tu—tu—te—te* is characteristic of the hymn style: cf. Cat. 34. 13 ff., 61. 51 ff.; Lucr. i. 6 ff.; Hor. *Od.* i. 10; and see E. Norden, *Agnostos Theos* (Berlin, 1913), 150 ff.

nubigenas . . . bimembris: the Centaurs: see on vii. 674 ff. According to Macrobius (vi. 5. 13), Cornificius had coined the adjective with his *centauros foedare bimembres*.

294. Pholum . . . mactas: the verb (see on vii. 93) awkwardly emphasizes what was not a very creditable exploit: when Hercules went to hunt the Erymanthian boar in Thessaly, Pholus was his host whom he killed in the course of a brawl with his fellow Centaurs (Apollod. ii. 5. 4). Virgil uses a different story in *Geo.* ii. 455 ff., where Pholus and Hylaeus meet their deaths in the fight between the Centaurs and the Lapiths.

mactas : for the present see on vii. 363.

294 f. Cresia . . . prodigia : the wild bull sent by Poseidon to ravage Crete.

295. uastum . . . leonem: for *uastus* see on vii. 302: the epithet becomes conventional: cf. Prop. ii. 19. 21 'uastos . . . temptare leones'; Man. iv. 176 'uasti . . . natura leonis', v. 228, 701; Sen. *Phaedra* 318.

297. semesa cruento: the gruesome picture hardly fits the usual representation of Cerberus: in Hesiod (*Theog.* 311 f.) he gobbles up anyone who tries to escape from Hades, but usually he is a watchdog, not a man-eater.

semesa: see on 194.

298. facies, 'shapes': see on vii. 448.

Typhoeus: the hundred-headed giant Typhoeus does not explicitly appear elsewhere as one of Hercules' adversaries, but the hero's own account of his exploits in Euripides, *H.F.* 1266 ff. includes λέοντας ἢ τρισωμάτους / Τυφῶνας ἢ Γίγαντας, and one story (cf. Pind. *N.* i. 67 ff.) made him help the gods in their battle against the giants in the Phlegraean plain.

299. arduus arma tenens, 'towering weapons in hand': cf. 683 'arduus agmen agens': for a similar description cf. vii. 784 '(Turnus) uertitur arma tenens et toto uertice supra est'.

rationis egentem : the phrase is Lucretian (iv. 502).

300. Lernaeus . . . anguis: the nine-headed Hydra (cf. vii. 658) of the marshes of Lerna in the Argolid.

301. uera Iouis proles: i.e. his ancestry is proved by his prowess: cf. vi. 322 'deum certissima proles', iv. 12 'nec uana fides genus esse deorum'; Prop. iv. 6. 60 'sum deus: est nostri sanguinis ista fides'.

decus addite diuis: i.e. 'qui additus es decus diuis': the construction supports 'canibus date praeda' at ix. 485 (cf. x. 507 'o dolor atque decus magnum rediture parenti'): for the thought cf. Hor. *Od.* ii. 19. 13 f. 'beatae coniugis (sc. Ariadnae) additum / stellis honorem'.

302. pede . . . secundo: cf. x. 255 'Phrygibusque adsis pede, diua, secundo'.

304. speluncam . . . ipsum, 'Cacus' cave and its master'.

305. resultant, 're-echo': so, more fully, v. 150 'pulsati colles clamore resultant': more naturally the echo is the subject in *Geo.* iv. 50 'uocisque offensa resultat imago'.

307. obsitus aeuo: *obsitus* is 'planted with', 'overgrown with' (so with *arbustis* Lucr. v. 1378, *frugibus* Cic. *Leg.* ii. 63), and so metaphorically 'covered with': cf. Ter. *Eun.* 236 'pannis annisque obsitum'; Livy ii. 23. 3 'obsita erat squalore uestis': similarly Plautus, *Men.* 756 f., has 'consitus sum / senectute'.

308. tenebat: kept them at his side in his slow progress; for *ingredi* used (like *incedere*) of a slow, deliberate motion cf. vi. 156 f. 'Aeneas maesto defixus lumina uultu / ingreditur linquens antrum': contrast x. 763 'turbidus ingreditur campo'.

310. facilis oculos: Manilius borrows the phrase, i. 649 'circumfer faciles oculos'.

311. capitur, 'is charmed': cf. *Geo.* iv. 348 'carmine . . . captae'.

312. monimenta, 'memorials': cf. 356, iii. 102 'ueterum . . . monimenta uirorum'; Cat. 11. 10 'Caesaris uisens monimenta magni'; Prop. iv. 6. 17 'Actia Iuleae pelagus monimenta carinae'. *monimentum* is what 'tells a story' and reminds (*monet*) those who see it of its associations: so of tokens which carry personal associations, *Aen.* iii. 486 (of Andromache's handiwork) 'manuum . . . monimenta mearum', iv. 497 f. 'abolere nefandi / cuncta uiri monimenta', xii. 945 'saeui monimenta doloris'.

313. Romanae conditor arcis: a glance into the future: Evander's settlement is the nucleus of the Palatine of Romulus and of Augustus.

314 ff. The myth of the successive ages of mankind appears first in Hesiod (*W.D.* 109 ff.): there the Golden Race of men is the first creation, living in primitive innocence, peace, and plenty, while Cronos ruled the world from Olympus: that is the conception of the *Saturnia regna* (Saturn being identified with Cronos) which Virgil implies in vii. 203 ff., as he does in *Eclogue* 4 and in *Geo.* i. 125 ff., on which Ovid enlarges in *Met.* i. 89 ff., and which becomes a commonplace in later literature. Here the conception is a different one and the setting is local: man's first condition in Italy was savage and Saturn, not now the all-ruling Cronos, but the god-king expelled from Olympus who has taken refuge in Italy (see on vii. 47 ff.), imposes the rule of law on its people and gives Italy its Golden Age. For a collection of the relevant texts and an account of the forms of the myth, see A. O. Lovejoy and G. Boas, *Primitivism and Related Ideas in Antiquity* (New York, 1965), 24 ff.

314. indigenae Fauni: see on vii. 47 ff. The multiplicity of Fauni is inconsistent with the place which Virgil has given to a singular Faunus in his pedigree of the Latin kings: here perhaps he has in mind Lucr. iv. 580 f. (of echoing places) 'haec loca capripedes satyros nymphasque tenere / finitimi fingunt et Faunos esse loquuntur'.

315. truncis ... nata: for the legend of the creation of man from inanimate nature, which finds particular forms in the myths of Prometheus and Deucalion (*Geo.* i. 62 f. 'uacuum lapides iactauit in orbem / unde homines nati, durum genus' —where *durum* has the same point as *duro* here—men are as tough as the wood and stones they spring from), cf. Lucr. v. 925 f. 'genus humanum multo fuit illud in aruis / durius, ut decuit, tellus quod dura creasset'; Juv. 6. 11 ff. 'aliter tunc orbe nouo caeloque recenti / uiuebant homines, qui rupto robore nati / compositiue luto nullos habuere parentes'.

316. neque mos neque cultus: *mos* is the system of social convention on which a settled way of life is based, *cultus* the acquisition of the arts of life.

317. componere, 'store away': cf. Hor. *Ep.* i. 1. 12 'condo et compono quae mox depromere possim'; Tib. i. 1. 77 f. 'composito securus aceruo / despiciam dites'. The verb appears in a different sense in 322: see on vii. 491.

318. rami: i.e. the berries or acorns from the branches.
    asper uictu uenatus, 'hunting with its hard fare': cf. i. 445 'facilem uictu ... gentem'.

319 f. Saturnus ... arma Iouis fugiens: for Saturn and the identification of him with Cronos see on vii. 47 ff.

322. composuit: i.e. made them into an ordered society: cf. iii. 387 'urbem componere', and see on 317 above.

323. maluit: i.e. decided that it be called Latium rather than anything else.

latuisset: for etymologies in Virgil see on vii. 3, 684: according to Servius, Varro had derived *Latium* from *latere* but offered the curious explanation 'quod latet Italia inter praecipitia Alpium et Appennini'.

325. sic explains *aurea*, 'so true was it that . . .'. The alliteration on *p* and *d* in this line and the next is conspicuous.

326. decolor: in the succeeding age the gold is 'tarnished.

327. belli rabies: cf. vii. 461 'insania belli', ix. 63 f. 'edendi . . . rabies'.

amor . . . habendi: cf. *Geo.* iv. 177 'innatus apes amor urget habendi'; Hor. *Ep.* i. 7. 75 'amore senescit habendi'.

328. manus Ausonia: see on vii. 39.

Sicanae: see on vii. 795.

329. nomen posuit, 'again and again Saturn's land gave up its name': Virgil is now thinking not of Latium but of the whole country and of those other names which he himself gives to it—Ausonia (vii. 55), Oenotria (vii. 85), Italia.

330. reges asperque . . . Thybris: for *-que* introducing a particular name after a general expression cf. vii. 535 'corpora multa uirum circa seniorque Galaesus'. The phrase *asper immani corpore* comes from Lucr. v. 33 'asper, acerba tuens, immani corpore serpens', a line which Virgil remembers in two other places (ix. 794, *Geo.* iii. 149).

As Servius' note here shows, the legends of the eponymous hero of the Tiber were manifold: in Livy (i. 3. 8), as Tiberinus, he appears in the royal dynasty of Alba Longa: Varro (*L.L.* v. 30) makes him Thebris, an Etruscan king of Veii, but knows of other stories. On the name of Tiber in Virgil see on vii. 30: he finds no difficulty in giving the same name here to the hero after whom the river is said to be called and in line 72 above to the immanent deity who is the river.

331 f. cognomine . . . diximus, 'from whom we Italians' (Virgil forgets that the speaker is an immigrant) 'called the river Thybris by way of name': for the ablative cf. xii. 845 'dicuntur geminae pestes cognomine Dirae'; for *cognomen* of a significant name see on vii. 3 and 671.

332. Albula: this 'original' name of Tiber, discovered or invented by antiquarians, appears, with a similar rationalizing story of the change of name, in Varro (*L.L.* v. 30, *Men.* 415) and later in Livy (i. 3. 8) and Dionysius (i. 71. 2).

333. pulsum patria: the reason for Evander's exile is uncertain: parricide, matricide, local hostility, a famine are the kind of explanations offered.

sequentem: see on vii. 606.

334. Fortuna ... fatum: *fortuna omnipotens*, the supreme power of chance, and *ineluctabile fatum*, the inevitable decree of destiny, are different (and indeed opposed) conceptions: Virgil seems to be identifying them here as he does in some other places where *fortuna* takes the place of an expected *fatum*, what is *fatum* by destiny being regarded from the standpoint of the human agent as his *fortuna*. See C. Bailey, *Religion in Virgil*, 234 ff.

335 f. matris ... Carmentis: Carmentis (or Carmenta: Livy has both forms, *-a* at i. 7. 8, *-is* at v. 47. 2) was a primitive Italian deity who still had her *flamen* and her January festival at Rome in Virgil's day and after it. Her associations were with childbirth (Ovid, *F.* i. 617 ff.: so Varro *ap.* Gell. xvi. 16. 4): the attribution of prophetic powers to her was no doubt based on a popular etymology of her name (cf. Ovid, *F.* i. 467 'quae nomen habes a carmine ductum'). In the Hellenizing Italian legend of Evander she takes the place (Dion. Hal. i. 31. 1; Plut. *Rom.* 21. 2) of the nymph, variously called Themis and Nicostrata, who is Evander's mother in Greek legend (Strabo v. 3. 3; Paus. viii. 43. 2), and comes with him to Latium, where she prophesies the rebirth of Troy and the glories of Rome (Ovid, *F.* i. 465 ff.). It is somewhat surprising that Virgil makes no dramatic use of a prophecy so closely related to his theme and mentions it only incidentally in line 340 without dwelling on its occasion or its import.

336. auctor Apollo: Apollo is the inspirer of the prophetess as in xii. 405 f. ('nihil auctor Apollo / subuenit') of the physician.

337 ff. Throughout this romantic account of Aeneas' sightseeing Virgil is anticipating later history—Asylum, *sedes Tarpeia*, Forum and Carinae all belong to later times, and *quam memorant* (339), *rettulit* (343), *nunc* and *olim* (348), *lautis* (361), are comments from the poet's own point of view —nor does he distinguish clearly, in his antiquarian enthusiasm, between what was to be seen in Evander's day and what was still to come: Evander had no reason to draw Aeneas' attention to the *ingens lucus* (342) for its own sake—its interest for Virgil's reader was what Evander did not know, that Romulus was to make it his Asylum. But he avoids explicit anachronism except in *monstrat ... portam*: while the altar of Carmentis at the foot of the Capitoline might plausibly be assigned to Evander's time, the adjoining gate which was called after it belonged to the wall of Servius.

337. dehinc is here disyllabic as at iii. 464, v. 722, xii. 87: at i. 131, 256, vi. 678, ix. 480 it becomes a monosyllable by synizesis.

339. memorant, 'call': cf. i. 327 'o quam te memorem, uirgo?'.
   honorem: the accusative is 'in apposition to the sentence';
   see on 683.
340 f. cecinit . . . Pallanteum : see on 335 f.
341. Pallanteum: see on 51 ff. For the spondaic ending see on
   vii. 631.
342. lucum ingentem: see on vii. 29.
   acer: a common epithet, with the implication of active
   energy (cf. 441, 614), usually related immediately to the
   situation (e.g. x. 308 f. 'rapit acer / totam aciem in Teucros',
   xii. 938 f. 'stetit acer in armis / Aeneas').
342 f. asylum rettulit: for the 'refuge' in a hollow between the
   two summits of the Capitoline hill which Romulus was said
   to have established to supply inhabitants for his new town,
   see Livy i. 8. 5; Plut. *Rom.* 9. At v. 596 ff., 'hunc morem
   cursus atque haec certamina primus / Ascanius, . . . / ret-
   tulit', the verb means 'reproduced from a model' (i.e.
   Trojan precedents) and probably it should be so understood
   here: whatever the primitive origins of this 'place of refuge'
   may have been, the fact that it is always called by the Greek
   name itself shows that Roman antiquarians supposed it to
   be modelled on those ἄσυλα which were a common feature
   of Greek life in legendary and in historical times.
343. The *Lupercal* was a cave at the southern end of the
   Palatine, the centre of the rites of the Lupercalia on 15
   February when, after sacrifice particularly prescribed, two
   troops of patrician Luperci, dressed in goat-skins, ran up
   and down the Via Sacra below the Palatine (in later times:
   originally probably round the hill), striking the bystanders
   with goat-skin whips. No ceremony in the Roman calendar
   was more primitive—the fact that it was not associated with
   any god itself points to a very early origin—or more obscure,
   and none had a longer history: Augustus took steps to regu-
   late it and control its excesses (Suet. *Aug.* 31. 4) and it was
   still an occasion of public diversion at the end of the fifth
   century, when Pope Gelasius, troubled by the disorders con-
   nected with it, turned it into the festival of the Purification
   of the Virgin. Its origin and purpose have been much dis-
   cussed: whether it was a piece of fertility magic (as the
   Romans themselves believed: see Ovid's account of it, *F.*
   ii. 267 ff.) or began as a pastoral ritual for the protection of
   the flocks, and whatever lies behind the name 'Luperci',
   there is no reason to doubt that Roman etymologists hap-
   pened to be right in deriving the name from *lupus*: that
   element in it was enough to encourage Hellenizing anti-
   quarians into identifying the rite with the Arcadian cult of

Pan *Λυκαῖος* (see L. R. Farnell, *Cults of the Greek States*
[Oxford, 1896–1909], v. 431 ff.), who derived his title from
the Arcadian mountain *Λυκαῖος*, his alleged birthplace: hence
here the Lupercal is 'named, after Arcadian custom, as be-
longing to Lycaean Pan' (cf. Livy i. 5. 2). In Ovid the identi-
fication of Pan with the Italian Faunus (see on vii. 47 ff.)
leads to the appearance of Faunus, with the extraordinary
title of 'Faunus Lycaeus', as the deity of the rite. See K.
Latte, *Röm. Rel.* 84 ff.; A. M. Franklin, *The Lupercalia* (New
York, 1921); A. K. Michels, *T.A.P.A.* lxxxiv (1953), 35 ff.

344. Parrhasio: i.e. *Arcadio* (cf. xi. 31 'Parrhasio Euandro').
The name Parrhasia for a region of Arcadia is already in
Homer (*Il.* ii. 608): in Latin poetry (and especially in Ovid)
the adjective becomes a stock literary equivalent of *Arcadius*.

345. nec non et: see on vii. 521.

345 f. Argileti . . . Argi: the Argiletum lay in the low ground
south of the Quirinal: in historical times it was a trading
quarter, where Cicero owned shops (*Att.* xii. 32. 3) and Mar-
tial's bookseller had his premises (i. 3. 1). The name clearly
meant 'clay-pits' (from *argilla*: a parallel formation to *ar-
boretum, quercetum, dumetum*), but popular etymology inter-
preted it as *Argi-letum* and invented an *aition* for it in the
story of an Argus who was Evander's guest and was killed
by Evander's people for seeking to dethrone his host.
Varro, *L.L.* v. 157, impartially offers both the true explana-
tion and the invention. For the spondaic ending see on vii.
631.

346. testaturque locum: i.e. calls on the place to tell its story:
the personification implied is that of such formulas as Cat.
64. 357 'testis erit magnis uirtutibus unda Scamandri';
Prop. iii. 7. 21 'sunt Agamemnonias testantia litora curas';
Hor. *Od* iv. 4. 37 f. 'quid debeas, o Roma, Neronibus, / testis
Metaurum flumen'; Tib. i. 7. 11.

347. Tarpeiam sedem: again Virgil anticipates: the *Tarpeia
sedes*—the *arx Tarpeia* of 652—is the Capitolium, and legend
derived the name from the betrayal of the citadel to the
Sabines by Tarpeia in the time of Romulus (Varro, *L.L.* v. 41;
Livy i. 11. 5–9; Prop. iv. 4).

Capitolia is a regular 'plural of convenience' in dactylic
verse (like *Palatia, Geo.* i. 499).

348. aurea: i.e. with gilded roof: cf. Prop. iv. 1. 5 (in a similar
contrast) 'fictilibus creuere deis haec aurea templa', ii. 31. 1 f.
The gilding of the Capitoline temple roof was a feature of the
rebuilding after the fire of 83 B.C. which had not then found
universal approval (Pliny, *N.H.* xxxiii. 57).

349 f. iam tum is emphatically repeated: even in these far-off

times, before the building of the temples we know, this was
a hallowed place: cf. vii. 643.

religio . . . dira, 'sinister awe': for *dirus* see on vii. 22, for
religio on vii. 172: cf. 597 f. 'ingens . . . lucus . . . / religione
patrum late sacer'. Seneca, quoting from the passage, de-
velops the idea (*Ep.* 41. 3): 'si tibi occurrit vetustis arboribus
et solitam altitudinem egressis frequens lucus et conspectum
caeli ramorum aliorum alios protegentium summouens ob-
tentu, illa proceritas siluae et secretum loci et admiratio
umbrae in aperto tam densae atque continuae fidem tibi
numinis facit'.

352. quis deus: see on vii. 38.

ipsum : i.e. in visible presence: cf. 31, *Geo.* i. 328 f.

353 f. cum saepe . . . concuteret: for the idiomatic use of *cum
saepe* for *cum, ut saepe fit*, cf. i. 148 f. 'ueluti magno in populo
cum saepe coorta est / seditio'; Lucr. iv. 34 f. 'in somnis
cum saepe figuras / contuimur miras'; so *Aen.* x. 723 'ceu
saepe', v. 273 'qualis saepe': for other examples see Munro
on Lucr. v. 1231. *uiderunt cum concuteret* can be substituted
for the normal *uiderunt concutientem* even in prose.

354. aegida concuteret: two different conceptions of the
divine αἰγίς appear in Homer—the result, probably, of the
concurrence in the word of two homonyms, the one meaning
'hurricane' (as in Aesch. *Choeph.* 593), the other 'goat-skin'
(Eur. *Cycl.* 360)—and Virgil has taken over both. In *Il.* iv.
167 ff. the αἰγίς of Zeus is something which he takes up and
brandishes (ἐπισείει) in his hand to dismay mankind: it is
dark (ἐρεμνή), like the storm-clouds, and it was made for him
by χαλκεὺς Ἥφαιστος (*Il.* xv. 308 ff.): so Apollo, when he has
it, takes it in his hand to shake (*Il.* xv. 229 ff.). The hurricane
is represented as a weapon wielded by the god. That is
clearly Virgil's picture of Jupiter's *aegis* here, where both
nigrantem and *concuteret* translate Homer. But elsewhere
(*Il.* xvii. 593 ff.) the αἰγίς of Zeus is not dark but radiant
(μαρμαρέη) and it is fringed (θυσσανόεσσα), and that picture is
elaborated when Athena has it: it seems to be conceived as
something worn, with a tasselled fringe (*Il.* ii. 447 f.) and with
the Gorgon's head on it: she throws it about her shoulders
(*Il.* v. 738 ff.) and Ares strikes her on it (*Il.* xxi. 400 f.): so in
the description of Athena in Aesch. *Eum.* 404, ῥοιβδοῦσα
κόλπον αἰγίδος suggests a garment hanging from the shoulders
and filling with the wind. This is the form taken by repre-
sentations of the *aegis* in art, where it is a sort of breast-
armour bearing the Gorgon's head in the centre, surrounded
by wreathed snakes (so it was in the Parthenon statue: Paus.
i. 24. 7 καί οἱ κατὰ τὸ στέρνον ἡ κεφάλη Μεδούσης) and this is the

aegis horrifica which Virgil describes in 435 ff. as being made for Pallas by the Cyclopes.

355. disiectis: cf. 290.

356. ueterum ... monimenta uirorum: so iii. 102: for *monimenta* see on 312, for *ueterum* on vii. 204.

357 f. Varro's account (in Augustine, *Ciu. Dei.* vii. 4) was that when Saturn came to Latium (cf. 323) Janus, who was then reigning there, received him and divided his kingdom with him, retaining his own settlement on the Janiculum while Saturn established his on what was later to become the Capitoline hill (cf. Ovid, *F.* i. 235 ff.; Fest. 430 L.; Macr. i. 7. 19 ff.). There is no evidence to support the view that the name Janiculum here belongs to one of the summits of the Capitoline, Saturnia being the other: Ovid (*F.* i. 241 f.)· certainly supposed Janus' citadel to be on the ridge across the Tiber which was the Janiculum in historical times. But the use of *huic* and *illi* to refer to the more distant and the nearer object respectively is awkward.

357. Ianus pater: see on 394 and cf. Hor. *Ep.* i. 16. 59 'Iane pater', *Sat.* ii. 6. 20 'Matutine pater, seu Iane libentius audis'.

358. fuerat, 'had been before it was changed': for this idiomatic use of the pluperfect defining a past state as prior to a past event which is not expressed cf. vii. 532 f. 'natorum Tyrrhi fuerat qui maximus (before he was killed), Almo, / sternitur' (similarly xii. 513 ff. 'neci ... mittit ... Menoeten, / Arcada, piscosae cui circum flumina Lernae / ars fuerat'), v. 397 f. 'si mihi quae quondam fuerat (before I grew old) ... si nunc foret illa iuuentas', x. 613 f. 'si mihi, quae quondam fuerat (before you changed) ... / uis in amore foret'. So, e.g., Ovid, *Tr.* iii. 11. 25 'non sum ego quod fueram'. See K.–S. ii. 1. p. 141.

359. talibus ... dictis: ablative of attendant circumstances, *dictis* being substantival as in vii. 249, 284.

360 f. uidebant ... mugire: Virgil has the same combination at iv. 490 f. 'mugire uidebis / sub pedibus terram et descendere montibus ornos'. For the conflation of sight and sound in a single image cf. Lucr. i. 255 f. 'laetas urbis pueris florere uidemus / frondiferasque nouis auibus canere undique siluas'; Prop. ii. 16. 49 'uidistis toto sonitus percurrere caelo'. See Norden on *Aen.* vi. 256 ff.: the evidence of Augustine that *uide* was freely used of perception other than that of sight (*Conf.* x. 35 'dicimus autem non solum uide quid luceat, ... sed etiam uide quid sonet, uide quid oleat, uide quid sapiat') refers to a more colloquial usage (which is shared by English 'see' and 'look').

361. Romano ... Carinis: both phrases are anticipatory. The point of the epithet *lautis*, 'smart', 'grand', contrasted with *pauperis* is clear: the Carinae, on the western end of the Esquiline, was in later times a fashionable residential quarter, where Pompey, Antony, and Quintus Cicero among others had houses. But the adjective, which begins as a colloquialism and usually has a familiar, sometimes a disparaging, tone, is surprising in this context.

Virgil does not say where Evander's quarters are, but *subibant* (359) perhaps suggests climbing and the view of the Forum and Carinae points to a site on the slope of the Palatine. If that is what he means, there is another foreshadowing of the future: for in his own time, as Warde Fowler points out, that was the position of Augustus' house (Suet. *Aug.* 72; Ovid, *Tr.* iii. 1. 31 ff.).

363. subiit: for the lengthening see on vii. 174.

cepit, 'had room for him': cf. ix. 644 'nec te Troia capit'; Juv. 10. 148 'hic est quem non capit Africa'.

364. aude . . . contemnere, 'have the moral courage to', 'make up your mind to': cf. Hor. *Ep.* i. 2. 40 'sapere aude'. The notion of effort is continued in *finge*: cf. *Geo.* ii. 407; Hor. *Ep.* i. 2. 64 f.

364 f. te quoque dignum finge deo: the reference of *deo* is difficult. Seneca, who quotes the passage twice (*Ep.* 18. 12 f., 34. 11), reads Stoic doctrine into it and expands with 'nemo alius est deo dignus quam qui opes contempsit'. But it is not clear that Virgil himself had in mind Stoic views of deity and of the duty of man to conform to the divine reason which directs the universe. It would be natural to refer *deo* to Hercules—'mould yourself to be worthy of your great predecessor, now a god'—but for the presence of *quoque*: that may be what Virgil intends if *quoque* merely points the correspondence (as καί might do) or if a *quoque* which would be appropriate in the first clause—'(tu quoque) aude contemnere opes', 'have the courage to do as he did'—is illogically inserted in the second.

Henry's view that *deus* is Jupiter and refers to the descent from him of both Hercules and Aeneas is untenable. Hercules' divine parentage has indeed been mentioned at line 301, but humility achieved by spiritual effort is not a quality obviously connected with a divine pedigree.

Juvenal alludes to the passage in an apology for an unpretentious meal: 11. 60 f. 'cum sis conuiua mihi promissus, habebis / Euandrum, uenies Tirynthius'.

365. ueni: see on vii. 470.

366. subter fastigia tecti, 'under the gabled roof': in ii. 302 f. 'summi fastigia tecti / ascensu supero' (cf. 458 'euado ad summi fastigia culminis') the phrase is used of Priam's palace; for *angusti* cf. *Geo.* iv. 296 'angustique imbrice tecti'.

367. ingentem is emphatically placed to contrast with *angusti*.

368. pelle Libystidis ursae: the same phrase is used of Acestes' dress in v. 37. The adjective is not found elsewhere and the form points to a Hellenistic source (the only occurrence in extant Greek is Ap. Rhod. iv. 1753 ἠπείροιο Λιβυστίδος): even if Africa is to be credited with bears in heroic times (Pliny believed it had none in historical times, *N.H.* viii. 228), the literary epithet is implausible in this context.

369. nox ruit, 'comes hurrying on': cf. ii. 250 f. 'ruit Oceano nox / inuoluens umbra magna terramque polumque', vi. 539: similarly of day, x. 256 f. 'interea reuoluta ruebat / matura iam luce dies'.

370-406. *Venus uses her blandishments on Vulcan and appeals to him to make arms for her son.*

The scene has its Homeric prototypes in *Il.* xviii. 428 ff. (Thetis' appeal to Hephaestus for arms for Achilles) and xiv. 159 ff. (Hera's exercise of her wiles on Zeus).

370. mater: for the emphatic position ('with a mother's concern') cf. *Geo.* iv. 357 'percussa noua mentem formidine mater': similarly xii. 412 'genetrix'.

371. duro . . . tumultu: cf. vii. 806 f. 'proelia . . . dura', x. 146 'duri certamina belli'.

372. aureo: see on vii. 33.

372 f. haec . . . incipit: for the ellipse cf. xi. 705.

373. dictis . . . amorem, 'breathes love into her words': there is perhaps a reminiscence of Lucr. i. 38 ff. 'hunc tu, diua, tuo recubantem corpore sancto / circumfusa super, suauis ex ore loquelas / funde'.

375. debita: i.e. owed (by destiny) to the destroyers, due for destruction (cf. Livy xxiv. 25. 3 'debitos iam morti destinatosque'): for a similar elliptical use cf. ix. 107 f. 'tempora Parcae / debita complerant'.

377. artis opisque tuae, 'arms that were within your skill and your resources': cf. i. 600 f. 'grates persoluere dignas / non opis est nostrae'.

377 f. nec te . . . exercere labores, 'put you or your endeavours to work': cf. 411 f. 'famulasque . . . longo / exercet penso'. Garrod's proposal of *incassum uetitos*—'I did not wish (it would have been vain) that you should ply forbidden labours' —neatly anticipates and gives point to Vulcan's rejoinder in 398: you should have asked me, says Vulcan; the fates did not forbid it as you thought. But there is no reason to suspect the text.

378–80. labores . . . laborem: for the fortuitous repetition of a word in a different sense see on vii. 491, 509.

379. Priami . . . natis: Venus is no doubt thinking primarily of her obligation to Paris for his judgement in her favour.

381. Iouis imperiis: cf. v. 726 'imperio Iouis huc uenio'.

382. eadem, 'after all': this common use of *idem* points a contrast between two inconsistent attributes or lines of conduct in the same person.

sanctum mihi numen: an unexpected description for Venus to apply to Vulcan in this context, but compare her address to her own son, Cupid, with the same sort of cajolery, at i. 666 'ad te confugio et supplex tua numina posco'. Macrobius (i. 24. 7) represents a critic as being shocked by Venus' appeal to her divine husband Vulcan on behalf of her son by the mortal Anchises: for Virgil there is no more impropriety here than in i. 667, where she speaks to Cupid of Aeneas as 'frater tuus'.

If a line ends in two disyllables, then the almost invariable pattern of the Virgilian hexameter, which shows the ictus of the verse and the speech-accent of the words coinciding in the last two feet, is liable to be disturbed by a conflict between ictus and accent in the fifth foot. That conflict is avoided when the first of the disyllables is enclitic (like an unemphatic personal pronoun) or forms with the preceding or the following word a word-group which is treated in speech as a single unit under one accent: so here *sanctúm-mihi*, x. 849 *miseró-mihi demum*, xii. 317 *iám-mihi sacra*, and so, e.g., i. 199 *hís-quoque finem*, 498 *pér-iuga Cynthi*, vi. 30 *tú-quoque magnam*, 123 *áb-Ioue summo*, x. 302 *puppís-tua Tarchon*, 400 *moráe-fuit Ilo*, xi. 562 *rapidúm-super amnem*, xii. 295 *atque ita-fátur*. But there are a number of cases in which there is marked conflict and the reason for departure from the norm is not clear: e.g. x. 440 *medium secat agmen*, xi. 143 *lucet uia longo*, 170 *magni Phryges et quam*. See E. Norden, *Aeneis VI*, p. 447; L. P. Wilkinson in *C.Q.* xxxiv (1940), 34 ff.

383. genetrix nato: the correlatives emphasize the bonds of affection between mother and son: cf. x. 600 'fratrem ne desere frater'.

filia Nerei: i.e. Thetis. In Virgil the genitive termination of Greek proper names in *-eus* is always monosyllabic *-ei*: cf. i. 41 *Oilei*, 120 *Ilionei*, xi. 262 *Protei*, 265 *Idomenei*.

384. Tithonia . . . coniunx: i.e. Eos, who in the cyclic *Aethiopis* appealed to Hephaestus for arms for her son Memnon.

385 f. moenia . . . ferrum acuant: an even bolder personification than vii. 629 f. 'urbes / tela nouant'.

clausis . . . portis: because they are at war: similarly of peace Hor. *Od.* iii. 5. 23 'portasque non clausas', *A.P.* 199 'apertis . . . portis'.

386. in me: Venus identifies herself with her protégés.

387 f. lacertis . . . amplexu: for the double ablative see on 219 f.

388. repente placed in contrast to *cunctantem* stresses the immediate effect of those allurements which Venus had exercised before (*solitam . . . notus*).

389. flammam . . . medullas: cf. iv. 66 'est mollis flamma medullas'; Cat. 64. 92 f. 'concepit corpore flammam / funditus atque imis exarsit tota medullis'.

390. labefacta: a favourite word of Lucretius': cf. iv. 1114 (in a similar reference) 'membra uoluptatis dum ui labefacta liquescunt', i. 492, v. 653.

  per ossa cucurrit: cf. ii. 120 f., vi. 54 f., xii. 447 f.: see on vii. 355.

391. olim, 'at times', 'from time to time': *olim*, a temporal adverbial form corresponding to *olle*, may refer to the past (as it most often does), to the future (e.g. i. 20, iv. 627), or to an indefinite time, as here: for this last archaic use cf. v. 124 ff. 'saxum . . . quod tumidis summersum tunditur olim / fluctibus', *Geo.* ii. 403 f. 'ac iam olim, seras posuit cum uinea frondes / . . . / iam tum acer curas uenientem extendit in annum / rusticus', iii. 303 f. 'cum frigidus olim / iam cadit extremoque inrorat Aquarius anno', iv. 421 'deprensis olim statio tutissima nautis'.

391 f. tonitru . . . nimbos, 'a rift of fire burst open by thunder runs flashing with sparkling light through the clouds'. The rhythm suggests taking *corusco* with *tonitru*, but while *coruscus* may refer to quick, trembling motion as well as to flashing light (so i. 164 f. 'siluis scaena coruscis / . . . imminet', xii. 701 f. 'coruscis / cum fremit (Appenninus) ilicibus'), it does not fit *tonitrus* in either sense. *lumine* needs an epithet more than *tonitrus* does and the lines look like a reminiscence of Lucr. vi. 282 ff. 'maturum tum quasi fulmen / perscindit subito nubem, ferturque coruscis / omnia luminibus lustrans loca percitus ardor'.

393. sensit: for the absolute use cf. iii. 669 'sensit, et ad sonitum uocis uestigia torsit'.

394. pater is 'generale omnium deorum', as Servius (on *Geo.* ii. 4) rightly says: so again of Vulcan, 454; similarly 'pater Tiberinus' (*Geo.* iv. 369), 'pater Appenninus' (*Aen.* xii. 703).

  aeterno . . . deuinctus amore: the phrase is clearly a reminiscence of Lucr. i. 34 (of Mars overwhelmed by love for Venus) 'aeterno deuictus uulnere amoris' which Virgil has varied by a change of verb.

aeterno, 'life-long' or 'age-long' rather than 'eternal': the love of immortals may indeed be eternal, but *aeternus* (originally *aeuiternus*) commonly refers to the span of life: cf. xi. 583 f. '(Camilla) aeternum telorum et uirginitatis amorem / intemerata colit', iv. 99 f. 'quin potius pacem aeternam pactosque hymenaeos / exercemus?'; Ter. *Eun.* 872 f. 'spero aeternam inter nos gratiam / fore'; Cic. *Sull.* 28 'cum mihi uni cum omnibus improbis aeternum uideam bellum esse susceptum'.

395. ex alto, 'why do you look so far back for a plea?': cf. Accius 160 R. 'cur uetera tam ex alto adpetissis discidia?'; Cic. *Fam.* iii. 5. 1 'quae de nostris officiis ... scripserim ... quoniam ex alto repetita sint': similarly *altius, Geo.* iv. 285. For *causa,* 'plea', cf. ix. 219 'causas nequiquam nectis inanis'.

395 f. fiducia cessit quo tibi?: cf. ii. 595 'quonam nostri tibi cura recessit?'. For the genitive cf. i. 132 'generis ... fiducia'.

396 f. fuisset ... fuisset: the repetition seems to emphasize the correspondence between the desire of Venus and Vulcan's ability to comply: cf. 271 f.

398. nec fata uetabant: for the conceptions of fate in Virgil see on vii. 313 ff.

402. electro: for the spondaic ending see on vii. 631. *electrum,* which is amber in *Ecl.* 8. 54, *Geo.* iii. 522, is here (as in 624) a metal—an alloy of gold and silver (according to Pliny, *N.H.* xxxiii. 80, in the proportion of four to one), which took its name from its resemblance in colour to amber: cf. Homer, *Od.* iv. 72 f.

403. animae: the wind of the bellows, the *aurae* of 449: for *animae* used of wind cf. Lucr. v. 1230 'uentorum ... paces animasque secundas'; Hor. *Od.* iv. 12. 2 'impellunt animae lintea Thraciae'.

absiste: Vulcan's vigorous undertaking—the vigour seems to be stressed by the assonance of *quicquid ... quod ... quantum*—breaks off, without the expected *promitto* or *accipias,* in an excited anacoluthon.

404. indubitare, 'cease from mistrusting my powers by your prayers': the compound first occurs here. For the infinitive with *absisto,* first found in Virgil, cf. vi. 399 'absiste moueri', xii. 676 'absiste morari'.

405. optatos ... amplexus: cf. Cat. 64. 372 'optatos animi coniungite amores'. (*optatus* is a favourite word of Catullus' in contexts of love: cf. 62. 30, 64. 31, 141, 328, 66. 79.)

405 f. petiuit ... per membra soporem: cf. 30 'dedit per membra quietem'.

407–53. *Vulcan rises early to go to his forge where his workmen, the Cyclopes, are busy: he orders them to leave the various tasks on which they are engaged and press on with a new piece of work, the arms which he has promised for Aeneas.*

407 f. ubi prima quies ... somnum: 'in the mid course of departing night when first repose had banished sleep', i.e. as soon as the sleeper had rested enough and was ready to rise, when night had reached the middle of her course and had begun to move from the sky. For *ubi prima* representing *ubi primum* cf. ii. 268 f. 'tempus erat quo prima quies mortalibus aegris / incipit', iii. 69 'ubi prima fides pelago'. For *abactae* without past force taking the place of a present participle see on 636; the notion is made more explicit in iii. 512 f. 'necdum orbem medium Nox Horis acta subibat: / haud segnis strato surgit' (where the sleeper rises just before, as here just after, the middle of the night): cf. also v. 721 'Nox atra polum bigis subuecta tenebat', 835 f. 'iamque fere mediam caeli Nox umida metam / contigerat'.

408 ff. cum femina ... natos: to this vignette of the woman rising early to spin, charmingly vivid but curiously inappropriate in the context as an indication of time and incongruous when it is turned into a simile at line 414, three epic similes in which the same motive is used, in quite different contexts, by Homer and Apollonius, have contributed: the rekindling of the fire comes from Ap. Rhod. iii. 291 ff. ὡς δὲ γυνὴ μαλερῷ περὶ κάρφεα χεύατο δαλῷ / χερνῆτις, τῇπερ ταλασήια ἔργα μέμηλεν, / ὣς κεν ὑπωρόφιον νύκτωρ σέλας ἐντύναιτο, / ἄγχι μάλ' ἐγρομένη· τὸ δ' ἀθέσφατον ἐξ ὀλίγοιο / δαλοῦ ἀνεγρόμενον σὺν κάρφεα πάντ' ἀμαθύνει (where the comparison is with the fire of love kindled in Medea's heart); the woman's hard lot comes from iv. 1062 ff. οἷον ὅτε κλωστῆρα γυνὴ ταλαεργὸς ἑλίσσει / ἐννυχίη, τῇ δ' ἀμφὶ κινύρεται ὀρφανὰ τέκνα, / χηροσύνῃ πόσιος· σταλάει δ' ἐπὶ δάκρυ παρειάς / μνωομένης οἵη μιν ἐπισμυγερὴ λάβεν αἶσα (where the comparison is with Medea's tears); the last words come from *Il.* xii. 433 ff. ἀλλ' ἔχον ὥς τε τάλαντα γυνὴ χερνῆτις ἀληθής, / ἥ τε σταθμὸν ἔχουσα καὶ εἴριον ἀμφὶς ἀνέλκει / ἰσάζουσ', ἵνα παισὶν ἀεικέα μισθὸν ἄρηται (where the point is the spinner's weighing of her wool). Virgil's picture is of a widow working to maintain her children and—a characteristically Roman addition—to preserve her own good name as *uniuira*: for the prejudice against a second marriage cf. Prop. iv. 11. 36 and the frequent occurrence of *uniuira* as a title of respect in sepulchral inscriptions; Dido's declaration in iv. 15 ff. represents the same feeling.

The repeated alliteration in these lines is striking.

409 f. tolerare ... impositum, 'whose burden it is to support

life by means of the distaff and Minerva's humble work'.
For the metonymy of *Minerua* applied to spinning and
weaving, see on vii. 113: for the adjective cf. Tib. ii. 1. 65
'assiduae textrix . . . Mineruae'; Ovid, *Met.* iv. 33 'intem-
pestiua . . . Minerua'. The meaning 'fine' for *tenui* (cf. vii. 14
'tenuis . . . telas') does not suit this context: it is rather
'humble', 'unpretentious' (cf. *Geo.* i. 177 'tenuis . . . curas',
iv. 6 'in tenui labor').

410. sopitos suscitat ignis: cf. 542 f. 'sopitas ignibus aras /
excitat': similarly in other scenes from humble life, Ovid,
Met. viii. 641 f. '(Baucis) inque foco tepidum cinerem dimouit
et ignes / suscitat hesternos'; *Moretum* 8 ff.

411. ad lumina 'by the firelight' or 'by torchlight': cf. *Geo.* i.
291 (a similar scene) 'hiberni ad luminis ignis', *Aen.* iv. 513
'ad lunam'.

411 f. famulas . . . penso: cf. *Geo.* i. 390 'nocturna . . . car-
pentes pensa puellae'.

413. educere, 'bring up': the use of *educere* as a synonym of
educare, which is not uncommon in prose, is made necessary
in hexameters by the metrical difficulty of most forms of
educare (*educat*, which Virgil has at x. 518, is an exception):
see on vii. 762.

414. ignipotens: the epithet for Vulcan is found first in Virgil,
but the compound (cf. ix. 717 'armipotens', xi. 8 'bellipo-
tens') belongs to a type favoured by earlier poets.

416 ff. insula . . . erigitur . . . quam . . . hoc tunc: for this nar-
rative formula see on vii. 563 ff.

   insula : the island associated with the activities of the
divine smith in the West, the nearest to Sicily of the group
of seven volcanic islands (the largest of them was its neigh-
bour Lipare, where popular belief placed the home of Aeolus,
ruler of the winds) which lies between Vesuvius and Etna,
was called Hiera, 'the sacred island', by the Greeks (e.g.
Thuc. iii. 88), Volcania (cf. 422) by the Romans. (It retains
that name, as Vulcano, today.) But Vulcan's forge and its
labour-force of Cyclopes (who appear first in Hesiod in that
function) is sometimes placed under Etna itself (e.g. *Geo.* iv.
173) and Virgil can call the cavern-workshops *Aetnaea* and
the workmen *Aetnaei* here without being committed to any
precise view of the subterranean topography of the region.
The whole passage is reminiscent of a similar scene in Calli-
machus, *Hymn.* 3. 46 ff., where, however, the forge in which
the Cyclopes work is in Lipare.

416. Sĭcănium: so iii. 692 *Sĭcănio*, but v. 24 *Sĭcānos*, 293,
vii. 795 *Sĭcāni*: for the variation of quantity see on vii. 85,
359.

418. exesa: cf. *Geo.* iv. 418 f. 'specus ingens / exesi latere in montis'.
419. incudibus: for the local ablative attached to a noun see on vii. 140.
420 f. The alliteration on *s* represents the sound of the hissing metal as in *Geo.* iv. 262 ('mare sollicitum stridit refluentibus undis') it represents that of the sea.
421. stricturae: *stringere* is technically 'to smelt', i.e. to run molten iron through moulds (hence the appropriateness of the verb) into ingots (cf. Cat. 66. 50 'ferri stringere duritiem'; Pers. 2. 66 f. 'stringere uenas / feruentis massae crudo de puluere') and *stricturae* are the ingots or bars of pig-iron which hiss as they are cooled in the tank (cf. 450 f. 'stridentia tingunt / aera lacu').

Chalybum here, as in x. 174 ('Chalybum . . . metallis'), is a literary cliché: the Chalybes (who appear in Xenophon's itinerary, *Anab.* v. 5. 1, as a real tribe of ironworkers on the south-eastern shore of the Black Sea) are in literature from Aeschylus (*Sept.* 728) onwards the legendary discoverers of iron-working. (The common noun χάλυψ, 'steel', which makes its first appearance in Latin here (446), seems to have had its origin in the proper name.) Cf. Ap. Rhod. ii. 1001 ff.; Cat. 66. 48.
423. hoc: the explicit testimony of Servius on this line (repeated in a confused note on i. 4) and of Priscian (*Gramm. Lat.* K. iii. 64. 7), that Virgil here used the archaic form of the adverb is the more puzzling since the normal *huc* appears many times elsewhere (seven times in this book): so far as euphony is concerned, cf. *Geo.* iv. 62 'huc tu', *Aen.* x. 680 'nunc huc nunc'.
424. uasto: see on vii. 302.
425. Brontes ('thunderer') and Steropes ('lightener') as names for Cyclopes come direct from Hesiod, *Theog.* 140 Βρόντην τε Στερόπην τε, as the lengthening of the first -*que* in imitation of Greek practice clearly shows: see on vii. 186. Pyracmon ('fire-anvil'), substituted here for Hesiod's Arges as the third member of the trio, is found nowhere else.

nudus: as foundrymen (within the current limits of convention) have always been: cf. *Geo.* i. 58 '(mittunt) Chalybes nudi ferrum'.
426 f. his . . . erat, 'they had a thunderbolt shaped by their hands, part already finished': *his* should probably be taken thus as dative masculine in spite of the awkward proximity of *manibus*. *informare* is to give an object its initial shape, *polire* to 'finish' any piece of workmanship, not necessarily metal (cf. Varro, *R.R.* i. 2. 10 'regie polita aedificia'; Enn.

Ann. 319 f. V. 'causa poliendi / agri'): but Virgil uses *polire* of metal in 436 below and here he probably has Apollonius' παμφαίνων (see on 429) in mind.

427. quae plurima, 'one of the many which . . .': the formula is Homeric: e.g. *Od.* v. 421 f. κῆτος . . . οἷά τε πολλὰ τρέφει κλυτὸς Ἀμφιτρίτη, viii. 160 ἄθλων, οἷά τε πολλὰ μετ' ἀνθρώποισι πέλονται. But the idiom is not unknown in prose: cf., e.g., Cic. *Mil.* 9 'si tempus est ullum iure hominis necandi, quae multa sunt'.

429. imbris torti radios: Virgil represents the constituents of tempest, rain, cloud, fire, and wind, as the shafts (*radii*, ἀκτῖνες) which are combined to make up the thunderbolt as it is conventionally portrayed in art: the idea comes from Apollonius, i. 730 ff., where the Cyclopes are Ζηνὶ κεραυνὸν ἄνακτι ποιεύμενοι· ὃς τόσον ἤδη / παμφαίνων ἐτέτυκτο, μιῆς δ' ἔτι δεύετο μοῦνον / ἀκτῖνος (which they make from fire). With characteristic confusion of physical and non-physical, he makes flash and crash, terror and flaming rage, ingredients in its composition. *imbris torti* is rain discharged as a missile (cf. iv. 208 'fulmina torques'): similarly ix. 670 f. 'Iuppiter horridus Austris / torquet aquosam hiemem'. Virgil no doubt is thinking of hail, but *torti* does not mean 'constricti et coacti in grandinem' (Servius).

432. flammisque sequacibus iras: for the plural *irae* see on vii. 445: in the descriptive ablative attached to it a metaphor is made actual.

434. instabant, 'were pressing on with': a neologism, says Servius, but Novius had said (61 R.) 'instat mercaturam: spero, rem faciet': Virgil has a similar transitive use of *properare* below (454 'haec . . . properat') and in the similar context of *Geo.* iv. 170 f. 'lentis Cyclopes fulmina massis / cum properant'.

435 ff. aegida . . . collo: see on 354.

435. horriferam: the irregularly formed compound belongs to earlier poetry: Pacuvius, Accius, and Lucretius had all used it.

   turbatae : a word of which Virgil makes varied and effective use: of Pallas here when her serenity is disconcerted by her enemies; of Aeneas, his composure shaken by the realities of war (viii. 29 'tristi turbatus pectora bello': so of Latinus, xi. 470 'tristi turbatus tempore'); of the panic of men caught in a trap (ix. 538: cf. xi 618); of horses shying in terror (vii. 767, ix. 124); of the consternation of the cornered Cacus (viii. 223); of the Trojans demoralized at the sight of Turnus (ix. 735); of Juturna shattered by the sudden knowledge of her brother's doom (xii. 160 'incertam et tristi turbatam uulnere mentis'); most effectively of all, of the gallant unsuspecting Camilla when she sees death before her eyes (xi. 796 'subita turbatam morte').

436. squamis . . . auroque: the same hendiadys (see on vii. 15, 142) as in ix. 707 'duplici squama lorica fidelis et auro'.

polibant: see on 426 f. above. For the form see on vii. 485.

437. ipsam marks the central figure.

439. auferte labores: for the concrete use of *labor*, cf. vii. 248 'Iliadumque labor uestes', ii. 306 'sata laeta boumque labores'.

441. acri . . . uiro, 'a man of mettle': cf. xi. 47 f. 'metuensque moneret / acris esse uiros': and see on 342 'Romulus acer'.

442. omni arte magistra, 'the guidance of all your skill': cf. xii. 427 f. 'non haec . . . arte magistra / proueniunt'.

443. praecipitate moras: xii. 699 'praecipitatque moras omnis' suggests that the notion is 'sweep obstacles away before you'.

445. sortiti : probably participial, 'they set to work speedily and dividing the work fairly among them': for the co-ordination of adverb and adjectival phrase cf. iv. 102 f. 'communem hunc ergo populum paribusque regamus / auspiciis', v. 498 'extremus galeaque ima subsedit Acestes', vi. 640 f. 'largior hic campos aether et lumine uestit / purpureo'. The whimsical notion of demarcation of work—*pariter sortiti* is explained in 447 ff.—does not appear in the other descriptions of the divine foundry.

446. uulnificus: see on vii. 324.

chalybs : see on 421.

uasta fornace: cf. Lucr. vi. 681 'uastis Aetnae fornacibus'. For *uastus* see on vii. 302.

447. unum omnia contra: 'by itself opposing all the missiles of the Latins', probably (in view of the use of *contra tela* elsewhere: ix. 552, xi. 282), rather than 'countervailing against' (which the emphatic juxtaposition of *unum omnia* might suggest: cf. iii. 435 'unum illud . . . proque omnibus unum', 'as good as all else').

448 f. septenos orbibus orbis impediunt: *orbes* must be the circular layers of which the shield is composed, the πτύχες of the Homeric shield—Ajax's shield (*Il.* vii. 245 ff.) has seven of hide and one of metal, Achilles' (*Il.* xx. 269 ff.) five πτύχες of three different metals: Turnus' shield too has seven layers (*septemplex*, xii. 925)—and *orbibus orbis impedire* must mean binding these layers to one another. (For somewhat similar uses of *impedire* cf. Hor. *Od.* i. 4. 9 'caput impedire myrto', *Sat.* i. 6. 27 f. 'medium impediit crus / pellibus'.) Virgil uses the phrase 'orbibus orbis impediunt' at v. 584 f. in an entirely different context of the equestrian manœuvres in which the riders weave intersecting circles in a pattern. (For his habit of repeating a phrase with entirely changed meaning see on vii. 509.) For *septenos* see on vii. 538: the layers of the shield make up a 'set' of seven.

449–52. The lines are repeated, with the change of four words (*uentosis* for *taurinis*, *antrum* for *Aetnam*, *multa* for *magna*, and *massam* for *ferrum*) from the simile of *Geo.* iv. 171–5.

450 f. stridentia . . . lacu: cf. Ovid, *Met.* ix. 170 f. 'gelido ceu quondam lamina candens / tincta lacu stridit'. *lacus* is no heroic euphuism but the ordinary word for the blacksmith's tank, as it is for the vintner's vat.

452. The heavily spondaic rhythm is expressive of the physical effort.

453. in numerum, 'in time': cf. *Ecl.* 6. 27 f. 'in numerum . . . ludere': see on 260.

454–519. *Next morning Evander tells Aeneas that he cannot provide assistance himself but that it can be found in Etruria, where the people of Caere have deposed their king Mezentius, who has taken refuge with Turnus. Wishing to pursue him there and advised by oracles to look for a foreign leader, they had appealed to Evander, who had told them that he himself was prevented by age and his son Pallas by his half-Italian birth. He now urges Aeneas to present himself as their leader and offers to send Pallas with him.*

454. haec . . . properat: for the transitive use cf. *Geo.* iv. 170 f. (in the same context) 'Cyclopes fulmina massis / cum properant', *Aen.* xii. 425 'arma . . . properate', *Geo.* i. 260 'forent quae mox caelo properanda sereno'.

pater . . . Lemnius: cf. 394: when Hephaestus was thrown out of heaven by Zeus, he fell on Lemnos (*Il.* i. 593): the island was his resort (*Od.* viii. 283), and his workshops were sometimes placed there (Cic. *N.D.* iii. 55 'Lemni fabricae traditur praefuisse').

Aeoliis : cf. 416.

455. lux . . . alma : cf. iii. 311. The contrast between the all-night activity in the divine workshops and the gentle peace of early morning in rural Pallanteum is effective.

456. matutini uolucrum . . . cantus: the swallows or martins twittering under the eaves: the *culmen* is the roof of the *humile tectum* under which they lodge (cf. *Geo.* iv. 307 'garrula . . . tignis nidum suspendat hirundo'): for the ὑπόρθριαι φωναί of the λάλη χελιδών waking the sleeper, cf. Ps.-Anacr. 9. 9. The crowing of the cock, the conventional herald of the dawn in literature from Hesiod onwards (of which Silius uses the phrase, xiv. 22), is less likely here, not because cocks in heroic times would be an anachronism but because *sub culmine* does not suit the cock's habits (and Virgil's

contemporaries at any rate kept their fowls in low sheds:
Varro, *R.R.* iii. 9. 6).

457 ff. The description follows the Homeric pattern of *Il.* ii.
42 ff. (ἕζετο δ' ὀρθωθείς, μαλακὸν δ' ἔνδυνε χιτῶνα | . . . | ποσσὶ δ' ὑπὸ
λιπαροῖσιν ἐδήσατο καλὰ πέδιλα, | ἀμφὶ δ' ἄρ' ὤμοισιν βάλετο ξίφος
ἀργυρόηλον: cf. *Od.* ii. 2 ff.) with the characteristic addition of
the 'ornamental' local epithets.

457. tunicaque inducitur artus, 'clothes his limbs with a tunic':
for the 'middle' use see on vii. 503.

458 f. Tyrrhena . . . Tegeaeum: the reference of the second
epithet is simple: *Tegeaeus* is *Arcadius* (cf. v. 299) and Evan-
der is an Arcadian. The first probably refers, as Servius sug-
gests, to the belief that the senatorial shoe with its straps
(a simplification, perhaps, of the shoe with upturned toes,
calceus repandus, which survived in religious use) had its
origin, as it may well have had, in Etruscan royal or priestly
dress. (Pollux vii. 92 gives Τυρρηνικὰ πέδιλα as a technical term
for sandals with wooden soles and gilded straps, adding that
Phidias' famous statue represented Athena as wearing them.)
For *uincula* of a shoe cf. iv. 518 'unum exuta pedem uinclis'.

459. umeris: cf. ὤμοισι in *Il.* ii. 45 quoted above: the sword-
belt holding the sword at the left side passed over the right
shoulder.

460. demissa is proleptic, 'flinging it back to hang on the left':
cf. vii. 666, where *torquens* is used of the same action. For
tergum, 'hide', see on vii. 20.

461. nec non et: see on vii. 521.

461 f. gemini custodes . . . canes : another Homeric touch;
Telemachus walks with his dogs, *Od.* ii. 11 οὐκ οἶος, ἅμα τῷ γε
κύνες πόδας ἀργοὶ ἕποντο (cf. xvii. 62).

461. limine ab alto : the conventional epithet for a princely
dwelling (cf. xi. 235 'alta . . . limina', of Latinus' home)
is strikingly inconsistent with the *humili tecto* of 455, but
that does not justify the change to *arto* proposed by Mark-
land.

462. gressum . . . erilem: cf. vii. 490 'mensae . . . erili' and the
common 'filius erilis' of comedy: see on vii. 1.

463. sedem et secreta: i.e. *sedem secretam*, his private quarters;
for *secreta* cf. *Geo.* iv. 403 'secreta senis' (of Proteus' lair),
Aen. vi. 10 'secreta Sibyllae'.

At 366 Evander lodged Aeneas in his own house: here he
seems to go out to find his guest in other quarters. Consistency
can be secured if *limine ab alto* is to be taken closely with
custodes (*canes*) and the dogs that guard the door go with
their master through the house.

464. promissi muneris: i.e. the help he had promised at 170 f.

heros: that the position of the word is meant to carry special emphasis, as Conington suggests, may be doubted: Virgil has *heros* in this position eighteen times and only once in another.

465. matutinus: for the personal use of the adjective of time (so in Homer ἠοῖος, ἑσπέριος, and χθιζός) cf. *Geo.* iii. 537 f. 'lupus . . . nocturnus obambulat', *Aen.* iv. 303 'nocturnusque uocat clamore Cithaeron'; Hor. *Epod.* 16. 51 'uespertinus circumgemit ursus ouile'.

se . . . agebat, 'was bestirring himself': cf. vi. 337, ix. 696.

467 f. mediis . . . aedibus: Virgil is no doubt thinking here, as in ii. 512, of the Roman house with its central atrium.

468. licito: i.e. the free talk for which they have not had opportunity before.

469. For Virgil's incomplete lines see on vii. 129.

472. pro nomine tanto: 'our strength is small in comparison with our great name' rather than 'in comparison with your great name': a touch of characteristic self-complacence on Evander's part is more effective than mere flattery.

473. Tusco . . . amni: i.e. the Tiber, rising in Etruria: so x. 199.

474. Rutulus: it is surprising to find the Rutulians threatening Evander on his unprotected side at a time when they have been mobilized against the Trojans (vii. 793 ff.).

475 f. opulentaque regnis . . . castra, 'armies rich in kingdoms': a bold phrase—and an extravagant one: Etruria had its kingdoms, twelve by tradition, but only one of them is in prospect here.

476. quam . . . salutem: for the construction cf. i. 187 f. 'arcumque . . . celerisque sagittas / . . . quae tela gerebat Achates', iv. 262 ff. 'ensis erat Tyrioque ardebat murice laena / . . . diues quae munera Dido / fecerat'.

477. fatis . . . poscentibus: for *poscere* see on 12.

478. saxo . . . fundata uetusto : cf. iii. 84 'templa dei saxo . . . structa uetusto'.

479. urbis Agyllinae sedes: for the defining genitive see on vii. 209. Agylla was the earlier name of the Etruscan hill-town of Caere, thirty miles north of Rome.

479 f. Lydia . . . gens: the tradition that the Etruscans were immigrants from Lydia goes back to Herodotus (i. 94), who dates their migration, led by the king's son Tyrrhenus at a time of famine in Lydia, to the period of the Trojan War. Thereafter it is an accepted commonplace: the only dissentient is Dionysius (i. 30), who rejects it on grounds which are not unreasonable but inadequate. For Virgil himself the Tiber, the *Tuscus amnis* of 473, is *Lydius Thybris* (ii. 781 f.), and the Etruscans are *Lydi* (ix. 11: cf. x. 155); for Catullus (31. 13) the waves of Benacus are *Lydiae* because the empire of the Etruscans had extended over the Po basin before they were dislodged by the Gauls in the fourth century. A deputation from Sardis appearing before the Senate in A.D. 26 claims kinship with Etruria (Tac. *Ann.* iv. 55. 7); and Seneca can say epigrammatically 'Tuscos Asia sibi uindicat' (*Dial.* 12. 7. 2). The tradition of Asiatic origin has not been decisively proved or disproved by archaeological and other evidence: it may have had a basis in a westward migration, in the unsettlement which followed the fall of Mycenaean civilization, of a people from Asia Minor which imposed itself on a local population to produce the highly developed Etruscan culture of early historical times. See M. Pallottino, *The Etruscans* (Eng. tr., Penguin Books, 1955), 53 ff.; H. H. Scullard, *The Etruscan Cities and Rome* (London, 1967), 34 ff.

485 ff. mortua . . . necabat: this Etruscan torture is not Virgil's invention; Cicero describes it in a fragment of the *Hortensius* (95 M.) preserved by Augustine: 'fit ut . . . uerum sit illud quod est apud Aristotelem, simili nos affectos esse supplicio atque eos qui quondam cum in praedonum Etruscorum manus incidissent, crudelitate excogitata necabantur; quorum corpora uiua cum mortuis, aduersa aduersis accommodata, quam aptissime colligabantur: sic nostros animos cum corporibus copulatos ut uiuos cum mortuis esse coniunctos'.

486. -que . . . atque: for the rare combination cf. *Geo.* i. 182, iii. 434: the only earlier example is Lucr. v. 31.

487. tormenti genus: for the accusative 'in apposition to the sentence' see on 683; the phrase is strangely prosaic.

488. sic is resumptive, summing up the circumstantial phrases which precede: see on vii. 668.

489. infanda furentem, 'in his unutterable madness': cf. 248 'insueta rudentem'.

491. ignem . . . iactant: cf. ii. 478 'flammas ad culmina iactant'.

493. confugere . . . defendier: for the 'historic' infinitive see on vii. 15; for the infinitive in *-ier*, on vii. 70.

494. furiis: see on 219 f.

495. praesenti Marte, 'with immediate war'.

497. fremunt . . . puppes: the transference from men to ships of the verb expressing inarticulate noise (see on vii. 389) is an easy one (cf. 717 'laetitia ludisque uiae plausuque fremebant'): with *iubent* a new general subject ('they call for battle') might be understood (cf. 552 'ducunt', vii. 79 'canebant'), but Virgil has as bold an example of transference at 385 f. 'quae moenia clausis / ferrum acuant portis': see also on 107 f.

condensae : a favourite adjective of Lucretius'.

Virgil's account of Etruscan movements is more picturesque than clear. The force which was impatiently preparing to embark from Etruscan shores (497) has withdrawn from the sea (504 ff.). Waiting for a leader, it is drawn up on land—somewhere near to the site of Rome, it seems, and even within sight of it (*hoc campo,* Evander says): but when Aeneas goes to take command he finds it encamped near Caere itself, in a sheltered valley where it can be seen only from the protecting hills (597 ff.), and when he sets out from the gates of Pallanteum (585 ff.), there is no mention of the immediate obstacle which his troop of cavalry faced, the Tiber.

499. fata canens: for *canere* of prophetic utterance see on vii. 79.

Maeoniae: the conventional poetic synonym for Lydia goes back to Homer's name for the country (*Il.* iii. 401). For the Lydian origins of the Etruscans see on 479 f.

500. flos . . . uirtusque uirum: Servius comments 'Ennianum'. In Enn. *Ann.* 308 V. 'flos delibatus populi' ('picked flower') the metaphor is more explicit: for ἄνθος similarly used cf. Aesch. *Agam.* 197 ἄνθος Ἀργείων, *Pers.* 59 ἄνθος Περσίδος αἴας. For *ueterum uirum* cf. 356 'ueterum . . . monimenta uirorum': for the alliteration v. 754 'bello uiuida uirtus', xi. 386 'possit quid uiuida uirtus', x. 609 f. 'uiuida bello / dextra uiris'.

502. subiungere: the metaphor is from yoking animals (cf. *Ecl.* 5. 29 'curru subiungere tigris'): in prose usage an adverbial phrase (*sub imperium, sub ius*) is attached.

503. optate, 'choose', as in i. 425 'optare locum tecto', iii. 109 'optauitque locum regno', vii. 273.

505. oratores, 'spokesmen': see on vii. 153.

506. Tarchon is in legend the son (or the brother) of the Tyrrhenus who brought the Etruscans from Lydia (see on 479 f.), the reputed founder of Tarquinii: for the variations of the legend, see Mielentz in P.–W. Virgil is vague about the status of Tarchon—in 555 he is *rex Tyrrhenus*—and about the polity of Etruria in general. He uses the form *Tarchon* nine times, *Tarcho* (elided) once (603).

507. succedam: the indirect jussive depends on the sense of the preceding lines.

508. tarda gelu . . . senectus: cf. v. 395 f. 'gelidus tardante senecta / sanguis hebet'.

saeclisque effeta, 'worn out by the passing generations': for the metaphor cf. vii. 440 'uerique effeta'.

509. inuidet: opposed to *indulget* in 512; for the point cf. v. 415 f. 'aemula . . . senectus'.

serae . . . uires, 'strength that is too far gone for deeds of valour': *serus* is the metaphorical opposite of *uiridis*: cf. Sil. iii. 255 'consilio uiridis sed belli serus'.

510 f. mixtus . . . traheret, 'blended with a Sabellian mother's blood he draws a share of his native land from Italy': so in vi. 762 Silvius, half Trojan and half Italian, is 'Italo commixtus sanguine'.

513. ingredere, 'enter upon your task': for the solemn adjuration cf. *Geo.* i. 42.

515. Pallanta adiungam: the sending of Pallas is perhaps suggested by Apollonius, ii. 802 ff., when King Lycus sends his son with Jason.

516. graue Martis opus: the phrase is suggested by Homer's μέγα ἔργον Ἄρηος (*Il.* xi. 734).

518. huic: i.e. *Pallanti*: Evander gives Pallas 200 of his men to serve with Aeneas and Pallas gives as many on his own account.

518 f. robora pubis lecta: a reminiscence of Cat. 64. 4 'lecti iuuenes, Argiuae robora pubis'.

520–84. *A sudden sign from heaven and a vision of arms in the sky give Aeneas reassurance. After offering sacrifice and sending a message back to Ascanius he makes ready to set out for the Etruscan camp and Evander bids a sad farewell to his son.*

520 ff. uix ea fatus erat . . . dedisset, 'He had just spoken and with set faces they were pondering deeply (and would have continued so) had not Venus given a sign': *uix ea fatus erat* would be expected to be taken up by a *cum*-clause (or a paratactic sentence) expressing the sudden phenomenon of the heavenly sign (a very common type of structure in Virgil: cf., e.g., i. 586, ii. 692, vi. 190, xi. 296): but the interruption of the semi-parenthetical *defixique . . . tenebant*, emphasizing the despondency of the Trojans, continued in *multaque . . . putabant*, leads to the substitution of a conditional construction of a common elliptical type, in which an imperfect indicative in the apodosis is followed by *nisi* and a pluperfect subjunctive (cf., e.g., vi. 358 ff. 'iam tuta tenebam, / ni gens crudelis . . . inuasisset').

520. defixique ora tenebant: cf. ii. 1 'intentique ora tenebant'.
522. suo tristi cum corde: see on 72.

Why are the Trojan leaders gloomy when they have just been promised Etruscan help? It is enough that they see a hard struggle before them and have not yet had the promised (534) reassurance from Venus. Warde Fowler sug-

gests that Aeneas' gloom is 'premonitory', foreshadowing
what is to happen later in the poem: he is cast down by
concern for Pallas, whom his father has put in his charge,
and the patronymic *Anchisiades* is a deliberate suggestion
of the thought of father and son. He supports this view from
x. 822 f., where *Anchisiades* reflects the thought that is in
Aeneas' mind (as Virgil himself says) when he kills Lausus,
and from vi. 331, where he suggests that *Anchisa satus* im-
plies that Aeneas is thinking what might have been his
father's fate. But the argument is weakened by the fact that
Virgil elsewhere uses *Anchisiades* and *Anchisa satus* in quite
unemotional contexts, e.g. at v. 407 and vii. 152, where they
have no particular relevance.

523. aperto: the appearance of thunder and lightning in a
clear sky (for *aperto* cf. i. 155) makes its significance: cf. *Geo.*
i. 487 'caelo . . . sereno'; Hor. *Od.* i. 34. 7 'per purum'; Ovid,
F. iii. 369 'tonuit sine nube deus'.

526. Tyrrhenusque tubae . . . clangor: for the transference of
epithet cf. Lucr. v. 24 f. 'Nemeaeus . . . hiatus / . . . leonis'.
The appropriateness of the ornamental epithet to this Etrus-
can context may be accidental: for 'Tyrrhenian' is a con-
ventional epithet of the trumpet in Greek tragedy (Aesch.
Eum. 567 f.; Soph. *Ajax* 17; Eur. *Phoen.* 1377 f., *Rhes.* 988 f.).

528. inter nubem: i.e. the sky is clear but the divine armour
is seen resting on a cloud as deity itself appears—Venus at
608 ('inter . . . nimbos'), Apollo at ix. 640 ('nube sedens'),
Juno at xii. 792 ('de nube tuentem'), Cybele and her atten-
dant train at ix. 111 f.

529. rutilare uident et . . . tonare: the combination of *tonare*
with *uident* is made easier by the preceding *rutilare*: but see
on 360 f.

530. heros here perhaps reminds the reader of Aeneas' semi-
divine descent: but see on 464.

531. promissa parentis: the promise (*cecinit*, 534, suggests a
prophecy) has not been mentioned before.

532. profecto repeats and reinforces *uero* (for *ne uero* cf. xi. 278).
Virgil does not use the adverb *profecto* elsewhere, but that
the word is to be taken as the participle and construed with
the next line is very unlikely: it would have little point in
the context, certainly not enough to justify the emphasis
put on it by a break in the line.

533. ego poscor Olympo: the punctuation was a question for
Servius, but rhythm and rhetoric both make it certain that
Olympo is to be taken as ablative (or dative) of agent with
poscor, 'I am called by heaven': cf. 12 'fatis regem se dicere
posci'.

534. missuram: for the omission of the subject of the infinitive (*se*) cf. ii. 433, xi. 712, xii. 655, 762: it is not uncommon, where no ambiguity arises, not only in the informal language of comedy but also in formal prose (e.g. Cic. *Tusc.* ii. 40, *Clu.* 176: see K.-S. ii. 1, p. 701).

535. ingrueret, of gathering menace: cf. ii. 301 'armorumque ingruit horror' (where see Austin's note), xii. 284 'ferreus ingruit imber', 628 'ingruit Aeneas Italis'.

536. For Virgil's incomplete lines see on vii. 129.

537. quantae ... caedes: the fact that *caedes* may be regarded as a 'poetic' plural makes the use of *quantus* easier, but *quantus* is found elsewhere with a plural noun when *quot* would be expected: cf. Hor. *Od.* i. 15. 9 ff. 'heu ... quanta moues funera Dardanae / genti'. Propertius even writes *quanta milia* (i. 5. 10): for such illogical substitution of the quantitative for the numerical adjective (which becomes frequent in later Latin) see D. R. Shackleton Bailey, *Propertiana*, 270; Housman on Man. v. 170.

539. The line is repeated from i. 101, where 'Simois' is the subject, and is a reminiscence of *Il.* xxi. 235 f. (of Scamander) πάντα δ' ὄρινε ῥέεθρα κυκώμενος, ὦσε δὲ νεκροὺς / πολλούς. So far as Tiber is concerned, the idea appears again in Latinus' words at xii. 35 f. 'recalent nostro Thybrina fluenta / sanguine adhuc'—with equal inappropriateness. No battle is represented as taking place, or as being likely to take place, on the Tiber: Virgil has let Homer's Scamander dictate to him.

540. pater: see on vii. 685.

542 f. Herculeis ... penatis, 'wakes the slumbering altar with Herculean fire and happily worships yesterday's Lar and the humble Penates': i.e. he rekindles the embers on the altar of Hercules and repeats the sacrifice to the *lares* and *penates* of his host in which he had presumably taken part on his first coming.

543. paruosque penatis: the gods of Evander's humble household, with simple images of wood or earthenware: so in Hor. *Od.* iii. 23. 15 f. the 'lares' of the rustic Phidyle are 'paruos ... deos'.

544. adit: in worship, as in Lucr. v. 1229 'diuum pacem uotis adit'; Prop. iii. 21. 18 'undisonos nunc prece adire deos'; Cic. *N.D.* i. 77 'deos ipsos ... adire'.

    mactat ... bidentis : see on vii. 93.

545. Euandrus: Virgil has this form five times, *Euander* only once (x. 515).

548 f. prona ... aqua is repeated in *secundo amni*; cf. *Geo.* i. 203 'prono ... amni'.

549. segnis: i.e. idling with the current without using their oars. Virgil says nothing of the return of these messengers to cheer the hard-pressed Trojans in Latium who have lost their fleet. On the other hand a relieving land-force of Arcadian and Etruscan cavalry sent by Evander, of which there is no mention here, makes its appearance at x. 238 f.

552. ducunt exsortem (equum): they (i.e. Evander's people) bring a special gift for Aeneas: *exsors* (like ἐξαίρετος) originally refers to a prize which is reserved for the leader when booty is distributed by lot to his men: cf. ix. 270 f. (Ascanius promises Turnus' horse as a special gift for Nisus) 'ipsum illum . . . / excipiam sorti, iam nunc tua praemia': at v. 534 the adjective is transferred to the recipient of a special prize.

553. aureis: see on vii. 33, 142.

555. ocius: the comparative entirely supplants the archaic positive *ociter*.

556 f. propius . . . timor, 'fear comes closer because of the danger and the shape of Mars looms larger'.

557. it timor: the emphatic *it* at the opening of the line is a Virgilian mannerism: cf. iv. 130 'it portis', 404 'it nigrum campis agmen', ix. 434 'it cruor', 499 'it gemitus', 664 'it clamor', xi. 192 'it caelo clamor', xii. 452 'it mare per medium'. So at the beginning of a sentence within the line: iv. 443 'it stridor', 665 'it clamor', vii. 637 'it bello tessera signum', xii. 592 'it fumus ad auras', 609 'it scissa ueste Latinus'. On Virgil's use of *ire* see also on vii. 223.

   imago is a favourite word of Virgil's: sometimes it refers to a concrete shape seen by the eye (x. 456 'Turni uenientis imago') or in a dream (iv. 351 ff. 'patris Anchisae . . . imago', v. 636 'Cassandrae . . . imago'), sometimes to a 'replica' (iii. 489 'Astyanactis imago', x. 643 the phantom-Aeneas created by Juno), sometimes to an abstract idea or picture in the mind (vi. 405, ix. 294, x. 824 'pietatis imago', xii. 560 'pugnae accendit maioris imago').

558. euntis: i.e. *Pallantis*, as *pater* is enough to show, though Pallas has not been mentioned for fifty lines.

559. haeret: see on 124 'inhaesit'.

   inexpletus lacrimans: the use of the adjective accompanying a participle can be paralleled from *Geo.* ii. 377 'grauis incumbens', iv. 370 'saxosusque sonans Hypanis' (where, as here, early readers wished to substitute an adverbial accusative), *Aen.* iii. 70 'lenis crepitans', v. 764 'creber . . . aspirans', though in all these cases the adverbial connection is less strong. For *inexpletus*, 'insatiable', see on vii. 11.

560 ff. Evander's lament for his lost youth has its Homeric prototype in Nestor's two long speeches of reminiscence:

Il. vii. 132 ff. αἲ γάρ ... / ἡβῷμ' ὡς ὅτ' ἐπ' ὠκυρόῳ Κελάδοντι μάχοντο,
κ.τ.λ., xi. 670 ff. εἴθ' ὡς ἡβώοιμι βίη δέ μοι ἔμπεδος εἴη, / ὡς ὁπότ'
Ἠλείοισι καὶ ἡμῖν νεῖκος ἐτύχθη / ἀμφὶ βοηλασίῃ, ὅτ' ἐγὼ κτάνον Ἰτυμονῆα,
κ.τ.λ.

The wish is vividly presented as capable of realization
(*referat*: 'O that Jupiter would give me back my youth'):
in the apodosis Evander naturally passes (568 *diuellerer*) to
the tense of an unrealizable condition, '(if he did—and he
cannot) I would never be parted'.

561 f. qualis eram has its antecedent in the sense of the pre-
vious line, as if it had been preceded by *o si talis sim*.

primam aciem, the enemy's front rank, is suggested by
Nestor's ὁ δέ ... / ἔβλητ' ἐν πρώτοισιν ἐμῆς ἀπὸ χειρός(*Il.* xi. 674 f.).
But *scutorum incendi aceruos* is a Roman touch: for the cus-
tom of burning the *spolia* of a defeated enemy (magical in
origin: the victor must destroy the power of the strange arms)
see, e.g., Livy viii. 30. 8, xxiii. 46. 5, xxx. 6. 9.

Praeneste is normally neuter (as it is at vii. 682), but
Juvenal repeats the feminine (3. 190 'gelida Praeneste').
For *ipse* giving precision to a location cf. iii. 5 f. 'sub ipsa /
Antandro'.

563. Erulum: the story of this Italian monster is otherwise
unknown.

564. Feronia: see on vii. 800.

565. terna arma mouenda: three lives imply three bodies and
Evander had to attack each in turn and kill the monster
three times. For *terna* ('one for each of three') see on vii. 538.

566. leto sternendus: *leto* is presumably dative (cf. xii. 464
'sternere morti') and *leto sternere* an extension of the for-
mulas *morti dare, morti mittere* which are as old as Plautus
and which may originally imply a personification. For the
datives *leto, morti, Orco* with *dare, mittere, demittere, deicere*
see J. H. Waszink, *Mnem.* xix (1966), 249 ff.

568 f. usquam ... umquam: as Page says ad loc., the unique
repetition perhaps suggests passionate emphasis.

570 ff. huic capiti is naturally taken as a periphrasis for *mihi*,
a stately equivalent of the *hic homo* of colloquial speech
(Ter. *Heaut.* 356; Hor. *Sat.* i. 9. 47) though the attachment of
an adjective (*finitimo* here: 'me, his neighbour') is un-
paralleled: for *caput* cf. iv. 354, 640. *urbem* must refer to
Evander's city: attacks by Mezentius on his own subjects ta
Caere could not be thought to concern Evander directly
enough to justify *insultans*. But in that case *uiduasset* is a
surprisingly strong expression: there has been nothing to
suggest that Evander's people have been decimated by
attacks from Etruria, and Evander himself has spoken (473)

of the barrier of the Tiber which protects him on the Etruscan side. For the metaphorical use of *uiduare* cf. Hor. *Od*. ii. 9. 8 'foliis uiduantur orni': it may well have been suggested here by *Il*. v. 642 Ἰλίου ἐξαλάπαξε πόλιν, χήρωσε δ' ἀγυιάς.

570 f. dedisset funera: cf. *Geo*. iii. 246 f., *Aen*. xii. 383. Virgil makes very free use of the 'causative' sense of *dare* (the result of the coalescence in *dare* of the roots corresponding to διδόναι, 'give', and τιθέναι, 'put', 'make'): so, e.g., ii. 310, xi. 613 f. (*ruinam*), ii. 482 (*fenestram*), vi. 76 (*finem*), vii. 567 (*sonitum*), xi. 384 (*stragis aceruos*), xii. 575 (*cuneum*), 681 (*saltum*), and so with a predicative participle xii. 436 f. 'te . . . / defensum dabit'.

573. Arcadii . . . regis: a curious periphrasis for the speaker himself; in *Arcadii* Evander seems to be making his exiled condition a claim to Jupiter's mercy.

574 f. numina . . . fata: for the combination cf. 511 f. 'cuius et annis / et generi fatum indulget, quem numina poscunt'; and for the change from *fata* to a personified Fortuna (578) see on 334.

576. eum: see on vii. 63.

579. crudelem abrumpere uitam, 'break off a life that gives me pain': Euryalus' mother repeats the phrase, ix. 497: cf. iv. 631 'inuisam . . . abrumpere lucem'.

580. dum curae ambiguae: i.e. while my anxious thoughts still look both ways.

581. care puer: Virgil has the vocative *puer* for *mi fili* only twice, here and at xii. 435, where also it has an emotional overtone: he has *nate* twenty-five times.

sera uoluptas, 'pleasure of my latter years': so Euryalus' mother calls her son 'senectae / sera meae requies' (ix. 481 f.): there is no implication that the son is late-born.

583. digressu . . . supremo: for the ablative see on 215.

585–607. *Aeneas and his new allies make their way to the Etruscan camp*.

585. iamque adeo: *adeo* emphasizes a new stage in the progress of events (cf. ii. 567, v. 268, 864): see on vii. 427.

588. it: Markland's emendation removes a weak repetition of *in* and restores Virgilian idiom (see on 557): cf. xi. 89 f. 'post bellator equus . . . / it lacrimans guttisque umectat grandibus ora', xii. 164 'bigis it Turnus in albis'.

pictis . . . armis: cf. vii. 796, xi. 660, xii. 281: probably not painted but inlaid with gold and silver, like the Sabine shields of Livy ix. 40. 2 (so *pingere* is often used of gold and silver embroidery).

589. qualis . . . Lucifer: the comparison of the hero to a star is

a commonplace of eulogy, but here Virgil has in mind *Il.*
v. 5 f. ἀστέρ' ὀπωρινῷ ἐναλίγκιον ὅς τε μάλιστα / λαμπρὸν παμφαίνῃσι
λελουμένος Ὠκεανοῖο, though he has replaced Sirius by Lucifer.

590. Venus: cf. Cic. *N.D.* ii. 53 'stella Veneris quae Φωσφόρος
Graece, Lucifer Latine dicitur': Lucifer is Venus' favourite
star because in his other aspect of Hesperus, the evening
star, he ushers in the marriage night (*Ecl.* 8. 30; Cat. 62.
20 ff.).

592. pauidae repeats the idea of 556: with fear at their hearts,
since they know the meaning of war, 'bellaque matribus /
detestata' (Hor. *Od.* i. 1. 24 f.; cf. *Aen.* xi. 215 ff.), the women
looked out from the walls (cf. xi. 877) as the Trojan women
do in Homer (*Il.* iii. 146 ff., xxii. 462 ff.) or the mother and
daughter in Hor. *Od.* iii. 2. 6 ff.

594. olli brings the cavalcade before the reader's eye: for the
form see on vii. 458.

    quae proxima meta uiarum, 'where the end of the journey
is nearest', i.e. by the shortest way: cf. iii. 714 'longarum
haec meta uiarum'.

595. it clamor: see on 557.

596. Here and in the similarly suggestive line xi. 875 'quadri-
pedumque putrem cursu quatit ungula campum' Virgil
develops a suggestion from Ennius, who had written (*Ann.*
277 V.) 'summo sonitu quatit ungula terram' and (439 V.)
'it eques et plausu caua concutit ungula terram'. *quadri-
pedare* is to gallop, lifting all four feet at once, and Ennius
had already used the verb, *Sc.* 184 V. 'sublime iter quadru-
pedantes flammam halitantes'. Virgil here transfers the
epithet to *sonitu*: at xi. 614 f. 'perfractaque quadripedan-
tum / pectora pectoribus rumpunt' it may be no more than
a variant for the *quadripes* which Virgil often uses.

597 ff. est . . . lucus . . . haud procul hinc: see on vii. 563 ff.
The whole description is unrealistic (and perplexed Servius
accordingly): the *nemus* in which the Trojans establish
themselves is on water surrounded by hills, but they look
down from hills on the Etruscans encamped on the level.

597. Caeritis is probably an irregular genitive of *Caere*, the
name of the town, rather than the regular genitive of the
adjective *Caeres* used as the name of the river (for the de-
fining genitive see on 231): at x. 183 Virgil has *Caerēte* as
the ablative.

598. religione . . . sacer: cf. vii. 170 ff. 'tectum augustum . . . /
horrendum siluis et religione parentum', 607 f. 'Belli portae
. . . / religione sacrae'.

598 f. colles . . . caui, 'encircling hills': *cauus* is often a relative
term, expressing not the hollowness of an object but the fact

that it surrounds, conceals, or protects something within it: so i. 516 'nube caua', ii. 53 'cauae . . . cauernae', 360 'nox atra caua circumuolat umbra', ix. 46 'cauis . . . turribus', 633 'caua tempora', x. 475 'uaginaque caua'; Cat. 17. 4 'cauaque in palude recumbat', 64. 259 'obscura cauis celebrabant orgia cistis'; Prop. iii. 14. 12 'cauo protegit aere caput' (of a helmet); Ovid, *Tr.* iv. 8. 17 'in caua ducuntur quassae naualia puppes' ('the shelter of the dock').

599. nigra: for *niger* of foliage cf. Hor. *Od.* i. 21. 7 f. 'nigris . . . Erymanthi / siluis', iv. 4. 57 f. 'ilex tonsa bipennibus / nigrae feraci frondis in Algido', iv. 12. 11 f. 'nigri / colles Arcadiae': so Pind. *P.* 1. 27 Αἴτνας ἐν μελαμφύλλοις . . . κορυφαῖς.

abiete: for the trisyllabic value see on vii. 175, for the collective singular viii. 34.

600. fama est: see on vii. 48.

ueteres : *uetus*, as often, conveys a romantic colour of legendary antiquity: see on vii. 204.

Pelasgos: elsewhere in Virgil *Pelasgus* is always a synonym of *Graecus*: so in the mouth of Dido i. 624, of Sinon ii. 83, of Aeneas vi. 503; that use, based on Homer's Πελασγικὸν Ἄργος, became commonplace in Alexandrian poetry and had been taken over by Ennius (*Ann.* 17 V.). Here he is following the Hellenizing antiquarian tradition represented by Dionysius (i. 17) which found a place in Italy for the Pelasgi (the name, probably, of a North Aegean people scattered by early migrations which later Greek historians came to apply indiscriminately to any pre-Hellenic populations of Greece) by making them the predecessors in Etruria of the Lydian immigrants (see on 479 f.). Whoever they were, the prehistoric inhabitants of Caere could not have been worshipping a god with the Latin name of Silvanus, a spirit of the wild woodland who later became a deity of the farmer.

603 f. tuta . . . locis, 'defended by its situation'—though it was on level ground and overlooked by hills (604 f.).

604 f. uideri iam poterat . . . et . . . tendebat: for the characteristically Virgilian structure see on vii. 7.

605. legio, 'muster', of any armed force: cf. vii. 681 'legio . . . agrestis', ix. 174, 368, xii. 121.

tendebat, 'pitched their tents': cf. ii. 29 'hic saeuus tendebat Achilles'; Ovid, *Her.* i. 35 'illic Aeacides, illic tendebat Ulixes': the verb is a military technical term in this use (so, e.g., Caesar, *B.G.* vi. 37 'qui sub uallo tenderent mercatores').

606. bello lecta, 'picked for war': see on vii. 482.

607. equos et corpora curant: an expansion of the technical term for the resting of troops, *corpora curare*; cf. *Geo.* iv. 187, *Aen.* iii. 511.

608–731. *Venus brings Aeneas his new armour: on the shield he sees depicted the whole history of Rome from the birth of the twins to the triumph of Octavian.*

608. The goddess appears amid clouds (cf. 528) which enhance her radiance (*candida*).

609. reducta: the valley running into the hills is a cliché of natural description: cf. vi. 703; Hor. *Od.* i. 17. 17, *Epod.* 2. 11.

610. procul egelido secretum flumine: the intensive use of *egelidus* (*ualde gelidus*: cf. *edurus*) is repeated by Manilius (v. 131) and later taken up by Ausonius. In Catullus (46. 1 'egelidos tepores') *egelidus* is 'with the chill off' and so it is in Ovid's precious 'et gelidum Borean egelidumque Notum' (*Am.* ii. 11. 10) and later in the technical use of Celsus (iv. 18. 3 'aqua neque ea ipsa frigida, sed potius egelida danda est'), Pliny (*N.H.* xxxi. 4) and Suetonius (*Aug.* 82 'egelida aqua uel sole multo tepefacta').

611. For the structure of the line see on vii. 7: for *ultro* ('to his surprise') see on vii. 236.

612. promissa ... arte: the reference is to Vulcan's promise in 401 ff., but Aeneas, though he has already been promised these arms by his mother (see on 531), does not know of her appeal to Vulcan.

617 ff. So when Thetis brings her son the promised arms (*Il.* xix. 18 ff.) Achilles τέρπετο δ' ἐν χείρεσσιν ἔχων θεοῦ ἀγλαὰ δῶρα. / αὐτὰρ ἐπεὶ φρεσὶν ᾗσι τετάρπετο δαίδαλα λεύσσων, κ.τ.λ.

617. honore, 'gift', probably, as the word is often used (see 61) of offerings.

618. expleri nequit: cf. 265 'nequeunt expleri corda'.

620. flammasque uomentem: like the Chimaera on Turnus' helmet, vii. 785 ff.: cf. 680 f. 'tempora flammas / laeta uomunt', x. 271 'uastos umbo uomit aureus ignis'.

621. fatiferum: cf. ix. 631 'fatifer arcus'.

  ex aere rigentem, 'stiff with bronze': for the use of *ex* ('as a result of') cf., e.g., Quint. viii. 3. 66 'ex uino uacillantes'.

622. sanguineam: the adjective vividly represents the colour of the bronze: for the emotive use of *ingens* see on vii. 29.

622 f. qualis ... refulget: the comparison is suggested by Apollonius' description of the golden fleece, iv. 125 νεφέλῃ ἐναλίγκιον, ἥ τ' ἀνιόντος / ἠελίου φλογερῇσιν ἐρεύθεται ἀκτίνεσσιν.

624. electro: see on 402.

  recocto: i.e. refined by repeated smelting.

625. textum: the 'fabric' of the shield: *texere* is freely extended from weaving to other kinds of intricate fabric, especially

carpentry: cf. xi. 326 'texamus robore nauis (so Enn. *Sc.*
65 f. V. 'mari magno classis cita / texitur'; Cat. 64. 10
'pinea . . . texta carinae'); *Aen.* ii. 186 (of the wooden horse)
'roboribus textis', v. 589 (of a maze) 'parietibus textum
caecis iter'.

626 ff. As Virgil gave a new meaning and dramatic relevance
to the Catalogue in Book VII which he borrowed from
Homer's epic pattern, so he does with the Shield. Homer's
Shield of Achilles (*Il.* xviii. 483 ff.) is a pictorial survey of the
life of his time in town and country: Virgil's Shield is a
prophetic pageant of Roman history which serves his drama-
tic design and enhances his theme. That he was conscious,
and might expect his readers to be conscious, of a topical
analogy in the golden shield which was set up in the senate
house in 27 B.C. to commemorate the virtues of Augustus
(*Res Gestae* 34; *C.I.L.* ix. 5811) is an unnecessary hypothesis:
the Homeric precedent and the possibility of exploiting it,
reshaped, for his own purpose were justification enough for
the episode.

Two features of Virgil's handling of the Shield are note-
worthy. One, which he shares with Homer, concerns his
manner: while he professes to be describing a work of art,
and even (unlike Homer) alludes to technique in the appro-
priate use of metals, his pictures come to life before his eyes
and transcend the limitations of art: the scenes become
scenes of action, with movements and circumstances which
art could not represent. The other concerns his matter: the
survey of history is a highly selective one. The descriptions
of Actium and Augustus' triumph, the climax to which it
leads, occupy more than half its length. The theme is *pugnata
in ordine bella*, but of these all that appear are the early wars
of Rome with her Sabine and Etruscan neighbours, with
some of the romantic legends attached to them, and the
invasion of the Gauls. The later wars, even, most strikingly,
the war with Carthage, the most critical struggle in which
she engaged, go unnoticed: their place is taken by a briefly
sketched scene of traditional ritual and the crowded space
of history between 392 and 31 B.C. is awkwardly bridged by
an underworld scene presenting Catiline and Cato. As for the
disposition of the scenes on the shield, where the whole of
earlier history, it seems, is in the upper part, the underworld
in the lower, and the central space is occupied by Actium
and Augustus, it represents (what is sometimes forgotten)
a poet's symbolic imagination, not an art critic's description.

627. haud uatum ignarus: Vulcan is given no powers of fore-
sight and is represented as obtaining his knowledge of the

future from the *uates* who are the mouthpieces of those gods who can declare it.

628 f. genus ... stirpis: cf. iv. 622 'stirpem et genus omne futurum', *Geo*. iv. 282 'genus ... nouae stirpis'.

629. ab Ascanio: cf. i. 729 f. 'Belus et omnes / a Belo'.

    pugnata: the participle may be regarded as taking its time, illogically but naturally, from the writer's standpoint— the wars are *pugnata* to Virgil—or as an aoristic timeless use like that of 636 'magnis Circensibus actis' (see note there). For the use as subject in the passive of what would be an internal object in the active (*bellum pugnare*) cf. x. 370 'deuictaque bella'.

630 f. fecerat ... procubuisse: nouns (*genus, bella*) are combined with infinitival clauses as objects of *fecerat*. For this use of the infinitive in descriptions of works of art cf., e.g., Ovid, *Met*. vi. 108 f. 'fecit et Asterien aquila luctante teneri, / fecit olorinis Ledam recubare sub alis': similarly of representations in literature, e.g. Cic. *N.D*. iii. 41 'quem ... Homerus apud inferos conueniri facit ab Ulixe', *Tusc*. iv. 35 'poetae impendere apud inferos saxum Tantalo faciunt'. The tense of *procubuisse* is strictly true: 'represented as having thrown herself down'.

630. Mauortis in antro: i.e. traditionally the Lupercal on the Palatine (see on 343).

633. tereti ceruice reflexa: Lucr. i. 35 'tereti ceruice reposta' confirms the ablative *reflexa* (and Virgil has *reflexa ceruice* again at x. 535 f.).

634. mulcere alternos, 'stroking them (with her tongue) turn about'.

    fingere: Ovid's description repeats the verb, *F*. ii. 417 'et cauda teneris blanditur alumnis / et fingit lingua corpora bina sua', crediting the wolf with the habit of licking the young into shape which ancient zoologists ascribe to the bear (Aelian, *N.H*. ii. 19; Pliny, *N.H*. viii. 126): so Virgil said of his own method of composition 'carmen se ursae modo parere et lambendo demum effingere' (*Vita Donati* 22: cf. Gell. xvii. 10. 2).

635. sine more: indecently, in defiance of convention; see on vii. 377.

636. consessu caueae: the Lucretian phrase (iv. 78 'consessum caueai') is used again of the games in Sicily, v. 340.

    magnis Circensibus: the tradition represented by Livy (i. 9) attached the rape of the Sabine women to the festival of the Consualia, to which indeed races had been added in historical times. Virgil seems to be identifying the occasion with the *ludi Romani* or *ludi magni* of later times, a Septem-

ber celebration which was evolved out of votive games held
after campaigns.

actis, 'when the games were held', 'at the holding of the
games': for this timeless use given to the past participle
passive (in default of a present) cf. *Geo*. i. 293 f. 'longum
cantu solata laborem / . . . percurrit pectine telas', 339 'sacra
refer Cereri laetis operatus in herbis', ii. 140 f. 'haec loca non
tauri . . . / inuertere satis immanis dentibus hydri', *Aen.*
viii. 407 f. 'medio iam noctis abactae / curriculo', xi. 37 f.
'ingentem gemitum tunsis . . . tollunt / pectoribus'.

637. nouum, 'sudden': for *nouus* used of a startling pheno-
menon cf. i. 450 f. 'noua res oblata timorem / leniit', iii.
591 f. 'ignoti noua forma uiri . . . / procedit', (perhaps) vii.
554 'sanguis nouus imbuit arma', ix. 110, 731 'noua lux
oculis offulsit' (cf. Prop. iv. 6. 29 f. 'noua flamma / luxit'):
similarly of mental phenomena, ii. 228 f. 'nouus per pectora
cunctis / insinuat pauor', v. 670 'quis furor iste nouus?',
Geo. iv. 357 'percussa noua . . . formidine'.

638. Romulidis: see on vii. 616.

Curibusque seueris: the Sabine town of Cures was the
home of the Sabine leader Titus Tatius, the legendary rival
of Romulus (Livy i. 10): for the proverbial strictness and
simplicity of the Sabine way of life cf. Livy i. 18. 4 '(Numa)
instructum . . . disciplina tetrica ac tristi ueterum Sabi-
norum quo genere nullum quondam incorruptius fuit'; Hor.
Ep. ii. 1. 12 'rigidis . . . Sabinis'.

641. caesa . . . porca: Quintilian curiously credits Virgil with
having invented the feminine to secure dignity: viii. 3. 19
'caesa . . . porca fecit elegans fictio nominis quod, si fuisset
porco, uile erat'. Varro uses *porcus* in describing the fetial
ceremony (*R.R.* ii. 4. 9 'foedus cum feritur porcus occiditur')
as does Livy (i. 24. 8, ix. 5. 3). The form *porca* (for *porcus
femina*) occurs in Cato (*R.R.* 134) and again in Festus 266 L.
'(pax) porca caesa in foedere firmari solet'.

642. Mettum: the story of the punishment of the *dictator* of
Alba who made a treaty with Tullus Hostilius, third king of
Rome, and then deserted him in face of the enemy is given
by Livy i. 28, where his name (a Latinization of the Oscan
title *meddix*) is Mettius.

citae . . . in diuersa : for the participial use cf. Hor. *Epod.*
9. 20 'puppes sinistrorsum citae'.

643. distulerant: the action is represented as preceding that of
raptabat: cf. i. 483 f. 'raptauerat . . . uendebat'.

dictis . . . maneres, 'you should have kept to your word',
the jussive *dictis maneas* (cf. ii. 160 'tu modo promissis
maneas') being thrown back into past time. The 'past jussive'

or 'retrospective command' is common in comedy (e.g. Plaut. *Pseud.* 437 'tu ne faceres tale', 'you should not have done a thing like that'; Ter. *Hec.* 230 'quae hic erant curares') and in Cicero (e.g. *Sest.* 54 'quod si meis incommodis laetabantur, urbis tamen periculo commouerentur'): after Cicero it is rare. The pluperfect is often found (mostly in Cicero) replacing the imperfect to emphasize the past reference (e.g. *Verr.* ii. 3. 195 'quid facere debuisti? ... quod superaret pecuniae rettulisses'): so in Virgil iv. 604 'quem metui moritura? faces in castra tulissem', 678 'eadem me ad fata uocasses', xi. 162 'obruerent ... dedissem'. See K.–S. ii. 1, p. 187; Madvig on Cic. *Fin.* ii. 35.

646. nec non: see on vii. 521.

    Porsenna: the Etruscan name is *Porsĕna* in Horace (*Epod.* 16. 4), Silius, and Martial.

646 ff. Virgil follows the tradition represented by Livy (ii. 9) that on the abolition of the monarchy the expelled Tarquinius Superbus appealed to Lars Porsenna, the Etruscan ruler of Clusium, who besieged Rome but, having failed to take it, thanks to the heroism of Horatius Cocles, admiringly recognized its liberty and withdrew. That account is a figment of Roman patriotism: there is no evidence for a connection with Tarquin; Porsenna was a powerful neighbour who saw his chance and in fact captured Rome (Tac. *Hist.* iii. 72. 1; Pliny, *N.H.* xxxiv. 139).

    Virgil compresses the patriotic stories of Horatius Cocles (Livy ii. 10), who held the Tiber crossing of the Pons Sublicius while his countrymen cut it behind him ('rem ausus plus famae habituram ad posteros quam fidei', says Livy: the story may be a rationalization of a religious ritual), and Cloelia (Livy, ii. 13), one of a band of women given as hostages to Porsenna who escaped back across the Tiber (on a horse, in some versions, and not 'uinclis ruptis' but, says Livy, 'frustrata custodes').

    For the jingle *iubebat ... premebat ... ruebant*, closely followed by *tenebat* (653) and *canebat ... tenebant* (656-7), see on vii. 187 f.

648. Aeneadae (see on vii. 616): the name is used from the writer's point of view; Aeneas did not recognize these as his descendants.

    in ferrum ... ruebant, 'were rushing to take up the steel' (cf. ix. 182 'in bella ruebant') or 'were rushing headlong on the steel': and cf. *Geo.* ii. 503 f. 'ruuntque / in ferrum'.

649. indignanti similem: i.e. he was depicted as angry and threatening: similarly on an embroidered cloak (v. 254) Ganymede is shown 'anhelanti similis'.

650. aspiceres, 'one could have seen': so 676 'uideres': at 691 Virgil has the more vivid potential present 'credas'.

652 ff. For the story of the saving of the Capitol from the Gauls, traditionally in 390 B.C., thanks to the alarm raised by the sacred geese and the prompt defence of Manlius, see Livy v. 47.

652. in summo, on the upper part of the shield: so 675 'in medio'.

Tarpeiae . . . arcis: see on 347.

653. tenebat: cf. xii. 705 f. 'quique alta tenebant / moenia': the use of the same verb for the defender here and for the repulsed attackers in 657 is awkward.

654. This line is giving a background to the story of Manlius and the reference must be to a building on the Capitoline. The *casa Romuli*, a straw-thatched hut (cf. Ovid, *F*. iii. 183 f. 'quae fuerit nostri, si quaeris, regia nati, / aspice de canna straminibusque domum') which was preserved with reverent care in historical times and restored when it suffered from time and weather, was on the Palatine (Dion. Hal. i. 79. 11; Plut. *Rom*. 20. 4: cf. Prop. iv. 1. 9 f.), but there seems to have been a replica of it on the Capitoline (Sen. *Contr*. ii. 1. 5; Vitr. ii. 1. 5: S. B. Platner and T. Ashby, *A Topographical Dict. of Ancient Rome* [Oxford, 1929], 101–2) which may have suggested Virgil's reference. *horrebat* may well combine a reference to the straw surface represented in the metal with a suggestion of primitive simplicity (see on vii. 746 'horrida'). *recens* is difficult: if it means 'new from the maker's hand' (and so bright and sharp in effect), it is awkwardly used of a building which claimed to be a relic of the distant past.

655. atque introduces a dramatic turn: see on vii. 29.

auratis . . . argenteus: the contrasting metals reproduce the contrast of natural colour: so below, the dolphins and the foam are silver on a gold sea.

657. tenebant, 'were on the point of gaining' (cf. vi. 358 'iam tuta tenebam'): even if the truth, suppressed by tradition, was that the Gauls did occupy the Capitol—and that is doubtful (see Ogilvie on Livy v. 39)—this cannot be quoted as evidence for it.

658. dono noctis opacae: cf. Ovid, *Met*. x. 476 'caecae munere noctis': but the darkness cannot have been represented.

659 ff. aurea . . . aurea . . . auro : for the pictorial repetition see on vii. 278 f.

659. ollis: see on vii. 458.

aurea uestis is naturally taken to refer to the Gauls' dress and to be repeated in *lucent sagulis* (Silius perhaps took it so:

his Celts have 'auro uirgatae uestes', iv. 155), but Servius
refers it to beards and there is some evidence to support that
possibility. (1) Festus (506 L.) cites *uesticeps* as meaning
'uestitus pubertate' and *inuestis* as its opposite: in Gellius
v. 19. 7 *uesticeps* is a technical term for the minimum age for
adrogatio: the words are taken up by archaizing writers, both
by Apuleius (*Met.* v. 28, *Apol.* 98), *uesticeps* by Tertullian (*de
An.* 56. 5) and Ausonius (p. 265 P.). (2) The use of *uestire* in
reference to the hair on the face (160 'mihi prima genas
uestibat flore iuuentas'; Lucr. v. 888 f. 'iuuentas / . . . molli
uestit lanugine malas') and of *uestis* itself in Lucr. v. 672 f.
'imperat aetas / . . . impubem molli pubescere ueste' may be
more than poetic metaphors and preserve an archaic use.

660. **uirgatis,** 'striped' (the tigress is *uirgata* in Sen. *Phaedra*
344): in a similar context Propertius gives a northern chief-
tain *uirgatae bracae* (iv. 10. 43).

661. **auro innectuntur:** their necks are in silver and they wear
the gold *torques* which gave the younger Manlius his cogno-
men in 361 B.C. (Livy vii. 10. 11): cf. Prop. iv. 10. 44.

662. **gaesa:** this word for a type of *iaculum* is Celtic and *gaesa*
are Gaulish weapons in Caesar (*B.G.* iii. 4. 1).

   scutis protecti . . . longis: but not broad enough, according
to Livy, xxxviii. 21. 4 'scuta longa ceterum ad amplitudinem
corporum parum lata . . . male tegebant Gallos'.

663-6. The scenes from early Roman history are abruptly suc-
ceeded by a vignette from ancient ritual—the dancing priests
of Mars and the mysterious Luperci (see on 343). The Luperci
separate the Salii from their attributes, survivals of primi-
tive accoutrements—the conical headpiece (*apex*) of olive
wood topped by a tuft of wool, which they shared with the
flamines, and the magic shields (*ancilia*: cf. vii. 188) which
were said to have been made in the time of Numa, one which
had fallen from the sky being matched by eleven others.

665 f. **ducebant sacra,** 'formed religious processions', an exten-
sion of the use in *pompam ducere, funus ducere.*

   pilentis: the right of Roman *matronae* to ride in carriages
at religious ceremonies (Livy v. 25. 8 f.; Diod. xiv. 116. 9:
cf. Ovid, *F.* i. 617 ff.) was traditionally a reward for their
contribution of their jewellery to the treasury in 395 B.C.

666. **mollibus:** i.e. cushioned: cf. xi. 64 'molle feretrum'.

666 ff. The gap between earlier history and the crisis of Actium
is hastily bridged by a picture of the underworld with the
figures of Catiline, the representative of the forces of anarchy,
and Cato, the stern upholder of morality and social order,
taking the place, the one of the *scelerati*, the other of a Minos,
in the mythical picture—the latter in a not altogether con-

vincing role, since the *pii*, whose Elysian seclusion he no
doubt shares, do not need a judge. The tribute to Cato is in
line with the eulogy for which Cicero set the pattern and is
no more extravagant, within poetic convention, than the
plain prose of Velleius (ii. 35. 2 'homo Virtuti simillimus et
per omnia ingenio diis quam hominibus propior'): that the
implacable opponent of Julius Caesar and the uncompromis-
ing champion of the lost cause of the Republic, in criticism
of whom Augustus himself wrote (Suet. *Aug.* 85. 1), should
receive this tribute in a prelude to the *laudes Augusti* and
the panegyric of the new regime is the less surprising when
one remembers that Horace chose to include *Catonis nobile
letum* (*Od.* i. 12. 35 f.) in a very similar context, a parade of
exempla from Roman history leading up to a panegyric on the
princeps as its crowning glory.

668. minaci, 'beetling': cf. i. 162 f. 'geminique minantur / in
caelum scopuli'. Catiline's punishment is suggested by that
of Prometheus, chained to his Caucasian rock: the notion
of the Furies as Catiline's tormentors agrees with the Greek
conception of the Erinyes as punishers of domestic crime
but is curiously at variance with Virgil's own picture of them
at vii. 324 ff., in which their activity is that of stimulating it.
See on vii. 324 ff., with the references there, however, to the
'Greek' conception at vi. 571 ff. and 605 ff.

670. secretos, 'in a place apart': cf. vi. 477 f. (the abode of the
war heroes) 'arua tenebant / ultima, quae bello clari secreta
frequentant'.

671. haec inter: the scenes of history are depicted in the upper
part of the shield (652), the underworld in the lower (666
'hinc procul'): between is the sea and in the midst of it the
battle scene of Actium.

672. spumabant: a necessary correction of *spumabat*, with
which *caerula* ('in blue') would have to be an adjective
parallel to *aurea* ('in gold'). There is no question of blue:
the waves are gold (677), the foam silver, and the contrast is
the same as in 655 and in 659–61: *caerula* must be plural,
'waves', as in iii. 208 'torquent spumas et caerula uerrunt'.

673. in orbem, 'in a ring', 'ringwise': for the modal use of *in*,
see on 260.

675. aeratas: technically the word refers to the bronze beak
of a warship (cf. Caes. *B.C.* ii. 3 'cum classe nauium xvi,
in quibus paucae erant aeratae') but it becomes a conven-
tional epithet of sea-going vessels: cf. x. 223 'aeratae ...
prorae' (so v. 198 'aerea puppis', i. 35 'spumas salis aere
ruebant'); Hor. *Od.* ii. 16. 21 'aeratas ... nauis', iii. 1. 39
'aerata triremi'.

Actia bella stands in loose apposition to *aeratas classis*:
cf. *Geo*. ii. 97 'sunt et Amminneae uites, firmissima uina'.
Virgil prefers the form of the adjective without adjectival
suffix (see on vii. 219) to *Actiacus*.

676. **cernere erat**: cf. vi. 596: the use of *est* for *licet* is a Graecism
based on the common use of ἐστι: it is rare but is already
found with *uidere* in an Atellane fragment (Mummius 1 R.)
and in Horace (*Sat*. i. 2. 101). See E. Wölfflin, *A.L.L*. ii. 135 f.

677. **feruĕre**, 'bustling': cf. Accius 482 R. 'classis aditu occludi-
tur: feruit'; Lucr. ii. 40 f. 'tuas legiones per loca campi /
feruere cum uideas': so of the bustle of the bees, *Geo*. iv. 169,
and of the ants, *Aen*. iv. 407. Virgil uses only the archaic
third conjugation form in the infinitive *feruere*: so he has only
fulgĕre and *effulgĕre*.

Leucaten: the geography is not to be taken seriously.
Actium was the southern of the two promontories which
closed the Ambracian Gulf: Leucate was some thirty miles
to the south of it, the dangerous southern tip of the large
island of Leucas lying off the coast and close to it at its
northern end. Virgil is here combining the two as he has
already done at iii. 274 ff., when Aeneas himself lands at
Leucate (274) and is at Actium. Confusion was assisted by
the fact that both promontories had temples of Apollo:
Apollo Leucadius is the denizen of Leucate in Ovid, *Tr*.
v. 2. 76 but the god of Actium in Prop. iii. 11. 69. (See R. B.
Lloyd, *A.J.P*. lxxv [1954], 292 ff.) But Leucate was indeed
of importance in the campaign: Antony had a squadron
based there to cover his in-shore supply-route: Agrippa de-
stroyed it and occupied Leucas, forcing Antony to use the
seaward route outside Cephallenia (Dio. l. 13. 5).

678. **Augustus . . . Caesar**: that Octavian did not receive the
title of Augustus until January 27 B.C. is no objection to
taking the word as his title here, as in Horace, *Od*. ii. 9. 19 f.
'cantemus Augusti tropaea / Caesaris': Propertius uses it so
in the same context (iv. 6. 29). But the emphatic position of
the word here and at vi. 792 suggests that in both places
Virgil is stressing its religious associations: see on vii. 153.

Italos is deliberately opposed to *ope barbarica uariisque
armis* in 685: Octavian is leading a national cause and his
country and her gods are with him.

679. **penatibus et magnis dis**: cf. iii. 11 f. 'feror exsul in altum /
cum sociis natoque penatibus et magnis dis': the stately
spondaic cadence and the monosyllabic ending are a reminis-
cence of Ennius, *Ann*. 201 V. 'dono, ducite, doque uolentibus
cum magnis dis' (see on vii. 592, 631). According to Varro
(cited by Servius on iii. 12) *di magni* was a name for the

Penates and the base of a statue bore the inscription 'magnis diis'. This suggests that in Virgil's phrase one title supplements the other and that the reference of both is to the *penates publici* who had a share in the temple of Vesta (Tac. *Ann.* xv. 41. 1) but also had their own shrine in the Velia, restored by Augustus (*Res Gestae* 19) and were identified with the *penates* brought from Troy with Aeneas. See G. Wissowa, *Hermes* xxii (1887), 29 ff.; S. Weinstock in P.–W. s.v. Penates; R. B. Lloyd in *A.J.P.* lxxvii (1956), 38 ff.

680. celsa in puppi: Augustus stands on the stern (as Aeneas does in x. 261 and the captains do in v. 132 f.), and the ship's tutelary deities had their images there: cf. x. 171 'aurato fulgebat Apolline puppis'; Ovid. *Her.* 16. 114 'accipit et pictos puppis adunca deos'; Pers. 6. 30 'ingentes de puppe dei': so Eur. *I.A.* 239 ff. χρυσέαις δ' εἰκόσιν κατ' ἄκρα Νηρῆδες ἔστασαν θεαί, | πρύμναις σῆμ' Ἀχιλλείου στρατοῦ.

680 f. tempora flammas laeta uomunt: cf. 620, but here the flame does not rise from the warrior's helmet: Augustus is bare-headed and a radiance shines from his 'exultant brow'. The manifestation of divine favour in a halo of fire which plays about the kingly head has many parallels in legend in Rome (e.g. in the story of Servius Tullius, Livy i. 39. 1) and among other peoples: for Greek examples see Gow on Theoc. 24. 22; A. B. Cook, *Zeus* (Cambridge, 1914–40), ii. 114.

681. aperitur, 'comes into view': cf. iii. 275 'formidatus nautis aperitur Apollo' (i.e. Apollo's temple at Actium). The active is used in the same sense, iii. 206 'aperire procul montis': both uses (like that of *abscondere*, 'lose sight of', iii. 291) are no doubt technical.

patrium . . . sidus: on, or above, his head appears 'his father's star'—the comet seen at the funeral games held in honour of Julius which was exploited by Augustan propaganda as the sign of his apotheosis and appeared on coinage of Augustus (H. Mattingly, *Coins of the Rom. Emp. in the B.M.* [London, 1923], i, pl. 6, nos. 6–8): cf. *Ecl.* 9. 47; Hor. *Od.* i. 12. 46 ff.; Suet. *Jul.* 88; Plut. *Caes.* 69. 3; Pliny, *N.H.* ii. 93: Propertius' account of Actium makes Julius look down on the battle from his star (iv. 6. 59).

682. parte alia: for the formula of vivid description of a work of art cf. i. 474; Cat. 64. 251.

uentis . . . secundis: the phrase is no doubt conventional here, but weather played an important part in the action: after Antony, blockaded in the gulf, decided to fight his way out, bad weather delayed the engagement for four days.

683. arduus agmen agens: Agrippa too is on his stern. He was in fact in command of the Roman fleet, leading it from the

left, facing Antony on his own right, and engaging him there
when he came out and marshalled his force. The rest of the
fleets were never engaged : Antony's centre and left, and
most of his right, either deserted or surrendered. On the
tactics of the battle see W. W. Tarn, *J.R.S.* xxi (1931),
173 ff.; G. W. Richardson, *J.R.S.* xxvii (1937), 153 ff.; J.
Kromayer, *Hermes* lxviii (1933), 361 ff.; J. M. Carter, *The
Battle of Actium* (London, 1970).

arduus: see on vii. 624.

belli insigne superbum stands in loose apposition to the
following words. The accusative is regularly so used 'in
apposition to a sentence', to expand its sense or comment on
it, in Greek poetry (e.g. *Il.* xxiv. 734 f. ἤ τις Ἀχαιῶν | ῥίψει χειρὸς
ἑλὼν ἀπὸ πύργου, λυγρὸν ὄλεθρον: Eur. *Or.* 1105 Ἑλένην κτάνωμεν,
Μενέλεῳ λύπην πικράν); a similar use of the nominative is also
found (Eur. *Heracl.* 71 f. βιαζόμεσθα καὶ στέφη μιαίνεται, | πόλει τ'
ὄνειδος καὶ θεῶν ἀτιμία): many of the examples are of neuters and
so ambiguous. In prose it is confined to formal phrases like τὸ
λεγόμενον, τὸ κεφάλαιον. In Latin the idiom does not appear before
Sallust (*Hist.* iv. 69. 8 'Eumenem . . . prodidere Antiocho,
pacis mercedem') and Lucretius (vi. 391 f. 'flammas ut ful-
guris halent / pectore perfixo, documen mortalibus acre'):
apart from colourless phrases like *rem difficilem, rem dictu
paruam* conveying an author's comment, it is infrequent
before Tacitus, who uses it very freely: most of the examples
which are not ambiguous (like Cic. *Phil.* ii. 85 'non enim
abiectum (diadema) sustuleras, sed attuleras domo, medita-
tum et cogitatum scelus') are in the accusative and the nomi-
native is very rare. The other Virgilian examples are all, like
this one, in the neuter: viii. 487 'tormenti genus', vi. 222 f.
'subiere feretro, / triste ministerium', ix. 52 f. 'iaculum . . .
emittit in auras, / principium pugnae', x. 187 f. 'olorinae
surgunt de uertice pennae / (crimen, Amor, uestrum), 310 f.
'turmas inuasit agrestis / Aeneas, omen pugnae', xi. 62 f.
'intersintque patris lacrimis, solacia luctus / exigua ingentis'.
This example is exceptional in that the appositional phrase
stands before the main clause: but cf. Prop. iv. 6. 63 f. 'illa
petit Nilum cumba male nixa fugaci, / hoc unum, iusso non
moritura die', and in Greek, Eur. *H.F.* 992 f. μυδροκτύπον μίμημ',
ὑπὲρ κάρα βαλὼν / ξύλον καθῆκε. See K.–S. ii. 1, pp. 247 f.

684. tempora nauali . . . rostrata corona: the *corona naualis* or
classica, a golden crown decorated with representations of
ships' *rostra*, was indeed an *insigne superbum* (or *unicum
decus*, as Seneca calls it, *Ben.* iii. 32. 4). If Velleius (ii. 81. 3)
is right, Agrippa had been the first winner of it for his defeat
of Sex. Pompeius in 36 B.C.; if Pliny (*N.H.* xvi. 7), the second,

the first having been M. Varro in Pompey's campaign against
the pirates in 67 B.C.

685. ope barbarica: a phrase from Ennius' *Andromacha*, *Sc.*
94 ff. V. 'uidi ego te (sc. Priami domum) adstantem ope
barbarica / tectis caelatis laqueatis / auro ebore instructam
regifice'. *barbarica* with its suggestion of Oriental wealth and
splendour stands in contrast to the Italian emphasis of
678 f. It is, however, used elsewhere without disparagement:
the description of the royal palace at Troy in ii. 504 ('bar-
barico postes auro spoliisque superbi') and that in Ennius
are spoken by Trojans, the one by Aeneas himself, the other
by Andromache: so in Greek tragedy Hecuba (Eur. *Hec.* 1200)
and a Persian messenger (Aesch. *Pers.* 255) use βάρβαρος
of their own people. *uariis*, repeated in 723, vividly represents
the heterogeneity of Antony's levies. It is significant that
Virgil leaves entirely out of sight the fact that a large part of
Antony's strength consisted of legionary troops (he had
20,000 of them on his ships), that his commanders were
Roman, and that he had a large following of Roman senators.
Propertius glances at it to make the point that Cleopatra was
using Roman arms against Romans (iv. 6. 22 'pilaque
feminea turpiter acta manu'): but it is the scandal of that
situation which concerns him, not its political significance,
which was far greater than that of the support of Asia.

686 ff. uictor ab Aurorae populis, 'returning triumphant from
the nations of the Dawn': cf. Ovid, *Met.* ix. 136 f. 'uictor ab
Oechalia Cenaeo sacra parabat / uota Ioui'. Designed (as
Servius observed) to enhance the glory of Octavian, the
description, which makes Antony into another Alexander, has
little or no foundation. Antony, still Octavian's colleague,
had conquered Armenia in 34 B.C., reporting his victory to
Rome and celebrating it in Alexandria, but his attempt on
Parthia in 36 B.C. had been a costly failure and he had never
been near the shores of the Indian Ocean (*litus rubrum*, the
Oceanus ruber of Horace, *Od.* i. 35. 32). But he had attached
to himself the client-princes of inner Asia Minor and the
Levant, whom he had put or maintained in power, and,
when a confrontation with Octavian was imminent, he
called on these to provide, as the price of his patronage,
contingents of men for the decisive contest (Plut. *Ant.* 61).

688. Bactra, the capital of the semi-Hellenized kingdom of
Bactria (the region of northern Afghanistan and southern
Turkestan), the centre of a prosperous trade with the further
East, is for the Augustan poets a name of romance and
mystery, an Eldorado awaiting conquest: cf. *Geo.* ii. 138;
Hor. *Od.* iii. 29. 28; Prop. iii. 1. 16, iv. 3. 63. But with Bactria

Antony had no more to do than with those other lands of fabulous wealth, India and Sheba (705 f.). Cleopatra may have sought to inspire an unwilling Antony with the design of an Asiatic confederation: there is no evidence that she did, but, if she did, the design never took shape.

Aegyptia coniunx: it is a tribute to the success of the campaign of propaganda directed against Antony that the Augustan poets never use Cleopatra's name: she is *mulier* or *femina* (the woman who has made men her slaves: Prop. iv. 6. 57, 65; Hor. *Epod.* 9. 11 ff.) or *regina* (696: a title of odious associations to a Roman ear), *monstrum* (with its sinister implication, Hor. *Od.* i. 37. 21). Antony's marriage to a foreigner is an outrage (*nefas*: for the parenthetical use cf. vii. 73, x. 673) to Roman feeling (cf. Hor. *Od.* iii. 5. 5 'milesne Crassi coniuge barbara / turpis maritus uixit') and *Aegyptia* is calculated to suggest the depravities of Egyptian court life. See H. Volkmann, *Cleopatra: a Study in Politics and Propaganda* (London, 1958); I. Becher, *Das Bild der Kleopatra in der griech. und latein. Literatur* (Berlin, 1966).

689 ff. It is idle to inquire how the engagement and the rout were represented on the shield: the picture has become a story.

689. reductis: the rowers pull their oars back against their chests: cf. v. 141 'adductis . . . lacertis' of the same action.

690. The line is repeated from v. 143: the three-pronged beak appears regularly in representations on coins.

692. Cycladas: the same comparison is prosaically put by Dio (l. 33. 8): εἴκασεν ἄν τις ἰδὼν τὰ γιγνόμενα . . . τείχεσί τισιν ἢ καὶ νήσοις πολλαῖς καὶ πυκναῖς ἐκ θαλάσσης πολιορκουμέναις.

693. tanta mole: the comparisons of the preceding lines and Propertius' phrase 'stetit aequore moles / pinea' (iv. 6. 19 f.) make it clear that *moles* refers to the ships (cf. v. 118, 223 'ingenti mole Chimaeram')—'such is the bulk of the towered ships with which they attack'—though the attachment of one ablatival phrase to another is awkward. The tradition of Actium (like that of the Armada) made much of the difference in bulk between the opposing fleets, contrasting Antony's floating monsters with the light *Liburnae* of whose speed and manœuvrability Agrippa and Octavian made effective use: see Dio. l. 29. 2; Prop. iv. 6. 47 ff.; Veg. iv. 33: for a warning against taking it at face value see C. G. Starr, *The Roman Imperial Navy*² (Cambridge, 1960), 8.

turritis puppibus: the erection of towers on a ship's deck was a familiar device, as old as Thucydides (vii. 25. 6): cf. Caes. *B.G.* iii. 14. 4, *B.C.* i. 26; Pliny, *N.H.* xxxii. 1. 3. But Dio makes particular mention of the towers on Antony's ships, l. 23. 3 καὶ ἐπ' αὐτὰ (sc. τὰ σκάφη), πύργους τε ὑψηλοὺς ἐπικατεσκεύασε καὶ πλῆθος ἀνθρώπων ἐπανεβίβασεν ὥστε καθάπερ ἀπὸ τειχῶν αὐτοὺς μάχεσθαι (cf. Plut. *Ant.* 66. 2), and Horace's words to Maecenas in *Epod.* 1. 1 f., 'ibis Liburnis inter alta nauium, / amice, propugnacula', suggest that word of them had reached Rome before the battle. They added confusion to the rout, when crews were throwing them overboard in a desperate attempt to lighten ship (Dio l. 33. 4).

694. stuppea flamma: i.e. flaming tow (cf. vii. 462 f. 'flamma ... / uirgea') attached to *tela*: an authentic detail: Dio l. 34. 2 gives a long and vivid account of the havoc wrought by Octavian on Antony's ships with fire-bolts and fire-pots.

telisque uolatile ferrum, 'the flying iron of their shafts': for the characteristically Virgilian complex of adjective and ablative see on vii. 639 f.

695. arua ... Neptunia: perhaps an Ennian phrase; cf. Cic. *Arat.* 129 'Neptunia prata'. For the use of the adjective see on vii. 1.

696. regina: Cleopatra is *regina* also for Horace, *Od.* i. 37. 7 and Propertius, iii. 11. 39: when she was at Rome, under Julius Caesar's protection, in 44 B.C., Cicero, writing to Atticus, had used the same invidious description (*Att.* xv. 15. 2 'reginam odi', xiv. 8. 1, 20. 2).

in mediis: the suggestion that Cleopatra was in the thick of the fray is untrue: during the engagement her squadron was lying in the rear and from there she broke through to make her escape (Dio. l. 33. 1). The *sistrum* was an Oriental rattle-like instrument of metal rods set in a frame and shaken in the hand which is regularly associated with Isis-worship (cf., e.g., Ovid, *Am.* ii. 13. 11, *A.A.* iii. 635; Juv. 13. 93): that Cleopatra used it as a call to battle is a picturesque fiction which Propertius borrows (iii. 11. 43 'Romanamque tubam (ausa) crepitanti pellere sistro') and Lucan exaggerates (x. 63 'terruit illa suo, si fas, Capitolia sistro').

697. necdum etiam: for the combination cf. i. 25; Cat. 64. 55; Prop. ii. 10. 25; Man. i. 73.

geminos ... anguis: Horace (*Od.* i. 37. 27) and Propertius (iii. 11. 53) both use the plural, but the historians speak of one snake: so Suet. *Aug.* 17. 4, Dio li. 14. 1 and Plut. *Ant.* 85–6, who adds that the asp was represented on the image of Cleopatra which was carried in Octavian's triumphal procession. Virgil's *gemini* should no doubt be taken in connection with the pair of snakes which appears in other scenes—crowning the head of the Fury (vii. 450) and attacking Laocoon (ii. 203 f.) and the infant Hercules (viii. 289)—and may well have been suggested by conventional representation in art.

698. omnigenum: for the genitive form see on vii. 189.

deum monstra: for *monstrum* see on vii. 21: for the genitive cf. vi. 285 'uariarum monstra ferarum' and, in the language of familiar abuse, Plaut. *Poen.* 273 'monstrum mulieris'; Ter. *Eun.* 696 'monstrum hominis'.

latrator : the Egyptian god Anubis was represented in the form of a dog: Propertius takes up the phrase in the same context, iii. 11. 41 'ausa Ioui nostro latrantem opponere Anubim'.

699 ff. The strange gods of Egypt are represented as arrayed against the Roman pantheon. The reasons for the mention of Neptune, whose element is the scene of the conflict, and Venus, patron of the Julian house, are obvious: Minerva is perhaps chosen to represent the Capitoline triad, since Jupiter, the ultimate arbiter of events, and Juno, who in the poem has been concerned to thwart the destiny of Rome, cannot well appear in this context. (See C. Bailey, *Religion in Virgil*, 156.) The powers that concern themselves with war next enter the scene—Mars, not here in the capacity of a Roman deity but as the war-god, Homer's Ἄρης βροτόλοιγος, who inspires the struggle, the Furies, whose business is to promote strife, coming from the underworld to hover in the air, Discordia, the Ἔρις who joins the fray in Homer (*Il.* iv. 440), and the wild figure of Bellona.

701. caelatus ferro: a third metal is added (not very intelligibly) to the gold and silver of the shield to represent appropriately the god whose symbol is *ferrum*. *caelare* is properly to use the chisel, and iron cannot be chased, but Propertius similarly extends it to statuary in bronze (iv. 2. 61 'formae caelator aenae').

Dirae: for these grim (*tristes*) sisters and their role in Virgil as promoters of strife, see on vii. 324 ff.: so Tisiphone appears in the battle in Latium (x. 761) and *tristis Erinys* at the sack of Troy (ii. 337).

703. Bellona: see on vii. 319. Here, as in that passage, she is a personification of war, but her *sanguineum flagellum* is perhaps suggested not by the μάστιξ which Ares wields in Aesch. *Agam.* 642 but by the self-wounding rites practised by the fanatical devotees of the Oriental goddess ('gaudens Bellona cruentis' of Hor. *Sat.* ii. 3. 223) with whom Bellona had become identified (cf. Tib. i. 6. 43 ff.).

704. Apollo, whose temple had long stood on the promontory of Actium (Thuc. i. 29. 3) and was enlarged by Augustus in commemoration of his victory (Suet. *Aug.* 18. 2; Dio. li. 1. 2), enters the field as he does in Propertius, iv. 6. 27 ff. Here he puts the finishing touch to a struggle in which the gods are already arrayed: in Propertius he delivers a speech of encouragement to Octavian before opening the fight with his own bow.

705. eo terrore: see on vii. 595. For *eo* see on vii. 62.

705 f. Indi . . . Sabaei: see on 686 ff.: Antony had not drawn troops either from the Far East or from the region in South Arabia where the Sabaeans inhabited the country of Sheba, the modern Yemen. For the same romantic combination in another context cf. *Geo.* ii. 116 f. 'sola India nigrum / fert hebenum, solis est turea uirga Sabaeis'.

707 f. uidebatur, 'she was to be seen' (in the picture) spreading sail and just in the act of letting the sheets run loose (cf. x. 229 'uelis immitte rudentis'). *iam iamque* expresses an action so imminent that it seems to have happened; cf. ii. 530 'iam iamque manu tenet', xii. 940 f. 'iam iamque magis cunctantem flectere sermo / coeperat'; Cic. *Att.* vii. 20. 1 'illum ruere nuntiant et iam iamque adesse', xvi. 9 'iam iamque uideo bellum'; Caes. *B.C.* i. 14. 1 'Caesar enim aduentare iam iamque et adesse eius equites falso nuntiabantur'.

709. pallentem morte futura: so in iv. 644 Dido is 'pallida morte futura'.

710. fecerat . . . ferri: see on 630 f.

Iapyge: the WNW. wind blowing off Iapygia, i.e. Calabria, which could speed the remnants of the fleet towards Egypt as it could speed Virgil on his journey to Greece (Hor. *Od.* i. 3. 4).

712. sinus can have a double reference, to the recesses of the river (*latebrosa flumina*) and to the folds of the robe which the river-god wears. For the identification of river-god and river cf. 62 ff. where Tiber, appearing to Aeneas in human shape, says 'ego sum pleno quem flumine cernis / stringentem ripas'.

tota ueste uocantem: cf. Ovid, *Met.* vi. 298 ff. 'quam toto corpore mater / tota ueste tegens . . . clamauit'.

712. caeruleum is the river-god's conventional colour: see on vii. 346.

714. at turns the reader's eye back from the emphatically placed *uictos* to the victor.

triplici . . . triumpho: Octavian's triumph was held on three successive days of August 29 B.C.: the first day was for the campaigns in Illyricum and the north, the second for Actium, the third for the conquest of Egypt (Suet. *Aug.* 22; Dio li. 21. 6).

715. uotum immortale sacrabat, 'solemnly made an undying vow': both the tense of *sacrabat* and the parallel expressions *legem sacrare* (a *lex sacrata* is a law made with solemn sanc-

tions against violation, e.g. Livy ii. 33. 3; Cic. *Dom.* 43: cf.
Cic. *Balb.* 33 *sanctionem sacrare*) and *foedus sacrare* (Livy
xxxviii. 33. 9) show that Octavian is being represented in the
act of making the vow, not as fulfilling it.

716. ter centum is an indefinite large number: cf., e.g., iv. 510,
vii. 275. Augustus himself claims no more than twelve new
temples (*Res Gestae* 19); he restored a further 82.

717. fremebant: for Virgil's use of *fremere* see on vii. 389.

718 f. The lines refer in general terms to a *supplicatio*, a cere-
mony proclaimed by the Senate or the magistrates on occa-
sions of national thanksgiving (earlier in times of national
emergency) when for one day or several the temples were
opened and their cult-statues exhibited on *puluinaria* and
the whole adult population visited them in turn with their
prayers. *supplicationes* were a familiar feature of Augustus'
reign: he claims that they were held on fifty-five occasions
to a total of 890 days (*Res Gestae* 4).

720 ff. In the last scene of the Shield, in which a triumphant
Caesar receives the homage of an obedient world on the steps
of the temple of Apollo which he built, Virgil moves from em-
bellished history to magnificent imagination. At Octavian's
triumph in August 29 B.C., the representatives of the con-
quered were paraded: Cleopatra escaped that indignity, but
her children did not, and nine captive princes were in the
procession (*Res Gestae* 4). But the great temple of Apollo
on the Palatine, which had been begun before Actium and
commemorated the victory over Sextus Pompeius in 36 B.C.,
was not dedicated until October 28 B.C., a year later, and
the picture of the submissive nations marching in a long
procession (722) before it is fantasy. In a crowded catalogue
of romantic names peoples who may be thought to have been
exhibited in Octavian's triumph consort on the one hand
with a mysterious legendary race and on the other with the
remote inhabitants of unknown lands whose names are
only names, reflecting the vague dreams of distant conquest
in which the politic flattery of Augustus' poets indulged (as
Virgil himself does in *Geo.* iii. 26 ff., *Aen.* vi. 792 ff., Horace
in *Od.* i. 12. 53 ff., iv. 14. 41 ff., Propertius in iii. 4. 1) but
which he (though he had diplomatic dealings with Scythian
and Indian potentates: Suet. *Aug.* 21, *Res Gestae* 31) was
wise enough not to share.

720. candentis is indeed an appropriate epithet for Apollo (cf.
Hor. *Od.* i. 2. 31 f. 'nube candentis umeros amictus / augur
Apollo'), but here the god is, as often, identified with his
temple (cf. iii. 275 'aperitur Apollo'): that was of white
marble and *candentis* reinforces *niveo*.

721 f. superbis postibus: cf. ii. 504 'barbarico postes auro spoliisque superbi'.

722. uictae ... gentes: cf. Hor. *Od.* ii. 9. 21 f. 'Medumque flumen gentibus additum / uictis minores uoluere uertices'.

724. Nomadum: the Berber tribes of the Atlas region are given (as in iv. 320) the Greek name Νομάδες (originally a description of their way of life), which was Latinized as *Numidae*. North Africa had been on Antony's side (Plut. *Ant.* 61) and operations there earned a triumph for L. Autronius Paetus in 28 B.C.

discinctos: the loose robes of Africa are contrasted with the neatness of Roman military dress: cf. Livy xxxv. 11. 7 (of Numidian cavalry) 'nihil primo adspectu contemptius: equi hominesque paululi et graciles, discinctus et inermis eques'; Sil. iii. 235 f. (of Carthaginian troops) 'uestigia nuda sinusque / cingere inassuetum'. (So in Plaut. *Poen.* 1008, a Carthaginian is unceremoniously addressed as 'tu qui zonam non habes'.) The contrast is the sharper because for Roman troops to lose their belts and be made *discincti* was a military punishment: cf. Livy xxvii. 13. 9; Suet. *Aug.* 24. 2; Val. Max. ii. 7. 9.

Mulciber: the old title of Vulcan, of unknown origin, occurs only here in Virgil. (See Mielentz in P.–W. s.v.)

725. Lelegas Carasque: the highly Hellenized region of Caria had been part of the province of Asia since 129 B.C.: Roman Asia had been on Antony's side, but in the settlement after Actium Octavian was more concerned to rehabilitate the communities whose resources Antony had annexed than to triumph over them. The Leleges were a prehistoric people of the Asian coast, who are particularly associated with Caria (in Homer they are with the Carians as allies of Troy, *Il.* x. 428 f. πρὸς μὲν ἁλὸς Κᾶρες καὶ Παίονες ἀγκυλότοξοι / καὶ Λέλεγες: cf. Herod. i. 171. 1): they may have been the predecessors of the Carians and conquered by them, but for ancient ethnographers, who found traces of them not only in the islands but also in various parts of mainland Greece (cf. Strabo vii. 7. 2), they were as ubiquitous as the equally mysterious Pelasgi. (See W. Aly, *Phil.* lxviii [1909], 428 ff.; P. Kretschmer, *Glotta* xxxii [1953], 161 ff.) Their appearance here is a piece of learned allusion: Ovid repeats it by pairing them with the Carians in *Met.* ix. 645, though in viii. 6 *Lelegeius* is 'Megarian'.

Gelonos: the Geloni, a Scythian people of the region between Dnieper and Don, about whose precise location Pliny (*N.H.* iv. 88) is as uncertain as Herodotus (iv. 108) had been, are on the fringe of the world for Horace (*Od*. ii. 20. 18 f. 'ultimi Geloni', iii. 4. 35 'pharetratos Gelonos') and for Virgil himself in *Geo*. ii. 115.

726 ff. Euphrates ... Rhenusque bicornis ... Araxes: the river-names reflect the practice of carrying images of river-gods among representations of conquered territories in triumphal processions: cf. Prop. ii. 1. 31 f. (of this triumph) 'aut canerem Aegyptum et Nilum, cum attractus in urbem / septem captiuis debilis ibat aquis'; Ovid, *Pont*. iii. 4. 107 f. 'squalidus immissos fracta sub harundine crines / Rhenus et infectas sanguine portet aquas', *Tr*. iv. 2. 41 f. 'cornibus hic fractis uiridi male tectus ab ulua / decolor ipse suo sanguine Rhenus erat', *A.A*. i. 223; Tac. *Ann*. ii. 41 'uecta spolia, captiui, simulacra montium, fluminum, proeliorum'.

726. ibat ... undis: cf. Prop. ii. 1. 32 quoted above.

727. Morini: the Morini were a tribe of Belgica, in the region of Boulogne, which had been subdued by Julius Caesar; the suppression of a rising among them, and among the Germanic Suebi to the east, who had crossed the Rhine—and are represented by *Rhenus* here—earned a triumph for C. Carrinas in 29 B.C. and the two tribes were also included in Octavian's triumph of the same year (Dio li. 21. 6). The conventional description *extremi hominum* (which survives in Pliny, *N.H*. xix. 8) is the less appropriate since it was in their country that Julius had made his base for crossing to Britain in 55 B.C. (*B.G*. iv. 21. 3): it is Britain that is the world's end for Catullus (11. 11 f., 29. 4, 12) and for Virgil himself (*Ecl*. 1. 66) and the design of invading Britain which Augustus was believed to have when he went to Gaul in 27 B.C. had drawn attention afresh to the lands beyond the Channel (cf. Hor. *Od*. i. 35. 29 f.; Dio liii. 22. 5, 25. 2: see A. Momigliano in *J.R.S*. xl [1950], 39 ff.; P. A. Brunt in *J.R.S*. liii [1963], 173 ff.).

   bicornis: see on 77.

728. Dahae: a nomadic people of the region east of the Caspian: *indomiti* they no doubt were, but that description fits ill with *uictae gentes*.

   pontem indignatus Araxes: the great river of Armenia, flowing into the Caspian. Antony had crossed it in 36 B.C. on his Parthian expedition and had recrossed it in defeat: Augustus was never in the region and the statement in DServius that he bridged the Araxes is an invention based on Virgil's words. The Araxes resents being bridged as the waves of the Portus Julius resent its break-water (*Geo*. ii. 161 f. 'portus Lucrinoque addita claustra / atque indignatum magnis stridoribus aequor') or the winds resent imprisonment

in Aeolus' cave (*Aen.* i. 55 f. 'indignantes magno cum mur-
mure montis / circum claustra fremunt').

730. The subject is taken up from 617–19, from which the verb
miratur is repeated.

    rerum belongs in sense both to *ignarus* and to *imagine*,
'knowing nothing of the events he takes pleasure in the
representation of them'.

731. famamque et fata, 'lifts on his shoulder the glorious des-
tiny of his descendants': cf. vii. 79 'inlustrem fama fatisque
canebant'.

APPENDIX

ALLITERATION

ALLITERATION (the technical term for the deliberate repetition of initial sounds is an invention of fifteenth-century scholarship) was a natural habit of Latin speech serving to give an utterance solemnity or emphasis, force or point. It was a feature of archaic religious formulas (e.g. in the prayer quoted by Cato 141. 3, 'pastores pecuaque salua seruassis') and it maintained itself in legal and in official phrases (e.g. 'manu mancipio', 'loca lautia', 'datum donatum dedicatum'), in proverbial sayings (e.g. 'laterem lauare', 'ad rastros res redit') and in many stereotyped expressions of ordinary usage. Literature accepted it as a stylistic device from the beginning. It appears in the native Saturnian verse, imposing a pattern on one or other hemistich or linking the two (e.g. Naev. 5 Baehr. 'eorum sectam sequuntur multi mortales', 31 'prima incedit Cereris Proserpina puer', 34 'scopas atque uerbenas sagmina sumpserunt', 57 'magnae metus tumultus pectora possidit') in a formative scheme as marked, though not as regular and rigid, as that of early English alliterative verse. When Ennius set himself to give the Greek hexameter a Latin form, he took over this indigenous and traditional ornament and established it in the pattern of his verse. His hexameters, and his iambics, are full of alliteration, and a high proportion of his lines exhibit the device in greater or less degree. Sometimes a single alliteration extends over a whole line (e.g. *Ann.* 9 V. 'quae caua corpore caeruleo cortina receptat', 32 'accipe daque fidem foedusque feri bene firmum', 621 'machina multa minax minitatur maxima muris'); sometimes one alliteration in the first hemistich is balanced by another in the second (e.g. 71 'hinc campum celeri passu permensa parumper', 273 'rem repetunt regnumque petunt, uadunt solida ui', *Sc.* 185 'constitit credo Scamander, arbores uento uacant'). With him, as in *Beowulf* or *Piers Plowman*, the purpose of the device is not imitative: in these lines the alliteration does not echo the sense but is a stylistic pattern which is cultivated for its own sake and which may dictate the poet's choice of words. This conventional technique of the early literary language, continued both in the tragedy of Ennius' successors and in comedy, passes to Lucretius and Cicero and to Virgil: after him the device in its traditional form disappears.

The suggestive power of sounds in Virgil's verse is plain to any reader: the effect of the play of sounds, consonants and vowels, in reflecting and reinforcing an image or a mood is often immediate and unmistakable. Alliteration may sometimes contribute to that effect (as it does, e.g., in vii. 567, with its accumulation of s's and t's, or in 632), but that need not be its function; its suggestiveness may be of another kind and to expect to be able to read an expressive value into it and ascribe distinctive 'meanings' to different sounds is to misunderstand its purpose. How Virgil felt that the repeated alliterations of xi. 44–7 served to heighten the pathos with which these lines are charged we cannot know: there can be no doubt that he was using the device to that end, but there is no question of imitative effect. When Norden confidently describes the repeated *u* in the lines 'inualidus, uiris ultra sortemque senectae' (vi. 114) and 'continuo auditae uoces uagitus et ingens' (vi. 426) as 'der Laut des starken Wehs', the description is misleading: the same alliteration appears, even more emphatic, in lines of a totally different complexion, 'Teucrosque uocari / aut uocem mutare uiros aut uertere uestem' (xii. 824 f.) and unprejudiced reflection may suggest that the frequency with which the poets choose the *u*-sound for alliterative effects is not unrelated to the frequency of *u* as an initial sound in the basic words of their vocabulary. It is significant that many of Virgil's alliterative phrases had been used already by Lucretius and Ennius and that some are repeated by Virgil himself. In some lines an alliteration in each hemistich (e.g. vi. 15 'praepetibus pennis ausus se credere caelo, 683 'fataque fortunasque uirum moresque manusque') conforms closely to an Ennian pattern; sometimes an alliteration is developed over two lines with Ennian lavishness (e.g. ix. 775 f. 'Crethea Musarum comitem, cui carmina semper / et citharae cordi numerosque intendere neruis'). There is no common factor of expressive effect in the five alliterative line-endings 'casus Cassandra canebat' (iii. 183), 'capta cupidine coniunx' (vii. 189), 'custodia credita campi' (vii. 486), 'candenti corpore cycnum' (ix. 563), 'comitatus classe cateruas' (x. 194): the common factor is a literary continuity in the restrained use of a stylistic pattern which had belonged to the conventions of poetry since the time when Ennius wrote 'in conspectum corde cupitus' (*Ann.* 48 V.) and whose origins were even older.

See E. Wölfflin, 'Über die alliterierenden Verbindungen der lateinischen Sprache', *Sitz. Bay. Akad.* (1881, II), 1 ff. (*Ausgewählte Schriften* [Leipzig, 1933], 225 ff.); id., *A.L.L.* xiv,

515 ff.; A. Cordier, *L'Allitération latine: le procédé dans l'Énéide de Virgile* (Paris, 1969); J. Marouzeau, *Traité de stylistique latine*, 45 ff.; L. P. Wilkinson, *Golden Latin Artistry*, 25 ff., 49 ff., 56 ff.; C. E. S. Headlam, 'The Art of Virgil's Poetry', *C.R.* xxxiv (1920), 23 ff.

INDEXES

*References are to the notes on lines in Book VII
unless prefixed by* 'viii'.

(1) INDEX NOMINVM

(2) INDEX VERBORVM

caput, viii. 65, 570 ff. (*huic capiti*)
carpere (of sleep), 414
cateia, 741
cauus, viii. 598 f.
cedere, 635 f.
cedrus, 178
Ceres ('corn'), 113; viii. 181
chalybs, viii. 421
cinctus Gabinus, 612
circa, 535
clarus (adverbial), 141 f.
classis ('levy'), 716
cognomen ('significant name'), 3, 671
componere, viii. 317, 322
conclamare, 504
concutere, 338; viii. 3
coniurare, viii. 5
continuo, 68
coquere (metaphor), 345
cordi, 326
cornipes, 779
coronare (*uina*), 147
crudescere, 788
cultus, viii. 316
cum (*lumine*), 130
cum (*tuo cum flumine sancto*), viii. 72
cum saepe, viii. 353 f.

daedalus, 282
dare (causative), viii. 570 f.
debellator, 651
dehinc, viii. 337
deinde, 135
delatus, 411
dicto parere, 433
didere, 144
dirus, 22, 324
discinctus, viii. 724 •
dolo, 664
ducere, 634 ('mould'); viii. 665 f. (*sacra*)
durus, viii. 315

ecce autem, 286

edere, viii. 137
educere, 762; viii. 413
effetus (with gen.), 440
effudere ('throw'), 780
egelidus, viii. 610
egregius, 556
electrum, viii. 402
enim ('indeed'), viii. 84
est (for *licet*), viii. 676
est locus . . . hic, 563 ff.
et/aut, -que/-ue, 131
et tum, 92
et (with first of two co-ordinate clauses), 327
eunt res, 592
ex ('as a result of'), viii. 621
examen, 703 f.
exire (from source), viii. 65
exposcere, 155
exsors, viii. 552

facies ('shape'), 448
falx, 179
fasces, 174
fata, fatum, 239 ('oracle'), 293 f., 313 ff.; viii. 334
fatigare, 582; viii. 94
fauere, viii. 173
felix ('fruitful'), 725
ferre (*se*), viii. 199
feruere, viii. 677
ferus, 489
flauus, 31 f.
florere (of radiance), 804
foedare (of wounding), 575
forte, 112
fortuna laborum, 559
fragosus, 566 f.
fremere, 389
fuit ('is no more'), 413
fuluus, 76
fundere ('give birth to'), viii. 139

gaesum, viii. 662
galerus, 688
gemere (of wild beasts), 15

marmor, 28
mater (emphatic), viii. 370
matutinus, viii. 465
medius, (intensive) 169, 372, 397,
  (of mediation) 536
memini (with infin.), 206
mensa, 116
mensae perpetuae, 176
mensae secundae, viii. 283
mephitis, 84
-met, 309
Minerua ('spinning and weav-
  ing'), viii. 409 f.
modis miris, 89
moliri, 127
mollis ('leafy'), 390
monere ('remind'), 41
monimentum, viii. 312
monstrum, 21, 269 ('warning')
mos, viii. 316
mouere, 312

ne (with imperative), 96
nec minus interea, 572
nec non et, 521
nemus, 29
neque enim, 581
nequiquam, 652
nitidus, 275
nomen, 3, 337, 723
notus ('familiar'), 491
nouerca, viii. 288
nouus ('sudden'), viii. 637
numen, 584; viii. 78
numerus, 211, 274

o, 360
ob ('in the cause of'), 182
obscenus, 417
obsitus, viii. 307
ocius, viii. 555
olim, viii. 391
ollus, -e, 458; viii. 391
opportunus, viii. 235
optare, 273
optatus, viii. 405

ora ('region'), 564
orare ('speak'), 446
orator, 153
orbis, 223 f.; viii. 448 f.
orgia, 403
oriens, 51
orsa ('first words'), 435 f.

pallidus, viii. 244 f.
paratus ('ready-made'), 97
pascere crinem, 391
pater (of gods), viii. 394
pecten, 14
penates parui, viii. 543
per mutua, 66
pertemptare, 355
peruersus, 584
pictus, 252, 431, 796; viii. 588
pietas, 5, 21
pinna, 159
pius, 5
plaga, 225 ff.
polire, viii. 426 f.
polluere, 467
ponere (intrans.), 27
porca, viii. 641
portus (metaphor), 598
poscere, 155, 272; viii. 12
posse ('bring oneself to'), 309
potens, 56 (of wealth), 541 (with
  gen.)
primus (reinforcing phrase of
  'beginning'), 40
profecto (adv.), viii. 532
proficisci (metaphor), viii. 51
pronuba, 319
properare, 56 f. (with noun-cl.);
  viii. 454 (trans.)
propius, viii. 78
proprium dare, 331
proruptus (middle voice), 459
pubes, 105

quadra, 115
quadripedare, viii. 596
quae plurima, viii. 427

(3) INDEX RERVM

name, 209; viii. 231; partitive, with neut. plur. adj., viii. 221

Golden Age myth, 47 ff., 203 f.; viii. 314 ff.

halo as sign of divine favour, viii. 680 f.

hendiadys, 15

Hercules-cult, viii. 184–279, 285

horse-taboo at Aricia, 761 ff.

imperfect ('was all along'), 128

incomplete lines, 129

inconsistencies, 36, 46, 63, 123, 171, 178, 203 f., 366, 617, 664 ff., 711 f., 803 ff.; viii. 41, 55, 314, 461, 463, 539, 549

'incubation' oracle, 87 ff.

indicative: in apodosis of elliptical condition, viii. 520 ff.; for deliberative subjunctive, 359; with *aspice ut*, viii. 190 ff.

infinitive: after verb, 35 f., 214, 239; viii. 404; after verbal phrase, 591; 'historic', 15

intransitive use of transitive verbs, 27

invocation of Muses, 37–45, 641 ff.

Italy, names for, 39, 47 ff., 85; viii. 329

Iulium sidus, viii. 681

litotes, 261; viii. 49

ludi Romani, viii. 636

Lupercalia, viii. 51 ff., 343

metonymy, 113, 388; viii. 91, 181, 409 f.

METRE and PROSODY:
anapaestic rhythm, 479
break after third foot, 625
caesura: feminine in second and third feet, 724; trochaic in fourth and fifth feet, 27, 45

dactylic words forming fourth and fifth feet, viii. 239

ending: double disyllable, viii. 382; monosyllable, 592; quadrisyllable, 344, 398; rhyme('grammatical'),187f.; spondee in fifth foot, 631, 634

hiatus, 178

hypermetre, 160

spondaic rhythm reinforcing sense, 27, 164, 170, 588 f., 631, 634; viii. 452, 679

Asia, 701 f.; *conubia*, 96; *dehinc*, viii. 337; *Diana*, 306; *excitus*, 623; *Italus*, 85; *Lauinia*, 359; *praeustus*, 524; *Sicanius*, *Sicani*, viii. 416; *supra*, 32 f.

consonantal *i* and *u*, 175, 237; viii. 194

lengthening of short final syllables, 174, 186 (-*que*), 398

synizesis, 33, 262; viii. 337

'middle' voice, 459, 503, 569

name, emotive use of speaker's own, 401 f.

names of heroes, 532

numbers: 'distributive', 538; 'heroic', 153, 275; viii. 716; 'magical', 141

omission of part of *esse*, 300

parataxis, 287–9

parenthesis, 110

participle: aoristic 'timeless', viii. 629, 636; negatived, 11

'pathetic fallacy', 514 ff.

Penates and *di magni*, viii. 679

perfect: 'gnomic', 689 f.; instantaneous action, 394; viii. 219

personification, 629 f., 802; viii. 107 f., 346, 385 f., 497, 728